Democracy Declassified

Democracy Declassified

The Secrecy Dilemma in National Security

MICHAEL P. COLARESI

OXFORD
UNIVERSITY PRESS

Oxford University Press is a department of the University of Oxford.
It furthers the University's objective of excellence in research, scholarship,
and education by publishing worldwide.

Oxford New York
Auckland Cape Town Dar es Salaam Hong Kong Karachi
Kuala Lumpur Madrid Melbourne Mexico City Nairobi
New Delhi Shanghai Taipei Toronto

With offices in
Argentina Austria Brazil Chile Czech Republic France Greece
Guatemala Hungary Italy Japan Poland Portugal Singapore
South Korea Switzerland Thailand Turkey Ukraine Vietnam

Oxford is a registered trade mark of Oxford University Press
in the UK and certain other countries.

Published in the United States of America by
Oxford University Press
198 Madison Avenue, New York, NY 10016

Library of Congress Cataloging-in-Publication Data
Colaresi, Michael P., 1976–
    Democracy declassified : oversight and the secrecy dilemma in liberal states / Michael P. Colaresi.
      p.   cm
    Includes bibliographical references and index.
    ISBN 978–0–19–938977–3 (hardcover : alk. paper) 1. Official secrets. 2. Government information.
3. Security classification (Government documents) 4. Democracy. 5. National security. 6. Internal security.
7. Government accountability. I. Title.
    JF1525.S4C64 2014
    352.3'79—dc23
                            2014004960

9 8 7 6 5 4 3 2 1

Printed in the United States of America
on acid-free paper

CONTENTS

To Graham, Landon and Chandra Colaresi

ACKNOWLEDGMENTS

This book has been a long time in the making, and my debts have risen exponentially as the years have ticked by. At each stage of this project, from inception to publication, I have benefited from the generosity of scholars, friends, and my family that I will be unable to fully articulate here or adequately repay. But I will try.

Many people have patiently listened or read as I droned on about intelligence oversight in Norway or the Standing Orders of Parliament in Greece and offered crucial guidance about how to better approach and advance the topic. I received terrific feedback as the project began to take shape in colloquia at Binghamton, Rice, Penn State, and Illinois. Ben Fordham, Bret Ashley Leeds, Doug Lemke, and Paul Diehl deserve special thanks for their advice and insights. I also benefited greatly from being a part of Sabine Carey's working group at the Center for the Study of Civil War at the Peace Research Institute of Oslo. Through a series of meetings over two years, I was able to learn from discussions with Sabine, as well as Kristian Gleditsch, Scott Gates, Håvard Hegre, Lisa Hultman, Neil Mitchell, Nils Petter Gleditsch, Gerald Schneider, and many others.

Discussions with Henk Goemans and Joachim Rennstich were very helpful as I began thinking about the tension between secrecy and accountability. At several times over the last few years, Sara Mitchell provided valuable advice on how to improve the clarity of my work. Erik Gartzke traded detailed emails with me that prodded me to rethink and improve several parts of my arguments. Bruce Bueno de Mesquita was very helpful at two crucial times in this process. I presented my first paper on the topic of secrecy and accountability at a conference in Hawaii where Bruce was the discussant. He challenged the arguments I made while providing encouragement that the topic had possibilities. Years later, after giving a talk at MSU, he was nice enough to chat with me in his hotel lobby about the project as it was coming closer to completion. He gave me valuable advice that I put to use in Chapters 5 and 6 in particular. Bruce Russett's work, and in particular his book *Controlling the Sword*, has provided important waypoints in my thinking about liberal conceptions of democratic foreign policy and how we might weave an understanding of secrecy into the threads of accountability. Similarly, I have benefited greatly from feedback from Dan Reiter. Aidan Wills was kind enough to talk to me on the phone about his work on intelligence oversight around the globe.

I have had the good fortune to be advised by and to work with Bill Thompson and Karen Rasler. They both have continued to provide me with terrific guidance for which I remain very grateful. While at Michigan State University, I have benefited from current and former colleagues who have discussed parts of the project with me, including Burt Monroe, Darren Davis, Brian Silver, Corwin Schmidt, Eric Juenke, and Tom Hammond. Cristina Bodea, Benjamin Appel, and Jakana Thomas each deserve special appreciation for reading chapters and providing valuable feedback, as well as for putting up with how I teach PLS 860. Chuck Ostrom was also very supportive of the project throughout. Several former and current graduate students also provided help in thinking about secrecy in international relations as well as research assistance, including Kristopher Grady, David Dreyer, Johann Park, Petra Hendrickson, Hyun-Jin Choi, Brian Crothers, and Masaaki Higashijima. I owe a large debt of gratitude to Ric Hula, who was the chair for most of my time at MSU working on this topic. I began this book when I was an assistant professor, and Ric not only helped to hire me but consistently supported my work despite the risks that starting a large, new project like this entailed.

I would like to thank Angela Chnapko at Oxford University Press for her belief in the project and her time and effort in seeing the manuscript move toward publication. I learned a great deal from the reviews I received on the manuscript. Each reader provided detailed and specific feedback that helped make this a better book. I owe a particular debt of gratitude to Anonymous Reader #1, whose identity is a secret (but I have my guesses). When I first submitted the manuscript to a publisher, I was quite hopeful. What I got in return a few months later included a 20-page single-spaced reader report on how to improve my argument and presentation. The reader report was obviously from a terrific mind and a generous scholar who was willing to spend an enormous amount of time both challenging and nurturing another person's work. I was very lucky to get that report, as it helped me rewrite Chapters 3–6 and 10 in particular, but also more generally guided me to see more clearly the components of the secrecy dilemma as well as connections between my interest in national security secrecy and other works. The arguments in this book evolved from two articles, one published in 2006 in *International Organizations* and another in 2012 in the *American Journal of Political Science*. The respective editors, Lisa Martin and Rick Wilson, gave me useful feedback that not only improved those manuscripts but aided me in this larger undertaking.

Steve Kautz deserves my deep appreciation. He has been the greatest of colleagues and friends throughout the writing of this book. He has read more drafts of these chapters than anyone else, and he has spent what must amount to months of his time working to help me mend broken arguments and unwind mixed, or is that twisted, metaphors. Most important to me, he believed in the idea of the book, if not in the placement, of my commas.

I want to end by thanking the people that contributed the most to this project: my wife Chandra and our two children Landon and Graham. Their faith that I could finish this book and that someone might actually publish it, despite all observable evidence to the contrary, sustained me through the sometimes frustrating process of improving the manuscript. They supported me with their humor, wit, kindness, optimism, and love. To borrow a sentiment from Abraham Lincoln, if this book has anything worthy to say, it is because I have a family that believed in me and I did not have the heart to let them down. For all they have done for me, I dedicate this book to them.

Michael P. Colaresi
East Lansing, Michigan
April 10, 2014

Democracy Declassified

1

Introduction

THE SECRECY DILEMMA

This book begins with an ambitious aim, to solve a practical dilemma of democratic governance that has been left unresolved by constitutional framers, democratic theorists, and international relations scholars: the problem posed by the necessity of national security secrets for public accountability and consent.

I argue that the crux of the *secrecy dilemma* in democracies is this: How can the public be confident that foreign policy programs advocated by the executive will enhance security if that same leader also has the power to selectively reveal and hide relevant information? The capacity to keep secrets is useful for security, but it can also be abused for nonsecurity ends. The same classification and counterintelligence powers that can hide security vulnerabilities and reduce threats to the public can also cover up executive incompetence and corruption or undercut legitimate domestic political opposition. The secrecy dilemma has been redacted in previous accounts of democratic foreign policy. I aim to bring to light the tensions and interconnections between national security secrecy and public consent to find potential solutions to the dilemma.

Over centuries, theorists from Immanuel Kant[1] and Jeremy Bentham[2] through James Madison,[3] to Dennis Thompson[4] and Sissela Bok,[5] have pondered the unique difficulties that democratic political leaders and their constituents face when formulating and judging foreign policy, since the very success of the policy might depend upon keeping some information from competitors and thus also from the public. Yet, to date, there have been few theoretical or practical answers as to what mechanisms can ease this secrecy dilemma in democracies.

One reason for this gap is that recent international relations scholars, while being keenly interested in the means by which democratic governments can operate on the international stage, have ignored the role that either national security secrecy or public accountability and consent plays in these polities.[6] Where liberal theorists accentuate the benefits of an open marketplace of ideas and accountability for reducing executive abuse of power in democracies, they overlook the transparency costs of releasing national security information. Thus, liberal proponents have minimized the capacity for secrecy in democracies. On the other hand, critics of democratic accountability on national security issues usefully point out the potential for secrecy powers to be abused by a leader, but then underappreciate how these potential abuses of national security secrecy can deflate consent and lead to insecurity. If leaders can deceive the public about the benefits of their policies by covering up corruption or incompetence, why should skeptical members of the public support investments that may be squandered? If current perspectives are our guides, we have to assume that the capacity for either secrecy or public consent is expendable.

Worryingly, these scholarly assumptions are mirrored in simplistic commentaries on the unauthorized release of national security information as either heroic or villainous. For example, some have reacted to the Edward Snowden and Bradley Manning leaks in the United States by claiming that the publication of national security information has significant public costs in terms of security and thus that leakers are criminals.[7] Others respond that the public, in a democracy, must know what the government is doing to hold it accountable and thus that leakers are public heroes.[8]

Of course, both polemics contain only part of the story. There are times when the public accepts secrecy and nevertheless offers consent to national security policies. A majority of the Israeli public has not only supported the development of nuclear weapons for decades, but also stated in opinion polls that they would prefer not to know about the capabilities.[9] In the United States, one writer suggests that "when it comes to certain sensitive subjects in the realm of security, the American people have voluntarily chosen to keep themselves uninformed about what their elected government is doing in their name."[10] This view was dramatically illustrated when Senator John Stennis was approached in 1973 by CIA Director James Schlesinger to discuss an upcoming covert operation. Stennis reportedly responded, "Don't tell me. Just go ahead and do it, but I don't want to know."[11]

Yet blind support in democracies is exploitable by executives and is often short-lived.[12] While Stennis was refusing to hear details of secret operations, other politicians such as Senator Stuart Symington and Representative Lucien Nedzi, and more publicly Senator Frank Church and Representative Otis Pike, were skeptical and made names for themselves by investigating executive abuse of national security secrecy related to Watergate, government surveillance, assassination programs, and Vietnam.[13] These criticisms of executive actions led to a rethinking of investments in Vietnam and elsewhere.[14]

COMBINING PRIVATE INFORMATION AND PUBLIC CONSENT

Three clues suggest at the outset that combining the usefulness of private information and public consent into a theory of democratic foreign policy success may be fruitful. First, the ability to keep secrets in democracies is not an exception, but the rule. All democracies around the world codify an executive's discretion to keep national security secrets.[15] Thus, the existence of national security secrecy indicates that information on foreign policy is treated distinctly from most information on domestic policy issues across democratic contexts. If democratic governments are aware of the potentially significant transparency costs that can accrue without a capacity to keep some national security secrets, perhaps scholars should be also.[16]

Second, despite this capacity for secrecy, democracies not only have survived in the twentieth and early twenty-first centuries, they have thrived.[17] Both the number of democracies and the proportion of the Earth's territory and wealth that is controlled by democracies have risen over the last 50 years.[18] Research shows that democracies tend to make reliable international partners (Leeds 1999), present credible international obstacles to rivals (Schultz 2001), and win more of their wars (Reiter and Stam 2002).[19] While the foreign policy record for democracies is far from perfect, practically speaking, at least a subset of democracies seem to be doing something right, or at least better than the competition.

A third signpost pointing toward a more useful analysis of the secrecy dilemma is that policymakers in democracies themselves do not choose to forgo either the discretion of secrecy or the power of public consent. Instead, they often stumble over the opaque gaps between accountability and secrecy when trying to have both. For example, the Nixon administration became obsessed with keeping information from leaking out to the public in the aftermath of the publication of the Pentagon Papers while at the same time believing that the details of the now public report might help to rally voters toward their preferred foreign policy goals.[20] Similarly, the Obama administration has been stern in its warnings that public revelations of NSA surveillance programs "cause harm to [US] national security interests" while at the same time suggesting that President Obama "welcomes" public debate on the subject.[21] These types of contradictions have led to such anomalies as one famous leaker in the United States, Herbert Yardley, having inspired, on the one hand, threats of prosecution and a tightening of laws to increase the capacity for secrecy in the United States and, on the other hand, a place in the National Security Agency's hall of honor.[22]

The time is ripe to focus on the role that national security secrecy plays in democracies. New technologies have allowed executives discretion over previously impossible levels and depths of digital surveillance, as well as lethal targeted attacks around the globe using drones. While these technologies might have prodigious security uses, they also have the potential for potent abuse. At the same time, the growing absolute scale of leaking, enabled by related digital technologies, should not give the public a false sense of transparency. The United States made over 95 million classification decisions in fiscal year 2012 alone.[23] At this pace of classification, it took the government less than two and a half days to generate more secrets than contained in the three quantitively largest leaks in US history combined.[24] Moreover, even if national security leaking continues to grow, the dilemma for democracies only worsens. If democracy must pay increasing transparency costs over time, the foreign policy advantages discussed above will erode. Organizations like Wikileaks, which attempted to publicize previously secret information and mass leaks from Edward Snowden, do not alter the secrecy dilemma; they reveal it.[25]

A false choice between unconditional constraints on secrecy due to distrust or living with the potential for abuse of secrecy in exchange for the promise of security is increasingly unattractive. As a first step toward a solution, we must understand the twists and turns of the secrecy dilemma and their cascading consequences for foreign policy effectiveness in democracies.

TRANSPARENCY COSTS AND THE CAPACITY FOR SECRECY

The secrecy dilemma arises directly from the transparency costs that can accrue in international politics. If all information could be revealed to citizens, and thus potential enemies too, on demand, without public costs, then the dilemma would disappear into the normal process of accountability in democratic politics. However, I argue, following a long tradition of practical scholarship, that revealing foreign policy information—such as troop strength estimates and specific vulnerabilities, negotiating positions, the content of decoded enemy communications, and the means and capabilities that obtained them—is likely to undercut the public benefit of the policy. The transparency costs of not being able to anticipate, deceive, or suppress the capabilities of a potential competitor are why democracies not only have a capacity for secrecy, but use (and sometimes abuse) it.

Many signature foreign policy successes of democracies relied upon secrecy. Operation Overlord and Operation Husky in WWII were victories for the allies in large part due to deception and secrecy.[26] The Cuban Missile Crisis was a success for the United States because the Kennedy administration had access—through Colonel Oleg Penkovsky,[27] a spy in Moscow—to details of the weapons under construction that allowed the United States to quickly recognize the threat and plan a response before the USSR was made aware of their knowledge of the missile program in Cuba.[28] In 1967, over the course of only a few hours, Israel launched an airstrike on the Egyptian air force that, due to prior intelligence and the element of surprise, destroyed approximately 300 Egyptian planes at a cost of only 19 Israeli aircraft.[29] More recently, in 2011, the killing of Osama bin Laden in Pakistan was planned and carried out in secrecy with the use of previously undisclosed helicopter technology.[30]

Foreign policy transparency would have allowed a potential threat to either block the anticipated moves or increase the costs of militarized action. Had the decision to try to capture or kill bin Laden been announced beforehand, not only would the Al Qaeda leader have had the opportunity to flee, but Pakistan might have moved to stop or at least delay the operation. If Defense Minister Moshe Dayan had announced to the public that Israel had extensive knowledge of exactly where Egyptian planes and defenses were located before the attack, perhaps to shore up domestic support for the action, the Egyptian leadership not only would have had advance warning of an attack but could have moved their strategic assets and begun searching for where the information breach occurred. In addition, had the Soviet Union been able to block US access to the spy before the crucial information was transmitted to the Unites States, Moscow might have been able to complete construction of the batteries and change the strategic situation before the United States could respond.[31]

It is these transparency costs that justify the construction and maintenance of the capacity for secrecy in democracies around the world. The fact of transparency costs does not imply that secrecy in any particular case is alway beneficial. In the 1956 Suez crisis, secret British and French collusion with Israel was seen as largely delegitimizing and played a role in US pressure to cease the operation. What is important is that executives have significant justifications to be empowered to keep some secrets—they must have the capacity for national security secrecy. They may or may not use that capacity in a given case, but the very existence of secrecy institutions has significant consequences for democratic foreign policy.[32]

The Potential Abuses of Secrecy

Once a secrecy capacity exists, the public cannot benefit from the uses of classification while monitoring the content of what is kept from them, as the information would then no longer be secret. This means that the capacity for secrecy has the potential to be abused for nonsecurity motives, as the institutions that can anticipate, deceive, and suppress the capabilities of an interstate threat can also target domestic opposition and cover up incompetence and corruption. By the 1970s, it was clear that US national security secrecy had been abused to spy on potential opposition voices and senators, as well as to attempt to cover up Watergate.[33] In France, at the turn of the twentieth century, the same bureau that kept the secrets of France's technologically advanced artillery, the Statistics Section, also violated citizens' rights, forged documents, and perpetuated outright deceptions to cover up corruption and incompetence in the Dreyfus Affair. During World War I, the United Kingdom used famous writers, including *Winnie-the-Pooh* author A. A. Milne, to concoct false stories in newspapers to deceive the public into believing that the war was progressing better than it was. This was an improvement over British deceptions during the Boer War, which included a staged attack on a fake Red Cross tent on Hampstead Heath in London that was passed off in newsreel footage as an example of enemy atrocities.[34]

While evidence of actual abuse of national security powers for nonsecurity motives can be found across democracies, from the revelations of the McDonald Commission in Canada through to the Lund Report in Norway and the Church and Pike Committees in the United States,[35] the larger point is that the public is unable to monitor the content of classification decisions and have it remain secret. The very existence of the capacity to keep secrets, even if it were rarely used, could lead to public worries of abuse. Thus, the potential for the abuse of the capacity for secrecy has direct ramifications for generating public consent in democracies.

INFORMATION AND PUBLIC CONSENT

The capacity for secrecy is only one part of the secrecy dilemma. In a democracy, the public must also consent to the policies and investments necessary to execute policy. Even if the public cannot view what goes on behind the veil of classification, it is public consent to supplying the blood, bucks, and ballots that takes policy from the drawing board to the Situation Room. Thus, an executive, armed with substantial capabilities for secrecy and even military might, is still beholden in a democracy to the public for support. Public skepticism, instead of consent, for investment in foreign policy priorities not only decreases troop morale and security, but also decreases the probability that the political leaders proposing the investment will remain in office. Democratic successes from World War II to the capturing of bin Laden were only possible because a majority of the public did not withhold their support for investments in security or threaten to punish political leaders that carried out these policies. Democratic leaders would have been much less likely to land on the beaches of Normandy and Sicily, encircle Cuba, preemptively strike Egypt, or enter Pakistan if more of their respective voters had doubted that the security benefits were worth the costs. Even in peacetime, if the public does not support political decisions to take a tough negotiating stance, foster alliances, and prepare for rising challenges around the globe, a threatened country's foreign policy is likely to suffer, along with the prospects of leaders that warn of these threats.

Liberal theorists have long identified public accountability and consent not as a weakness but as a core strength of democracies.[36] Yet to understand how secrecy can give rise to and perpetuate public skepticism, we need to be more specific about the role that information would play in generating public consent in democracies if there were no transparency costs. Within what liberal theorists have called the robust marketplace of ideas,[37] the public is assumed to have access to information on the expected costs and benefits of competing policy proposals and, on this basis, to then make a choice as to which policy is preferred. This type of decision-making can happen in real time and can be evaluated in opinion polls or more formally during elections. If a leader chooses to support or implement policies that are suboptimal from the public's perspective, due to either incompetence or private motives, that leader can be replaced. This process of public monitoring of expected costs and benefits provides an incentive for leaders to supply citizens greater net benefits to ensure their survival in office. While disagreements will remain, available information reduces the incentives for leaders to cheat the public and increases citizen support for beneficial policies.[38] However, if the public has less information, due to secrecy, then this has consequences for public consent.

Secrecy and Skepticism

The reality of the capacity for secrecy in democracies disrupts the marketplace of ideas as information asymmetries arise between the leadership and the public. The public no longer can monitor the costs and benefits of policy proposals and thus has a more difficult time identifying policies that might be incompetent or corrupt. Moreover, because the public knows that leaders can abuse national security secrecy for their own ends—covering up mistakes or corruption and manipulating the revealed costs and benefits of policies—even the partial release of information may not be convincing.

Even if a leader is rightly promoting a security-enhancing policy—based on intelligence identifying a growing external threat—the capacity for secrecy makes it more difficult for that leader to convince the public to support investments that will reduce or meet that challenge. President Obama has argued that the myriad NSA spying programs that were partially revealed to the public in 2013 were in the public interest and were not being abused for nonsecurity aims and that if the public could only see the classified information, they would agree. He stated that he was "comfortable that the program currently is not being *abused*" and that he was "comfortable that if the American people examined exactly what was taking place, how it was being *used*, [and] what the safeguards were, they would say, 'You know what? These folks are following the law.'" President Obama admitted, however, that he too "would be concerned . . . if [he] weren't inside the government." An Associated Press report on President Obama's comments noted that "[b]ecause the program remains classified, however, it's impossible for Americans to conduct that analysis beyond the assurances his administration has given."[39] This anecdote is not unique. Leaders in France before both World Wars, as well as the Nixon administration in negotiations over Cyprus, also faced considerable public doubt for potentially public-security-enhancing policies.[40]

A leader might attempt to reveal the intelligence that led to the threat assessment to raise public support, but this creates two related problems. First, and most obviously, not only does publicizing the previously secret information raise transparency costs that can undercut foreign policy, as discussed above, but because of these costs, the public itself might not support transparency. For example, the *Economist* magazine chastised the US government for its announcement of an Al Qaeda threat in August 2013 by writing that "[A]l Qaeda has been given precious information about American surveillance capabilities that will help it keep communications more secure in [the] future."[41] Second, even if a leader reveals information to the public, the public cannot be assured that other essential facts and information that remain classified would not change the interpretation of the information presented. When French leaders called for more spending on heavy artillery and training before World War I, they were chided as secretly being in the pay of the armaments industry or warmongers. Nixon and Kissinger released reams of classified documents to try and convince the US public and Congress to support their policy in Cyprus, to little effect. In addition, after the French released partial information about rumored atrocities in Algeria, many rightfully doubted that this was the whole story.[42] Recent justifications for surveillance programs in the United States based on the number of attacks averted have likewise been met with skepticism that "there is no evidence that the oft-cited figure is accurate."[43] Together, these factors can lead policymakers to accept unpreparedness and insecurity in the face of public skepticism. As Kennan once wrote, "the truth is sometimes a poor competitor in the market place of ideas—complicated, unsatisfying, full of dilemmas, always vulnerable to misinterpretation and abuse."[44]

The secrecy dilemma and the problem of public skepticism are not insoluble, since there are success stories that prove that the public can be persuaded by executives to consent to investments in useful security despite secrecy. I argue that we can learn from these patterns of consent and investment versus skepticism and underinvestment to understand how democracies have innovated to partially bridge the gap in accountability created by national security secrecy.

SOLVING THE DILEMMA

Unlike critics of liberal international relations theories, I do not argue that secrecy necessarily negates the benefits of public consent in democracies. It simply complicates the mobilization of consent and calls for institutional innovations. Two previously underappreciated sets of forces make democratic accountability on national security policy possible while maintaining immediate and necessary secrecy. The first is transparency cost deflation, the process whereby secrets tend to lose their value over time as sources are moved out of harm's way, contexts change, or a rival learns the information anyway. For example, because the Soviet Union learned of the spying of Colonel Penkovsky during the Cuban Missile Crisis from their own network of informants in the United States, his secrets had less value. Similarly, the transparency costs of revealing the locations of the D-Day landing in Operation Overlord declined significantly over the ensuing months.[45] Due to transparency cost deflation, while real-time accountability is rendered ineffective by justifiable classification, retrospective information on the costs and benefits of actions can be relatively cheap in comparison. However, lower ex post transparency costs only tell us that the price of publicly digging up classified secrets declines over time; they do not supply the tools to do the digging.

The second set of forces are national security oversight institutions that empower actors outside of the executive with tools to investigate national security issues and publicize information. The purpose of these institutional innovations is to allow for investigations into previously secret information and to reveal executive abuses of secrecy powers such as the covering-up of incompetence or corruption. These tools include (a) freedom of information laws that provide a balance test for the release of foreign policy information to the public and allow an extra-executive body to review denials, (b) legislative committees that carve out space for legislators to investigate national security issues and intelligence agencies informed by witnesses, experts, and significant professional staffs, and (c) protections of press freedom so that the press can independently scrape away at secrecy. I will show how these three tools of national security oversight work together to raise the probability that executive abuse will be uncovered retrospectively and thus increase the probability of consent to investments.

Oversight Constrains and Convinces

Oversight institutions simultaneously constrain the executive and allow for more effective mobilization of public consent. Oversight on national security policy issues will take more time than revelation of information on nonsecurity issues, due to transparency costs and, relatedly the greater depth at which national security secrets are buried within the executive. Yet, an abuse of secrecy can still be punished by the public. This conditional punishment can take the forms of removing a leader from office, punishing the offending executive's party at the ballot box, overturning policies associated with the leader, and harsh judgments on the legacy of an executive.[46] Since the existence of these institutions and the potential punishment of abuse they represent are not themselves secrets, executives can be at least partially deterred from executive corruption or incompetence by the possibility of future revelation of wrongdoing.[47] In turn, these retrospective constraints on an executive increase the public's confidence that secrecy is not being abused, which reduces the reasons for skepticism and the withholding of consent in the first place. Declining transparency costs supply the will, while oversight institutions provide the way, for public accountability in democracies on national security policy.

Of course, these retrospective constraints depend on the usefulness of the oversight tools, which vary considerably across democracies. To explore this heterogeneity and analyze its consequences, I have collected, for the first time, a systematic catalog of national security accountability institutions in democracies over the last 30 years. Some democracies, such as Canada, Croatia, Sweden, Norway, and the Netherlands, among others, haver erected strong protections for immediate national security secrecy as well as the capacity for retrospective investigation of national security policy on the part of the legislature, the press, and citizens. These countries benefit from using classified information to prepare for new threats, to bluff and sneak, without delegating power to an unaccountable executive with impunity.

Since not all democracies have embraced national security oversight, some are left at a relative disadvantage compared to democracies with strong oversight mechanisms. I show that states that are solidly democratic and accountable on domestic issues, such as Greece, Italy, and Ireland, provide the executive with wide latitude to avoid public accountability specifically on national security issues. In contrast to democracies that have developed oversight mechanisms, these unaccountable democracies systematically either suffer greater transparency costs, releasing valuable national security information to mobilize the public, or miss international opportunities due to lack of public support. This heterogeneity in oversight institutions means that some democracies should be able to execute foreign policy that is fueled by both private information and public consent, while other democracies that lack these institutions should sputter due to either insufficient investments or lack of secrecy.

Evaluating the Solution

This potential solution leads to three sets of observable implications that I analyze in this book. First, as argued, retrospective oversight institutions should lead to greater public support during international crises. Because there is a greater probability of abuse being revealed, ex post, with stronger oversight institutions, citizens have less reason to distrust that crisis actions are not in the public interest. I compare public support during international crises within three cases. Two of these, occurred in the United States and France, which have seen different changes in relevant oversight institutions. I utilize the United Kingdom as a control because it did not see meaningful changes in national security oversight institutions but did implement institutional changes that should not have affected national security oversight. In the data, we observe that positive changes in oversight institutions led to higher levels of support in the United States and France, controlling for several important factors, and that alternative changes did not lead to evidence of similar changes in the United Kingdom.

Second, while public support is increasing as retrospective oversight improves, the secrecy dilemma and a focus on national security oversight predict that oversight institutions should have both a mobilizing and a constraining effect on military spending. With very low oversight, the public and legislature form beliefs about what price they are willing to pay for the security policy offered by a leader but are skeptical about leadership calls for unexpected changes in spending, because this spending could be abused for nonsecurity purposes. With increasing oversight, this abuse is less likely, and the public and legislature are more willing to pay a higher price because they believe that their investments will pay off in public security benefits. This is the mobilizing effect. For cases with moderate amounts of oversight, military spending is invested in a mix of security and nonsecurity goods because the leadership can get away with some overspending, as oversight still misses significant corruption, but not enough that the public withdraws their support. As oversight continues to increase, however, and becomes more effective, it drives out greater amounts of overspending and abuse on nonsecurity projects. This is the constraining effect. In aggregate, we should see a curvilinear change in spending as oversight institutions are empowered, on average, where at first the mobilizing effect is dominant and then, after a peak, the constraining effect is apparent. Data on military spending across democracies provide evidence consistent with both the mobilizing and the constraining effect.

Third, if democracies with national security oversight institutions are investing in security while paying lower transparency costs and having greater public consent than democracies that lack effective oversight, then these advantages should be apparent in foreign policy outcomes. I provide evidence that improving national security oversight institutions increases the probability of a democracy winning a dispute with a non-democracy. This oversight advantage stems from two sources, each traceable to the original roots of the secrecy dilemma. On the one hand, democracies with national security oversight are, on average, better prepared in terms of material capabilities, relative to their opponents, than democracies that lack oversight, suggesting that these states are able to generate greater public consent for investments in security. On the other hand, these material capabilities do not fully explain the oversight advantage. Democracies with oversight have better outcomes in disputes than one would predict by looking at the material capability ratios and other observable indicators. These sets of findings are consistent with the idea that democracies with national security oversight institutions are paying lower transparency costs and utilizing private information effectively to augment their material capabilities. Together, these results suggest that national security oversight institutions deserve greater attention in analyses of democratic foreign policy.

KEY CONTRIBUTIONS FROM DECIPHERING THE SECRECY DILEMMA

This book contributes to our theoretical, empirical, and practical understanding of how democratic foreign policy and international relations function. First, partially resolving the secrecy dilemma involves an emendation, not a refutation, of liberal international relations theory. Transparent information on the costs and benefits of alternative policies plays a critical role in liberal explanations of democratic successes.[48] Therefore, secrecy necessarily challenges this immediate transparency assumption. However, where critics assume that secrecy renders the mechanisms of democracy, and particularly accountability and public consent, either dangerous or ignorable, I argue that the capacity for secrecy on national security policy highlights the necessity of public consent in democracies. Without the ability to verify information and reveal potential abuse, the public has fewer reasons to believe that a leader's policy is in the public interest. The capacity for secrecy increases, not decreases, the need for domestic institutions that can constrain an executive from clandestine corruption and incompetence. My solution involves moving beyond previous assumptions that see all democracies as equally and everywhere transparent, or limiting the role of secrecy to self-contained covert operations, or similarly circumscribed categories. Using the secrecy dilemma and national security oversight as a platform, this book offers new theories of public mobilization, military spending, and democratic foreign policy success.

When secrecy is incorporated into a theory of public consent in democracies, several criticisms of liberal international relations theories become less potent. For example, it has been argued by many that the rally-around-the-flag effect in the United States and abroad illustrates blind patriotism on the part of the public that can be manipulated by elites.[49] However, I show that public support for executive foreign policy decisions is entirely consistent with a rational public that understands that the executive has an informational advantage on international affairs but may be punished for abusing that advantage.[50]

A similar debate, engaging belligerents as diverse as de Tocqueville and Presidents Kennedy and Lincoln, has raged for centuries concerning the foreign policy efficacy of democracies. A focus on oversight institutions reframes this debate by highlighting the diversity across democracies. While elections are a bedrock feature across democracies, they are not enough to ensure accountability and the benefits of public consent. Lacking relevant information, democracies' potential for degenerating into public skepticism and insecurity cannot be ignored, as critics attest. However, the story does not stop there. We now have evidence that democracies with strong oversight institutions are among the most effective at winning their disputes and dispatching their enemies.[51]

In addition, the secrecy dilemma is relevant to the growing research on the bargaining model of war.[52] This perspective assumes that private information is held by states and that this private information is one key reason that states fail to find a peaceful bargain instead of going to war. However, the bargaining model does not explore the justifications for secrecy and whether democracies, along with their greater transparency on domestic issues, necessarily transfer to the national security realm. The discussion in Chapters 3 and 4 fills these gaps in explaining why the capacity for secrecy exists, even in democracies. As I argue, the existence of secrecy complicates assumptions that transparency in all democratic states makes them more credible than non-democracies.[53] Further, a focus on the secrecy dilemma challenges the usefulness of the assumption in the bargaining model that a leader of a state always represents the state interests and never personal interests. Most of the literature on the bargaining model assumes that leaders do not have private interests in national security policy or overt conflict. Yet, if national security policy can be abused to cover up corruption or incompetence, then there may be utility in replacing the simple fiction of a unitary state actor with a more complete picture of potentially selfish leaders bargaining with their domestic constituents while simultaneously dealing with their external environment.

Empirically, this book investigates important innovations in oversight institutions across time and the globe. Despite their vanguard importance, attention to these national security oversight innovations has been scant and diffuse—scant because many international relations researchers have either assumed away oversight or, just as often, assumed that it is constant in all democracies around the world, and diffuse because the new innovations in national security laws have been largely written about in country-specific terms. In the United Kingdom, there has been significant coverage of the implementation of new freedom of information laws and changes to parliamentary committee structures[54]; likewise, there are a number of books written about US innovations in legislative intelligence oversight.[55] This book contributes a metric for systematic international comparisons between democracies across meaningful institutional dimensions and an analysis of the consequences of oversight across democracies. Just as the art of a tile mosaic floor may be underfoot but unnoticed until you scale an appropriate height, the contours and landscapes of democratic foreign policy institutions have been well worn without being fully appreciated. This view yields new empirical relationships and understandings of democratic foreign policy success and failures.

There are also practical policy contributions from understanding the secrecy dilemma and potential solutions. Leaders in democracies often are buffeted by the skepticism-inducing effects of executive secrecy on public consent. While some have argued in the United States and the United Kingdom that new threats need to be met with a unitary executive armed with speed and dispatch, I show that without proper oversight and checks and balances, an executive loses the ability to convince citizens to consent to critical investments. Instead of an investment of unchecked power in an executive during times of international duress, proper retrospective checks need to be instituted to constrain the potential misuse of power. Innovating oversight has worked in the past and is likely to work in the future. Since 9/11, both in the United States and abroad, there has been a movement to empower executives to more robustly combat international and transnational threats. However, as explicated in this book, empowering an executive to keep secrets and spy on, coerce, torture, and in some cases kill citizens provides new avenues for potential abuse. Further, if these escalations in executive power are not counterbalanced by improvements in oversight, the consequence is likely to be an enervated rather than empowered executive. If the executive has considerable foreign policy tools that can be wielded for either public security or private gain with impunity, there may be little reason for opposition partisans to mobilize behind a leader's preferred policy. We will see in this book that a unitary executive in a democracy is in fact a solitary one.

In the wake of revelations about National Security Agency capabilities and programs that stretch from collecting metadata from US citizens' cell phones to listening in on Angela Merkel's phone and tapping Internet communications around the globe, these lessons may be increasingly important. The ability for the government to potentially track and surveil vast portions of the population increases the scale of potential abuse. Argument that recent leaks do not reveal significant corruption of the current programs does not assure the public that this will not change going forward. Reassurance must come from overseers outside of the executive who are empowered to investigate the potential abuse of these new technologies.[56] Without oversight, skepticism can undermine the uses of these technologies through both defunding of initiatives and the erection of legal constraints from even partaking in useful practices. Skepticism of abuse and distrust of the executive and security services kept France from benefiting from inter-war technological advances and led to the splitting up of intelligence services so as to reduce their capabilities. Already in the United States, there are discussions of cutting programs and reorganizing the NSA led by several senators.[57]

Elites that argue against national security oversight institutions, such as strong legislative committee powers, on the grounds that they will lead to insecurity have the democratic world backward. Retrospectively transparent democracies are more agile at avoiding unfavorable international positions and are more effective on the battlefield. The argument is not that legislative committees manage foreign policy, but instead that by reducing the abuse of secrecy, they allow the executive to prepare for future threats by both keeping secrets and investing in security. In the absence of retrospective oversight, public distrust can reduce investments for military preparations and lead to the outlawing and divestment of programs that could have legitimate security uses. The potential scale and vectors of abuse, which might continue to change with available technologies, must be met with innovations in oversight.

THE CODEBOOK

To introduce, (partially) solve, and empirically explore the secrecy dilemma, I proceed in five parts. Part I reviews the role of transparency in previous liberal theories of democratic foreign policy success and argues that the capacity for secrecy in democracies should be incorporated in liberal theories. Part II suggests that the capacity for secrecy in democracy can be both used and abused and that the potential abuses have consequences for public consent. Part III presents a partial solution to the dilemma utilizing national security oversight institutions. The consequences of national security oversight institutions are explored empirically in a series of chapters in Part IV. The final section, Part V, takes the lessons from empirical results on the uses of national security oversight and applies them to current debates over leaking, oversight institutions, and executive powers around the world.[58]

Part I

DEMOCRACY CLASSIFIED: THE USES OF SECRECY

This part introduces the tension between private information and public mobilization in democracies. Specifically, I make the case in Chapter 2 ("Theories of Democratic Transparency and Foreign Policy Success") that previous theories of democratic foreign policy success have unreasonably limited meaningful transparency costs, while critics have assumed away the benefit of public consent in democracies. Therefore, both have largely ignored the secrecy dilemma.

However, the assumption of on-demand public information related to national security policy is difficult to sustain. Even in liberal theories where secrecy is given a tangential role, as in discussions of covert actions,[59] I find that since the public cannot view the content of information that is kept secret, a capacity for secrecy at the discretion of an executive is introduced.

I argue in Chapter 3 ("Not So Exceptional: The Theory, Uses, and Reality of National Security Secrecy in Democracies") that the capacity to allow an executive in a democracy to keep secrets has justifications in theory, history, and current institutional practice. Liberal theorists such as Immanuel Kant and Jeremy Bentham admitted national-security-relevant exceptions to their arguments for democratic transparency. Further, I show how, in practice, secrecy has allowed states to anticipate and deceive, as well as suppress the capabilities of, rivals using historical examples. The chapter ends with a survey of secrecy laws in contemporary democracies. I find that national security secrecy is a fact of democratic politics.

Part II

The Abuses of Secrecy and Public Consent

Once the capacity for secrecy in democracies has been established, the question then becomes what that means for democratic foreign policy and public consent. Chapter 4 ("The Potential Abuses of National Security Secrecy") highlights the fact that the capacity for secrecy can be abused, and the public is aware of this inescapable fact. The executive can use classification powers to deceive the public about the relative costs and benefits of policies. Moreover, counterintelligence tools, part of the capacity for secrecy, can be mobilized to track and suppress domestic opposition. I show that the capacity for secrecy in France led both to the production of the revolutionary 75-mm gun (a use) and to the Dreyfus Affair (an abuse) nearly simultaneously. Similarly, in the United States, the same capacity for secrecy was used for Project Azorian while being abused in the Watergate scandal.

In Chapter 5 ("The Consequences of Potential Abuse for Public Consent") I illustrate how the capacity for secrecy, and thus abuse, can render an executive unconvincing to the public and therefore lead to insufficient consent for investments in security. This dynamic played out in the decades between Dreyfus and World War I, where France became paralyzed by distrust and skepticism of potential abuses as the German threat strengthened. A similar, but less dramatic, story that unfolded in the United States as opposition to US policy in Cyprus in 1974 mirrored French distrust in the executive and even utilized some of the same arguments to withdraw commitments. In both cases, those that were skeptical of a leader could not be sure that calls to arms were in the public interest as opposed to the private interest of that leader or their party. How then do democracies thrive in the international system despite secrecy and its concomitant public accountability deficits?

Part III

Democracy Declassified: the Dilemma and Oversight

The answer to this question forms the basis of Chapter 6 ("Solving the Secrecy Dilemma"). A series of institutional innovations around the democratic globe have partially resolved the tension between national security secrecy and public accountability. When stymied by partisan gridlock and distrust, at specific times in history, elites have written new rules of the game that help to break the stalemate. For example, distrust between the Hats and Caps in Sweden precipitated the world's first freedom of information law, and extreme polarization in the United States during the Civil War gave birth to an experiment in legislative oversight, the Committee on the Conduct of the War. While each of these early innovations was rudimentary and severely flawed, they each attempted to create oversight of national security policy outside of the executive. From these humble beginnings, modern national security oversight was born and blossomed. This was particularly clear in the United States in the mid-1970s. These innovations help to explain why the United States was able to recover from Watergate and continue to compete in the final stretches of the Cold War, while France, which in contrast did not improve its oversight, suffered not only a costly stalemate in World War I, but defeat and occupation in World War II. Oversight institutions do not provide real-time, on-demand access to the public, since classification remains. However, they do take advantage of declining transparency costs over time and the possibility that leaders care about their position, party, policies, and legacy.

I lay out the empirical predictions of this theory of retrospective oversight in Chapter 7 ("The Consequences of National Security Oversight in Democracies") and compare its predictions on partisan polarization, military spending, and foreign policy success to other perspectives. These predictions highlight the constraining and mobilizing effects of oversight institutions, along with the fruitful combination of lower transparency costs and public consent in democracies with robust oversight.

Part IV

The Evidence

In the next part, we begin to empirically evaluate the usefulness of this new perspective. Does a focus on retrospective oversight of national security in democracies explain additional facts as compared to simpler theories that ignore these institutions and dynamics? Chapter 8 ("A View of National Security Oversight Institutions") presents a new catalog of national security institutions in democracies from 1970 to 2006. This chapter presents the geographic and over-time trends in these institutions. Most important, the data show that oversight has been expanding in democracies over time, on average, and that this trend appears across the globe. However, there is great variation in the level of oversight in different regions. Additionally, here we see that while in the late 1970s the United States had moderate investigative institutions, it was above other democracies on national security oversight. Over the last three decades, however, the United States has fallen behind other states that have continued to innovate, particularly on legislative oversight. These data are then used in the next chapter to examine the consequences for oversight.

With the theory of democratic oversight and new data on national security-specific oversight institutions, I move to an exposition of the real-world consequences of retrospective oversight. Chapter 9 ("Revealing Evidence: Support, Spending, and Success") includes three sets of investigations on how oversight affects support, spending, and success in democratic foreign policy. The first set of analyses explores how specific changes in retrospective institutions mobilize public support for military conflict, or do not, in France, the United States, and Great Britain. I present evidence that public support for military action has increased since the strengthening of French institutions in 1979 and since the improvements in US Freedom of Information laws in 1974 and co-temporal increases in legislative oversight in Washington. In contrast, over the same period of time (from 1959 to 2001) the United Kingdom did not significantly increase oversight, although it did institute some superficial changes around the time of the US and French improvements. As predicted, the United Kingdom has not seen a significant increase in its ability to generate public support in a crisis. Improved ex post oversight therefore allows leaders to get the benefit of the doubt from the public, a priori.

The second set of analyses provides evidence of the paradoxical but productive influence of oversight on military spending. I show that oversight institutions both propel military spending (what I term the mobilization effect) and constrain spending. As expected, states (such as the United Kingdom) that have modest but incomplete oversight in the national security realm have the highest military spending as a proportion of GDP. Here the public has some reassurance that large-scale corruption will be punished, but the elites know that there is still room for overspending on party and personal prerogatives. In comparison, states with historically high levels of oversight, such as the Netherlands, where the constraining effect of oversight should be stronger, tend to spend less than those democracies that have modest oversight, but more than democracies that lack any measurable national security oversight powers.

Next, I illustrate that the partial solution to the secrecy dilemma outlined leads to better outcomes for democracies that have strong national security institutions. When crises break out, democracies with national security oversight win a greater number of their foreign policy disputes as compared to democracies that lack these institutions. As expected, democracies that lack significant oversight have an increased tendency, relative to states with stronger oversight, to be targeted in a crisis when they are at a material disadvantage. Retrospective oversight turns out to be a force multiplier, allowing an executive to maneuver stealthily, with less public skepticism that the associated cost is not worth the benefit. Even if we measure foreign policy ability by the macabre measure of net fatalities, democracies with oversight substantively contribute to our understanding of foreign policy outcomes for democracies.

Taken together, the chapters in this section provide strong and consistent evidence that democracies that build and maintain oversight institutions are better able to manage foreign policies that promote the national interest as compared to democracies that lack these institutions.

Part V

CONCLUSION: IMPLICATIONS AND INNOVATIONS

In Part V (Conclusion), Chapter 10 ("Implications and Innovations"), I review the secrecy dilemma and draw out several implications relevant to debates about national security leaks, institutional changes, innovations in oversight, and executive powers. Secrecy, classification, and transparency costs have been in the news, as the public has attempted to understand policies involving everything from drones to the tapping of telephones in the United States and abroad. Less noticed has been a trend toward stronger freedom of information laws and stronger legislative oversight around the world.

I further discuss some challenges to effective oversight, as well as the moves in some countries to create bodies of experts that report to parliament. Over the last few decades, the Security Intelligence Review Committee (SIRC) in Canada, the Norwegian Parliamentary Oversight Committee (EOS), and the Review Committee on the Intelligence and Security Services (CTIVD) in the Netherlands, among others, have attempted to provide parliaments with expert advice on national security matters that either takes the place of targeted oversight by elected legislatures (as in Canada) or augments existing oversight institutions (as in the Netherlands).

These innovations have come at a useful time, as a focus on improved retrospective oversight has the potential to reinvigorate bipartisan foreign policy cooperation in democracies without undercutting the speed, dispatch, and discretion supplied by an executive to foreign policy decision-making. Thus, this book represents an effort to plot the development of democratic national security oversight in the past, understand the empirical consequences of these oversight institutions, and then apply those lessons to contemporary democracies.

PART I

Democracy Classified:
The Uses of Secrecy

2
—

Theories of Democratic Transparency and Foreign Policy Success

The spread of democratic forms of government around the world has spurred important and influential research on the role that domestic institutions play in the foreign policy processes of states.[1] One keystone of these arguments stretching back to Immanuel Kant has been that the process of public accountability allows democracies to execute efficient and successful foreign policy. While not uncontested,[2] research on elections and open flows of information to the public has yielded not only evidence of a democratic peace,[3] but other important empirical breakthroughs on foreign policy outcomes. These discoveries have centered on the foreign policy benefits of democracy, producing a growing consensus that democratic states win more of their wars,[4] successfully force rivals to back down in crises,[5] and effectively manage territorial disputes.[6]

Yet the fact that democracies keep national security secrets complicates our understanding of what role public accountability plays in democratic foreign policy success. How can the public know which national security policies to support and which to oppose if relevant information on the costs and benefits of foreign policy options is secret? Similarly, how can leaders, empowered with the ability to decide which information to reveal and what to keep secret, sell policies to members of the public, and particularly opposition partisans, if they cannot reveal the justifications for their proposals without endangering success? This is the secrecy dilemma in democratic foreign policy.

The purpose of this book is to identify and attempt to solve this secrecy dilemma. I argue for a liberal theory of democratic foreign policy that synthesizes the benefits of public accountability with the capacity for executive secrecy, rather than simply trading secrecy for accountability, or vice versa. To accomplish this, we need to appreciate the joint importance of the capacity for secrecy and the ability to generate public consent in democracies.

I begin with secrecy and transparency costs. The current chapter examines important liberal theories of democratic foreign policy success, as well as salient criticisms related to national security secrecy and accountability. A debate has been raised about the limits of transparency in democracies, specifically on national security issues. Many scholars have minimized the importance of democratic secrecy, assuming that the public has sufficient information to hold leaders to account for policies, both foreign and domestic, that have higher net costs to the public compared to alternatives.[7] In this set of arguments, secrecy is a marginal exception that does not impede democratic transparency and the benefits of public accountability.

Another set of scholars takes the opposite view of secrecy, emphasizing that national security policy is and must be conducted in secret. Here secrecy is the rule, not the exception.[8] To these critics, foreign policy secrecy obviates public accountability as either a scam or a danger. If the public does not have information on what policies are in their interest, how can they hold incompetent or corrupt leaders to account without descending into blind opposition or bellicosity? Where the first perspective minimizes the importance of secrecy in emphasizing the benefits of public accountability, the alternative perspective minimizes public accountability in the face of national security secrecy in democracy.

In making these strong but opposing assumptions, both perspectives miss the secrecy dilemma in democratic foreign policy. I then argue that attempts to minimize or assume away national security secrecy in democracies are limited by their reliance on the specific content of acceptable secrets, instead of focusing on the institutional capacity for secrecy itself.

Chapter 4 moves on to show why in theory and in practice the institutional capacity to keep secrets exists in democracies, and it also shows that this ability to limit publication is just as useful to the public as pure transparency would be to a potential enemy. Taken together, the first two chapters provide a justification for why we should take the capacity for secrecy in democracies seriously. This then serves as a launching pad for analyzing the consequences of national security secrecy in democracies for public consent in Chapters 4 and 5.

LIBERAL INTERNATIONAL RELATIONS THEORIES
OF DEMOCRATIC SUCCESS

Liberal international relations scholars have articulated several reasons that states with democratic institutions might formulate more effective[9] foreign policy as compared to non-democracies. These are commonly organized into two types of arguments: those that rely on norms of action and those that stress political institutions in democracies. Normatively based theories argue that leaders as well as citizens in democratic states hold specific sets of beliefs, values, and patterns of behavior that lead to more propitious outcomes. Reiter and Stam evocatively write that these types of arguments rely upon a "spirit" of democracy,[10] and they propose that the norm of allowing individual initiative in democracies could play a role in democratic war victories. Others[11] suggest that norms of peaceful conflict resolution lead to more cooperative outcomes for democracies.[12] A related set of arguments suggests that democracies have a norm of sticking together and bailing each other out of trouble.[13] These norm-based theories have received mixed empirical support and have been criticized for the difficulty in measuring norms.[14]

The second set of theories, the structural variants, are of more direct interest to the present study. Reiter and Stam suggest that domestic accountability institutions are the "skeleton" of democracy."[15] Democratic institutions allow for leaders to be held to account by the public for policies or proposals with which they disagree. In turn, this public accountability deters leaders from undertaking publicly costly policies that do not yield a net benefit for enough citizens.

The public benefits of democratic accountability rely upon two conceptually distinct but interdependent and crucial mechanisms: elections and information. First, government transparency and publicly available information through freedom of information laws, legislative oversight, and press freedom decrease the potential for the misuse of executive office by increasing the probability of catching corrupt or inept politicians, as well as lowering the cost to citizens and non-governmental groups of investigating political actions.[16] Second, electoral competition among elites to win elections increases the potential cost of promoting public-loss policies, conditional on those net losses being identified by voters.[17] These two pieces of the accountability puzzle—information and competitive elections—are interdependent. Without institutions that identify and publicize the actual and potential misuse of an executive office, elections can be held but will fail to punish those leaders that promote private interest policies at public cost. Similarly, without elections, it becomes much more difficult for the public to punish executive corruption or mistakes.

The Role of Transparency in Public Accountablity

Several important and influential works ground themselves in this structural theory of democracy[18] and thus assume that democratic accountability institutions,
and their ability to reduce executive corruption and incompetence, apply equally
to international security matters and domestic issues, with few caveats. This is
seen in the theoretical justifications provided in several high-profile and influential arguments for democratic foreign policy effectiveness,[19] which can be traced
back to Immanuel Kant in his First Definitive Article for Perpetual Peace (1795).
He writes[20]:

> [I]f the consent of the citizens is required in order to decide that war should
> be declared . . . nothing is more natural than that they would be very cau-
> tious in commencing such a poor game, decreeing for themselves all the
> calamities of war . . . . But, on the other hand, in a constitution which is not
> republican . . . a declaration of war is the easiest thing in the world to decide
> upon, because war does not require of the ruler, who is the proprietor and
> not a member of the state, the least sacrifice of the pleasures of his table, the
> chase, his country houses, his court functions, and the like. He may, there-
> fore, resolve on war as on a pleasure party for the most trivial reasons, and
> with perfect indifference leave the justification which decency requires to
> the diplomatic corps who are ever ready to provide it.[21]

Kant's argument about the institutions of consent has been utilized to extend
the logic of domestic accountability in democracies to foreign policy and international security issues. Unencumbered by democratic elections, leaders will be
able to push the costs of any policy, including war, onto the public, while hoard-
ing the potential benefits and avoiding political punishment. In contrast, if the
public, at a minimum, is able to punish leaders that fail to act in the public interest, costly policies due to incompetence or corruption will likely be deterred.
A key component of this argument is that citizens have sufficient information to
accurately calculate the costs and benefits of competing policy options; and thus
while they are "cautious," the public still calculates to "decide that war should be
declared" or not.

The Kantian accountability assumption, and this specific passage in particular, has been cited approvingly by influential international relations scholars such
as Bruce Russett,[22] Bruce Bueno de Mesquita,[23] Michael Doyle,[24] David Lake,[25]
and Kenneth Schultz.[26] For example, recent influential scholarship[27] argues that
states with broad enfranchisement and institutional rules that necessitate a large
coalition to keep a leader in power reduce the incentives for private-interest
and non-security-yielding foreign policy choices. Further, this is true equally for

domestic politics that may generate public health and grow employment, as well as foreign policies such as military spending decisions and crisis diplomacy.

Likewise, Lake,[28] in his pathbreaking study on democratic advantages, approvingly cites Kant when analyzing how democratic institutions reduce the rents that executives can potentially extract from the public in return for protection and other services. He states that "states can also act opportunistically against their own societies by artificially increasing demand for their services through extortion or racketeering. Extortion occurs when states magnify, exaggerate or 'oversell' foreign threats to society, whether by supplying incomplete information or outright deception."[29] He then notes that this rent-seeking activity of the executive is severely limited when the public can "monitor its performance and acquire information on the strategies it is pursuing, its real costs of protection production, the level of foreign threat, and the like."[30] He notes that monitoring and accountability are thus much easier in democracies than in autocracies,[31] and he further states that his argument "subsumes many of Kant's essential insights."[32] Lake also explicitly states that he views the constraints on executive rent seeking in democracies as equal across the domestic–foreign policy divide when he writes that there is not any "apparent reason why societal constraints on the state should differ significantly across areas of service."[33] By avoiding significant amounts of potential rent seeking through democratic transparency and accountability, democratic foreign policy is suggested to be more effective in providing public protection and winning conflict at a reasonable expense (pp. 28–30).[34]

Another important work, by Kenneth Schultz,[35] on democratic foreign policy credibility, involves a distinct mechanism for democratic efficiency but utilizes a similar assumption of transparency. Schultz argues that democracies' ability to credibly threaten uses of force follows from "public contestation . . . the two components [of which] are—publicity and competition," which he cites as the hallmarks of democracy. He notes that "[t]he public nature of democratic politics ensures that the process of decision making is observable by foreign states and can thus influence international behavior."[36] Schultz explicitly assumes that those outside of the executive have access to and can publicize "policy-relevant information"[37] that includes, but is not limited to, "the material outcomes of war, including the likelihood of victory and the expected costs, information about voters' willingness to trade off these costs for the good in question, and information about the likely political consequences of different crisis outcomes."[38]

For Schultz, public and opposition access to information allows a more credible signal to be sent from a democracy, as opposed to a non-democracy that can hide information and bluff in an international negotiation. Schultz illuminates the assumption of equal accountability on domestic and national security policy as he cites approvingly the works of Robert Dahl and Seymour Lipset concerning the domestic politics of democracies that make no issue-specific distinction.[39] Schultz spends a significant portion of one chapter defending the notion that extra-executive actors have equal access to relevant information.[40] Likewise, John Ikenberry contends that democracies are able to generate greater cooperation from other states due to the transparency of their governance structure. He assumes that in democracy "secrecy is seen to be the exception, not the norm."[41]

The Marketplace of Ideas: How Thick?

Perhaps the most sophisticated attempt to grapple with the role of national security information and structural transparency in democracies is embedded within Reiter and Stam's[42] discussion of democratic victory in war. They discuss several mechanisms that might link domestic institutions to war-fighting efficiency. Most generally, Reiter and Stam argue that democracies maintain a robust marketplace for ideas, building on the ideas of Schumpeter and Mill, and that this strong version of democratic transparency provides deeper underpinnings for understanding democratic efficiency. Again, like others, they explicitly reference Kant,[43] as well as Milton, Jefferson, and Mill,[44] in suggesting that democracies are defined by the transmission of information to the public and among the public so that informed citizen consent is built. Transparency institutions like a free press allow for open debate about the public benefits and costs of competing policies.

In foreign policy, just as in domestic policy,[45] Reiter and Stam suggest that elite decisions over policies, such as which wars to initiate, can be hampered by insufficient prospective discussion of alternatives if there is no democratic marketplace of ideas. In dictatorships where opposition viewpoints are highly costly to espouse and unlikely to be transmitted broadly, poor decisions are more likely to result because ideas have not been vetted and alternatives compared. In the marketplace of ideas in democracies, however, it is hypothesized that ideas and opinions do battle with each other openly and evenly, so that the better ideas are the ones that survive this scrutiny. Importantly, "better" is defined clearly as the ideas that maximize well-being such that the public "captures benefits while minimizing costs."[46] Therefore, as facts become publicly known, leaders make decisions about war and foreign policy, as "they do about any other policy issue."[47] This transparency, in turn, leads to superior international outcomes, such as winning a greater percentage of wars. The "marketplace of ideas" argument places a premium on public transparency across the domestic/foreign policy divide, as well as emphasizing the inability of an executive to hold an informational advantage over the public, except in limited circumstances.

A potentially less ambitious argument about democratic foreign policy success suggests that the marketplace of ideas is not as fully developed as previously discussed, and instead ensures simply that victory or defeat in war is strictly observable to the public and further that the public will punish defeat electorally. Reiter and Stam[48] argue here that the observability of victory coupled with public distaste for defeat leads rational leaders to avoid risky wars that would not be victorious, unless they can duck domestic punishment. In this watered-down formulation, the correlation between democracy and war victory comes about because leaders are more careful about the conflicts they choose in democracies and less careful in non-democracies due to the different probabilities of losing office and being punished by the public conditional on defeat.

This is a significantly more limited claim for transparency. While there are several problems with retreating to this limited informational content of the democratic marketplace of ideas, which will be discussed below, at present we need to understand the distinctions between these versions of the marketplace of ideas. Later, I will argue for a potentially useful middle ground that blends insights from the thick and thin versions of the marketplace of ideas. The thin marketplace assumes that the amount of relevant publicly available information can be collapsed to a simple signal, victory versus defeat. The thicker version, as we have seen, assumes that costs and benefits of competing policy proposals are available to the public. Relying simply on transparent signals of victory and defeat is also of limited relevance outside of the relatively rare set of interactions—wars—in contrast to the richer information content in the thick version of the marketplace.

There is another key difference between the thick and thin versions of the marketplace of ideas in democracies. The thick marketplace of ideas assumes a world where the public has real-time access to information that identifies publicly beneficial policies and those that are not and can then prospectively consent to policies that are carried forward. The thin version of the marketplace of ideas works backward in time. Victory or defeat is only observed ex post, but the leadership wants to avoid being punished for defeat, so they avoid difficult conflicts.

Following Kant's lead and applying the concept of democratic accountability, in both its thin and thick versions, to foreign policy has yielded significant empirical breakthroughs. As noted above, researchers have uncovered empirical evidence linking democratic institutions to lower propensities for conflict,[49] reduced defense spending,[50] enhanced credibility to threaten and negotiate,[51] and a higher propensity to win international wars,[52] in addition to a proclivity toward a separate peace.[53]

Except in rare instances, these liberal theories have not clearly delineated whether democratic transparency is more usefully characterized by thinner or thicker informational content and what role secrecy might play in public accountability on national security issues in democracies. Instead, they have assumed that the marketplace of ideas is thick enough to ensure that successful policies are chosen in a democracy. As we will see in the next section, the hushing-up of secrecy has created an opening for critics of democratic success.[54]

CRITICS AND THE CAPACITY FOR SECRECY IN DEMOCRACIES

Despite the empirical evidence of democratic effectiveness, several critics have pointed out two potentially weak links in the logical chain starting with democratic elections and transparency and stretching toward distinctive foreign policy behavior.[55] As the logic of democratic accountability has been imported from domestic-centric theories of political efficiency, the exigencies of national security secrecy and the capacity to keep secrets[56] have been either ignored altogether or sidelined as relatively unimportant.

Transparency Costs and Democracies

The first and simplest critique of public accountability in democracies is that its concomitant transparency takes a significant toll on foreign policy. By being public, democracies cannot keep necessary secrets and thus are at a military disadvantage. Gabriel Almond, following arguments by de Tocqueville,[57] contends that a democracy's lack of secrecy would inhibit effectiveness. In this analysis, democracies are indeed transparent, but this transparency is a significant drag on foreign policy effectiveness, rather than a boon, due to transparency costs. When the public is informed of the costs and benefits of various foreign policy alternatives, potential enemies become aware of vulnerabilities and weaknesses and further can anticipate democratic actions. In short, transparency costs the public, rather than fostering success.

The empirical prediction of this argument—that democracies should be less effective at foreign policy—however, is not consistent with the empirical evidence to date on democratic success discussed above. Additional countervailing evidence against this critique would be observations of democracies having a capacity to keep national security secrets.[58] However, the presence of secrecy institutions in democracies, while assuaging the concerns of Almond and de Tocqueville, would not necessarily increase our confidence in the mechanisms of public accountability and a robust marketplace of ideas.

Deception Instead of Accountabiity

More recent scholarship has taken a different and in some way deeper line of attack. Desch,[59] Schuessler,[60] and Downes[61] each criticize theories of democratic foreign policy efficiency for ignoring the reality of national security classification powers and secrecy in democracies and placing their theoretical bets unwisely on transparency and accountability. This perspective agrees with Almond that transparency costs exist, but it disagrees about whether democracies actually pay them. Instead, due to the potential for transparency costs if national security information were available in real time, democracies, just like autocracies, keep significant secrets for the public that allow leaders to evade public opinion.[62] Desch offers a clear articulation of this perspective when he argues,

> There are also good logical reasons to think that the relationship between democratic leaders and publics is exactly the reverse of that posited by the democratic triumphalists. Rather than the public being the key independent actor constraining the leadership, it is the leadership that really matters in the decision to go to war, with the public easily led along. This is the case because all leaders, democratic or not, are likely to have greater expertise than the general public, particularly in the abstruse area of national security affairs. It is also perfectly rational for most citizens in a democracy to remain "ignorant" in these realms . . . *Finally, democratic leaders can maintain secrecy about costs, benefits, and probabilities of war because much of the information necessary to judge those things is "private" (internal to the government) and can be kept from becoming public knowledge.*[63]

Likewise, Schuessler[64] suggests that "[r]ather than press their case in the marketplace of ideas . . . leaders will be tempted to preempt debate by shifting blame for hostilities onto the adversary." Leaders do this, according to Schuessler, through deception, in which one crucial component is "concealment, where a leader withholds vital information" from the public.[65] The critics take this argument to its extreme, arguing that since leaders control information, they are able to "manufacture consent" and thus "they no longer have to take public opinion into account and can pick fights as casually as their nondemocratic counterparts."[66]

Downes,[67] in a similar criticism of the assumption of a robust marketplace of ideas and public accountability in democracies, notes that "leaders may seek to conceal the potential costs of wars of choice from the public in order to build support for going to war in the first place"(p. 48). When explaining why Johnson chose to escalate the Vietnam War in the manner that occurred, Downes points to the importance of the executive's ability to keep secrets from the public. He writes that Johnson did not want a public discussion of war to drown out the passage of his Great Society legislation and that this "was the crucial factor that explains why Johnson escalated the war the way he did: slowly, incrementally, and most of all, secretly."[68] Therefore, the marketplace of ideas, as well as the ability of the public to identify the specific costs and benefits of distinct policy options, was obscured.

Neither Desch, Schuessler, and Downes nor other critics[69] have any doubt that executives in democracies not only have the capacity to keep secrets from their publics, but can selectively hide and reveal information so as to deceive the public. Since publicly available information is one of the keystones of the democratic accountability argument that was discussed above, this argument has significant consequences for the analysis of democratic foreign policy. The presence of meaningful information asymmetries that favor a leader over the public has the potential to empty the marketplace of ideas of the information necessary for the public to identify which policies are in their interest. Secrecy thus has the potential to sever the theoretical link between democratic institutions and foreign policy success. How can public security be fostered by the public if they are ignorant of the expected costs and benefits of policy options, as Desch contends[70]?

WHAT SECRETS? ASSUMPTIONS TO IGNORE OR LIMIT THE ROLE OF SECRECY

Given these subsequent criticisms, we need to undertake a damage assessment. In what ways does the recognition of a capacity for secrecy in democracies challenge liberal theories of democratic success? It is important to note that the previous theories of democratic efficiency, despite all resting on the logic of public accountability, each have slightly different theoretical arguments and thus vulnerabilities concerning the role of secrecy and the extreme transparency. These potential vulnerabilities populate a limited range from the extreme assumption of complete transparency for the costs and benefits of all national security policy options to the still significant assumption that secrecy might exist but is a special and limited case that can be ignored in most instances.

Most clearly, Bruce Bueno de Mesquita and colleagues[71] include transparency as an assumption in their model. The public benefits and costs of various policy options are formally assumed to be known to all.[72] A recognition of the capacity for national security secrecy would then challenge researchers to rethink the connections between democratic institutions and public benefits on security issues.

An Incomplete Defense of Transparency

The work of Kenneth Schultz goes farther by not simply assuming that the public has significant information about an array of foreign policy actions, short of war and including war, as well as their payoffs; he also expends considerable ink erecting defenses of the assumption of public transparency. Schultz admits that his theory requires that contending political actors "have useful information upon which to base their strategies . . . information that is relevant in international crises includes information pertaining to the material outcomes of war, including the likelihood of victory, and the expected costs, information about voters' willingness to trade off these costs for the good in question, and information about the likely political consequences of different crisis outcomes."[73]

His defense of this democratic transparency has three interconnected parts. First, he acknowledges that, indeed, the party holding the executive branch at a given time has access to significant foreign policy information. Schultz calls this "an obvious statement,"[74] and thus in this regard is in agreement with democratic efficiency critics—those in power have significant privileged access to information on national security. However, he departs from the critics by going on to argue, second, that those outside of government have access to functionally equivalent amounts of relevant information. He contends that this is the case because the party that holds power rotates over time. Therefore, today's opposition party is yesterday's government. For Schultz, this means that the opposition party has at least dated information about the international situation.[75] He adds that legislative oversight through committees involves minority parties and enhances the level of information available to opposition party members.[76] He does not argue, however, that any of these mechanisms provides real-time information on the context of threats and opportunities to those outside of the executive.[77] Third, and finally, Schultz argues that information on the international situation does not change very much over time; therefore, the dated information from the last time the opposition held power is still relevant.[78] For example, Schultz notes that most conflicts in international affairs occur within the context of ongoing international rivalries that can be decades old.[79]

Schultz should be commended for engaging in a partial defense of the role that democratic transparency plays within his theory of democratic credibility. Yet, his argument does not emerge from these criticisms unscathed and thus cannot be the last word on the subject of democratic national security transparency. A leader of a party who happens to be in control of the executive does not share foreign policy secrets with the whole of their party. If there are foreign policy secrets held in the executive, they are not automatically disseminated to the party. Executives from Lincoln through Obama and from Pitt to Thatcher have kept secrets related to the expected costs and benefits of foreign policy initiatives, including deployments, the relative competence of military leadership, the details of engagements, and other relevant intelligence, from members of their own party.[80] In fact, this intra-party secrecy is demanded by law, as the institutions of classification policy mean that only a select number of leaders within the executive have access to relevant national security information. A politician that divulged secrets to all fellow party members, whether they were in government or not, would be accused of sacrificing national security secrets to partisan ends.

Additionally, even if old information were shared, as Schultz suggests, despite the illegality of that sharing, new information that arrived in the meantime would still not be available outside of the executive. This is a significant disadvantage because everyone would know that it is only the current executive who has access to new information, and that new information may be highly valuable. The idea that old information is equally valuable in estimating the costs and benefits of various contemporaneous policy options as up-to-date intelligence estimates is not supported by the voluminous literature on the importance of efficient intelligence services.[81] Even within international rivalries, new information arrives that alters the strategic situation. In 1967, Israel had a strategic intelligence advantage, but by 1973 the situation had changed. During this time, Ben Gurion's faction from Rafi was absent from the executive, save for the brief national unity government. In Japan, a party other than the LDP was in power for only 11 months between 1955 and 2009.

There are other objections to the assumption that rotation in office provides transparency. It is often the case that even specific opposition party members, when they learn controversial facts, are likely to suppress that information for a time, as Senator Jay Rockefeller did in the United States when he objected to the NSA wire-tapping changes. He did not go public, and instead wrote a private letter to Vice President Cheney and reportedly locked a copy "in a sealed envelope in the secure space of the Senate Intelligence Committee." He stated in the letter that, "given the security restrictions associated with this information, and my inability to consult with staff and councel on my own, I feel unable to fully evaluate, much less endorse, these activities . . . without more information and the ability to draw on independent legal or technical experience, I simply cannot satisfy lingering concerns."[82] The memo is simply one example, but it does suggest that opposition members neither have access to sufficient information nor can share the limited information they do have with others in real time.[83]

Limiting Secrecy to Covert Action

Several other scholars that discuss the benefits of democratic transparency are aware that secrecy plays a potential role in national security policy, although that role is limited. The question then becomes whether these limits convincingly cordon off the arguments of critics. As we will see, given the nature of secrets, this is difficult ground to defend. For example, Lake, in his previously cited discussion of democratic efficiency, includes a footnote that reads, "monitoring costs will be higher, however, where the state can persuade society that 'national security' considerations require a higher degree of secrecy."[84] This idea is not discussed further, but it is an interesting exception. It suggests that secrecy can in certain cases interdict transparency specifically on national security issues, and it also connects secrecy with persuading the public to trust the leadership. These will be key themes of what follows.

Even more overtly, Reiter and Stam[85] write about one type of secrecy in democracies, covert actions, while at the same time arguing against the uses of secrecy. Building on the work of Forsyth,[86] Reiter and Stam note that democracies at times have utilized covert actions to keep foreign policy decisions and actions from becoming public. They further note that the supposed poor record of covert actions is a function of there being private information and failing to take advantage of the marketplace of ideas in democracies.[87] Instead of transparency costs, Reiter and Stam suggest that "[a]dvocates of secrecy overstate its benefits." They specifically point out that scientific innovations benefit from open access to information and suggest that the Manhattan Project benefited from this openness. Further, they make strong points about the necessity of public consent in democracies.[88]

While these are all valid points, they do not cleanly parry the thrusts from transparency critics. First, in Reiter and Stam's analysis, the capacity for secrecy must at least implicitly have been granted to executives in democracies, or else no actions could even potentially be covert. This begs the question of why, then, this capacity for secrecy is only used for self-contained covert actions. Second, covert actions and secrecy in general are partitioned from foreign policy. The Manhattan Project used some open source material, but it was one of the largest secrets kept in the United States, as even Truman was unaware of the project as Vice President. In fact, the critics' argument is not that transparency is not beneficial; it is instead that leaders can and do keep national security secrets. The Manhattan project and covert actions are examples of this potential for secrecy and the concomitant limitations on public information. There are two general problems with limiting the role of national security secrecy in democracies toward inconsequence in our models of democratic transparency: limits unenforceable by the public and meaningful transparency costs to the public.

Unenforceable Limits on the Content of Secrets

First, it is difficult to understand how the public could patrol the content of specific secrets. There is nothing within the impressive theoretical architecture assembled by Lake or Reiter and Stam that suggests why classification powers would be solely limited to covert actions or other narrow circumstances. There is evidence in these theories that secrecy is possible, for covert action, for example. If the capacity to interdict transparency exists, what restrains the use of that capacity to these limited cases? As we will see in Chapter 4, the same French Statistics Section covered up both the secret of the French 75-mm gun and political incompetence and abuses during the Dreyfus Affair.[89]

Limits based on content are difficult to enforce because the dynamics of information are such that once you know, you cannot unknow.[90] Therefore, once the executive has the ability to collect secrets, the public cannot check the content of the specific secrets—for they then would not be secrets.[91] A document that is classified and kept from the public could be the very thing the public would want a government to keep secret (e.g., nuclear codes, cryptographic breakthroughs, military strengths and weaknesses, sources and methods, etc.), but it could also be evidence of policies that were perpetuated at public cost without public benefits due to either incompetence or corruption (e.g., spying on opposition figures, overspending on weapons procurement, covering up a previous policy mistake or information that is politically inconvenient, etc.). As Mill reminds us, the public cannot "check or encourage what they were not permitted to see." Two serious case-study explorations of the uses of secrecy in democracy to date both suggest that executives can keep important information from the public and that these secrets go beyond simple operational concerns and are often motived by domestic political considerations instead of legitimate security.[92]

Meaningful Transparency Costs

An additional problem is that the uses of secrecy that fit these limitations, such as of covert action, tend to focus only on violent actions meant to be kept from public view that are unconnected to other foreign policy interactions.[93] Yet, as many have argued,[94] keeping actions and information out of public view is utilized as part of nearly every overt military operation and diplomatic negotiation. In the next chapter, I explore how keeping secrets has aided (a) diplomatic negotiations at the Washington Naval Conference, (b) traditional military battles as in the Battle of the Coral Sea and in the allied retaking of Italy and France, (c) during the nuclear arms race in the Cold War, and (d) in the production of the United States' stealth technology advantage. Without secrecy, there would have been significant transparency costs in these cases.[95]

Completely covert violent actions separate from other operations, such as secret assassination plots outside of a given war, may be a special limiting case, and they may indeed be more risky than other operational plans; however, the use of secrecy is not limited to such instances. It may be the case that advocates of secrecy overstate the benefits when they criticize public accountability, but that does not mean that the benefits of a capacity for secrecy are as limited as liberal theories of democratic foreign policy success suggest.

A RETREAT TO MISSION ACCOMPLISHED?

The question remains whether the thin marketplace of ideas is less vulnerable to these criticisms. In this case, one might argue that the democratic public knows just enough to hold leaders to account for defeats, even with secrecy. The core assumption in this limited variant is that both democratic and autocratic states can easily identify whether a war was a win or a loss.[96] Thus, at the coarse level of whether we got them or they got us, thick democratic transparency plays little role.

As noted above, however, this thin version of the marketplace has thus far been limited in its applicability only to wars, where defeat and victory are argued to be easily observable. One expects that such international interactions as diplomatic negotiations or even lower-level crises where no overt occupation occurs do not reveal victory as easily. For example, there were wide-ranging disagreements about the benefits of various START treaties in the United States during the Cold War and the twists and turns of the Middle East agreements, particularly within Israel, that remained unsettled due to ambiguities in publicly available information.[97] Similarly, the usefulness of specific alliance commitments may not be obvious to the public.[98]

Yet, while the assumption of transparent outcomes in the limited case of international war might seem unrelated to arguments for the capacity for secrecy in democracies (it is difficult not to notice foreign tanks running through your streets or houses burning), winning or losing a war cannot be disconnected from the utility it generates for political actors. If achieving publicized war aims always and everywhere guaranteed a net public gain in security and losses a net public deficit, relative to staying out of a conflict, the connection between outcomes and utility would be less problematic, but still open for debate. For example, it is always possible that an alternative strategy could have generated greater gains at the same costs or the same gains at lower cost, and thus had higher public net utility even in victory.[99]

But at a deeper level, there are many possibilities for a disjuncture between a victorious outcome as measured by whether a specific material war aim is judged to be achieved or not and measuring the concomitant net utility to the public. In fact, if we define successful foreign policy as something that has a net benefit to the public, relative to alternatives, we are right back in the same thicket of potential deception that critics highlighted. Capturing a neighboring capitol can appear to be a tactical victory, but if the operation does not yield a benefit net of the costs, the public would have been better off not initiating that tactic. Egyptian intervention in Yemen included early gains, for example, in the Ramadan offensive in February 1963, but it became clear over time that any regional prestige gains were far lower than the costs. Even from the other side of the conflict, the

Saudi government was able to eventually forestall Egyptian aims in Yemen, but at the cost of a split in the leadership.[100]

The reverse situation is also possible: a tactical defeat—for example, losing an outlying base—might bring longer-term security gains. In the first Taiwan Straits Crisis, Taipei lost several outlying islands that were difficult to defend. However, they not only held on to Quemoy and Matsu, which were strategically more important, but also gained a defense pact with the United States. In the next Taiwan crisis 3 years later, significant US support was crucial to holding on to territory, as was the fact that the limited Taiwanese assets were not stretched across a greater strategic perimeter.[101] The difficulty in mapping war events to net national security benefits is also illustrated by the recent US–Iraq War. Immediate military victory and occupation of Baghdad did not necessarily reap significant security gains for the US public.[102]

This suggests that while publics around the world may be able to view some material outcomes of specific battles and engagements, particularly if they are fought on the home front, it is more difficult to translate those observations into expectations of whether the public actually won or lost in terms of net security.[103] If the public cannot directly view costs and benefits of policies, as well as alternatives, then deception once again becomes possible.

Additionally, there are also ongoing disagreements concerning what the war outcome actually was in specific cases, such as the 1956 Sinai conflict[104] and Vietnam.[105] Disagreements on whether a war was a victory or not for a particular side, while understandable, suggest that outcomes may not be as clear-cut as this perspective hypothesizes, or at least are not wholly separable from other information that may or may not be publicly available. Even greater disagreements and ambiguity would be expected on policies less dramatic than war, such as negotiations, peace treaties, alliances, and crises resolved short of war.

This is not to argue that the observation of victory or defeat is inconsequential. However, when war aims are chosen by leaders, they may simply be revealed in part and thus open to deception. If democracies are merely better at winning inconsequential trials against weakened foes that do not generate significant public security gains, then even a correlation between democracy and victory could be hollow from the standpoint of public utility and security. On other other hand, if victory in war is evidence of net security benefits for the public, on average, we need to understand how citizens can tell the difference between victories that are hollow (or even costly) and those that carry net security benefits. For democracies to have this advantage over non-democracies, either the costs and benefits of all wars must be common knowledge across the world, regardless of domestic institutional context, but democracies must have the benefit of easily removing a leader from power, or there must be some informational advantage in some democracies on top of low-cost leadership removal.

A further discussion of this latter possibility will need to await our discussion in Chapter 6.

Common knowledge of both expected and occurring costs and benefits of conflicts is a much higher information threshold than simply observing "victory" or not. Reiter and Stam are open about this necessity in their work, as they note that publics care not only about outcomes, but also about the costs of obtaining those outcomes. They write that the public cares about "cheap victory" and affirmatively quote a historian who pointed out that "[t]he American public has wanted only one thing from its commanders in chief: quick wars for substantial victories with minimal costs."[106] They also go on to note that the public in a democracy is sensitive to costs in the form of casualties, and they cite research suggesting the public "as essentially stable, rational, and prudent, appropriately recognizing risks and interests in world affairs."[107] Therefore the "interests," which are benefits, are balanced against the "costs," connecting definitions of success explicitly to thicker information than merely the observation of a leader's declared aim being met or not.[108]

There is one additional problem with retreating to a thin marketplace of ideas. This argument might explain how democracies can avoid defeats, but it does not provide a process whereby these same liberal states can prepare for victory and gain net benefits. Fighting takes planning, preparation, and investment. The thick version of the marketplace of ideas suggests that a rich informational environment allows the public to consent to these investments in security and vet policies. The thin version provides no such mechanism for why the public would consent to investments in security and fighting capacity, or how the public might be assured that a specific weapons system or policy will increase public security at an efficient price. If we want to connect success, both within and outside of war, to the provision of net public security benefits, we must traverse back toward the thicker information content of the marketplace of ideas. Anticipating the discussion in Chapters 4 and 5, we will see that public consent to security investment and the capacity for secrecy sit side by side as key pillars of democratic foreign policy success. Yet, understanding how this consent is generated in democracies with executive classification powers entails more clearly valuing the role of national security information and secrecy in democracies, rather than limiting the issue or admitting defeat.

CONCLUDING WITH QUESTIONS

We are then left, after surveying the foundation of liberal arguments for democratic success, with significant questions about the role of the marketplace of ideas and national security secrecy in democracies. The capacity for secrecy appears to exist in some accounts, but how to police the limits on the use of that capacity is not spelled out. Further, the explicit uses of national security secrecy, to democracies, are left ambiguous. If secrecy is not ignorable, how can we resolve the inherent tension in liberal accounts of public consent emerging from a thick marketplace of ideas, particularly because the capacity for secrecy provides the executive at least partial control over what national security information is public and what remains classified?

To explore these questions further, I suggest that liberal theories of democratic success should not ignore transparency costs, but instead trace out the uses of secrecy and their implications for public consent. There is indeed a secrecy dilemma for democracies, but that does not mean that it cannot be partially solved.

The next chapter first looks back at the theoretical and practical justifications for providing a leader with the ability to keep secrets from the public. What we find is that even within the writings of the primary proponents of liberal publicity, including Kant, Mill, and Bentham, there are explicit justifications for legitimate national security secrecy. While no theorist alone explicated the secrecy dilemma, taken together these thinkers lay bare the core components of the dilemma for democracy: publicity is crucial to public accountability and consent, but that same publicity, on national security issues, can decrease public security. Yet, they provide no mechanism for overseeing whether the capacity for secrecy is being used or abused by executives.

The chapter then looks at examples to see whether the theoretical uses of secrecy are also mirrored in practice. In fact, the historical record reveals the value of secrecy that would be lost if democracies had no capacity to keep security-relevant information from the public. Both views from the theoretical and practical perspectives imply that the line between open transparency and any exception for secrecy may be more difficult to ignore than contemporary theories of democratic foreign policy success assume.[109] The next chapter ends by showing that the capacity for secrecy, and thus our dilemma, exists in democracies around the globe.

Not So Exceptional: The Theory, Uses, and Reality of National Security Secrecy in Democracies

While the information content available to the public in a mature democracy like the United Kingdom is unambiguously greater than what is available to analogous residents in a non-democracy such as North Korea, this does not imply that access to national security information is equal across democracies or that sufficient foreign policy information is available to support holding leaders to account for promoting suboptimal policies. My argument here is that the capacity for secrecy should not be ignored in democracies, nor should it be pigeonholed into a dimly lit corner of foreign policy. Instead, we should shine a broad spotlight on the capacity for democracies to keep secrets and the idea that this capacity is useful. Even though the light cannot reveal the content of specific secrets, the capacity itself has important consequences.

At the same time, we should not lock the notion of public accountability in democracies in a classified vault and throw away the key, as some critics advise. We cannot grapple with the dilemma of secrecy in democracies if one side assumes away the benefits of secrecy and the other ignores the benefits of public consent. As we will see, liberal theorists have much to add to this debate, even when we integrate secrecy into our understanding of democratic foreign policy success.

This chapter begins the task of exploring the justifications for national security secrecy in democracies, in terms of both the uses of secrecy and the transparency costs that might accrue to the public in its absence. Specifically, I will show that (1) even foundational liberal theorists such as Kant, Mill, Bentham, and Madison understood that democracies had reason to keep security-relevant secrets from the public; (2) on the ground, secrecy is useful both in crises and at times of peace to raise public security at reasonable cost in a broad range of cases; and finally (3) as a matter of fact, all democracies around the world allow executives to classify national security information. This calls into question the usefulness of democratic transparency assumptions embedded within current understandings of foreign-policy-relevant public accountability in democracies.[1]

EXCEPTIONS IN THEORY: KANT, MILL, BENTHAM, AND MADISON ON NATIONAL SECURITY SECRECY

Any list of the greatest proponents of liberal democracy must include Immanuel Kant, John Stuart Mill, Jeremy Bentham, and James Madison.[2] In fact, Michael Doyle, in his *Ways of War and Peace*, lists Kant, Mill, Bentham, and Madison among the first liberal thinkers he introduces.[3] These thinkers provide important intellectual roots for the liberal theories of democratic foreign policy success that were discussed in the previous chapter.

Upon inspection, we find that these theorists include explicit justifications for when secrecy is warranted in their work, despite the benefits of transparency. In particular, Kant, Mill, and Bentham note that it is possible that keeping secrets can save lives or increase public safety, with Mill and Bentham making explicit the connection between the need for national security secrecy and the capacity for governments to keep secrets.[4] However, it is Madison who most clearly connects the dots from these arguments into a fuller sketch of their logical contradictions for democratic governance. His insight is that the necessity of national security secrecy leads the government to have a sanctioned capacity to keep secrets and that this facility to manipulate and withhold information can distort public accountability.

Kant and Secrecy

As noted above, the work of Immanuel Kant has been used as a foundation supporting research on the role of democracy, international organizations, and trade in international affairs. Indeed, Kant went to great lengths to sketch the possibility of a fully open and public form of governance for states and expound on its potential benefits—namely, peace. In fact, he went so far as to state that "publicity" was one of the foundational principles of what was right and just.[5] However, even Kant includes exceptions to publicity in his writings.[6] In one of his last published articles, he included explicit "statutory" limits on publications that can be read by the public at large, "since unlimited freedom to proclaim any sort of opinion publicly is bound to be dangerous both to the government and to the public itself."[7] This is an explicit recognition of the capacity for the state to keep some information from becoming public knowledge and that complete transparency might have significant costs for the public itself. Other Kantian theorists have also noted Kant's exceptions for secrecy.[8] Elisabeth Ellis summarizes Kant's later writing on violent conflict as arguing that "the state will always have some legitimate interest in restricting potentially dangerous speech."[9]

Thus, from Kant we have not only the previously cited emphasis on public consent, but also exceptions for legitimate government secrets and censorship, despite his deep and abiding view of the importance of publicity. However, while he connected secrecy to the needs of the public in specific instances, he did not draw a specific connection to national security. Other theorists expounded on this connection more explicitly.

Mill and Bentham on Security and Secrecy

Beyond Kant, John Stuart Mill and Jeremy Bentham were pioneering proponents of publicity and government transparency, and they both illuminate the important role that publicity plays in public accountability. For as Mill puts it in the passage already quoted, "without publicity, how could they either check or encourage what they were not permitted to see?"[10] But Mill concedes, "Yet, that even this rule, sacred as it is, admits of possible exceptions, is acknowledged by all moralists; the chief of which is when the withholding of some fact (as of information from a malefactor, or of bad news from a person dangerously ill) would save an individual (especially an individual other than oneself) from great and unmerited evil."[11] For his part, Mill places high value on "security of person and place," noting that it "should be placed under central superintendence."[12] Thus, he argues that "[s]ecrecy is justifiable in many cases, imperative in some, and it is not cowardice to seek protection against evils which are honestly avoidable."[13] In discussing publicity, one explicit national security exemption for a state is where information can lead to "attacks directed against its own existence."[14]

Jeremy Bentham, another of the strongest early proponents of democratic transparency and an advocate of the role that informed consent can play in good governance, also carved out exceptions for national security information. Bentham wrote eloquently and convincingly in his pamphlet *Of Publicity* about the dangers of secrecy and the benefits of government openness. This work includes reasons that both legislatures and the head of state are better off with rules, votes, and opinions being public knowledge. The pamphlet ends, however, with a section entitled "Exceptions to the Rule of Publicity," of which he lists only three. The first is as follows: "Publicity ought to be suspended in those cases in which it . . . favors the projects of an enemy."[15] He continues that "it is not proper to make the law of publicity absolute, because it is impossible to foresee all the circumstances in which an assembly may find itself placed. Rules are made for a state of calm and security: they cannot be formed for a state of trouble and peril."[16] For both Mill and Bentham, transparency and publicity were foundational principles of a functioning democracy. However, on issues that could "favor the projects of the enemy" or involved "general maxims according to which war should be conducted," that foundation has a hole into which secrecy necessarily seeps. Mill and Bentham add to our understanding, beyond Kant's vague notion of "danger," in connecting the need for secrecy to designs of enemies and malefactors, particularly those who are foreign. Questions then arise: How big is this hole, and how do you know what is seeping through unseen by the public?

Madison's Worry: The Capacity for Secrecy and Public Accountability

It is to these questions that James Madison turned his attention in 1798 and 1799. Madison's views on representative government were similar to those of Mill and Bentham on publicity. While supporting the ratification of the US Constitution, he argued persuasively and eloquently for the use of checks and balances between branches of government and the important role that publicity played in accountability. When celebrating Kentucky's investment in public education, Madison wrote to W. T. Barry that "A popular Government, without popular information, or the means of acquiring it, is but a Prologue to a Farce or a Tragedy; or, perhaps both. Knowledge will forever govern ignorance: And a people who mean to be their own Governors must arm themselves with the power which knowledge gives."[17] For Madison, information animates the constitutional mechanisms of public accountability and allows citizens to rule themselves, as opposed to being trapped in the farce of supporting policies that are not in their own interest or the tragedy of opposing policies that would forward the public interest.

However, it was James Madison who clearly articulated the basic elements of the secrecy dilemma, if not the dilemma itself. When it came to the crucibles of war, peace, and diplomacy, Madison understood the connections among the necessity for national security secrets, the capacity for government to decide what is public information (and what is not), and the toll that could take on public accountability in democracies. In 1798, Madison wrote to Thomas Jefferson that "the management of foreign relations appears to be the most susceptible of abuse, of all the trusts committed to a Government, because they can be concealed or disclosed, or disclosed in such parts and at such times as will best suit particular views."[18] He argued a year later that the ultimate control of national security information by the executive meant that the "prerogative that superintends all foreign dangers . . . [can] exhibit and vary the pictures of them, at its pleasure."[19]

These arguments take the ideas of exceptions of Kant, Mill, and Bentham and deduce a logical conclusion. Executives' "prerogative that superintends all foreign dangers" meant that they had access to and control over information that the public did not. Further, this was understandable and legitimate because of the benefits of national security secrets in the first place to the public.[20] However, there was a cost to this capacity for secrecy. It allowed the information to "be concealed or disclosed in such parts and at such times as will best suit particular views" and the executive to "exhibit and vary the pictures" of threats and opportunities to the public "at its pleasure." Emma Rothschild writes that for Madison, excessive national security secrecy was "the only serious risk to liberty in America."[21]

Without publicly available information and without a thick marketplace of ideas, the popular government, however skillfully constructed, would either fall into blind support for a de facto king, making a farce of self-government, or fail to use the machinery of government to produce good public policy, which would be a tragedy. While he stated the problem succinctly, there is no evidence in the writings of Madison—or Kant, Mill, and Bentham, for that matter—that they were able to solve the dilemma between the necessity of some secrecy for public security on the one hand and accountability on the other.[22]

PRACTICAL USES: ANTICIPATION, DECEPTION, AND CAPABILITY SUPPRESSION

The legitimate uses of national security secrecy support the wisdom of the exceptions carved out by liberal thinkers over the years. Madison experienced this firsthand as the White House burned in 1814 after the British surprised him in attacking Washington, DC, instead of Baltimore. In fact, the President had planned to have a party at the White House the night it burned, the food for which was eaten by the British before they set the building ablaze.[23] These legitimate uses for secrecy are important because they justify the apparatus of national security secrecy in liberal democracies.[24] The uses of secrecy directly imply that there are relative transparency costs that would have to be paid if secrets could not be kept in democracies.

Codebreaking, encryption, and the accumulation of intelligence on the motives, location, and capacity of potential enemies and negotiation partners has proved invaluable over centuries. *The Art of War* by Sun Tzu devotes an entire chapter to the use of intelligence and spies. No less an authority on both war and democracy than George Washington noted, "There is nothing more necessary than good intelligence to frustrate a designing enemy and nothing requires greater pains to obtain."[25] In this section I explore the reasons that publicity exemptions exist for national security information.

To be clear, secrecy has costs. Not only does the classification of documents necessitate an infrastructure, but it has other pathologies, including information compartmentalization, group think, and corruption. However, most of these costs are common to all states and bureaucracies, not just democracies. Secrecy's deprecation of public consent and accountability, on the other hand, is uniquely relevant to democracies. Despite this, transparency costs mean that the ability to keep secrets is one component of foreign policy efficiency. As we will see, even as secrecy complicates mobilization, accountability, and democracy, eschewing all potential for secrecy is neither practical nor prudent.

It may be tempting at this point to partition secrets into different types—for example, secrets over operational matters versus strategic motives. However, this would obscure the point of this analysis. When a leader is given the capacity to keep secrets, that capacity can be used to classify both security and nonsecurity content. It is the capacity for secrecy, not the content of the information, that is the central concept of interest here.

Specifically, I will discuss how the capacity for secrecy can allow states to do at least three things that can substantially increase their foreign policy effectiveness: (1) anticipate a potential enemy or rival negotiator as in the Battle of the Coral Sea and Midway, the Washington Naval Conference, and the Cuban Missile Crisis; (2) deceive a rival as in Operation Mincemeat and Operation Overlord in World War II; and (3) suppress enemy capabilities as in the development of the US atomic bomb, for a time, and more successfully with stealth technology.

Anticipation and deception in many cases are sides of the same coin. Where anticipation robs an opponent of the element of surprise and private information, deception allows a state to maneuver unanticipated, and capability suppression decreases potential future threats. For example, at Pearl Harbor the Japanese navy was able to surprise the United States not only because Washington was deceived about both Japanese intentions and force location, but also because the Japanese had an aircraft-fired torpedo that could be utilized in shallow water.[26] The United States was unaware of this technology and thus believed that its ships were not as vulnerable as they were. In fact, there was a now in-famous message that was sent to the commander of the US Pacific Fleet, Admiral Husband E. Kimmel, in February 1941, that read in part, "based on known data regarding the present disposition and employment of Japanese naval and army forces, no move against Pearl Harbor appears imminent or planned for in the foreseeable future."[27] If the United States had been able to anticipate Japanese technology, intentions, and timing, a large portion of the fleet would not have been sitting idle in shallow water, and more appropriate countermeasures would have been taken.

Likewise, the United States was able to gain a tactical advantage in the 1991 Iraq War due to the accurate anticipation of Iraqi troop locations while deceiv-ing Baghdad as to where the main US thrust was aimed. Specifically, the United States made several fake amphibious attempts to land in and attack Kuwait City, while the main attack was to come at the southern border of Kuwait. Had the Iraqi forces instead been able to successfully anticipate where the US force was going to be concentrated, US casualties would have been much higher in retaking Kuwait. The capacity for the United States to keep these plans secret led to suc-cessful anticipation and deception in these cases and produced rather stunning international outcomes.[28]

Having the capacity to keep secrets also allows a state to suppress the tech-nical knowledge of operational advances in strategy, organization, and military capital of a rival, thus enhancing its own relative leverage. This capability sup-pression effect is analytically separable from deception and anticipation. Without secrecy, the details of the atomic bomb and other useful technologies would be freely available, enhancing capabilities around the world, for both other states and non-state actors. At the turn of the twentieth century, the French had devel-oped a revolutionary 75-mm gun with a recoil mechanism and break that allowed for more accurate and sustained fire, and they were eager to keep that infor-mation out of German hands, in particular.[29] Further, Biddle[30] makes the case that organizational knowledge is just as critical as information on military capital production. Lupfer writes that the United States often refused to publish memo-randa on battles even within the military security infrastructure for fear of secret lessons and countermeasures leaking out.[31] Thus, concealing useful information about the technologies of producing military materiel, along with the organiza-tional knowledge of how to dynamically deploy this military capital, can decrease the effectiveness of potential enemies.[32]

It will be helpful to look more closely at some examples of anticipation, de-ception, and capability suppression as we weigh the benefits of the facilities for secrecy in democracies. This is not to suggest that keeping specific information secret is always and everywhere beneficial. For example, keeping capabilities se-cret might lead a rival to doubt the credibility of a threat, when in fact they should back down.[33] However, the capacity of national secrecy is not something that should be ignored.

Anticipation

It is easiest to see the value of national security secrecy during wartime, although as we will see, secrecy can sow considerable foreign policy harvests during peacetime. As Sun Tzu writes, "what enables the intelligent government and a wise military leadership to overcome others and achieve extraordinary accomplishments is *foreknowledge*."[34] Several democratic successes and failures over the last 50 years have been directly attributable to the balance of intelligence on the field of battle. On the ground there is the practical and at times bloody importance of being able to uncover an enemy's plans and catch a rival by surprise. We can see the benefits of intelligence and anticipation in the War the in Pacific, the outcome of the Washington Naval Conference, and the Cuban Missile Crisis.

THE WAR IN THE PACIFIC
One of the most valuable intelligence triumphs of the last 70 years was the successful cracking of the Japanese naval code during World War II. Breaking an enemy code, unbeknownst to that rival, allows a state to anticipate actions and prepare the field of battle for success. Two examples of this process occurred during the War in the Pacific in 1942. Parker[35] makes the case that decoded signals intercepted from the Japanese Imperial Army, made possible by the clandestine cracking of the Imperial Japanese Navy's Ro code, alerted the United States to Tokyo's plans to move on Port Moresby and Tulagi in what became known as the Battle of the Coral Sea. In fact, the United States had more than a month's notice that Operation MO was being planned by the Japanese.[36] At the time, there were no US carrier groups in a position to defend these ports. In fact, even with the extreme advance warning, two out of the four US carriers in the Pacific did not make it to the battle. Having received advance warning of Operation MO and learning that the Japanese force was likely to be substantial, the Allied Powers dispatched a joint US–Australian force consisting of two US carriers, the Lexington and the Yorktown, to the area. The timing of the advance warning turned out to be enormously important. In preparing for their invasion of Port Moresby and Tulagi,[37] the Japanese had set up a line of submarines between the last known position of the US carrier fleet and Port Moresby. This is presented schematically in Figure 3.1. These submarines were to provide warning to the invasion force when the expected lone US carrier was on its way to respond to the attack. The Japanese believed incorrectly that the other three US carriers were far removed from the targets. However, unknown to the Japanese force, the United States had already moved two carrier groups on the other side of the Japanese

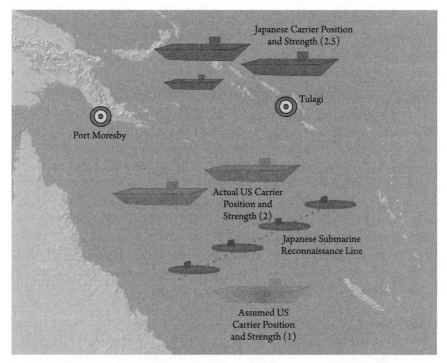

Figure 3.1 Representation of the Battle of the Coral Sea with approximate positions and strengths of forces. Not to scale.

submarine reconnaissance line toward the ports (see Figure 3.1). This allowed the United States the element of surprise, while depriving the Japanese of the same, and significantly evened the odds of the ensuing battle. While the Japanese navy still had the advantage of a light carrier in addition to other benefits, the arrival of both the Lexington and the Yorktown well before they were expected significantly changed the order of battle.

While the Japanese force was successful in its initial advances in May 1942, it suffered heavier-than-expected losses. Further, not knowing that the United States had two carrier groups in theater, the Japanese fleet moved to engage what it believed was an inferior US force. In the ensuing battle, Port Moresby was held by the Allies. Further, the sinking of the Shoho light carrier and the damage inflicted to the Shokaku and Zuikaku carrier groups depleted the Japanese Pacific force going forward.[38] At the time, the Japanese Navy had been advancing in the Pacific theater. The costs extracted at Coral Sea set the stage for the triumph at Midway that is credited as a turning point for the naval war. Had neither the Yorktown nor the Lexington been in theater, it is likely that Port Moresby would have been taken and, further, that the carriers would have arrived at the scene one at time, each then facing long odds.[39]

Similarly, the Allied Forces had significant advance warning prior to the battle of Midway. The Japanese continued to use their compromised Ro code, which was termed JN-25 by the United States. Decrypted messages referred to planning of an attack on "AF." It was not known what location this referred to, but Midway was one likely possibility. In an ingenious and daring feint, the United States sent out a false message from Midway stating that its water distillation facilities were malfunctioning. Sure enough, the United States quickly picked up a coded Japanese naval message that "AF" was short on water. In addition to the target of the planned invasion, cryptographic evidence also provided Admiral Nimitz with details of the battle plan and force. This allowed the United States to speed repairs on the carrier Yorktown, which had been damaged at Coral Sea, and return it to the Pacific theater to join the Enterprise and Hornet in the defense of Midway. Similarly, the United States learned that the Japanese fleet was dispersed into four parts with hundreds of miles separating important components from their carriers.

The Japanese had not broken US codes at the time and thus were largely unaware of both what the United States knew and the location of US carrier forces. Anticipation and the element of surprise were crucial for the United States, and without the ability to keep secrets, US costs would have been higher. While the Japanese carrier force was attacking Midway, unsuccessfully due in part to Allied reinforcements that had Arrived before the invasion began, the US carrier group was launching an air attack on the Japanese force.[40] The outcomes of Coral Sea and Midway allowed the United States to begin turning the tide of battle in the Pacific.[41]

THE WASHINGTON NAVAL CONFERENCE

Anticipation is also of dramatic value during peacetime. The ability to acquire clandestine information outside of war played critical roles, for example, in the Washington Naval Conference negotiations and the Cuban Missile Crisis, underscoring the wisdom contained within Federalist Paper 64, which reads, in part, "It seldom happens in the negotiation of treaties, of whatever nature, but that perfect secrecy and immediate despatch are sometimes requisite. These are cases where the most useful intelligence may be obtained, if the persons possessing it can be relieved from apprehensions of discovery." The Washington Naval Conference was an attempt to negotiate a de-escalation of the shipbuilding arms race that was accelerating in the early 1920s, particularly with regard to battleships. The main US aims at the conference were to slow Japanese expansion in the Pacific maritime theater of operations. The Japanese, one of nine parties at the talks, for their part wanted to secure a de-escalation of tensions with the United States and were willing to make compromises on battleship ratios to achieve this end. However, the United States had an invaluable tool at their disposal during the negotiations. The US Black Chamber, also known as the Cipher Bureau, under the leadership of Jonathan Yardley, had cracked the Japanese diplomatic code, which was distinct from the later naval code. This allowed US cryptographers to decode the specific instructions that Tokyo supplied to the negotiation team. The precise negotiation instructions that the United States was able to decrypt during the conference included this on November 28, 1921:

> Referring to your conference cablegram No. 74, we are of your opinion that it is necessary to avoid any clash with Great Britain and America, particularly America, in regard to the armament limitation question. You will to the utmost maintain a middle attitude and redouble your efforts to carry out our policy. In case of inevitable necessity, you will work to establish your second proposal of 10:6.5. If in spite of your utmost efforts, it becomes necessary in view of the situation and in the interests of general policy to fall back on your proposal No. 3, you will endeavor to limit the power of concentration and maneuver of the Pacific by a guarantee to reduce or at least to maintain the status quo of Pacific defenses and to make an adequate reservation which will make clear our intention in agreeing to a 10:6 ratio. [This] is to be avoided as far as possible.[42]

Therefore, during the early stages of the talks, President Harding's team, led by Secretary of State Charles Evans Hughes, knew what the Japanese bottom line was. Yardley wrote about the Washington Naval Conference negotiations that "stud poker is not a very difficult game after you see your opponent's hole card."[43] The Japanese had no such access to information that would enable them to anticipate how far US intentions and strategy could be bent short of conflict. While the negotiations took some time, Japan slowly backed down from their original 10:7 ratio offer to 10:6.5 and lower. The United States held fast and refused to accept anything less than what they knew was the most the Tokyo team would offer without breaking off negotiations. Indeed, the eventual agreement on armaments involved ratios of 10:10:6 with respect to the United States, the United Kingdom, and Japan's relative fleet tonnage. Secrecy provided net benefits during the negotiations that would have been impossible if the public had been aware of what the US government knew.[44] The United States had secured in peace, through the skillful use of intelligence and secrecy, something many nations fail to procure even in war: a relative decline in the capabilities of a rival.[45]

THE CUBAN MISSILE CRISIS
Similarly, two critical strands of US success in the Cuban Missile Crisis can be traced to dark corners of government action—one mechanical, the other human. First, Washington had been working since the early 1950s to design and build

a high-altitude reconnaissance aircraft that could fly over targets at an altitude that was unreachable to anti-aircraft missiles and fighter jets. Clarence Johnson at Lockheed Aircraft Corporation developed what became the eventual design in his Advanced Development Projects shop, also known as Skunk Works, in Burbank, California. The design was cutting edge and ahead of its time. In fact, the design was turned down by the Air Force when originally presented. However, it caught the attention of the CIA, who believed that it would make an ideal spyplane. Lockheed then received a secret $22.5 million contract for 20 planes, which were to be called the U-2, with the "U" standing for "utility." The planes could fly at 70,000 feet and necessitated that pilots wear space suits. The U-2 began its operational service in 1956.[46]

The U-2 spyplane used by the CIA and eventually accepted in the Air Force proved to be an extremely valuable intelligence-gathering tool. Further, in these early years of the Cold War, the Soviet Union did not fully appreciate the perception that it allowed. The U-2 provided intelligence on Soviet nuclear and conventional capabilities and even monitored French nuclear testing in 1964. However, no incident illustrates its worth so clearly as the pictures taken by Major Richard Heyser from his U-2 on October 14, 1962. In a flash, the Cuban Missile Crisis had begun. The U-2 pictures showed the early stages of a military construction project to build missile silos in Cuba that could be armed with nuclear warheads. These missiles, when operational, would have been able to reach Washington in a matter of minutes. While the President and his staff were deeply worried about the move, the warning allowed them time to formulate a response.[47]

The photographic evidence, however, was only one piece of the intelligence that alerted the United States to the growing threat in Cuba. In fact, the photographs might have been useless without information supplied by Colonel Oleg Penkovsky. Schecter and Deriabin[48] write that Penkovsky was a colonel in the GRU, the Soviet military intelligence agency, who approached a group of Americans in Moscow in 1960 offering them documents to be delivered to the CIA. While the CIA was slow to respond to Penkovsky, MI6 made contact. Penkovsky provided key information on Soviet operational plans and missile technology. This information was crucial to US efforts to understand what the Soviets were building in Cuba in October of 1962. While the U-2 was the high flier and took great pictures, Oleg Penkovsky's intelligence allowed Washington to interpret a set of low-resolution pixels taken at 65,000 feet as a threat to national security.[49]

The Soviet gambit to place missiles in Cuba was founded on the notion that the missiles could become operational before the United States detected them. Khrushchev wrote in 1970 that "it was during my visit to Bulgaria [in April 1962] that I had the idea of installing missiles with nuclear warheads in Cuba without letting the United States find out they were there until it was too late to do anything about them."[50] Khrushchev, it has been said, was convinced that the "palm trees" would provide adequate cover.[51]

In point of fact, the USSR almost got away with delivering and installing the missiles, through one Soviet technological achievement and two flukes. First, since 1957 the United States had been operating U-2s over Soviet territory. However, by 1960 the USSR had developed SA-2 SAM missile capabilities that could shoot down the U-2. The first successful hit on a U-2 came on May 1, 1960, when CIA pilot Francis Gary Powers was shot down over Sverdlovsk and captured. As a result, President Eisenhower scaled back U-2 flights, including a complete suspension of overflights of the USSR. Thus, the U-2 could no longer fly in 1962 with the relative impunity[52] enjoyed before May 1960.

Then two haphazard but highly important events occurred in 1962 that almost robbed the United States of the benefit of anticipation. First, on August 30, an Air Force–operated U-2 overflew Sakhalin Island in the Pacific, which is part of Russia, on accident. The United States was forced to formally apologize for this, and the incident increased Washington's sheepishness about overutilizing the U-2. Second, another U-2, this one operated by Taiwan, was shot down over China on September 9. Together, these two events, along with the 1960 U-2 downing, convinced Secretary of State Dean Rusk and National Security Adviser McGeorge Bundy that bimonthly Cuba overflights should be stopped. Thus, there were no U-2 flights over Cuba from September 5 until October 14, just when key components of both SS-4 and SS-5 missile systems were being delivered and constructed.

However, despite these delays, the United States was able to learn about the missiles before they were operational. This anticipation gave the United States time to seek negotiations, talks that eventually were successful and possibly prevented multiple mushroom clouds. It took the EXCOMM group, the team tasked with thinking through US strategy, a week to coalesce around the idea for a blockade, rather than a direct military strike. Had the United States remained unaware of the missiles until they were operational, it is much less likely that the crisis would have been defused in relative peace.[53] Intelligence allowed the United States to anticipate, just in the nick of time, the Soviet plans and, with difficulty, head them off. Kennedy is reported as saying the following on November 26 while presenting the Presidential Unit Citation to the 4080 Strategic Wing, and the 363 Tactical Reconnaissance Wing, which had housed the U-2 pilots and crews: "I may say, gentlemen, that you take excellent pictures and I have seen a good many of them, beginning with the photographs which were taken on the weekend in the middle of October which gave us the conclusive proof of the buildup of offensive weapons in Cuba."[54] The role of Penkovsky's information has not gone unappreciated. Former GRU Colonel Viktor Suvorov paid tribute when he wrote, "[H]istorians will remember with gratitude the name of the GRU Colonel Oleg Penkovsky. Thanks to his priceless information, the Cuban crisis was not transformed into a last World War."[55]

Deception

Similarly, the ability to deceive an enemy into false anticipation or inaction is highly useful and can only come with secrecy and stealth of operation. The usefulness of foreign policy deception is of course the punchline of the Trojan Horse tale. In more detail, Sextus Julius Frontinus, a Roman consul and provincial governor, wrote a series of books known as the *Strategmata*, which included hundreds of examples of ancient deceptions that were useful in battle. In the foreword, Frontius writes that "[t]he essential characteristic of [stratagem], resting, as it does, on skill and cleverness, is effective quite as much when the enemy is to be evaded as when he is to be crushed."[56] Two dramatic and highly influential modern cases in Europe during World War II can serve to illustrate the dramatic utility of deception. Operation Mincemeat preceded the US attack on Sicily, and Operation Overlord involved deception before, during, and after D-Day. The Allies' aim in each case was to deceive the enemy into defending against a pretended threat, thus opening the way to a less costly landing in continental Europe.[57]

OPERATION MINCEMEAT
In late 1942, the Allies were making gains in north Africa and were planning to open a southern front on the European continent. The obvious target for the initial crossing was Sicily due to the availability of air cover from Malta and the short maritime distance needing to be covered. However, the benefits of Sicily as an initial target were negated by the very fact that its attractiveness was obvious to the enemy. As Churchill put it with his usual tact, "Everyone but a bloody fool would know it was Sicily."[58] Thus, Berlin specifically planned for Sicily to be the head of the Allied crossing. To negate this anticipation, intelligence operatives in London began to create a scheme to deceive Berlin into thinking Greece rather than Sicily would be the epicenter of the Allied attack. If successful, this deception would mean less resistance in Sicily as the actual crossing progressed, as the Axis powers not only would be spread thin across thousands of miles, but would be slow to deploy to the point of actual attack.

The resulting Operation Mincemeat was both intricate and farfetched.[59] The general idea was simple enough: to orchestrate a scenario where the Germans would discover false plans for an Allied invasion of Greece, but take these plans as genuine.[60] However, the details of the operation were anything but simple. To carry out the plan in a convincing fashion, a false identity was created for one

William "Bill" Martin, who did not exist (yet). He was given a backstory involving a fiancee (complete with a picture, love letters, and a receipt for a very expensive ring), ticket stubs (from a London theater as well as bus transportation), and, most important, quality undergarments.[61] In his final fictional moments, he was supposed to have been carrying these secret plans for the (false) invasion of Greece when his plane was lost at sea near Spain.

A corpse was necessary to transmogrify the fiction into corporeal form. One was procured, preserved in dry ice, and outfitted with both the identifying information and the plans. On April 19, the HMS Seraph submarine left Scotland for the Spanish coast with the body aboard. At night on April 30, Major Martin was pushed overboard near a Spanish beach with airplane debris. The area was carefully targeted due to its proximity to an active German intelligence operative residing nearby who had Spanish contacts. The next day, British command issued orders to its consulates to locate the "lost" plans, but not to let anyone know of their immense value. On June 4, Major Martin's name was included among the names of British casualties published in the *Times*. The *rus de guerre* worked to perfection, as the imagined story weaved its way from the hands of a fisherman to the Spanish local government to German agents and eventually into Hitler's own defense strategy. Operation Mincemeat dovetailed with the larger Operation Barclay. Macintyre[62] reports that

> The deception swung into action on a range of fronts. Engineers began fabricating a bogus army in the eastern Mediterranean; double agents started feeding false information to their Abwehr handlers; plans were drawn up for counterfeit troop movements, fake radio traffic, recruitment of Greek interpreters and officers, and the acquisition of Greek maps and currency to indicate an impending assault on the Peloponnese.

In reaction, the German command significantly altered their defense posture in the south, opening up Sicily and heavily defending Greece and the Balkans, even after Mussolini protested such a move. The allies continued to sell the pretend attack on Greece by sending saboteurs to Greece to destroy railway lines and communication channels in the German ranks.[63] Bombing raids were spread out from Sardinia to Greece to further the confusion. The operational details of the pretended plan versus what became the actual invasion of Sicily (Operation Husky) are shown in Figure 3.2. As decoded messages from ULTRA confirmed the success of the deception, Churchill received the news that would soon pay dividends on the beaches of Sicily: "Mincemeat swallowed rod, line and sinker."[64] The ensuing Allied landing that began the Italian campaign has been called the most successful amphibious assault of the war.[65] Without secrecy, this useful deception would not have been possible.

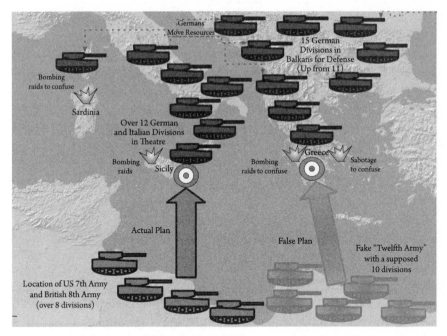

Figure 3.2 Representation of the Operation Mincemeat deception with approximate positions and strengths of forces. Not to scale.

OPERATION OVERLORD

The more well-known success of Operation Overlord, which came to a head on D-Day, was enabled by a similar deception, minus the gory transportation of fake plans. In early 1944, the Allied forces were preparing to make a larger and crucial landing on the European continent from the United Kingdom where forces were massing. Several possible landing spots were identified, including the beaches of Normandy and the Pas du Calais—which was an obvious spot due to its proximity to Great Britain—but also Eastern Europe and southern France. Ultimately, Normandy was chosen as the target.

Just as in Operation Mincemeat, the Allies were convinced that the success of the operation hinged on deceiving the Germans into defending the wrong beaches and holding up troops at strategically less important locales. There were actually two deception operations that occurred simultaneously as part of what became known as Operation Fortitude. The first, Fortitude North, was originally conceived of as an attempt to convince Berlin that an attack would come from Scotland into Scandinavia. However, reality interfered with this feint. It became clear to Allied logistic operators that the Scottish ports could not handle the needed capacity for such an invasion and that German intelligence officers would know this. The pretended units were then moved to Clyde on the west coast, and early stages of negotiations with Sweden were carried out. The negotiations were supposed to convince Berlin that a Norwegian invasion was in the offing. However, since the imaginary force had moved to Clyde, when the Germans picked up the radio traffic they believed, on balance, that the force was targeted at France.[66]

The second prong of the plan, Fortitude South, was more elaborate and successful. It was aimed at leaking false information to the German army and planting false clues on the ground that Pas de Calais was actually the target of the eventual D-Day crossing. The Pas de Calais was a logical choice, as its beaches were both easily in reach of the United Kingdom and difficult to defend. Fake tanks and landing craft, pretend encampments, and even a fictional army group were set up on the British coast opposite. Double agents were also used to pass information to the German intelligence establishment. Two other feints proved decisive. The Allies used fake radio signal traffic, as part of a subcomponent of the plan known as Quicksilver II, to mislead the German command about the concentration of the forces as well as bombing radar installation around the Pas de Calais.

As the Allies listened in to decoded German communications through Project ULTRA, they learned that Berlin believed not only that the Pas de Calais would be the main target of the invasion, but also that even after the Normandy invasion began, Hitler continued to believe that Normandy was the deception and Pas de Calais was the intended target.[67] This tied up key German resources that could have been mobilized against Allied positions. In fact, fully 22 German divisions were being held back to combat the fictional forces expected to land at Pas de Calais. With the success of Operation Overlord on D-Day and the subsequent breakout from the beaches, one historical writer has stated that "it may be doubted whether Overlord would have succeeded if the German Fifteenth Army had not been kept idle for those crucial weeks."[68]

Capability Suppression

A final use of secrecy, distinct from anticipation and deception, is simply the ability to suppress the capabilities of a potential enemy. Governments can spend billions of dollars attempting to gain an edge on the battlefield or the negotiation table. Without secrecy, these costly technological innovations, feedback on military effectiveness, and the like can diffuse across borders. Rival states can and sometimes do catch up to leading states in the flash of a photocopier or, more recently, with the insertion of a flash drive.[69] Two illustrative examples of the capability-suppressing effect of secrets involve nuclear and stealth technology. In one case, the United States has seen mixed success, allowing us to observe the consequences of transparency and the diffusion of key military technology.

When US secrecy was compromised through espionage, Soviet capabilities increased by the megaton. However, by keeping stealth technology under wraps, the United States maintained a decades-long, signature lead in low-observability technological capabilities. Stealth technology has paid off for the United States not only in Kosovo and the Gulf War but also in the raid that ultimately found and killed Osama bin Laden. Keeping nuclear secrets and stealth technology from potential enemies continues to be important today.

THE MANHATTAN PROJECT AND OPERATION ENORMOZ

Keeping nuclear technology secret from the Soviets was an important goal for the United States beginning in World War II. The ensuing decades would provide dramatic examples of the uses of secrets in suppressing enemy knowledge, but also direct transparency costs, when the USSR was able to learn valuable technological information.

The stark change from public science to private development of nuclear technology was evidenced in the publication patterns of US physicists during the 1930s and 1940s. Although leading US scientists were publishing papers during the inter-war years, this had come to halt, at least publicly, by 1939. The fact that physics in the United States had largely "gone dark" was noted by Russian scientist Georgy Flerov. He surmised, correctly, that the United States was working in secret on a nuclear weapon.[70] In fact, development of nuclear technology was accelerating in England, Germany, and the United States during that time. A letter written by Flerov brought this to the attention of Stalin in 1942.[71]

Thomas Kuhn has described science as the art of solving puzzles.[72] If that is the case, the race for the nuclear bomb was like being in a locked room with thousands of puzzles arrayed on tables. One could only exit the room if the right combination of puzzles were all solved simultaneously. However, the trick was not just to solve the puzzles, but to find the right puzzles to solve, since many of the puzzles had no solutions at all and were dead ends. Historians commenting on the Manhattan Project have attributed its success to knowing not only what to work on, but also what not to work on.[73]

From 1940 to 1945, with millions of dollars in backing, US scientists at the Manhattan Project solved several important puzzles related to the production of nuclear weapons.[74] The first design was a gun-type uranium weapon, which was worked on alongside a plutonium-based implosion weapon. Workable bombs were created from both designs. However, although the uranium gun-type weapon was dropped on Hiroshima in 1945 and had the simplest design, it was a theoretical dead end. The necessary uranium-235 was extremely costly and time-consuming to produce as compared to the relatively common uranium-238. Further, the explosive potential of U-235 was limited in the gun-type weapon. These limitations meant that both the yield of each bomb and the total number of bombs that the United States could produce over time by that design were limited.[75] The plutonium-based implosion design, on the other hand, which was much more complicated, turned out to be more efficient and practical to produce.[76] This was the type of bomb that was used at the Trinity test and dropped on Nagasaki. It had 40% greater destructive capacity than the gun-type "Little Boy" device and could be built much more quickly. The path to the production of the plutonium bomb took enormous resources and was delayed by the dead-end gun-type uranium weapon for the United States.

At the same time, the Soviet Union was simply watching what the United States was working out and taking notes. Richard Rhodes observed, when writing about early Soviet atomic spying, that "[o]ne tried, effective way to save time and expense was industrial espionage."[77] Using this prescription, Soviet intelligence personnel followed the United States around this metaphorical room, watching and learning. Soviet scientists were able to learn how to solve not only specific scientific enigmas, such as how to produce plutonium efficiently, but also which stumpers the United States had already learned were not worth solving— for example, the uranium-gun-type design. The United States spent 6 years and billions of dollars to produce their Trinity test in 1945; the Soviet Union, despite inferior resources, followed in 1949 with their own test of equal power, Joe-1, at significantly lower cost.[78] The CIA at the time was stunned by the Soviets' progress; in fact, several officials in Washington at first believed that the radiation fingerprint that was detected after the Soviet test must have come from a nuclear reactor accident. Specifically, American intelligence had predicted in 1949 that the USSR would not have a workable bomb until "the mid-1950s."[79] A failure to protect secrets, from an ally no less, had lost the United States its nuclear monopoly.[80]

How do we know that the Soviet Union used espionage to develop their bomb rather than home-spun ingenuity?[81] The evidence of espionage is overwhelming in this case. The United States both during and just after World War II was intercepting Soviet messages. The decoding and deciphering of these messages[82] has become known as the Venona program. The Soviets were very careful with their codes, and thus while thousands of messages were intercepted, only a fraction were readable by the United States even as late as the 1990s when the Venona program was publicly announced. However, over time, some were rendered accessible to Washington. The Venona telegrams together with evidence from Soviet archives make clear that intelligence and espionage allowed Moscow to learn through a Leica camera what the United States toiled with chalkboards, factories, and reactors to conjure. It was no coincidence that the Soviet solution turned out to be a carbon copy of the US "Fat Man" design.[83]

We now know that Operation Enormoz, the codename for Soviet spying within the US Manhattan Project, was indeed large scale and well placed from at least 1942 to 1949.[84] We also have significant evidence that Klaus Fuchs,[85] Theodore Hall,[86] Harry Gold, David Greenglass, Morton Sobell, Julius Rosenberg,[87] and George Koval[88] were part of a network that provided valuable information to the USSR about secret US nuclear programs. Additionally, Donald Maclean, one of the notorious Cambridge Five, was well placed to funnel technical secrets to Moscow in addition to high-level plans.[89]

As Haynes et al. make clear:

> Because of the information gained from Klaus Fuchs, David Greenglass, Theodore Hall, and several as-yet-unidentified spies [George Koval and others], the Soviet Union did not need to explore all the technical blind alleys that American and British scientists went down first; espionage revealed what worked and what did not. They did not have to expend enormous resources on the design and development of crucial technologies; espionage revealed the technical approaches that were practical and provided the data from expensive experiments free of charge. They did not have to depend on scientific insight for key conceptual breakthroughs; espionage revealed that implosion and plutonium offered tremendous savings in time and resources over the manufacture of a pure uranium bomb. Espionage saved the USSR great expense and industrial investment and thereby enabled the Soviets to build a successful atomic bomb years before they otherwise would have.[90]

Also interesting is that Soviet espionage appears to have dimmed in the early 1950s and allowed the United States to regain an atomic lead. From 1950 to at least 1953 and probably beyond, it appears that the USSR was lacking in access to the classified solutions involved in the development of the multi-megaton hydrogen bomb. Klaus Fuchs was identified in late 1948, the Rosenberg spy ring was broken up in 1949, Harry Gold's involvement was revealed in 1950, and we now know that George Koval left the United States in 1948.[91] This relative intelligence blackout for the USSR meant that when top US scientists Stanislaw Ulam and C. J. Everett concluded in 1950 that the single-layer (also known as the classical Super) design for a hydrogen bomb was unworkable, the Soviet Union continued to work on that flawed design for an additional two years.[92]

Additionally, when Teller, building on Ulam's work, came up with the "eureka" inspiration for the multi-megaton hydrogen bomb in 1951, solving in one swoop[93] at least two of the more complicated puzzles in the nuclear room, the USSR apparently did not learn about it. In fact, the USSR did not hit on (or emulate) the design until March of 1954.[94] So while the United States detonated a hydrogen bomb capable of producing a blast in the tens of megatons in 1952, the Soviet Union was still spending precious resources on a puzzle that had no useful solution. By keeping secrets, the United States gained a hydrogen

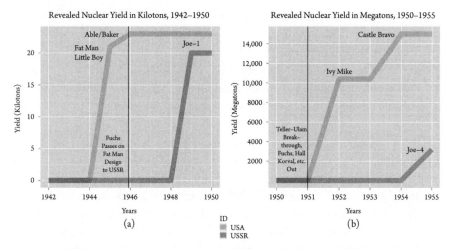

Figure 3.3 (a) Two time series of maximum yields in kilotons for US and USSR nuclear programs up to a given year, with major tests noted (1942–1950). (b) Two time series of maximum yields in megatons for US and USSR nuclear programs up to a given year, with major tests noted (1950–1955).

bomb capability that the USSR lacked . . . for a time.[95] Through a combination of espionage and industry, the nuclear arms race illustrates how suppressing the knowledge of an enemy can strengthen relative capabilities, and likewise how the revelation of that information—the failure of secrecy as suppression—can enhance a threat.

Figure 3.3 provides two brief graphical sketches of the early years of US–USSR atomic competition. Here I plot for each year the maximum nuclear yield that each state's program had revealed in an actual test up to that point.[96] While yields in kilo-/megatonnage are crude measures, they bring home the point forcefully here. Spying in the mid- to late 1940s allowed the USSR to catch up to US capabilities. Joe-1 was the product of both Soviet sweat and Hall and Fuchs' eyeballs. However, if we turn to Figure 3.3b, we see the effects of more robust secrecy in the United States. With Project Enormoz shrinking due to counterintelligence in the United States, USSR atomic spying during the early 1950s was less piercing. This allowed the United States to gain a megatonnage lead, leaping from the Fat Man design to Ivy Mike to Castle Bravo.[97] It was only in 1955 that the Soviet Union began to catch up.[98]

Interestingly, Soviet spying at the time yielded other capability benefits to the USSR. William Perl, a US scientist, provided Moscow with extraordinarily valuable intelligence on US advances in jet airplanes.[99] This led to the Soviet development of the MiG-15, which was far superior to what the United States believed the Soviets were capable of at the time of the Korean War. In fact,

The scientific and technical data they transmitted to Moscow saved the Soviet Union untold amounts of money and resources by transferring American technology, which enabled it to build an atomic bomb and deploy jet planes, radar, sonar, artillery proximity fuses, and many other military advances long before its own industry, strained by rapid growth and immense wartime damage, could have developed them independently.[100]

It is important to note that nuclear secrecy continues to play a capability-suppressing role even today, and for good reason. The thought of enemy states or terrorist organizations gaining a nuclear capacity has spurred countermeasures around the world.[101] One little-publicized story emphasizes the operational secrecy and vigilance necessary to suppress the destructive capability of terrorist groups; this story will also serve as a useful example in Chapter 4. In November 2009, the United States and Russia were working together to transport the last of Libya's weapons-grade uranium out of that country. In 2003 Libya had agreed to dispense with its nuclear capability, such as it was. However, as the uranium was being loaded into the cargo plane, the order was given by Tripoli to suspend the transport. Libya was going to use its last bit of leverage to extract diplomatic concessions from the United States. For over a month, with weapons-grade uranium sitting on a runway in Libya, Tripoli and Washington negotiated over terms. The danger, to the United States, was that there was a very small contingent guarding the uranium. In fact, diplomatic cables suggest that at one time there was only one guard on duty. Further, the uranium was placed next to a loading crane. As Max Fisher writes, "It would have been easy for anyone with a gun and a truck to drive up, overpower the guard, use the crane to load the casks onto the truck, and drive off into the vast Libyan desert."[102] Al Qaeda was known to have operated in the area.[103] Due to diplomatic, military, and operational secrecy, no terrorist group or other states seized on the nuclear vulnerability.

STEALTH TECHNOLOGY
A more successful case of secrecy suppressing enemy capabilities is the US development and guarding of stealth technology during the Cold War. The ability to design planes that would be militarily effective but have a low radar signature has been a goal of air force planners since the advent of radar in World War II. The ability to gain the element of surprise and strike far-off targets without enemy anti-aircraft defenses and fighters being alerted has been called the "holy grail" of Air Force technology.[104] In fact, Germany, late in World War II, began development of the Ho 229 V3, which would have had a very low radar signature relative to other planes at the time. The United States became highly interested in decreasing the observability of its aircraft in 1958, as part of the U-2 project. Specifically, the CIA was interested in reducing the radar signature of the spy

plane. However, the subsequent Project RAINBOW was a failure for technical reasons, and a new plane was designed. In the secret Skunk Work[105] labs at Lockheed, stealth technology progressed from the A-12 to the SR-71 Blackbird. The SR-71 included the use of stealth technologies that included a flattened shape and cesium-based fuel additives.[106]

However, the real breakthrough in stealth technology came from a Russian physicist and mathematician named Petr Ufimtsev. Ufimtsev had published a series of papers on the scattering of electromagnetic waves away from objects. The idea was that certain complicated physical shapes could diffract radar waves, leaving the object less visible by radar. The Soviet Union viewed the paper at the time to be of no military value and thus did not stop the publication of the results. What the Russians let slip through their fingers was caught by the Lockheed team. In secret, they designed computer programs, models, and testing equipment that proved the operational use of Ufimtsev's theory. The ideas became embedded in the classified projects to develop the F-117A and the B-2. In fact, the odd shape of the F-117A, which has led to its nickname—the Hopeless Diamond— is directly attributable to Ufimtsev's theory.[107] The F-117A was successful, not only because of its shape, but also because of its classified anti-radar paint coating.[108] Thus stealth technology secrets involved for starters the importance of Ufimtsev's work—practically, how to operationalize the work with intensive computer applications, as well as additional advances in radar-absorbent paints and materials that were unrelated to Ufimtsev's work.

At the same time, the Soviet Union was aware of US attempts at stealth technology but made little progress on their own.[109] They did, however, attempt to pierce the veil of secrecy around the stealth program as they had successfully with the atomic program as well as with jet engine technology earlier. The USSR called intelligence on engineering and technical matters the "XY Line" and had extremely valuable sources within the US aerospace industry.[110] However, these spies failed for decades to uncloak the secrets of stealth.

This does not mean that they were not close. In one instance in 1985, the top Soviet air official in the United States, Colonel Vladimir Izmaylov, approached a US Air Force officer who would have had access to significant sources of classified documents on, among other things, the stealth program. Izmaylov relayed to his superiors that the contact was successful and that over a series of months a sale of highly classified documents on stealth technology, the Strategic for approximately $41,000 was arranged. In Fort Washington, MD, on June 19, 1986, Izmaylov drove to a secluded wooded area where he was to pick up the documents and bury the money as part of a dead drop. However, as Izmaylov began burying a milk carton filled with $41,100, he was apprehended by FBI agents and later expelled from the country. It turned out that the US Air Force officer, when originally contacted by Izmaylov, had notified his superiors and was working as a double agent for months. The stealth secrets were safe that day. The FBI at the time said that if the GRU operation had been successful, the United States would have suffered "significant loss of highly classified weapons and programs systems materials to the Soviets."[111]

The Soviet Union was perhaps even closer to obtaining valuable secrets about the stealth program one year earlier, in 1984. Thomas Cavanagh, an engineer at Northrop Corporation who had access to classified information, attempted to contact the Soviet consulate to sell them stealth technology secrets. However, Cavanagh's attempt was intercepted by the FBI. The FBI then posed as KGB agents and agreed to buy Cavanagh's documents for $25,000. On December 18, 1984, Cavanagh was arrested after delivering the documents and accepting payment. At the time, FBI Director Webster was quoted as saying that the secret information that Cavanagh had possession of and attempted to sell to the Soviets was "the core of the Stealth technology [program]" and that it had "cost . . . over 1 million dollars an hour to develop."[112] In fact, by some estimates the United States spent well over $60 billion simply on the research and development of stealth technology during the Cold War. This does not include the cost of actually producing even one stealth aircraft for operational use.[113] Yet, in the case of stealth, the two ends of the espionage chain, supply and demand for information, failed to meet. Izmaylov's demand missed Cavanagh's critical supply, and the United States profited with continued capability suppression.

Figure 3.4 presents graphically the impressive lead in stealth technology that the United States has been able to maintain from the early 1980s until today. This plot shows the estimated relative radar cross section (RCS) for a few select Cold War and post–Cold War military aircraft.[114] The RCS for a plane is the amount of radar return that it generates from a given angle. In the 1970s the US F-15 and USSR Su-27 had similar radar signatures.[115] However, with the F-117A (shown) and the B-2 (not shown),[116] the United States was able to embed the stealth lessons from the SR-71 into deployable units. The RCS of the F-117A was over 100 times smaller than that of the F-15. The MiG-19, for comparison, was deployed two years after the first F-117A and still remained a remarkably noticeable aircraft on radar. Even in the post–Cold War era, the F-22 Raptor, which entered service in 2005, both is maneuverable and has impressive frontal stealth capabilities. For comparison, the Su-35 Flanker, which had yet to enter operational service for Russia as of 2011, contains far less stealth capability.[117]

The ability of the United States to harness stealth technology ahead of the rest of the world paid dividends most dramatically in the first Gulf War, but it also played a role in Panama and Kosovo. The air war against Baghdad began with

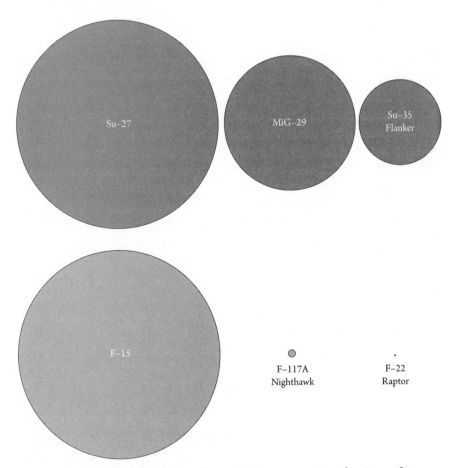

Figure 3.4 **Relative sizes of estimated frontal radar cross section of various military aircraft. Top**: USSR/Russia. **Bottom**: United States.

F-117As attacking positions that were heavily fortified with anti-aircraft defenses. Skunk Works engineers Ben Rich and Leo Janos wrote that "the only way the enemy knew the F-117A was in the sky above was when everything around him began blowing up."[118] While the F-117A supplied tactical surprise in Baghdad, the ability to keep the technology behind its design secret suppressed the capabilities of other states to threaten the United States. Apart from bombers and air superiority, aerospace stealth technology has recently facilitated one of the premier US foreign policy achievements of the post–Cold War world. While the details are still publicly unavailable, it appears from reports that specially designed stealth helicopters were used in the operation that killed Osama bin Laden in Abbottabad, Pakistan. Thus, stealth capability continues to pay dividends for the United States.

THE INSTITUTIONAL CAPACITY FOR SECRECY

As these examples make clear, democracies exist in a potentially competitive international arena. While international politics is by no means consistently zero-sum, opportunities exist to bully, exploit, and even invade other countries. If secrecy is useful for foreign policy effectiveness—as we have seen on the beaches of France and in counterintelligence operations in secluded woods in Maryland—and democracies are constitutionally unable to keep secrets, this will provide a tangible national security advantage to non-democracies. Non-democracies would have the ability to anticipate and deceive, while democracies would be left a step behind and perennially duped. This would fit the critiques of de Tocqueville that we visited earlier concerning democracies' inability to formulate effective foreign policy.

Luckily for those that value the institutions of democracy, this does not seem to be the case empirically. Democracies do maintain institutions that create and keep national security secrets. In fact, all democracies have rules allowing the executive to designate information as secret, allowing a part of the executive to act as a vault for that information, specifying penalties for revealing secret information and having counterintelligence powers to ward off enemies.

Not surprisingly, what has been justified in theory and necessary in practice is mirrored in law. Table 3-1 presents a sample of laws across democracies that punish the revelation of information that the executive deems to be national security secrets. Thus, *the capacity for executive secrecy* exists across democracies. What this means for public accountability in democracies—and the second strand of liberal critiques that doubt public accountability and the marketplace of ideas[119]—is an important question that will await discussion until Chapter 4. While we have seen that even liberal thinkers such as Kant, Mill, Bentham, and Madison carved out or worried about exceptions for national security secrecy in their defense of public transparency and that operationally secrecy has played an important role in international successes and failures this century, we can also see that actual laws on the books in democracies around the world provide for the legitimate capacity for executive secrecy.[120]

These laws set up three types of mechanisms. First, they specify that national security information can be classified and provide that power to the executive. They also specify what the penalties of publicly divulging secret information will be. This latter power includes counterintelligence operations to keep secrets. In Sweden, the 1980 Secrecy Act has over 160 sections and delineates national security information as being legitimately classifiable, sets out the classification scheme, denotes the executive as having the power to classify information for 2 to 70 years, and specifies the penalties for divulging state secrets. Sapo is the Swedish counterintelligence unit. In the United States, unlike in many other

Table 3-1. A SAMPLE OF NATIONAL SECURITY SECRECY LAWS IN DEMOCRACIES[a]

Albania	Law No. 8457 on Classified Information
Armenia	Law on State and Official Secrets, 1996, Dissemination of Mass Media (2003), stat. 146, 302, 306, 307, 302
Argentina	Article 2 and Article 16 of Intelligence Law, Article 17 of Data Protection Act
Australia	Crimes Act 1914, until 2004; then becomes patchwork
Austria	Law on the Security of Information (Informationssicherheitsgesetz)
Azerbaijan	1996 Law on State Secrets, 2004 Law on State Secrets, Article 68 of Penal Code
Belgium	Law on Security Classification and Authorizations, 1998
Bosnia and Herz.	Criminal Code 2003, 163–4
Bulgaria	Law for the Protection of Classified Information
Canada	Security of Information Act
Croatia	Criminal Code 144–146
Czech Republic	The Protection of Classified Information Act
Denmark	Criminal Statutes
Estonia	State Secrets Act
France	2004 Code du Patrimoine changed the 1979 Law on Archives, article 413–9
Georgia	Law on State Secrets, 1996
Germany	German Criminal Code Section 93–95, Abs 1 StGB
Greece	Penal Code S671
Hungary	Secrecy Act of 1995, Article 221 of the 1978 Criminal Code
Iceland	Criminal Code No. 19 91–92
India	Official Secrets Act, 1923
Ireland	Official Secrets Act, 1963
Israel	Chapter 76 of the Penal Code
Italy	Law 24, October 1977
Jamaica	Official Secrets Act, 1911
South Korea	Military Secrets Protection Act, 1993, pre-1993 OSA
Latvia	Section 94 of Criminal Code
Lithuania	Law on State Secrets and Official Secrets 1999, replaced Law on State Secrets and Their Protection
Macedonia	Law on Classified Information
Moldova	Criminal Code section 344–5, Law on State Secrets
Montenegro	Criminal Code, Section 425, 471
Netherlands	Criminal Code 98
New Zealand	1951 Official Secrets Act, Official Information Act in 1982
Norway	1998 Security Act (1998), Act on Defense Secrets (articles 90 and 91) plus crimal code
Peru	Article 330
Portugal	Law of State Secrecy

continued

Table 3-1. (CONTINUED)

Romania	Law on Protecting Classified Information, 2002
Serbia	Criminal Code, Lustration Law
Slovakia	Act for Protecting Classified Information, 2004
Slovenia	Classified Information Act
South Africa	Protection of Information Act of 1982
Spain	Law 9/1968, Law 13/1999, Law 11/2007
Sweden	1980 Secrecy Act, Secrecy Ordinance
Switzerland	Code penal miliaire (CPM) du 13 Juin 1927, Section 106, and Penal Code section 293
Tajikistan	Law on State Secrets, 2003
Turkey	Article 26 and 301
Uganda	Official Secrets Act, 1964
Ukraine	Law on state secrets, 1994, updated 1999
United Kingdom	Official Secrets Act, 1989, update of OSA, 1911
United States	1917 Espionage Act (ch 106, S 10(i), 40 Stat. 422), 18 USC S793, S794, S795, S661, 10 USC S1030, 50 USC S421

[a]Sources include individual country penal codes and constitutions, as well as Banisar 2004.

countries, the actual organization of classified information is decreed by executive order,[121] while the type of information that cannot be publicized and the penalties for publicizing sanctioned secrets have been delineated by law. At the most basic level, the US Constitution invests the president with foreign policy decision-making power in part to shield international secrets from the public transparency demanded by Congress.[122] For US citizens, the penalties for revealing classified information are spelled out in the Espionage Act of 1917, as well as in specific provisions in the Intelligence Identities Protection Act and the US Code on the "Disclosure of Classified Information."[123] The FBI has jurisdiction over domestic counterintelligence in the United States.[124]

The institutional tools for keeping secrets have not gathered dust in the hands of the executives. In the United States, the estimated cost of information classification was over $8.6 billion in 2008 alone and cannot be accurately bounded from above because the expense of keeping national security secrets within the Central Intelligence Agency, the Defense Intelligence Agency, the Office of the Director of National Intelligence, the National Geospatial-Intelligence Agency, the National Reconnaissance Office, and the National Security Agency is classified and not included in that figure.[125] Even the lower bound of $8.6 billion is 40% higher than government spending on the National Science Foundation and 14% higher than federal spending on the Environmental Protection Agency in the same year.[126] The scale of secrecy has prompted one expert, Steven

Aftergood of the Project on Government Secrecy, to say that the United States has "a department of government secrecy."[127] Even the case of the largest leak of classified documents in US history until 2011, the WikiLeaks release of the diplomatic cables, and the Iraq and Afghanistan war log comprise less than a quarter of 1% of all classification decisions recorded in ISOO reports over a similar time frame.[128]

The United States is not alone in delegating to the executive the power to keep national security secrets. Extensive provisions for national security secrecy are included not only in Swedish law, considered by some experts to be a model of government transparency, but also in that of the Netherlands, another country used as an example of transparency.[129] In addition, Great Britain uses a stringent Official Secrets Act (OSA) to contain national security information.[130] The OSA includes both regulations for information classification and penalties for divulging secret information. India has a similar OSA,[131] as do New Zealand and Ireland. Australia, like the United States, does not have a unified OSA, and instead punishes the revelation of secure information through various laws.[132]

While the laws in Table 3-1 vary in whether they emanate from executive orders that have been accepted by their relevant legislatures (e.g., the US classification scheme) or directly from the legislature (the UK OSA), they all share two common—and, for the present analysis, crucial—traits. They provide proof of an institutional capacity for secrecy in democracies such that there is a legal justification for keeping secrets, and they specify the penalties for divulging national security secrets. It was these executive orders and laws, as well as their predecessors, that allowed the United States to keep atomic and stealth secrets and to guard the information that Japanese codes had been broken both in 1911 and later in World War II, and they also allowed the United Kingdom to keep ULTRA secret and punish the atomic spy Klaus Fuchs.

Domestic Politics and the Capacity for Secrecy

The previous discussion necessitates a short analysis of where secrecy stops and whether the arguments above apply equally to domestic and national security policy. They do not, although the potential for abuse plays a key role in understanding the consequences for national security secrecy in democracies even for domestic politics.

First, keeping secrets is difficult if the public already knows something. Because we cannot intentionally forget information we already know, the only secrets that governments can hold are those facts, plans, technologies, opinions, theories, connections, and interpretations that reach them first or of which they can plausibly stop the transmission.[133] This means that the capacities to collect information and keep secrets are intrinsically related. This is why national security intelligence agencies are simultaneously collectors and classifiers.

On domestic matters, when there are many routes for information to reach the public without the intercession of the executive and without legitimate transparency costs, there are greater practical limits on the types of information that the government can keep secret before it reaches the public first. For example, the ability of an executive to suppress significant information on the state of the economy or tax policies is constrained because the public receives information on the economy from numerous private sources and even often their own eyes.

Second, since there are no obvious public transparency costs when releasing domestic political information—for example, on the state of the economy[134]— the government cannot resist revealing information on the costs and benefits of domestic policies without tipping its hand about having something embarrassing to hide.

The fact of legitimate transparency costs on national security policies helps to explain why the capacity for secrecy is highly relevant in that policy sphere but less directly relevant for information on purely domestic nonsecurity matters. If you already know something, it cannot be secret, and the leadership has less room to try and deceive the public about related information. Further, if the public is curious about what the government knows on a domestic subject, it is more difficult for the government to legitimately resist revelation.

However, there is no hard line between security and nonsecurity information because the public cannot view the content of secrets before they are classified, as discussed above. This means that there are still times when the capacity for national security information can be misused to hide domestic nonsecurity information, as in the Dreyfus Affair and the Watergate cover-up. This potential for abuse is analyzed further in the next chapter.

NATIONAL SECURITY SECRECY: JUSTIFIED, NECESSARY, INSTITUTIONALIZED

We have seen from the pens of theorists, through the guns of battle, to the gavels of law, that the ability to keep secrets is itself of value to the public. Public security depended on secrecy to anticipate events in the War of the Pacific, during the Cuban Missile Crisis, and at the Washington Naval Conference; to deceive in Operations Mincemeat and Overlord; and to reduce external threats involving atomic power and stealth technology in the Cold War and after.

Due to this secrecy, citizens go to the polls each election, in every democracy in the world, less informed about foreign policy than the executive they are supposed to be holding to account. Classification laws, loopholes in freedom of information laws, prior restraint, and pressure to censure stories distort the public's ability to process international information. Despite this fact, liberal international relations theorists have maintained that public consent is an important fount of democratic success. In this chapter we have seen that national security secrecy is an important component of successful foreign policy in war and in peace. But how can one give consent without information?

When Ronald Reagan asked Americans in 1980 whether they were better off today than they were four years ago, they could check their bank accounts and glance at their tax returns. The public had access to a considerable amount of information on their own economic well-being, as well as that of the nation at large. The analogous question for national security, explicitly raised by US Presidential candidate John Kerry in a 2003 CNN interview, "Are Americans safer today than they were three years ago?" is a more difficult proposition, by design, for a member of the public to answer. In fact, Kerry himself, in the same interview, explicitly described the difference between economic–domestic issues and those of national security. He explained that the public does not necessarily have "the kind of knowledge about our intelligence gathering that allows us to make the judgment that we are safer."[135]

We thus end this chapter where we began—with the question of what role the capacity for secrecy plays in democracies—but hopefully wiser. Elections become either (a) a farce, where the public thinks it is holding a leader to account but is actually itself being manipulated, (b) a tragedy, where the public fails to support policies in their own interest because they do not know any better, or (c) both simultaneously. The marketplace of ideas and publicity is central to liberal theories of democratic foreign policy and public consent. Yet, with significant evidence of the presence and necessity of national security secrecy in democracies, we need to explore the ramifications of the capacity for secrecy on this process.

However, the story does not stop with the uses of secrecy. This is only one-half of the secrecy dilemma. In the next chapter, I turn to an examination of the repercussions of the capacity for secrecy and, most important, on the potential for that capacity to be abused for nonsecurity goals. I illustrate that if we throw out the usefulness of the marketplace of ideas and accountability institutions, the capacity for secrecy creates potential problems for democracies. For example, the potential, and reality, of abuse can lead to public skepticism and the inability of a leader to signal beneficial security priorities. With the uses of secrecy come potential abuses. However, just as innovations in stealth technology and other technologies have changed the landscape of war, so have innovations in national security oversight institutions evolved to alter the landscape of the marketplace of ideas. Although these changes have largely evaded the radar of IR theorists to date, many democracies have found ways to gain the uses of secrecy while reducing the abuses. Understanding the uses of secrecy is the first piece of this puzzle, and the potential for abuse is the next.

PART II

The Abuses of Secrecy and Public Consent

The Potential Abuses of National Security Secrecy

The previous two chapters worked to establish one leg of the secrecy dilemma, the importance of the capacity for secrecy in democracies to foreign policy success. However, where past proponents of secrecy have used this leverage to disparage public accountability as either meaningless or dangerous, I will take a different tack.

In the next two chapters, I turn to the second leg of the secrecy dilemma, the costs of secrecy[1] for public consent. I suggest that the capacity for secrecy does not reduce the necessity of public consent and accountability in generating democratic successes. In democracies there is no substitute for public support for policies and investments. Someone must pay the bill for foreign policy, and while non-democracies can use overt repression to generate resources, this avenue is not open to democracies. As we will see, if one wants to understand democratic success, one must delve into the dilemma of how the public can consent to investing in security-enhancing policies without being deceived by leaders into paying for incompetence or corruption under the cover of secrecy.

This current chapter begins by illustrating that critics of democratic foreign policy efficiency disagree among themselves about the possibility of deceiving the public into consent for policies. One prominent group assumes that secrecy leads to successful deception and therefore treats the problem of generating

consent as ignorable. Others suggest that opposition is probable and thus democratic accountability should be abandoned for stronger executive control and
secrecy. Neither perspective answers the question that is fundamental to the
secrecy dilemma: Why would the public believe, or doubt, foreign policy statements made by an executive?

Yet to understand the importance of this question of consent, we need to
temporarily shift our focus from the public to the executive empowered with
discretion over the capacity for secrecy. What we see is that executives can use secrecy to raise net security benefits by avoiding transparency costs, but also abuse
secrecy for their own purposes. In fact, I show that while critics introduce the capacity for secrecy, they then largely ignore how that capacity could be utilized by
executives to cover up incompetence and corruption and thus hide evidence that
a policy will lead to net public costs.

I argue that the potential for executive abuse of secrecy is not ignorable in
democracies. In fact, incentives for executive abuse run in parallel to the uses
of secrecy discussed previously and extended below and thus emanate from
the same capacity for secrecy. Just as through the collection and classification
of information enemies can be deceived or have their actions anticipated and
capabilities suppressed, so too can the domestic public be deceived and opposition viewpoints suppressed under cover of official secrecy. With examples from
France during the Dreyfus Affair and from the United States during Watergate, I
show that uses and abuses can happen nearly simultaneously.

Understanding that executive abuse is possible allows us to appreciate the
public's decision to consent to or dissent from specific foreign policies in Chapter 5. From the public's view, when the leadership proposes a particular policy but
articulates that they cannot provide a full public disclosure of evidence for their
choices, the executive could be hiding inconvenient facts (an abuse) or could be
keeping legitimate secrets to save the public from paying transparency costs (a
use). Moreover, even if an executive reveals previously secret evidence, it may
not be believed, because it remains possible that this evidence is itself a deceit
and related to the covering up of abuse. The potential for abuse makes clear why
consent is not automatic and, if it were, why it could easily be manipulated at high
public costs.

Chapter 5 goes on to analyze the likely consequences of this potential for
abuse for public consent and democratic foreign policy investments. Public
skepticism of potential abuse can lead to costly opposition and delay to secrecy-
enhancing policies. I return to the French and US examples and illustrate
how the abuses of the Dreyfus Affair and Watergate generated skepticism and
public worries about future corruption and incompetence in national security
policy and eventually led to open opposition and the blocking of executive
proposals.

These specific democratic failures, and others like them, are not explained by critics who assumed a pliant public or doubted the ability of democracies to keep secrets. Further, the cause of the distrust and failure emerged directly from the executive power to selectively classify and reveal information and avoid accountability for abuse. Executives can suffer from dissent because the public worries about abuses. Increasing executive powers and secrecy, as some critics suggest, without somehow credibly assuring the public that abuses can be deterred is only likely to worsen this secrecy dilemma. Therefore, Chapter 5 ends with the secrecy dilemma fully exposed, but not yet solved.

IS DEMOCRACY DANGEROUS OR JUST IRRELEVANT?

In Chapter 2 we reviewed several cogent criticisms of the liberal assumption of domestic transparency, public accountability, and the marketplace of ideas. One set of these critiques argued that information asymmetries between leaders and the public meant that leaders could control the marketplace of ideas and avoid public accountability. Schuessler[2] argued that Roosevelt deceived the American public and orchestrated policy so as to "manufacture" support for conflict. Similarly, Downes hypothesizes that Johnson escalated the Vietnam war to protect his own domestic agenda, and he wrote that "the recent case of Iraq suggests ... [democracy] may prompt leaders to downplay or minimize the potential costs of conflict to *obtain public consent* for wars they want to fight for other reasons."[3] The chain of causation is clear in these critiques: leaders selectively reveal information to further their own preferred policies, and the public follows. Consent is not generated from a thick marketplace of ideas with transparency, open argumentation, and facts, but instead manufactured by selective deception.

Desch[4] argues that on national security policy, material capabilities trump any domestic institutional differences. Further, since the public is aware that it has little knowledge of the intricacies of international polities, citizens defer to elites. Leaders, therefore, drive policy in democracies just as they do in non-democracies, resulting in no measurable difference between states based on domestic institutional distinctions.[5] In fact, much of Desch's evidence consists of pointing out who had the operational advantage in anticipation and deception and how that, rather than regime type, correlates with military effectiveness.[6]

These critics are building on influential work from Waltz,[7] suggesting that the form of government a state maintains is irrelevant to foreign policy ability.[8] Waltz purported to show that despite institutional differences, the United States and the United Kingdom had similar foreign policy capabilities[9] and, further, that international anarchy forces all states into evolving functionally equivalent decision-making processes in order to survive.[10] Democracies and non-democracies alike can be invaded, attacked, and conquered. A tank runs just as well on election day as it does on any other day, and a properly deployed bomb destroys a dictator's palace with the same force of physics as it destroys a president's office or a parliament building. Military compulsion and international capabilities are the currency of international politics according to this world view. In order to survive in the harsh climate of the international system, all leaders must work toward the same end: security.[11]

However, not all critics of liberal arguments agree that domestic institutions are irrelevant. As we previewed in Chapter 3, Almond and Tocqueville doubted that democracies could formulate effective foreign policy because of transparency costs.[12] A second group, including Lippmann,[13] Morgenthau,[14] and more recently Ripsman[15] and Schweller,[16] suggests that democracy is dangerous for foreign policy, not due to transparency costs but because an uninformed public will dissent from necessary foreign policy. To these critics, domestic opposition to necessary national security priorities and moves enervates state power. Ripsman[17] makes the case succinctly for these democracy doubters when he argues that the Canadian public stopped their government from making the prudent choice to join the United States in the Iraq war.[18] In this telling, institutional constraints on an executive and specifically public accountability are like the Lilliputian ropes that bind Gulliver for a time. The public needlessly limits the range of action of a state and imposes counterproductive costs. The less the public knows of and has control over foreign policy, the better, according to this view.

Similar Perspectives, Different Diagnoses

While both sets of theorists—those that think democracy is irrelevant and those that believe democracy is dangerous—share the important assumption that leaders should not need domestic accountability institutions to enable them to pursue national security goals, there is a crucial tension between these criticisms of domestic foreign policy effectiveness. The irrelevantists assume that a leader can manufacture and "obtain" consent through the selective revelation of information and deception. The democracy alarmists, on the other hand, do not have confidence that the public can be made pliable. Instead, the ignorant public dissents, rather than consents, and thus blocks necessary actions such as raising spending or extending the terms of office for those that honestly promote security-enhancing policies.[19]

The fact that this contradiction exists between two perspectives that share such similarities is revealing. Both democratic irrelevantists and alarmists argue that a capacity for secrecy is needed for foreign policy success to allow for anticipation and deception as well as suppressing the capabilities of the enemy in a dangerous world.[20] Yet, they disagree about how to generate the necessary support for foreign policy. On the one hand, support is automatically provided if the leaders push the right buttons—the public is deceived and follows—and democracy itself is mere window dressing. In the alternative view, while the international context is equally ominous, the diagnosis is to despair of democracy. Here the institutions of democracy are not simply window dressing they are the shards from a broken policy process and must be mended into a more centralized and effective arrangement that approaches dictatorship.[21] In the one case, we can live with democracy, it just does not matter; in the other it is dangerous and an impediment to success.

The divergent diagnoses derive from the distinct assumptions about the public in each perspective. When translating relevant information into policy in a democracy, the public still must acquiesce or oppose, and the resulting policy outcome is dependent on the public's choice. It is simply that the one side places its theoretical bet on acquiescence and thus successful deception, and the other on skepticism and opposition. Neither perspective, however, offers an explanation for when and why the public will support or oppose particular policies. It is assumed in one case the public will support executive policies, and from the opposing perspective it is supposed the public will block initiatives. By introducing the capacity for secrecy and relaxing the assumption of pure democratic transparency, we are slipping into another assumption, of either subservient public consent or obdurate irrational opposition.

There are important reasons to push beyond looking at the public simply as an epiphenomenon or as a costly nuisance. First, democracy alarmists misdiagnose the causes of opposition in democracies. Blindly increasing executive power and decreasing mechanisms to hold a leader to account enervates rather than energizes foreign policy in democracies.[22] The cause of public skepticism and distrust on foreign policy issues is specifically that the executive has the discretion to abuse the capacity for secrecy. Therefore we need to better understand the potential abuses and whether they are separable from the uses of secrecy in reducing transparency costs. If the potential for abuse is the problem, increasing executive powers only exacerbates the problem of distrust.[23]

Second, given the known specter of abuse by the executive, why would the public choose to believe any attempted deceptions offered by the leader, as the irrelevantists assume? Since the public is aware that leaders have incentives to deceive them, there are reasons to specifically not offer their consent to paying for policies that entail significant costs. To further these points, below I offer several examples not only of the abuse of the capacity for secrecy, but later of public skepticism in the face of executive foreign policy initiatives.

THE POTENTIAL ABUSES OF SECRECY IN DEMOCRACIES

In the previous chapter, I argued that secrecy had three general uses: allowing for anticipation, deception, and suppressing the capabilities of potential rivals. In each illustration of these uses, the target of secrecy was the civilian and military leaders of other states. Thus, national security secrets were kept from the public as a means to an end, because telling the public would in turn alert the enemy. However, the capacity for secrecy does not have to be used simply to keep information from an enemy. While there are indeed national-security interest secrets,[24] such as the fact and details of breaking an enemy's or ally's codes, the location of an aircraft carrier, the state of a country's nuclear program, or the stealth capabilities that justify the official capacity for the executive to classify information away from public view, there is no reason to believe that all secrets are publicly beneficial national security secrets. In fact, there are specific reasons to expect that a leader with power to classify information has incentives to utilize that capacity for nonsecurity uses.

The capacity for secrecy has potential private nonsecurity benefits to a leader as compared to the security benefits detailed earlier. The same classification powers that hide the details of the stealth program in the United States can be used to deceive the public into believing that there are security benefits to a corrupt or mistaken policy. Further, the same counterintelligence capacity that keeps secrets, as well as intercepts agents attempting to steal information on stealth and other programs, can collect information on domestic opposition and covertly suppress the capabilities of the opposition. In these cases, the target of secrecy can be the domestic public and elites, not an external enemy. The same capacity that can help protect the public from security threats can undercut political opposition.

One of the key criticisms of the liberal marketplace of ideas and public accountability is that leaders can deceive the public through their use of informational advantages. While this is a useful corrective to theories that assume away information asymmetries between leaders and the public, it neglects to analyze the potential abuse of secrecy privileges by leaders and the consequences of public recognition of this fact. Specifically, leaders have the ability to keep information secret that will lower their costs or further their own interests, without necessarily increasing public security.

This incompleteness is apparent in the work of John Mearsheimer. In his book on lying in international relations, he suggests that there are "strategic lies" and "selfish lies"—with the former serving the national interest, and the latter an abuse of secrecy that serves the private interests of the leader. Thus, clearly, the potential for abuse exists. However, when it turns to the question of whether the public is successfully deceived, he writes, "I do not address the important question of when each kind of lie is likely to achieve its intended effect or not, mainly because I could not come up with a good answer."[25] Therefore, secrecy does not everywhere have to be used for the "national interest," but can further a leaders's private interests. Downes' discussion of Johnson's foreign policy[26] being motivated by domestic political circumstances, discussed above, is one example of nonsecurity motives for deception. Yet, we are left wanting for that "good answer" to when the public consents or dissents. This chapter begins to build an answer to this question that culminates in Chapter 5.

Deceiving the Public, Not Enemies

There are several examples of deception being utilized to cover up executive actions for net political gain, rather than security benefits, from around the democratic world. Illustrations from French policy in Algeria, as well as UK policy in the Boer War and World War I, are instructive. For example, Paris utilized censorship and classification powers in 1945 to make it appear that the French massacre at Setif[27] was an attack of "armed bands" with limited casualties. The truth was that the French military, including the air force, launched a large military operation to repress what had begun as a peaceful march for independence. Estimates of the dead were likely over 17,000. This occurred on V-E Day.[28]

Ten years later, when the Algerian revolt accelerated, the existence and scale of the French operation was similarly obscured by the government, who called it a "minor 'internal' difficulty," and strict censorship was enforced.[29] In 1957, Tom Brady of the New York Times wrote, "All information in Algeria is controlled by the French."[30] Smith[31] makes a forceful case that a succession of French leaders utilized censorship to deceive the French public about the costs of the Algerian campaign as well as the potential benefits. Information on casualties, the strength of the enemy, and organization of forces was kept from the public because, it has been argued, de Gaulle and others saw the Algerian issue as being useful to domestic plans to centralize authority and increase public support for his leadership.[32] The use of torture was also kept as a secret, and when the press attempted to report on some limited facts that had leaked, copies of newspapers and pamphlets were confiscated. Instead of these stories, the public was told that the troops were "reacting with courage" and how during raids "women and children were evacuated."[33]

Even in 1975, 13 years after Algerian independence, the French government was keeping embarrassing facts from the public relating to the case. For example, the Gorse report was ordered as a study of French aid payments to Algeria. The secret report found not only corruption and incompetence, but also that aid levels were much lower than the public believed. The government made the decision never to release the report.[34] The obfuscation on Algeria reached such heights that it was not until 1999 that the government officially recognized that there even had been a formal war.[35] One historical analysis suggests that leaders "relied to a very large extent on ruse, disinformation, and manipulation, as well as on some distinctly dirty tricks."[36] Therefore, for several historians, Algeria is an example of leaders keeping secrets from the public for nonsecurity ends, rather than to enhance the national interest.[37]

Similarly, the Boer War provides a stark example of government deception by the United Kingdom. First, the expected costs of the war were underplayed in the press on the eve of the war; then when casualty figures rose and mutinies began, these facts were covered up.[38] In addition, the influence of narrow political ambitions on the part of the High Commissioner for South Africa and other lobbying interests were kept out of official correspondence.[39] In one meeting, Lord Salisbury worried that "the one dangerous objection that is made to our policy is that we are doing the work for the capitalists."[40] The benefits of fighting the conflict were inflated by inventing fake atrocities by the Boer forces (and suppressing information on British-caused civilian hardships). The most infamous of these was when the British government staged a Boer attack on a Red Cross tent in Hampstead Heath, London, and passed it off as evidence of Boer barbarism in newsreel footage.[41] Incompetence at Mafeking was also covered up.[42] Knightley writes, "Britain was fooled . . . She never had a full and accurate picture of what was happening in South Africa."[43]

In World War I, the British government orchestrated even more deception in the press. The Secret Services Bureau was the progenitor of not only MI5 and MI6, which led to significant triumphs of secrecy such as Operation Mincemeat in the following decades, but also the lesser known Bureau MI7 and, in particular, MI7b.[44] MI7b was charged with planting positive stories in the press to keep public morale up during World War I. Famous writers were secretly paid to contribute, including Winnie-the-Pooh author A. A. Milne, as well as Cecil Street and H. B. C. Pollard, and their stories were passed to "willing newspaper proprietors."[45] In fact, Milne's activities were not even revealed to the public until 2012, when even his biographer was surprised.[46]

The organization operated in strict secrecy; at the end of the war, all materials on what information was produced and where it was placed were ordered destroyed because they were "too incriminating."[47] The very existence of the propaganda organization was supposed to be erased.[48] The only reason we now know some select details about this attempt to manipulate public opinion is that one employee illegally brought classified documents home after the war. These were forgotten until they were found by a relative decades later.[49] Arter writes that "the darkest secret of MI7b was that it existed because the Crown and Parliament had need of it . . . the enemy being public doubt, or skepticism, about the cost and the conduct of the war."[50] As the toll of the war grew and as strategic mismanagement and mistakes began to be recognized by leaders, and war profiteering and corruption internally investigated, the government needed "a large scale propaganda operation aimed at the British and the peoples of her Empire."[51] Thus, MI7b's goal was to exaggerate enemy atrocities while downplaying British wrongdoing. This had the effect of manipulating information to raise the expected benefits of fighting to the public. Perceptions of potential deception were to have consequences for the United Kingdom in the inter-war years.

MI7b did not protect secrecy to anticipate, deceive, or suppress the capabilities of the enemy, but instead kept information from the public to manipulate opinion and cover up net public costs. Many may defend this manipulation and propaganda as necessary for public security, and in certain cases it might be publicly beneficial. However, there is nothing to ensure that it is *always* or even often beneficial to the public. In fact, it is this ambiguity that fuels the dilemma of secrecy in democracies. If all secrets were selfish and nonsecurity-related, then evidence of secrecy would signal corruption and potential guilt, as in many domestic circumstances.[52] Likewise, if all secrets were necessary for national security and could not be used for selfish purposes or to cover up incompetence, then secrecy would not trigger distrust.

Public deception has also taken place in the arms industry, where national security secrecy has been used to hide public costs and embellish specific benefits. In India, during the 1980s, the capacity for secrecy was abused to hide flaws of preferred weapons systems, such as an inferior howitzer at an excessive price, an aircraft carrier ready for the scrap heap, and helicopters that could not safely fly. The Bofors AB scandal in India saw Prime Minister Rajiv Ghandi implicated in a scheme to collect and distribute bribes from the international purchase of howitzer guns that many argued were more expensive than and inferior to other choices. However, the company had strong political links to the Prime Minister.[53] Further, subsequent investigations have suggested that in a deal to buy the HMS Hermes from the United Kingdom, the Indian government paid more than double what it was worth[54] and that the British government was planning to scrap the vessel if India did not pay for it. Similarly, despite private doubts from advisors that Westland helicopters were ill-suited to their proposed missions, New Delhi spent £65 million on them. Only a few years later, the whole fleet had to be grounded for safety reasons and unloaded at a loss.[55] In each case the strengths of the weapon systems were embellished, while the weakness were downplayed.[56] Hungary, the Czech Republic, South Africa, and Austria have been embroiled in scandals involving bribes and deception in the purchase of Gripen fighter jets in the early 2000s.[57]

These examples illustrate the potential for the public to be deceived by an executive empowered with the capacity for secrecy to classify and reveal select information under the cloak of protecting the public from transparency costs. This was articulated bluntly in the United Kingdom when an investigation into bribes related to arms deals with Saudi Arabia was stopped in 2006, because of "the need to safeguard national and international security. It has been necessary to balance the need to maintain the rule of law against the wider public interest," according to the official statement by UK Attorney General Lord Goldsmith.[58] Further, deception of the public is not the only potential abuse of the capacity for secrecy.

Anticipating and Suppressing the Capabilities of Domestic Opposition

Keeping secrets is not simply a passive exercise. As Chapter 3 made clear, there are penalties for revealing classified information, and one part of the capacity for secrecy involves protecting secrets from revelation. As Born and Leigh warn, once you decide that you must have secrets to formulate and execute effective foreign policy, you must create agencies that work to collect those secrets and keep them from the prying eyes and spies of rivals and allies. This entails clandestine surveillance, infiltration, and disruption of groups, many times within a state.

Counterintelligence tools, which operate outside of the public view,[59] have been used to undercut political opposition and help leaders and parties stay in power. Examples in Canada, Norway, and the United States illustrate that the potential for abuse is institutional, not a function of a specific corrupt political culture or historical accident.[60]

In Canada, a Security Intelligence Review Committee (SIRC) report described that national security secrecy institutions had been abused in a "campaign of dirty tricks, consisting of break-ins, arson, and theft targeted at left-leaning press and political parties (including one that was poised to form [the next] government). A subsequent cover-up that was almost successful involved a deception that included lying to a Minister about the campaign. These kinds of stories might seem far-fetched and the stuff of spy-novel fantasy, but all of it is true. And all of it happened . . . *in Canada*"[emphasis in original].[61] The "spy-novel fantasy" culminated in what is known as the McDonald Commission,[62] which uncovered evidence that the Royal Canadian Mounted Police (RCMP), who at the time had the legal remit of both the US FBI and the CIA, were systematically disrupting domestic opposition to the government under the guise of national security. In a premonition of Watergate, the office of the Agence du Presse Libre du Quebec was burglarized in the early 1970s, with the RCMP behind the invasion. Similarly, the RCMP was found to have torched a barn near Montreal that was used as an office by Quebec intellectuals. In all, there was significant evidence that citizens that were associated with left-leaning positions or Quebec nationalism had been targeted for more than two decades by the RCMP Security services as an attempt to scuttle opposition.

A similar abusive dynamic was playing out in Norway around the same time, although the political corruption of security forces was not known publicly until the Lund Commission report in the 1990s. The Norwegian Police Security Services, the Norwegian Intelligence Service, and the Norwegian National Security Authority were found to have spied on and disrupted opposition groups ranging from anti-nuclear weapons groups to pacifists and communists. There were also specific linkages between the Norwegian Police Security Services and the Norwegian Labour Party,[63] which was dominant, holding the Prime Ministership for almost all of the period between 1935 and 1965 and then again from 1971 to 1981. In the conspiracy involving both the RCMP and the Norwegian security services, covert action, funded and organized for national security, was utilized instead to undercut domestic opposition and increase executive power.

Operation Shamrock in the United States provides another example of the capacity to keep secrets being turned against domestic opposition. In the 1950s, 1960s, and early 1970s, every telegram that left the United States from Western Union International, RCA Global, and other companies that were routed from or through New York, Washington, DC, San Francisco, and San Antonio were intercepted and read. This was uncovered by the Church Committee.[64] The committee discovered that these intercepts were used for political purposes in addition to national security ends. For example, the CIA used the records to track those that dissented on the Vietnam War and other policies, such as Martin Luther King.[65] Snider[66] writes that US citizens, particularly those that held opinions that challenged US official policy, were targeted in the program. This included anti-war and civil rights leaders. In 1973, at the height of the program, over 600 US citizens were on the watch list, and that information was used to anticipate opposition.[67]

As Shamrock was collecting intelligence on US citizens, another program, COINTELPRO, which was short for Counter Intelligence Program, was being run out of the FBI. COINTELPRO turned up publicly due to the investigations by the Church and Pike committees.[68] The Church committee's final report suggests that COINTELPRO began in 1956 with the goal of subverting domestic dissident groups that challenged the position of the executive in the United States. It finds that COINTELPRO was "a misnomer for domestic covert action" that was aimed at "defending the correctness of US foreign policy," among other status quo policies.[69] COINTELPRO attempted to break up groups as varied as anti-war protesters, the US Communist Party, the Black Panther organization, and the Southern Christian Leadership Conference. In addition, agents planted false stories in newspapers about group members, infiltrated groups, and suggested that leaders were working with the police, and they generally used "wartime counterintelligence" techniques against groups that actively opposed specific government policies. Counterintelligence was crucial in protecting atomic secrets and stealth, but these same tools were at times turned toward protecting the private interests of politicians from the opposition.

THE CAPACITY FOR BOTH USING AND ABUSING SECRECY

These examples serve to illustrate the potential for the capacity for secrecy, including the agencies that protect secrets, to be utilized against political opposition movements and to deceive the public. In these examples, the executive selectively revealed and classified information or decreased the prospects of political opposition groups and kept their actions secret. If the public had known about what information was being kept from them or targeting of opposition, this would have been very controversial. In fact, when revealed later, many of these abuses set off recriminations.[70]

Further, these examples illustrate that abuse does not have to have a corrupt villain motivating the plot, but can arise from incompetence and mistakes. Leaders such as de Gaulle often believe that their policies will be successful and that the benefits will eventually outweigh the costs. However, as in Algeria, this belief can be mistaken. These leaders then can use the capacity for secrecy to cover up evidence of their mistakes. While the motivations for these abuses—hiding corruption or incompetence—are different from a leader's point of view, from the public's perspective it is perceived that incompetence and outright corruption lead to similar outcomes: higher costs or lower benefits and the inability to hold the leader to account.

This potential for abuse does not exist separately from the uses of secrecy that justified having the capacity to keep information from public view in the first place. For example, if counterintelligence were only useful for suppressing domestic opposition (an abuse) and not for protecting stealth technologies (a use), then that part of the capacity could be excised. However, the same capacities for secrecy can be used for public gain and for abuse, sometimes nearly simultaneously. This duality has significant implications for public support of foreign policy and, in turn, foreign policy efficiency in democracies. Two examples clarify the intertwining of public benefits and private cover-ups within the capacity for secrecy: the Dreyfus Affair in the late nineteenth century and Watergate in the early to mid-1970s. In both of these cases, agencies existed to protect national security secrets. In France, one component of this capacity was the Statistics Section; in the United States, there was the CIA and FBI, along with other intelligence agencies. Both the Statistics Section and the CIA and FBI worked to produce and keep secret exceedingly valuable technologies—for example, the 75-mm gun in France and stealth technology (see Chapter 3) and Project Azorian in the United States. These are examples of the same capacities for secrecy being used and abused nearly simultaneously.

The 75-mm Gun and the Dreyfus Affair

In the late nineteenth century, France was shaken by a scandal involving the abuse of military intelligence. The roots of the scandal were submerged in a relatively new military counter intelligence group, known as the Statistics Section. This bureau was organized in 1871 and was led by Jean Sandherr. The avowed goal was to protect French military secrets and deceive international rivals, particularly the Germans, about French capabilities and plans. The Section worked in concert with Maurice Paleologue, who was head of the "Secret Affairs" division at the Ministry of Foreign Affairs. These two offices provided a significant capacity for secrecy in France.

One important target for intelligence was German military representative Count Maximillian von Schwartzkoppen, who was stationed at the German embassy in Paris. In fact, both the Statistics Section and the Secret Affairs division were tracking not only any German secrets they could purloin from the embassy, but also potential leaks to Count Schwartzkoppen from French operatives. One of the most important secrets these groups were protecting was the successful, and secret, development of the 75-mm artillery gun, known formally as the Materiel de 75 mm Mle 1897. This was an artillery piece that would be able to fire more quickly and more accurately than other contemporary weapons. Due to revolutionary technology put into action by the French, the 75-mm gun was a much more effective weapon than the German Feldkanone 96 gun. In particular, keeping the secret of its pneumatic recoil system worried French military planners. A German manufacturer had already worked out most of the details, but not all. The secret of the French design appears to have been successfully preserved even after the gun was publicly unveiled in 1899, and the weapon proved very useful in World War I, particularly at Verdun and in the Marne.[71]

However, this same capacity for secrecy that proved useful in one instance was directly abused in another. What came to be known as the Dreyfus Affair began simply enough. The French had employed a maid in the German embassy who was pretending to be "dim-witted" to provide them with the litter that she cleaned up after hours, including torn documents directly from von Schwartzkoppen's office trash can.[72] On September 26, 1894, a handwritten note, which came to be known as the bordereau, was brought to the Office of Statistics from von Schwartzkoppen's office. The content of the note implied that someone in the French military was offering to sell von Schwartzkoppen secrets relating to military plans and artillery developments. The document specifically referenced a unique hydraulic brake on the 120 "short" gun that the French forces were testing.

While this was neither as groundbreaking nor as secret as the development of the 75-mm gun,[73] the discovery of a possible highly placed traitor, particularly with information on the development of artillery, alarmed the highest echelons of French intelligence. Unfortunately, the investigation into who was the spy was bungled from the start. After collating information on who would have access to all of the promised documents mentioned in the bordereau, the investigators were stumped for suspects. By October 6, Sandherr and his deputies decided that it was possible that an intern with the artillery, rather than a permanent member of the general staff, might be to blame. The intern lists were analyzed concerning the "character" of potential suspects,[74] instead of ever ascertaining whether any had accessed or asked for direct access to the documents referred to in the letter procured from von Schwartzkoppen's litter basket.[75] One investigating officer looking over names of suspects noted that someone who he thought was "an unsatisfactory officer" was on the list, and another corroborated that this suspect was "a sly character."[76] The intern identified was Alfred Dreyfus. Dreyfus was with the artillery, and he was Jewish. The intelligence officers then performed an amateur comparison of Dreyfus' handwriting with the procured bordereau. While those in the Statistics Section worked to obtain more evidence of Dreyfus' guilt, the cabinet and leadership were informed and approved of the continuing investigation. There are varying theories about how dramatic a role the open anti-Semitism of the investigators played in Dreyfus being accused.[77]

The evidence used to implicate Dreyfus, in retrospect, was extremely thin. In total five people were asked to evaluate the handwriting on the bordereau, and three stated that it matched in parts an example from Dreyfus, but each agreed that there were significant discrepancies. Additionally, Dreyfus' position in artillery meant he could possibly have had access to the documents in question, but only if he had asked. It was never ascertained whether Dreyfus sought the mobilization plans discussed in the bordereau or the artillery manual mentioned. Other intelligence pointed to the traitor speaking German, which Dreyfus did, but so did many in the Statistics Section. Moreover, there were significant pieces of information that did not fit in implicating Dreyfus. The bordereau mentioned that the traitor would be on "maneuvers," while Dreyfus had not participated in any, nor was he scheduled to participate in any. In addition, Dreyfus was quite rich; thus the usual pecuniary motives for selling secrets did not seem to supply a motive.[78]

Despite the lack of additional information linking Dreyfus with the bordereau, the suspect was arrested on October 15. News of the arrest and Dreyfus' name leaked two weeks later. For a short while, the case appeared much stronger and more conclusively pointed to Dreyfus. An encoded Italian telegram from Alessandro Panizzardi at the Italian Embassy in Paris was intercepted. This transmission used a new cryptographic code, but it was provisionally cracked on November 6. Using this provisional code key, the telegram appeared to state "Captain Dreyfus has been arrested. The War Minister has proof of his relations with Germany. I have taken all precautions."[79] Yet, the codebreakers at Quai d'Orsay were not quite done. By November 10, a new code key was tried on the same document. This newer code key gave a quite different meaning and was much more innocuous. It stated, "If Captain Dreyfus has no relations with you, it would be advisable to instruct the Ambassador to publish an official denial to avoid comments in the Press."[80] While Sandherr preferred the first key solely because it substantiated his hunch of Dreyfus' guilt, the Foreign Office had a double agent in the Italian Embassy. This allowed the French Foreign Office to test which key was correct by having their agent send a message with recognizable names coded in the cypher. When the message was decoded by a cryptographic team that had no knowledge of the ruse, it proved that the second key, which did not incriminate Dreyfus, was the correct one. However, intelligence officials, and specifically Sandherr at the Statistics Section, ignored the second key, convinced as they were already of Dreyfus' guilt. They continued to use the first cypher as evidence against Dreyfus for years, despite knowing that it had been retracted by the cryptographic team.[81]

When discussing the allegations with Dreyfus' brother, Commandant du Paty, who was an agent in the Statistics Section, reportedly stated that "There is not one chance in a thousand that your brother is innocent."[82] However, in private, those pushing the investigation had their doubts about the clarity of the case. One historian writes that, "Knowing just how feeble these scraps were as evidence against Dreyfus, the prosecution decided that they would not be shown to the defense, but presented to the judges alone."[83] This led to the preparation of a "secret dossier" that was slipped to the judges as they were deliberating without the knowledge of the defense or the public. The Minister of War, General Auguste Mercier, approved of this tactic. As the accusations were publicized, the Statistics Section worked with the government, through Mercier, so that "if the judges themselves had misgivings about the legality of what was being done, 'national security' would be invoked as a justification."[84] Of note is that the secret dossier included the text of the false decryption of the message from the Italian Embassy. All those involved were worried that they would be ridiculed if it was shown that they had "jumped to the wrong conclusion in a precipitate way,"[85] but that only made them more careful in covering their tracks rather than rethinking their assumptions. At the trial, and after reading the "secret dossier," on December 22, not only did the judges unanimously exile Dreyfus, but the government changed the law so that the place of exile was the much less pleasant Devil's Island, off French Guyana, instead of New Caledonia, which was in the South Pacific.[86]

After Dreyfus was exiled and became ill, it began to appear to intelligence officers that the blundered investigation had implicated, convicted, and exiled the wrong person. The Statistics Section continued to get von Schwartzkoppen's refuse and piece together his correspondence. In March 1896, a blue piece of paper was reconstituted. This was a "petit bleu," which was the required form for sending letter telegrams at the time between post offices through a set of pneumatic tubes that were under the streets of Paris. This "petit bleu," which had not been sent, as well as another letter on ordinary paper, suggested that a meeting and trade of information was being planned between the author and von Schwartzkoppen. Most important, a name and address had to be given on the "petit bleu," and it read "Monsieur le Commandant Esterhazy, 27, rue de la Bienfaisance, Paris."[87] Esterhazy had himself been stationed in the Statistics Section as a German translator and was well known to the officers there. The handwriting on these letters did not match von Schwartzkoppen's.

In the interim, Sandherr became ill, and the new head of the Statistics Office, Lieutenant Colonel George Picquart, began an inquiry into the "petit bleu." For a time he was unable to find an example of Esterhazy's handwriting, and superiors refused to order the production of a specimen.[88] By August 1896, however, Esterhazy was applying for a post at the Ministry of War, and his application included handwritten sections. These were given to the Statistics Section and Picquart, who was leading the investigation himself. As Picquart looked at the writing, he is reported to have been "immediately struck by the similarity of the hand to that of the bordereau which had been so thoroughly scrutinized so many times."[89] When the handwriting was shown to those previously involved in the Dreyfus investigation, but with the names removed, they suggested that the new evidence was Dreyfus' handwriting, despite the fact that he was locked up on Devil's Island. Thus, the Statistics Section by August 1896 knew two things. Esterhazy was very likely a spy now working with the German embassy, and it was possible that he and not Dreyfus was previously spying for the Germans and had penned the original bordereau.

Picquart not only made these deductions, but also filled in the gaps left in the case when Dreyfus was exiled. He discovered that indeed Esterhazy had been on maneuvers, as stated, and that he had accessed several documents referred to in the bordereau. In addition, Esterhazy was said to be perpetually in need of money.[90] He also was able to reconstitute the "secret dossier" that had been ordered destroyed. Picquart's superiors, who already knew about the secret dossier and how it was used, were surprised that a copy still existed; General de Boisdeffre, Chief of the General Staff, supposedly asked, "Why was it not burned as agreed."[91] Here Picquart saw how weak the original case was against the unfortunate Dreyfus, particularly in relation to what he now knew about Esterhazy. However, the military and political leadership was united in deciding, against the council of Picquart, who wanted a renewed inquiry, that this new evidence should be suppressed.

The expressed motivation for this decision was the need for "military solidarity." The leadership further concluded that the revelation of Esterhazy's treason instead of Dreyfus' should be treated as "military secrets," according to the Minister of War General Jean-Baptiste Billot. When Picquart protested that the falsely accused Dreyfus was obviously innocent, General Gonse, Deputy Chief of the General Staff, is reported to have stated, "That is not something that should enter into our calculations. If you keep quiet, no one will know."[92] Read suggests that the logic for covering up the previous incompetence and mistakes was that "[w]ith the body politic corrupt and enfeebled by social and cultural fissures, the army embodied the unity and integrity of the nation. To make public the fact that the trial of Dreyfus had been fraudulent and its verdict unsound would so discredit the High Command that the army would be fatally weakened."[93] This was, of course, simply justification for avoiding blame. Regardless, over the next decade, the tools of national security and classification were diverted to attempt to keep the evidence proving Dreyfus' innocence from being known to the public.[94]

The cover-up was a spectacular, if ultimately another bungled, operation. It involved repeated reassignments of Picquart to locales as far away from Paris as possible, arresting those who would might expose the truth, and the forging of further evidence to deceive the public. The first step of this attempt at covering up the tragedy of Dreyfus' exile was unofficially exiling Picquart away from Paris, first to eastern France in October 1896, then to North Africa in December 1896, and then on to Indo-China. The stated justification for these moves was "to reorganize the intelligence networks."[95]

Picquart had no allies to protect him because those below him in the Statistics Section had helped prepare the false case against Dreyfus, while those above had explicitly approved those moves. Just before he was sent from Paris, Gonse and others worked to find out how much Picquart had learned. They decided that, "should the case against Dreyfus be reopened, some incontrovertible piece of evidence against him had to be found in the secret dossier."[96] Picquart's second deputy, Commandant Hubert Joseph Henry, worked to concoct that evidence, since it did not exist. He took a letter from the Italian military attache to von Schwartzkoppen, along with a piece of matching paper, also obtained from the Italian Embassy. Henry then forged an extra paragraph within the document and cut out the original content, which did not refer to Dreyfus. The new forged content read, "I have read that a deputy is to ask questions about Dreyfus. If someone in Rome asks for new explanations, I will say that I have never had any dealings with the Jew. If someone asks you, say the same for no one must ever know what happened with him."[97] This forgery was passed up to the Minister of War.[98]

In addition, the Statistics Section worked to frame Picquart as a leaker of classified information. Several facts about the Dreyfus case and cover-up had reached the press by 1896. The Statistics Section intercepted Picquart's mail and embellished a letter in Spanish, suggesting it was a coded message from regime opponents sympathetic to Dreyfus' cause. They also forged another document implicating Picquart directly in leaking information to newspapers critical of the leadership. Picquart was eventually charged as a forger of evidence against Esterhazy and imprisoned.

During this time, the Dreyfus family, which was correctly convinced of Alfred's innocence, had been working to generate public sympathy. By November 1896, they had learned about the existence of the secret dossier and the weakness of the evidence and had received a photograph of the bordereau, but they did not know about Esterhazy. While they were generally unsuccessful in getting publicity in the newspapers at this time for their cause, they did copy the bordereau onto posters all over Paris. This was to provide a break in the case and is perhaps an early example of crowd-sourcing information. On November 7, Jacques de Castro, a Parisian stockbroker, happened to be walking in Paris and saw one of the large posters of the bordereau. He found the handwriting in the bordereau identical to that of one of his clients, Commandant Esterhazy. He got word to the Dreyfus family through a mutual acquaintance.[99] While Picquart had told his story to his lawyer, and his lawyer to Auguste Scheurer-Kestner, Vice-President of the Senate and Senator for Life, both were sworn to secrecy. However, with Dreyfus' family now receiving Esterhazy's name from another source, both Picquart's lawyer and Scheurer-Kestner could confirm the information. Yet attempts to convince the President and Prime Minister were met with stonewalling.[100] In November 1897 a volley between the pro- and anti-Dreyfusard escalated in the press, with the one side attempting to move public opinion to understand Esterhazy's guilt and Dreyfus' innocence and the other side launching nationalist rhetoric and anti-Semitic tirades.

Eventually, more evidence found its way to the public until a new limited inquiry into whether Esterhazy was a spy started. The government, including the Prime Minister, President, and Minister of War, continued to stonewall. They worked to separate the Esterhazy evidence from the Dreyfus case and to preserve the "honour of the Army."[101] The Prime Minister announced that there "was no Dreyfus affair" and asked for a motion of support. In January 1897, Esterhazy was found not guilty and released. The next day the Senate removed Scheurer-Kestner as vice-president, and Georges Picquart, who was back in Paris, was "arrested on suspicion of imparting official secrets to a civilian and sent to the Mont-Valerien prison."[102] This has been described as an example of the public "being deceived by their leaders," and it was the capacity for secrecy that allowed it to happen. Pierre Miquel wrote that "[t]he Dreyfus Affair is above all about the manipulation of public opinion."[103]

The Dreyfus family continued to attempt to dig up the truth, with the help of many others, including Emile Zola, who supplied an impassioned defense of Dreyfus under the heading "J'accuse," and Georges Clemenceau. Even with these prominent friends, this was no easy task. At the same time, the Statistics Section and the Ministry of War worked to continue to deceive the public and suppress opposition. Emile Zola's writing on the topic garnerned an arrest, trial, and maximum sentence for libel in 1898. The forger of evidence against Picquart was found dead under suspicious circumstances. False information against Dreyfus, including what came to be known as the faux Henry, named after Statistics Section forger Commandant Henry,[104] was used in court and in the national assembly.

All the while the secret dossier and forged documents, making up much of the case against Dreyfus and Picquart, were classified. However, in July 1898, Minister of War Godefroy Cavaignac gave a rousing speech in the legislature about the evidence against Dreyfus where he quoted the forged documents in public for the first time. It was not until August of that year, two years after the forgery in 1896, that the faux Henry, as the Italian embassy letter was later referred to, was identified by another intelligence officer as a fake and brought to Cavaignac and Prime Minister Brisson.

This ignited a string of events in quick succession. While many in the government continued to press the case against Picquart and the opposition, Henry confessed his forgery to the Minister and committed suicide while in prison. Esterhazy was allowed to flee to England, and Cavaignac, who had given false testimony to the Senate, resigned. While Prime Minister Brisson offered a retrial of Dreyfus, the government ordered all of Emile Zola's furniture sold at auction to pay his fines. The next month the Brisson government fell after violent anti-Semitic rallies in Paris. It was not until 1899 that the verdict of 1894 was overturned. That same year Picquart was released from prison.[105]

Yet, even then, after the revelation of forgeries, false evidence, and the information on Esterhazy, the court martial of Dreyfus in a military court stood. The public was outraged, and with the support of the Prime Minister and the Cabinet, President Loubet pardoned Dreyfus. In November of that year, a general amnesty was passed for all those involved in the Dreyfus Affair, both the innocent who were still being pursued and those guilty of the cover-up. While Dreyfus was released in 1900, he was not cleared by an appeals court until 1906.[106]

The Dreyfus Affair illuminates the abuses of secrecy. The same group, the Statistics Section, that helped keep the secret of the 75-mm gun also kept from the public the incompetence of the leadership, including the Prime Minister and

President, for almost 6 years.[107] Understanding the Dreyfus Affair is important because it clearly shows that the capacity for secrecy, as exemplified by the Statistics Section, can be used and abused. Further, actions that might appear from the outside to be abuse, as Picquart's accusal of forgery to frame Esterhazy might have appeared, may be public-serving when placed in context. Similarly, actions that might appear public-serving, such as the robust prosecution of a traitor and defense of the "honor" of the army, can be abuse of those powers. In this case, the abuse included deceiving the public with false information and actively working to suppress opposition.

The potential for abuse has potentially tragic consequences for foreign policy in democracy. Both covering up incompetence and outright corruption have similar payoffs to the public—the benefits are outstripped by the costs, relative to alternatives. The Dreyfus Affair certainly had significant net public costs, as the net benefits of locking up someone innocent and allowing the actual spy to roam free for years were nil, while the costs were significant polarization and distrust.[108] The government attempted to make the case that "there was not one chance in a thousand" that Dreyfus was innocent and that conviction was necessary for the honor of the army. For years, many citizens believed the government, but that consent eroded into polarization and directly or indirectly brought down four governments. As we will review further below, this lack of public consent plagued France for decades after the Dreyfus Affair. Another, more modern example suggests that the shadow cast by the abuse of secrecy on public doubt and consent is not simply one peculiar case and continues to be relevant.

Project Azorian and Watergate

By the 1970s, the United States had developed an official capacity for secrecy that included several parts. The Central Intelligence Agency, which was organized after World War II with the passing of the National Security Act of 1947, focused on external threats.[109] The FBI, set up in 1908, had domestic policing powers and was responsible for counterterrorism within the United States and for a time in Latin America. Together with several military intelligence groups run through the Pentagon and the Department of State's Bureau of Intelligence and Research Unit, the CIA and FBI constituted what Loch Johnson would later call the United States' "secret power."[110]

During the presidency of Richard Nixon, both the uses and abuses of secrecy were operative, if not always immediately apparent to the public. The late 1960s saw the United States escalating its involvement in Vietnam against the backdrop of Cold War crises from the Middle East to Taiwan to Chile. In this threat environment, there were several important publicly beneficial secrets kept during this time. The development of the SR-71 and use of the U-2 spy plane, as outlined in the previous chapter, made significant, and classified, strides during this decade, as did satellite technology such as the Corona project.[111] The names of spies, such as high-ranking GRU officer General Dmitri Polyakov, who passed secrets to the United States from the 1960s to the 1980s,[112] and the information they provided was also highly classified. Additionally, the Soviet Union and the United States were accelerating their development and deployment of nuclear submarines. Intelligence on not only the capabilities of these subs, but also their placement, orders, and integration with other defenses was viewed as a top priority for both countries.[113]

Within this context, in 1968, the CIA learned[114] that a Soviet Golf-II submarine (designation K-129) patrolling the area northeast of Hawaii had sunk. The Soviet Union attempted a wide-scale search for the vessel but was unable to locate it. The K-129 was armed with three ballistic missiles that each carried nuclear warheads, as well as nuclear torpedoes. Also important was that the submarine would have highly valuable cryptographic information on Soviet communications. The US government saw in this tragedy a golden opportunity to learn more about Soviet capabilities, strategy, and codes. Using detailed sonar data, the United States undertook its own search and was able to locate the K-129, after the USSR aborted its attempt to locate the vessel. From 1968 until some time in 1974, the very fact that the United States knew that location were highly classified. However, perhaps the biggest secret related to K-129 was that the United States believed it could raise the submarine.[115]

On July 1, 1969, the CIA created Project Azorian,[116] headed by John Parangosky. Parangosky worked in the Skunk Works project run by Kelly Johnson, and he also helped develop technology for the Corona satellite program. President Nixon personally approved the project in August 1969. In secret, and under the guise of a Howard Hughes–sponsored expedition to mine manganese, a new ship, the Hughes Glomar Explorer, was built from scratch to conduct the deepest undersea salvage in history. The K-129 was photographed at over 16,000 feet in depth. From 1969 to 1974, a specially built ship and the training of the crew were accomplished under this cover story.

By the summer of 1974, the Glomar Explorer was launched from Long Beach, California. During the "mining operation," the Hughes Glomar Explorer was visited twice by Soviet vessels, one that launched a helicopter to take pictures of the vessel and another that collected trash that had floated overboard from the ship. However, the USSR still did not know the location of the K-129 and did not believe that the salvage operation was technologically feasible even if attempted.[117] Most important, the Hughes Glomar Explorer had been designed so that the entire operation occurred underwater and within a "moon pool" inside the ship. The submarine pieces were to be brought up into the hull of the ship from the bottom and thus would not be visible.

It is unclear how successful Operation Azorian was in terms of the specific items that were recovered, due to continuing classification of these details.[118] Recent accounts suggest that at least some nuclear torpedoes and useful information were obtained but that the nuclear ballistic missiles were not able to be brought up. After news broke, due to a leak 6 years after the start of the operation to build the Explorer, President Ford held a meeting on the topic, as well as on the potential for a follow-up mission known as Operation Matador. In this meeting, James Schlessinger, the Secretary of Defense, provided his assessment: "[t]his episode has been a major American accomplishment. The operation is a marvel—technically, and with maintaining secrecy."[119]

David Sharp, who was on-board the Glomar and has written a recent book on the subject, suggests that the greatest intelligence gain of the mission was not the specific items that were acquired, although those were useful, but the Soviet Union's confusion about what the United States now knew. Evidence suggests that Moscow was unable to learn what was recovered and what was not, and this necessitated costly changes.[120]

While Azorian was highly classified and there was significant success in keeping information on the mission secret, there is also evidence of transparency costs in this case. News broke publicly about some partial details in the press in 1975. These leaks did not provide the public with information on the costs and benefits of the action—those remained a secret—and one LA Times story even got the ocean wrong.[121] However, the follow-on mission had to be canceled.

During these same 6 years, significant abuses were occurring in parallel to Project Azorian using the same capacity for secrecy, but for different purposes.[122] The CIA operative who has penned the most complete history of Project Azorian and was intimately involved in its planning and execution, David Sharp, was a communications specialist during the Bay of Pigs fiasco with another CIA agent, Howard Hunt, of Watergate fame. In the wake of leaks on Vietnam such as the Pentagon Papers, President Nixon became, by some historians' judgments, "excessive" about secrecy.[123] The President created a "Special Investigative Unit," known as the "Plumbers," to plug leaks; this group included Howard Hunt. Nixon's abuse of the capacity for secrecy mirrored the Dreyfus Affair in several respects. Both involved executives and their close advisors working with those tasked with collecting and keeping secrecy—Gonse, Sandherr, and particularly Henry in France and ex-CIA officer Hunt, FBI director L. Patrick Gray, and CIA director Helms in the United States—to deceive the public and anticipate and suppress opposition, while insiders and outsiders—Picquart, Scheurer-Kestner, Zola, and others in France and Daniel Ellesberg, Mark Felt, the press, and various legislative committees in the United States—worked to reveal what was being covered up.

One of the early abuses in the Nixon White House was an attempt to gather "dirt" on Daniel Ellsberg. Ellsberg had leaked a classified study of Vietnam that he had worked on, which came to be known as the Pentagon Papers. The Pentagon Papers themselves revealed what many considered abuses of national security secrecy, as they included evidence that previous presidents had deceived the public about methods and intentions in Vietnam. For example, there was now confirmation, in a previously classified document, that President Johnson had worked to escalate the war while promising the public that this was not the case. John Prados wrote that the Pentagon Papers were "a body of authoritative information, of inside government deliberations that demonstrated, beyond questioning, the criticisms that antiwar activists had been making for years, not only were not wrong, but in fact, were not materially different from things that had been argued inside the US government."[124]

G. Gordon Liddy and Howard Hunt, a former CIA operative who was still connected to the agency,[125] broke into Ellsberg's doctor's office to try and find information to discredit the leaker on September 3, 1971. Other CIA officers, including Bernard Barker, who had worked with Hunt during the Bay of Pigs, were part of the burglary. These "operations," as they were referred to in the White House, were not only carried out in secrecy, but organized so that they would not be "traceable" to those that planned them.[126] The now infamous break-in at the Democratic headquarters at the Watergate Hotel, which also included Hunt, was part of a larger network of operations conducted by the CIA, the FBI, and the White House itself targeting opposition groups. These include wiretaps on prominent Democrats,[127] as well as the harassment of domestic groups that were deemed "subversive" by the CIA under Operation Chaos. This latter operation involved the harassment of opponents of the Vietnam War as well as other protest groups by the CIA, in violation of their charter.[128]

The summer of 1972 saw the CIA begin the secret construction of parts of the Hughes Glomar Explorer to collect legitimate national security information, along with a CIA-affiliated operative to burglarize a political office to try to collect illegal information for political gain. The attempt to cover up Watergate and these other operations is a clear illustration of an executive attempting to use secrecy to hide evidence of both incompetence and corruption from the public in the United States. The White House press secretary called the Watergate break-in a "third-rate burglary" at first, and when put under further pressure he stated that "certain elements may try to stretch this beyond what it is."[129] A few days later, President Nixon himself deceived the public when he stated to the press that "this kind of activity . . . has no place whatever in our electoral process or in our government process." He went on to promise in that same press conference that "the White House has no involvement whatever in this particular incident."[130] In private, the White House was planning how to keep information on their involvement from becoming public.[131]

Specifically, the White House attempted to use national security as a shield to prevent further revelations. A June 23, 1972, conversation between the President and H. R. Haldeman in the Oval Office suggested first that the head of the FBI, L. Patrick Gray, was working to try to cover up White House involvement and that a CIA cover story should be passed to FBI agents.[132] On another occasion, the President stated that he would suggest that Watergate was an "intelligence operation" that was needed "from the standpoint of security."[133] Evidence of this abuse has been called the "smoking gun" that led to Nixon's resignation.[134]

Just as Henry was the sharp point of broader deceptions and threats, including authoring forgeries and attempts to intimidate leakers, in the Dreyfus case, Hunt served that role for Nixon. Subsequent Senate investigations have uncovered that Hunt not only attempted to discredit Ellsberg and other whistleblowers but went so far as to forge State Department evidence that President Kennedy had ordered the killing of South Vietnam's leader Ngo Dinh Diem and his brother to hurt the Democrats' electoral chances in subsequent elections.[135]

The abuse and secrecy did not stop with Hunt. In 2007, after a new release of CIA documents on Watergate, Bob Woodward wrote, "[t]he CIA of that era was the perfect Watergate enabler, as these new documents suggest in telling detail." The documents were related to the White House communications with CIA Director Helms and in particular the government's use of the CIA to hide information from investigators. Woodward concludes that "[t]his was the Watergate-era CIA, with Helms ever serving the president, ever mindful, as Richard M. Nixon's secret White House tapes later revealed, that the president wanted the full story of Watergate locked away in government safes forever. And the CIA's role in that cover-up was always one of the murkiest parts of the story."[136] The FBI was also involved in the direct cover-up. FBI Director Gray worked with the CIA to try and delay interviews of CIA agents that had been identified as involved. More dramatically, Gray reports that he burned several documents relating to Hunt's activities working for the White House. In the White House on June 21, Gray was given several documents in manila folders and was told that "these should never see the light of day" and that they involved "secret" activities by Hunt, specifically.[137]

By 1974, as the Glomar Explorer was in the water, President Nixon had just resigned in the face of evidence of his involvement in domestic spying and the abuse of the capacity for secrecy in trying to deceive the public. These revelations then led to follow-on investigations of Operation Chaos and other programs.

Therefore, the capacity for secrecy in the United States was used in Project Azorian, but it was abused both in the Watergate cover-up and in the contemporaneous undercutting of domestic political opponents such as Ellsberg and prominent Democrats.

In the United States, there was a continuing fear that abuses of national security secrecy, following on the heels of revelations related to the Pentagon Papers and the Watergate investigation, would lead to public distrust of government and a lack of support for national security priorities. Like the Dreyfus Affair, the break-ins and cover-up served no public purpose, but they led to significant public costs—not only in investigative time and energy but, as in France, in distrust and cynicism. It was suggested by President Carter that the US public was "sick at heart" after Vietnam and Watergate.[138] During his presidency, Carter gave what came to be known as the "malaise speech," where he diagnosed the public with a distrust of government and a crisis of confidence in the nation.[139]

In 1980, President Reagan identified the "Vietnam Syndrome," which he believed afflicted the American public and made them doubt the "morality" of foreign policy. He believed that the Cold War would be lost, as Vietnam was, only if the United States failed "to win in the field of propaganda here in America." He went on to suggest that the public needed to support robust foreign policy, in both political support and military spending, because "we must have the means and the determination to prevail or we will not have what it takes to secure the peace."[140] The post-Watergate presidents knew that public polarization and distrust threatened investments in national security.[141]

In the next chapter, I explore the consequences of this potential abuse, both more generally and in the aftermath of the Dreyfus Affair and Watergate, for public support for national security policies. Public consent is not automatic, but it is necessary for investments in security. Skepticism and distrust can and do reduce foreign policy effectiveness in democracies if there is no mechanism to reassure the public that the capacity for secrecy is not being abused.

The Consequences of Potential Abuse for Public Consent

The potential abuse of secrecy that was exemplified in the Dreyfus Affair and Watergate has significant consequences for the process of generating public consent for foreign policy. The 1997/8 annual report from the Intelligence Select Committee in the United Kingdom aptly linked public support with the capacity for secrecy:

> It is vital that public confidence is maintained . . . [it] can be very fragile. That is the inevitable consequence of operation within the 'ring of secrecy', which prevents a more balanced public view of their activities and their value.[1]

This quote hits on the critical tension within a public that is called upon to supply consent in the form of money and active political support for foreign policy while being kept in the dark about the policy specifics. If the public could be assured that the money was going to be spent on their security and it was worth the return, it would clearly be in their interests to support these policies. However, as argued earlier, the public cannot be sure at any given time that their consent, be it political, pecuniary, or personnel, is being spent on public security. Because the marketplace of ideas is imperfect and the capacity for secrecy exists in democracies, leaders would have ample opportunity for abuse if the public blindly supported policies. However, the public does not blindly follow leadership priorities. Significant research has found deep and broad roots of opposition in democracies. Ben Fordham has suggested that disagreements about foreign policy goals are endemic in democracies.[2] Similarly, Kurt Gaubatz[3] makes the case that for every conflict the United States has considered becoming involved in, there has always been a significant subset of society that opposes it.

As the public has the ability to withhold consent, the potential abuse of national security powers leaves executives in a paradoxically precarious position in democracies. One might think to envy leaders that have the ability to keep national security secrets and use the public coffers to further their own political career. But the coffers have to get filled from somewhere, and as Reiter and Stam[4] rightly remind us, public consent is necessary for policies to be successful. Worrying about how to generate public consent is not a problem in non-democracies because repression, while costly in its own right, more than pays off for the executive. Repression allows a leader to extract the resources from the public that are necessary for power and corruption. In a democracy, a leader does not have repressive tools at his or her disposal.[5] Thus, while that leader is empowered with the capacity for secrecy, he or she still needs public consent and support to pass policies.[6]

The way that secrecy perpetuates and increases distrust and potentially reduces public consent was described by the Moynihan Committee on Secrecy: "[T]he failure to ensure timely access to government information, subject to carefully delineated exceptions, risks leaving the public uninformed of decisions of great consequence. As a result, there may be a heightened degree of cynicism and distrust of government."[7]

National security secrecy, ceteris paribus, robs the public of some of the tools they need to investigate whether a given foreign policy proposal, such as a military budget, is worth the asking price versus whether it is being proposed due to incompetence or nonsecurity motives. On domestic political issues, this is of less concern, because either transparency is the norm or excessive secrecy is itself a sign of malfeasance. One reason the Bush administration was admonished about keeping their energy commission lobbying list secret[8] was that few believed there were plausible public interest reasons to classify this information. On security affairs, secrecy is not prima facie evidence of a conspiracy. In fact, as in the case of the 75-mm gun, Project Azorian, and the examples in Chapter 3, secrecy is often crucial to increasing public security.

There are specific times and exceptional instances where consent is not difficult to generate, even in the specter of potential abuses of power. For example, moves by an external actor, such as a rival state, might exogenously signal a threat; or the public, due to previously available information, may already be convinced that a specific policy is useful. For example, the outbreak of the Korean War signaled a threat that moved public and elite opinion toward supporting more military spending.[9] Likewise, the 9/11 terrorist attacks also shifted public attitudes toward consenting to intervention in Afghanistan. In the Boer and Algerian Wars, the public was already prepared to support small-scale interventions to support their colonies, although larger investments were more controversial.[10]

Yet, in most cases previous public perceptions do not perfectly match international exigencies. A. J. P. Taylor wrote, "We are apt to say that a foreign policy is successful only when the country, or at any rate the governing class, is united behind it. In reality, every line of policy is repudiated by a section, often by an influential section, of the country concerned." In these cases, public skepticism of the policies put forth by an under-accountable leader can enervate, rather than energize, that executive's ability to mobilize resources to meet even meaningful international security threats. The question then becomes how a leader that may genuinely perceive external threats as becoming more ominous can overcome skepticism that threat levels are in fact rising or suspicions that the leader is inflating threats either for personal gain or due to the misreading of the situation. The larger the necessary investment or risk, the more public support will be necessary. The obverse situation is also of interest. How can a leader that sees threats declining convince the public that cooperative initiatives will be reciprocated and pay off rather than being taken advantage of? National security secrecy and a strengthened executive make this more difficult, but no less critical.[11]

RATIONALES FOR SKEPTICISM

Skeptical voices have been heard from the World Wars through the Vietnam conflict to the Iraq War. Skepticism generally takes two, reinforcing forms. First, those outside the executive, and particularly opposition partisans, might doubt that threats are being forecasted accurately. For example, before the October 2002 vote to authorize military force in Iraq, members of US President Bush's leadership team warned of a "mushroom cloud" if force was not used and suggested that the United States would be a likely target for a nuclear attack from Iraq.[12] On the other side, skeptics argued that these were scare tactics and that the war would be both costly and not in the public interest. During the debate in October 2003 Democratic Senator Robert Byrd provided a stark contrast in skepticism of the presidential case for war. He began by doubting the doomsday-threat level the administration was claiming. He stated:

If Saddam Hussein is such an imminent threat to the United States, why hasn't he attacked us already? The fact that Osama bin Laden attacked the United States does not, de facto, mean that Saddam Hussein is now in a lock and load position and is readying an attack on the United States. In truth, there is nothing in the deluge of Administration rhetoric over Iraq that is of such moment that it would preclude the Senate from setting its own timetable and taking the time for a thorough and informed discussion of this crucial issue.

He then went on to question the costs and benefits of the war:

A U.S. invasion of Iraq that proved successful and which resulted in the overthrow of the government would not be a simple effort. The aftermath of that effort would require a long term occupation. The President has said that he would overthrow Saddam Hussein and establish a new government that would recognize all interest groups in Iraq .... This kind of nation-building cannot be accomplished with the wave of a wand by some fairy godmother, even one with the full might and power of the world's last remaining superpower behind her. To follow through on the proposal outlined by the President would require the commitment of a large number of U.S. forces—forces that cannot be used for other missions, such as homeland defense—for an extended period of time .... It will cost billions of dollars to do this as well.

While Byrd's argument, and amendments, lost the subsequent votes, he spoke for a significant portion of the country.[13] In the House of Representatives, over 60% of Democrats voted against the resolution to authorize the President's use of force against Iraq, and 40% of Democrats in the Senate voted along with Senator Byrd against the authorization. In public opinion polling at the time, roughly between 50% and 40% of the public registered opposition to the resolution in some form.[14] Republican Senator Chuck Hagel reportedly told Secretary of State Colin Powell, "To say, 'Yes, I know there is evidence there, but I don't want to tell you any more about it,' that does not encourage any of us. Nor does it give the American public a heck of a lot of faith that, in fact, what anyone is saying is true."[15]

Second, these same critics might believe that present circumstances provide specific private benefits to the leadership, as opposed to offering national security benefits. Many Republican politicians claimed that Democratic US President Clinton was playing politics with national defense when he authorized a strike on Iraq in December of 1998 during the impeachment proceedings.

The Republican Senate Majority Leader went so far as to say that "the timing and the policy are subject to question." House Rules Committee Chairman Gerald Solomon said: "Never underestimate a desperate president . . . . What option is left for getting impeachment off the front page and maybe even postponed?"[16] Similar accusations were made by the opposition to Margaret Thatcher's government during the Falklands War. MP Nigel Spearing is quoted as saying, "The fleet is really that of HMS Government, whose purpose is not only to right the wrongs over the Falkland Islands but to retrieve the reputation of the Government."[17]

Sometimes skepticism goes so far as to beggar belief. In World War I, the UK exaggerated several German atrocities to try and magnify support for the war, as in the Bryce Commission report.[18] However, in World War II, remembering the previous exaggerations and deceptions, many in the British public believed that early reporting of the holocaust was simply propaganda. Reports on concentration camps and interviews with witnesses had been on the BBC for years, but it was only with mounting evidence after the Allied advance that the public saw the horror.[19] Writer and columnist Mollie Panter-Downes wrote of the skepticism: "Millions of comfortable families, too kind and lazy in those days to make the effort to believe what they conveniently looked upon as a newspaper propaganda stunt, now believe the horrifying, irrefutable evidence that even blurred printing on poor wartime paper has made too clear."[20] In point of fact, the British government made decisions not to emphasize the information, expecting either that the public would not believe it or that it would incite antisemitism instead of raising support for the war.[21]

FROM SKEPTICISM TO UNDERINVESTMENT

The absence of broad public consent for policies can and has undercut foreign policies. Quite simply, if the public cannot be convinced that resources are necessary for general goals and policies under the executive's discretion, then either the policy must be abandoned, possibly after a costly political fight, or, more often, the investment is trimmed down to reduce opposition. Either possibility can compromise security.[22] For example, there is a growing body of evidence that executive concerns about the lack of political support for conflict in Iraq led to significantly fewer troops on the ground to give the impression of a quick, easy victory.[23] Perhaps the most famous example of partisan conflict circumscribing military commitments is the Vietnam War, where Congress went so far as to cut off future funding.[24]

Partisan divisions and distrust can also be pronounced in domestic battles for armaments and defense spending to prepare for future rather than imminent threats. Partisan bickering in mid-1980s France over the Eurofighter and the eventual decision of the French to build their own fighter is one recent example.[25] In an impressive set of analyses of early Cold War defense policy in the United States, Benjamin Fordham[26] has found significant evidence that investments in both strategic and conventional forces were contentious and often scaled back for lack of political support. Fordham[27] also finds an interesting dynamic where opposition to national security policies was bought off by sacrificing domestic priorities.

During the inter-war years, unconvincing executive actions interacted with skeptical publics to produce underinvestment in security across several democracies.[28] Jackson[29] blames secrecy and continued distrust of the executive and military, in part, for France's failure to mobilize adequately during the inter-war years, particularly from 1934 to 1939. As the German threat increased, the French government received useful intelligence on Nazi intentions and capabilities, particularly from the army's Deuxieme Bureau. However, the public remained skeptical of government estimates of this threat, particularly after the Stavisky affair[30] revived memories of the abuse of the Dreyfus Affair in 1934. This lack of preparation, at least in part, accelerated their defeat in the subsequent conflict.[31] Public opposition to military spending and alliance ties in the United States in the 1930s also has this character, with Roosevelt's calls to arms and embrace of the lend-lease program being met with catcalls of "warmonger" by the opposition.[32] Similarly, in the United Kingdom, Germany's ascent went unchecked in part because the government did not believe, accurately in many historians' eyes, that the public would support the mobilization of a large expeditionary force.[33]

BACK TO DREYFUS AND WATERGATE

The dynamic of unconvincing executives facing public skepticism and either trimming back their policies or facing opposition was obvious in France after the Dreyfus Affair and in the United States during Watergate. In both cases, the previous abuse of secrecy and the national security apparatus led to public and elite doubts about the policy courses charted by the executive. Even further, elites were cognizant of this public distrust and often scaled back their policies, or covered up their costs, instead of facing public opposition. In France, distrust of the military led directly to a lack of trained military personnel and heavy artillery in World War I and early setbacks, despite robust alliance support from both Russia and the United Kingdom. Even after German bellicosity became more salient in 1911, opposition to rearmament was fierce and preparations were compromised.

In the United States, there was a short window where foreign policy followed a similar pattern of skepticism, arising from ambiguity in the strategic situation. Distrust of the executive on the issue of Vietnam had grown since the Tet Offensive in 1968 and the leaking of the Pentagon Papers in 1971. As outlined above, this dynamic helped to feed the Nixon administration's eventual abuses. Yet, the Cyprus Crisis of 1974 provided a more important test case. Unlike in Vietnam, the United States had a history of success in the Aegean, providing aid to Greece and Turkey, under the auspices of the Truman Doctrine, leading both to join NATO.

However, after Watergate, the unconvincing executive syndrome engulfed the White House and Congress. Skepticism of the President's and his team's motives led to Congress cutting off funding for a key policy initiative, aid to Turkey, even though the administration strongly believed, and tried to articulate, that slashing aid would be a foreign policy mistake for the United States. As predicted by the administration, the cuts resulted in the loss of US intelligence stations in Turkey, some of which were critical to monitoring Soviet actions and deployments, and significant distance between Washington and Ankara. It was only in 1978 that attempts were made to acknowledge and rectify the problems that this divestment caused.[34]

France After Dreyfus

After the Dreyfus Affair, the polarization of the French public accelerated, particularly in relation to the military and civilian leadership. Executive powers, symbolized most obviously by the Statistics Section and the army, were feared by those that hoped to build France into a democratic republic. For those that distrusted executive power, the abuse of the capacity was not potentialities but instead realities. Stevenson[35] describes that situation from 1900 to 1914: "French politicians saw the army as a potential threat to the republic." The distrust was acutely felt toward the Statistics Section, and it was officially disbanded. However, the capacity for secrecy continued in France, as the duties of collecting and keeping secrets were transferred to other agencies around the executive.[36] However, this did little to reassure the opposition partisans that national security tools, and secrecy, were being utilized for what they believed to be public ends.

The dimensions of skepticism extended across the political spectrum in France. On the one side were nationalists that believed that Germany was a menace that needed to be not only deterred but punished after the French defeat in 1870. This cadre of elites and supporters did not trust the left to support national security. Thus when the left was in power, the right argued that they were enervating French power for nonsecurity motives. Proposed leftist reforms of the military were opposed because nationalists worried that they were vehicles for anti-military sentiment and ideologically driven.[37] On the other pole were socialists, who from 1905 to 1911 had espoused a purely "anti-militaristic and anti-patriotic" stance and decried the use of "parasitic" international conflict, which misdirected public energies and funds toward non-public-serving goals.[38] These sentiments that were skeptical of executive power and national security investments were not marginal, as parties of the left controlled almost half of the Chamber of Deputies on average during this period.[39] Thus, any military prerogatives suggested by the right were viewed either as a waste of public funds or, worse, as threats to democratic institutions and workers. When the left offered counterproposals, the right argued that these deliberately weakened France.[40]

On balance, however, opposition to additional spending reigned from 1900 to 1911, with the civilian leadership and large sections of the public distrustful of the military leadership in particular.[41] This skepticism manifested itself in a lack of investment in security. Between 1895 and 1910, French military spending as a proportion of GDP had shrunk relative to the period between 1875 and 1890.[42] This was not true of Germany, which had raised military spending and personnel during this time.[43] One historian suggested that, after the Dreyfus Affair, "Parliament and the public were prepared to sanction French rearmament only if it could be justified as the only means of safeguarding national territory against an apocalyptic German 'onslaught.'"[44] However, there were wildly varying explanations of what defined the true threat, as well as how many troops and what appropriation of money would deter an "attaque brusquee" by the Germans.[45]

Therefore, French spending on defense remained inadequate even up to 1913.[46] France did not have an income tax until 1916; and, in turn, aggregate French military spending in Europe was considerably lower than that in Germany. This was particularly true because much of France's military spending went toward its colonies. Porch writes: "For more than a decade after 1900, France and her army had dozed."[47]

This underinvestment in security affected the size of the French army, military equipment, and strategy. The two-years law of 1905 reduced the time of service in the active military to two years, where it had been three. While this change also reduced the number of exemptions for military service, this did not make up for the decline in overall personnel. For example, by 1910 the number of reserve units available in France declined by more than 30%.[48] In addition, French military officers were "always far worse paid than their counterparts in Germany."[49] By 1908, half of the technical officers in artillery had resigned due to "poor career prospects."[50] Thus, while the infantry and army was not keeping pace quantitatively, it also fell behind in the quality of the officers it could recruit.

Whereas the impetus from defeat in the Franco-Prussian War stirred the innovation to develop the world's most advanced piece of artillery up to that point (the previously discussed 75-mm gun), post-Dreyfus investment in new artillery technology slowed to a crawl. The French military and political leadership were not ignorant of the uses of heavier artillery or the limitations of the 75-mm gun. The general staff knew that the Germans were investing in heavy artillery and that the 75's shot in a straight line and thus could not threaten artillery in defilade positions.[51] Heavy artillery, on the other hand, could strike the 75's that were out in the open. Stevenson writes: "Because of Parliamentary tight-fistedness and war ministry infighting, they had no equivalent of the German field howitzers."[52] Further, it took approximately 5 years to develop a new gun system. Yet from 1900 to 1911, the French failed to capitalize on the success of the 75-mm or to develop heavier weapons that could strike entrenched positions.[53]

The Agadir crisis in 1911, where Germany dispatched the gun boat Panther to Morocco in response to the annexing of Fez by Paris, brought the threat of conflict with Germany to the fore. This crisis had two immediate effects. First, it made French generals and politicians calculate that France was not prepared to fight and win a conflict against Germany. At this time, the largely defensive Plan XVI was the active French scheme if war were to break out with Germany. However, it was clear to the leadership that shortages in personnel made its successful execution unlikely.[54] Chief of Staff Joffre stated, modestly, that France "did not have even a 70 percent chance of victory" in a conflict with Germany at the time.[55] Second, the public became more aware of the German threat, with headlines about the crisis. In particular, public opinion turned more anti-German as the French offered concessions that many viewed as akin to being on the wrong end of "blackmailing."[56]

However, even after the Agadir crisis, with the Germans themselves helping to push the French public toward supporting investment in arms, progress in preparing for these threats was slow and incomplete. It took fully two years after Agadir to propose a law to increase military service, and in this interim Germany had increased their service and training requirements. The proposed French bill was known as the three-year law, as it increased active duty service back up to three years. The government wanted this bill passed as soon as possible, and without debate. However, instead of broad consent for longer military service, significant opposition to the bill emerged. Krumeich writes, "In the opening phase of the campaign (February–May 1913), the government, backed by the unconditional support of the far Right and other factions, tried to stir up feelings of hysterical fears as a means of pushing through the three-year bill as quickly as possible."[57] Opponents in return found it effective to "denounce the domestic reactionary and anti-republican motives behind the rearmament."[58] This line of skepticism was effective at weakening the case for the bill, as the government found the idea that "the defense bill was first and foremost a vehicle of domestic reactionary [nationalist] aspirations could never be completely dispelled."[59]

The fissures in trust between republicans and the military during the Dreyfus Affair were still clearly visible in this 1913 debate. To reinforce the right's support for the measure, the government argued that passage of the 1913 three-year bill would be "proof that the entire policy of the left-wing republican regime since the Dreyfus affair had been a failure." The bill was sold as repealing "the law of the Dreyfus men."[60] While this did increase support on the right, it widened the gap with the left, who continued to worry that the bill was being used for domestic political gain. These cracks in consent have been traced back to the previous abuses of secrecy by historians: "Troisiannistes (three-yearists) battled opponents of the law, just as Dreyfusards and anti-Dreyfusards had battled each other fourteen years earlier, and using much the same language."[61] In the barracks, the tension erupted into riots.[62]

In fact, there was reason for skepticism, even apart from residual distrust from the Dreyfus Affair. The government was less than forthcoming about its immediate motives for the three-year law. Krumeich[63] explains that political and military leaders wanted the three-year law to support a planned offensive strategy against Germany[64] but were able to "hide these motives from Parliament and the public" and "sell" the law as purely defensive.[65] The offensive strategy itself was a reaction to the weakness of French defenses and the lack of forecasted public support for additional investments. When an innovative defensive plan was devised by General Victor Michel in 1911 that called for significant mobilization of reserve troops and additional training, it was scoffed at as "looney."[66] In addition, the military distrusted the public to both politically support the number of troops necessary to mount a defense and militarily fight effectively alongside the professional army.[67]

Facing vociferous objections, the government allowed the law to be amended and even attempted to promise that the 1913 change was merely an extension of the emergency codicils in the 1905 law and was temporary.[68] Eventually, the law did pass, but it was weakened in the process and remained controversial. The class that was graduating its second year of service in 1913 was released, and two untrained classes were called up the next autumn. In addition, Parliament did not vote additional expenditures for the call-ups, preferring to wait until after the 1914 elections for fear of provoking an even greater public backlash. Regardless, despite weakening of the law and attempts to reduce the cost, the three-year call-up became a major election issue in May 1914, and Trosiannistes lost 50 seats.[69] This opposition reflected the deep suspicion of the public about the motivations of the bill, despite, as noted, Berlin having already increased its service requirement and having threatened France at Agadir.[70] Several historians have argued that in the way the three-year law was compromised and executed to avoid more public backlash, "it probably weakened the French army in the last year before the war by further thinning the already sparse supply of trained commissioned and non-commissioned officers."[71]

A similar dynamic can be found in debates and the resulting political dysfunction in trying to acquire heavy artillery as war grew closer. Large parliamentary blocs "consistently opposed funds for new weapons."[72] This opposition often was justified based on skepticism about the underlying, and potentially secret, motives of the spending programs. Porch writes that "the alacrity with which some politicians and soldiers called for the adoption of private industry [armaments], naturally led to the whispered charge that money was changing hands."[73] One strong proponent of spending on updated artillery, Charles Humbert, had given rousing speeches on the topic, but these had "lost much of their effect because many suspected that they sprang more from personal interest than from genuine concern for defense."[74] In turn, Humbert himself wrote to the President to ask "if the purchase by different ministry services of some defective, obsolete or excessively onerous materiel has not been motivated by the abusive action of certain very influential officers in the ministry [of War] looking to increase the benefits of some firms in which they secretly have a preponderant interest."[75] Due to this distrust, military plans for weapons of the future, like heavy artillery, were stillborn because it was believed that "no politician was ever likely to commit the government to a substantial program of armaments."[76]

Money and planning for heavy artillery thus became mired in executive committees and were abandoned or significantly trimmed by the legislature. The reporter for the Ministry of War stated that no additional money could be passed, even for heavy artillery, because it would have "blown an already overloaded political circuit."[77] At the start of World War I, Germany had an advantage of 848 to 308 in heavy artillery compared to France.[78] However, even this underrepresents French weakness, because the French guns were either obsolete versions of guns taken from forts or ineffective.[79] When taking firing range and targeting into account, the French "had practically no heavy artillery" by the start of World War I.[80]

The debate on the three-years law and lack of heavy artillery illuminated a more general problem in French policy after Dreyfus, and particularly after 1911. The worries about the abuse of national security information and secrecy—in the form of doubts about the necessity of policies, weapons systems, and spending as well as the nonsecurity motives for policy—reduced support for national security preparations. One prominent historian writes that "the Dreyfus Affair was not a hiccup in French civil-military relations from which the army quickly recovered," but instead had the effect of "throwing up a wall of distrust between the army and the republic."[81] Krumeich[82] reports that caught between the need to make up for years of lack of preparation and this continuing distrust of the military, many politicians considered "the defense issue a 'burning poker, so hot that many did not know by which end to pick it up.' " In fact, those that tried to pick up the defense issue were burned. Many that voted for the three-year law were voted out of office, and in 1911 alone, as the situation with Germany heated up, the Ministry of War changed hands three times.[83]

What emerged was a "disparity between defense requirements and the inability to explain these requirements to the people."[84] This process was the opposite of successful deception of the public to guard the national interest. The skeptical public was unconvinced by the executive, and underinvestment in security was the result. This underinvestment took the form of a "steady decline in French military strength. Bad training was the result of the lack of training areas and personnel. But rather than hard cash, politicians held out near useless palliatives—the social role was substituted for marksmanship, civil spirit for manoeuvre, 'military preparation' for training camps."[85]

The lack of public consent for the three-year commitment and heavy artillery had consequences for French national security. Krumeich sums up the situation: "The discrepancy between the reality and the ideological justification of French rearmament policy was to have serious consequences. The confusion in French internal affairs up to July 1914—the swing from the nationalist revival to the sweeping victory of the Left in the 1914 elections—can indeed be explained only by this disparity. It could even be said that the three-year law was not the apex of the nationalist revival but the beginning of its end."[86]

Instead of the public rallying under le drapeau tricolore, many dissembled, second-guessed, and opposed the government's plans. Moves toward the right, as when the compromised three-year bill was passed, were followed by hedges to the left. In the opening rounds of World War I, these deficiencies in personnel and materiel were evident as batteries of 75's were either mowed down or forced to retreat before their awesome power could be brought to bear, and casualties mounted. More than half of the over 1,400,000 French casualties were suffered before the winter of 1915.[87] Despite this, France was not defeated in the war, but it had failed to accomplish its offensive objectives in 1914 and thus suffered a destructive and long war. The diseases of polarization and distrust were not bled dry in World War I, as we will investigate in the next chapter.

The problem for France was best summed up by Radical leader Georges Clemenceau in 1914. He had previously been a supporter of the three-year law, but as disagreements and distrust from right to left undercut defense spending bills, preparations, and even governments, he gave a speech described as "equal in vehemence and rhetorical effect to Zola's J'accuse! [during the Dreyfus Affair]." Clemenceau observed that on national security, France could "be neither governed nor defended."[88] In fact, the lack of governance and security were inextricably linked through a lack of public consent for national security priorities.

The United States and the 1974 Cyprus Crisis

The Cyprus crisis, emerging in the wake of the Watergate scandal, provides a similar view of a skeptical public being unconvinced by an executive's foreign policy arguments. As Watergate led to US President Nixon's resignation in 1974, a military and diplomatic crisis broke out on the island of Cyprus. The island had been under British control until the Greek population of the island attempted to join Greece in 1955. This move was resisted both by the British and, more importantly and vigorously, by the Turkish minority on the island. By 1960, London had granted Cyprus independence, but under tense circumstances, with Greece still supporting unification with Cyprus, referred to as enonis,[89] and Turkey strictly opposed to this. Continuing tensions in 1964 and 1967 brought the United States in to negotiate for fear that Greek–Turkish tensions would weaken NATO, since both Turkey and Greece were members, and that moves by the Cypriot President Makarios to placate the Cypriot Communist Party signaled an opening for Moscow.[90]

After a coup in Greece in late November 1973, the new leadership, under General Dimitrious Ioannides, helped to engineer the overthrow of Makarios on July 15, 1974. Nikos Sampson was installed by the junta as President. The United States was acutely worried about the Turkish reaction.[91] In Ankara, Prime Minister Bülent Ecevit passed a message to the United States that since the coup had been "completely engineered by the Greek government," it was "completely unacceptable."[92] Due to the threat to the Turkish minority, Ecevit warned that he would "have to directly intervene with military force."[93] At the same time, Makarios, who had survived the coup by fleeing to a British base on Cyprus and was flown to London and then New York, was attempting to mobilize an international reaction to place him back in charge.[94]

Nixon dealt with the outbreak of the Cyprus crisis between meetings on the Watergate revelations that were engulfing his administration. The public revelations not only included the tracking of democratic opposition groups and the break-in, but now also encompassed wiretapping and the forgery and destruction of documents (see above). Yet, the United States had several specific security interests in Turkey and, to a lesser extent, Greece. Secretary of State Henry Kissinger argued that the United States wanted to keep the status quo, meaning avoiding a war between Greece and Turkey, as well as keeping the USSR's influence out of the region as much as possible. Toward this end, the United States suggested a compromise whereby Glafkos Clerides, the speaker of the Cypriot

Parliament, would take up executive power. However, this proposed unraveling of the coup was unacceptable to Athens, while the new Greek-installed regime in Cyprus was rejected by Ankara. In reaction to this stalemate, on July 20, Turkey began landing forces on Cyprus.[95]

The official US response to the Greek coup in Cyprus and ensuing Turkish invasion involved opposing public and private messages. Publicly, the United States issued a statement that "while criticizing the Turkish action, would put the blame for the war on Greece."[96] However, behind closed doors, Kissinger gave instructions to one subordinate "to be brutal towards the Turks in the sense that he can say that we will withdraw all military aid in the event there is an all-out war.'[97] Though Turkish Prime Minister Ecevit had been a student of Kissinger's at Harvard, Ankara remained determined to create a fait accompli on the ground that partitioned Cyprus. Increased US pressure, as well as stronger than expected Greek resistance in Cyprus, brought a short ceasefire and, quickly thereafter, on July 23, the overthrow of the coup leaders in Greece with a civilian government headed by Konstantinos Karmanlis. However, during the ceasefire, Turkey continued to maneuver toward what they called "double enosis," the partition of Cyprus into Greek and Turkish sections that would be run from Athens and Ankara, respectively.[98] On the same day that Gerald Ford took over the US Presidency from Nixon, the US State Department received intelligence reports that Turkey was planning to militarily seize a predetermined proportion of Cyprus.[99] Despite these developments, the United States wanted above all else to maintain solid relations with Turkey.

Kissinger understood that US–Turkey relations were strategically important and that there was no reason that US interests would not be served by a partition.[100] In a meeting with President Ford, Kissinger stated, "We certainly do not want a war between the two [Greece and Turkey], but if it comes to that, Turkey is more important to us and they have a political structure which could produce a Qadhafi . . . . There is no American reason why the Turks should not have one-third of Cyprus."[101] When an advisor suggested that the United States cut off military aid to Turkey if they renewed their offensive, Kissinger retorted, "We will not do that," and he asked in return, "What is the long-range advantage to the US [in cutting off aid]?"[102] Kissinger was willing to make a conditional threat to Turkey, so that US arms would not be used to fight an "all-out war" against a NATO ally, but he was adamant that partition should not trigger the same repercussions. Miller writes: "If, as was likely, the Greeks failed to cooperate, the United States was prepared to abandon them and tilt toward Turkey, standing by as Ankara used military force to oust Samson and accept the ultimate outcome: double enosis, partition, or an inter-communal solution imposed by Turkey."[103] Thus, even if the United States lost control of the diplomatic situation and Turkey was able to force a partition, the United States could maintain cooperation with Turkey.

There were further important reasons for the United States to "tilt" toward Ankara despite the particulars of potential Cypriot partition. At the time, there were several US intelligence stations in Turkey and Cyprus. These were important particularly for collecting technical information on Soviet missile tests and to support US deployments in the Middle East.[104] The problem for the new Ford administration was how to convince the public to continue a strong relationship with Turkey, despite their breaking of the ceasefire. Additionally, because of the sensitive nature of the intelligence bases, many of the specific benefits of cooperation with Turkey could not be publicly detailed.[105] On the other hand, because it had orchestrated the coup in Cyprus that set off the crisis, Greece was far from blameless.

Despite these reasons, US policy toward Turkey was about to be thrown on to the rocks of public skepticism. In August the script played out on the international scene in ways that did not surprise the US leadership. Turkey renewed its push for more of Cyprus on August 14, and within 48 hours Ankara had achieved its objectives.[106] Kissinger and Ford both agreed that the United States would not cut off military aid to Turkey as a consequence due to the importance of continued cooperation with Ankara. There was widespread agreement in the executive that if the United States cut off aid to Turkey or strongly sided with the Greeks, the intelligence bases and air force facilities in Turkey would be closed to the United States.[107] While Greece was greatly agitated by the moves orchestrated from Ankara, disorganization in the military severely constrained its options.[108]

As the international situation was moving toward double enosis, domestic surprises emerged for President Ford on the issue. Ford told Kissinger that he believed the public and Congress would stay out of the Cyprus issue and at least implicitly support US policy.[109] However, opposition began to grow in the United States for what was perceived as US support for Turkish military adventurism. Most of Nixon's and then Ford's tough threats to Turkey had been in private. Thus, it appeared to many that Nixon and then Ford, through Kissinger, had created the conditions for Ankara's move. This view gained steam when the coup leaders in Athens were replaced by Karamanlis, who made commitments to democratize Greece.

A speech by Congressman John Brademas in Boston on August 18, 1974, began by calling the Turkish moves "naked aggression by one country against a far smaller one." He applied blame to President Ford, stating, "[B]y action and inaction, the government of the United States has condoned and, it is not too much to say, given tacit support to these aggressive acts on the part of the government of Turkey." Brademas argued, in particular, that US policy in Turkey cost Americans money and paid little in public dividends. He continued: "[W]hat is, of course, particularly outrageous is that arms used by the Turkish forces have been supplied by the taxpayers of the United States and troops that have been carrying out these savage attacks have been trained with money supplied by the American people through our program of aid to Turkey." As for the benefits of the US policy, he asked, "[W]here are we today? The invasion and occupation . . . has had the most calamitous effects."[110] Because of these "calamitous effects," bills were introduced in the House and Senate to cut off military aid to Turkey.

In response to this opposition, Kissinger and Ford attempted to prove that they had not given Turkey the green light to invade, and they also felt that cutting off military aid to Ankara would be counterproductive to US interests. Kissinger, Ford, and CIA Director William Colby not only met with Congressmen Brademas, Peter Kyros, Gus Yatron, Paul Sarbanes, and Skip Bafalis, who made up the backbone of growing opposition, but also met with nearly a majority of Congress in a "massive" effort to avoid cutting off military aid to Turkey and defend the administration's position. Kissinger shared diplomatic cable traffic from DC to Ankara with several Congressmen, to little avail.[111] One report stated that "CIA director William Colby was dispatched to Capitol Hill with armloads of secret documents to demonstrate that our intelligence bases in Turkey were crucial to national security."[112]

These sanctioned leaks and arguments proved unconvincing. Miller writes that the Turkish invasion created "an instant credibility problem for the Ford administration."[113] The intelligence was mocked as merely "photos of Soviet ships steaming through the Bosporus Straits."[114] Kissinger and Ford themselves attested to the difficulty they had in persuading Congress and the public. On September 24, Kissinger told Turkish Foreign Minister Gunes, "We will meet with Congressional leaders on Friday, but it is to some extent out of my control. [Aid to Turkey] is being used against me politically."[115]

Indeed, echoing similar themes used by the left in France in 1913, opponents suggested that there were reasons to be suspicious that the underlying motives and competence of Nixon and Kissinger, and then Ford, were being hidden from the public.[116] Congressman John Brademas, who became a ringleader for the opposition, linked his distrust of the assurances from the White House to the abuses of Watergate. He stated, "[W]e have just emerged from what President Ford quite rightly described as the long nightmare of Watergate. During the last two years, the American people have been learning month by month of what we know to have been the most sordid pattern of lawlessness and corruption on the part of any administration in the near 200 year history of our country." He then went on to state, "[I]t must now be clear to all but the most biased observers that the so-called 'private diplomacy' of the Department of State has failed, and failed abysmally, to prevent the tragedy of last month."[117]

Brademas was not alone in his skepticism. Others directed volleys of distrust at Kissinger, suggesting that he was placing his own determination to hold on to power ahead of US national interest, he blustered, temporized, misused his department, and in the end had nothing to show but the creation of an enormous reservoir of ill will in the United States and in the eastern Mediterranean.[118]

Another line of attack, no less unfriendly to the administration, suggested that "incompetence not malevolence was the persistent hallmark of his eastern Mediterranean policy."[119] *New York Times* columnist William Shannon concluded that the Cyprus crisis was a manifestation of the CIA's "squalid involvement" in the Aegean which "nothing the US has gained in military 'security' in the Mediterranean in the past decade could justify." He suggested that "Cyprus ought not to be an American responsibility. The crisis there is no direct concern of the American President or the American People." This was a direct repudiation of the administration's case.[120]

Despite wrangling about specific dates, the bills cutting off Turkish aid and the ability to purchase US military equipment were overwhelmingly popular. For example, one bipartisan vote to pass the embargo and oppose Ford topped votes in support of the administration by almost 6 to 1 on October 17, 1974, in the House. The administration was able to finagle a few months' delay, until February 1975, under a compromise, but after that deadline the delivery of all military goods to Turkey, even those that were already paid for, ceased.[121] In return, Ankara expressed their "outrage" while closing all of the US facilities in Turkey, except one that was limited to NATO missions, and severely limited other forms of cooperation.[122] Even in July 1975, as Ford continued to point out how the ban was counter to US interests, Congress voted not to lift the embargo. This vote occurred despite the fact that the previous cutting off of aid had not led to the hypothesized Turkish concessions. Ford called this last vote "the single most irresponsible, short-sighted foreign policy decision Congress has made in all the years I'd been in Washington."[123] It would take 3 more years for negotiations, finally between the Carter White House and Congress, to reinstate Turkey as a legitimate buyer of US arms. Despite the situation in Cyprus not changing, the 1978 amendment to the Foreign Assistance Act allowing arms to be shipped to Turkey passed without difficulty.[124]

The Secrecy Dilemma in Democracies

The outlines of US policy during the 1974 Cyprus crisis, while less dramatic than the problems that France suffered after Dreyfus, follow a similar pattern. Manifest public and elite distrust of executive foreign policy, due to the potential for malevolence or incompetence, undercut support for foreign policy. The administration was unable to overcome this skepticism and distrust. Even as Ford released information on foreign bases to Congressmen, there were still doubts about "private diplomacy." In contrast to critics of liberal IR theories that assume leaders in democracies can easily achieve deception, Nixon and then Ford were constrained into a policy they believed harmed US interests. Yet, at the same time, this is also not a positive story for the marketplace of ideas in democracy. The revoking of the embargo in 1978 is an example of immediate public distrust and skepticism leading to outcomes that even critics eventually agree needed to be changed.

Another interesting corollary arising from this analysis of US and French policy is that good intelligence was not enough for foreign policy efficacy. The French had significant intelligence on German plans, capabilities, and intentions leading up to 1914. There are reports that one French spy with a flair for the dramatic was known as "the Avenger," because he wrapped his head in bandages to conceal his identity. Although the Avenger might not have passed information as dramatic as his appearance, through a variety of sources, France acquired information on German plans to eventually attack through Belgium and elude several French defensive positions.[125] They had copies of German war game plans, a 1912 document that detailed Germany's intention to move against France first if faced with the possibility of having to fight both France and Russia simultaneously, and German mobilization plans.[126] Thus, the early French debacles in 1914, despite alliance help from Russia and Britain, were not intelligence failures, broadly construed.[127] Similarly, the United States had very good intelligence on the fact that Turkey was going to push further into Cyprus, and also what Turkey's reaction would be to an arms embargo.[128]

Yet anticipation in these cases was simply wasted potential energy. Without public momentum to swing policy in an effective direction, the ideas of General Michel were derided as "looney" and Ford, Kissinger, and Casey's warnings were left on the shelf. Therefore, while there are uses of secrecy—underlying the justification for a capacity to keep information from the public—secrecy alone is insufficient in democracies to bring about success. Public support and preparation are also needed. Further, the dual necessities of a capacity for secrecy and a capacity to raise public consent in democracies are not independent. The capacity for secrecy allows for potential abuse, which, in turn, reduces the ability of an executive to gain public consent at times. This type of distrust is similar to what William G. Hyland, who was the director of the Bureau of Intelligence and Research during the Cyprus crisis, worried was isolationism, which he thought was "the Dracula of American foreign policy."[129]

These cases illustrate that critics who worried that democracies could be too transparent and thus ineffective got the diagnosis backward. It was secrecy that led to distrust and underinvestment in these cases, not transparency. Democracies can and do keep secrets, but this secrecy has costs for public consent. In both Watergate and the Dreyfus Affair, secrecy allowed leaders to abuse national security tools and generate greater distrust. Eventually this distrust continued as the potential for future abuse hung over the political arena and led to underinvestment, both through open opposition to policies, as most fully seen in the US 1974 Cyprus Crisis, and in reduced and deflated plans in anticipation of opposition, as in France.

CONCLUSION: A PROBLEM IN NEED OF A SOLUTION

In exploring how the capacity for secrecy allows for both the uses and abuses of secrecy—diving to recover Soviet submarines and hiring "Plumbers" against domestic opposition sometimes simultaneously—we have also tracked some specific foundations of rational skepticism in the public to blindly following, and potentially being deceived by, a leader. The intersection of secrecy and public consent marks the secrecy dilemma that all democracies face and sometimes fall prey to. For publicly beneficial national security policy, an executive needs the capacity for secrecy while also securing public consent. Yet with this capacity for secrecy comes the potential for abuse, as in the Dreyfus Affair, Watergate, and beyond. Moreover, these abuses lend credence to accusations such as those made by socialists in France and Democrats in the United States, to great political effect, that the capacity for secrecy is hiding corruption[130] and incompetence.

The resulting credibility deficit for an executive can, if unchecked, lead to tragic results for both the public and leaders. The public may get reduced security, due to an underinvestment in materiel, training, or personnel, or poor policy that leads to fewer options in the future. A leader may suffer through opposition, as did Ford—or, alternatively, eschew the political costs of fighting a losing battle to try and generate consent for spending and simply go along with the underinvestment. This latter strategy was the dominant story in France before World War I, even as Germany loudly signaled its threats at Agadir.

Despite the importance of the secrecy dilemma, there are strong reasons not to despair of democracy. Previous theories offered by the democracy irrelevantists and alarmists fail to explain key facts related to the secrecy dilemma. Those that believe that democracy is irrelevant to foreign policy suggest that the public can easily be deceived. Yet as we have seen, this is not always so—the public can be skeptical, and in these cases, democracy is not irrelevant. On the other hand, it is only by cherry-picking failures such as in France prior to World War I and in US policy after Watergate, while ignoring successes, that we can find weak support for the alarmist view. Even then, they misconstrue the causes of failure;

distrust and secrecy, not transparency costs, led to higher foreign policy costs. Further, alarmists cannot explain how enfeebled democracies would be able to produce the 75-mm gun in secrecy or execute Project Azorian, not to mention Operations Mincemeat and Overlord. As this chapter and the previous one have explored, both successes and failures are part of the story of democratic foreign policy. Relatedly, we should not lose sight of the empirical findings of Reiter and Stam, Schultz, and Huth and Allee, discussed previously, that many democracies have been able to formulate effective foreign policy.

These four chapters have constructed the footing for the secrecy dilemma by analyzing, instead of ignoring, the capacity for secrecy, and particularly its effect on public consent and support in democracies. I now turn to solutions. I argue that some, but by no means all, democracies have attempted to innovate their way out of this dilemma. While these solutions are necessarily partial, a fact I discuss below, they help us understand the variation in democratic foreign policy successes: why France suffered decades of setbacks after Dreyfus, but the United States recovered to correct their mistakes and survive the Cold War.

PART III

Democracy Declassified: The Dilemma and Oversight

Solving the Secrecy Dilemma

How can we solve the dilemma of private information for accountability and public consent? I suggest we look at the secrecy dilemma not as a static trade-off of security versus accountability, but instead as a dynamic struggle between an executive's justification for secrecy and the public's skepticism. Transparency costs and the availability of potential tools for revelation and accountability change over time. In this chapter I illustrate that specific configurations of ex post public information institutions can produce better international outcomes for some democracies by uniquely providing a mechanism to limit, although not eliminate, a leader's a priori incentives to abuse national security secrecy.

The complication, as the previous five chapters have argued, is that the public cannot retreive a valuable national security secret without an enemy also having access. Further, it is clear that the public cannot review the content of a secret and have that information remain secret. There is no Schrödinger's cat in foreign policy.

This direct juxtaposition of classification and transparency is not the only approach to at least partially unlocking the tension between secrecy and public consent. In fact, there are three important puzzle pieces: the benefits of publicity for generating public consent, the capacity for secrecy, and *time*. We have investigated the liberal argument for publicity and the marketplace of ideas and how that aids public consent, and also the necessity of the capacity for secrecy, despite its potential for abuse. Of course, publicity and secrecy do not fit together simultaneously. However, similar to the ability of an enzyme to speed a chemical reaction between two nonreacting elements, introducing the element of time unlocks the potential benefits of both the capacity for secrecy and public consent.

By carefully tracking how democracies around the world have experimented and innovated in the face of domestic distrust and opposition on security concerns, we can unearth the institutional layers of democratic foreign policy success. What we find is not simply uniform elections and immediate transparency—or, alternatively, unaccountable executives where democracy is mere window dressing. Instead, some, but by no means all, democracies around the world have crafted specific institutions that take advantage of immediate secrecy to fuel successful foreign policy while subjecting governments to ex post scrutiny. As IR theorists have assumed either that leaders do not need to be held accountable (ignoring consequences for abuse on public consent) or that leaders are held accountable simply by competitive elections as in domestic politics (ignoring the capacity for secrecy), underappreciated innovations in national security oversight have sprouted unevenly around the globe. For both researchers and the public, looking back provides clues to understanding democratic successes and failures. Although early freedom of information laws, protections for press freedom, and legislative oversight were marred with inefficiencies and in some cases even counterproductive, they were early sketches for more modern and successful institutions to help generate public consent in the shadow of the capacity for secrecy.

What we see is that several democracies have engineered rules and laws that are useful for retrospectively overseeing whether the capacity for secrecy was used for legitimate security purposes or misused. Just as the capacity for secrecy has been institutionalized in democracies to bury secrets from public view, institutional tools also exist for digging this information up ex post. One such innovation is a set of legislative committees specifically targeting oversight of national security, with powers of investigation and the ability to issue public reports. Similarly, freedom of information laws are also engineered to retrospectively reveal information. While these laws exempt national security information from the same rules that apply to most other government documents—respecting the capacity for secrecy—the exceptions are oftentimes balanced by mechanisms to declassify national security information that is in the public interest, as well as requiring the release of information after a specific time lag. Protections of press freedom also bring national security information to the public, although often after the fact. Together these national security oversight tools eventually pry information out of the executive for public view that provides citizens with evidence of whether policy has been used or abused.

This is not a return to the real-time efficiency of the thick marketplace of ideas, nor is it a retreat to the thin informational content of theories that assume that the public can only view victory or defeat. Instead, retrospective oversight builds on important components of both of these arguments that were discussed in Chapter 2. The oversight theory offered here relies on ex post investigation and punishment of abuse, consonant with the mechanisms in the thin marketplace. However, oversight institutions help to reveal richer information into the public debate over time, which approximates the content of the thicker version of the marketplace of ideas, but with a lag.

I argue that national security oversight institutions act more like risky lotteries for both the public and the executive. If an executive decides to abuse the capacity for secrecy—for example, to cover up a botched spy investigation and conviction—there is a chance that the public will learn about this, conditional on someone taking the time to investigate. The better the tools for national security oversight, the more likely an abusive leader will be caught. In fact, oversight was very weak in France, and this was one reason that Sandherr and Gonse were confident that they could manufacture a case against Dreyfus and not get caught.[1] In a complementary fashion, improved oversight increases the incentives of the press, legislators, and interested members of the public to undertake investigations. Once the United States set up intelligence committees in the House and Senate, they were active in investigating potential executive abuse.[2]

Retrospective investigation is useful, and is a credible threat to an executive, because the public security costs of revealing information decline over time. It is less costly to reveal information about a crisis after the crisis is over, as compared to revealing information in the heat of negotiations or even battle, as in Operation Overlord. Likewise, details on advanced military technology, such as high-altitude reconnaissance planes, would be costly to reveal to the public (and thus an enemy) before the weapon is used in battle. However, after other states have already seen or learned of its capabilities and potentially even captured an example, revelation to the public is less costly. The declining public value of specific secrets over time provides the opportunity for public consent to be generated at lower cost than immediate, real-time information revelation as expected by a fully transparent marketplace of ideas.[3]

These mechanisms for retrospective national security oversight provide the public with additional, although imperfect, confidence that an executive's announced policy will lead to public security benefits rather than be a reflection of the misuse of national security policy for nonsecurity ends. Without retrospective oversight, the public lacks assurances, outside of any preexisting information, that an investment will enhance security. With strong retrospective oversight, the public knows that leaders would be running the risk of being caught and politically punished[4] if they abused their classification powers to deceive the public for nonsecurity ends. This increases public consent for executive foreign policy priorities, without assuming away immediate transparency costs.

Building on this discussion, Chapter 7 moves to the consequences of national security oversight for public support in international crises, military spending, and success in disputes. I argue that oversight has both mobilizing and constraining effects that can be investigated empirically.

UR-VERSIGHT: LEARNING FROM HISTORY

Over the last 250 years, there have been numerous examples of leaders that have been stymied by the same public and elite opposition that paralyzed France in the early twentieth century and the United States in the 1974 Cyprus Crisis. Divisions between supporters of Gladstone and Disraeli, for example, scuttled war plans in Afghanistan, Home Rule in Ireland (twice), and public investment in the Suez Canal[5] and support to the Ottoman Empire to check Russian expansion over a 30-year period.[6] Distrust of the military in Costa Rica led to their disbanding in 1948.[7]

However, in a subset of these cases of partisan bickering and immobilization, there have been ventures to create mechanisms and institutions to retool accountability. These have been genuine attempts to form new "rules of the game" that break the prior deadlock and distrust. These rules are often interpreted in moral terms, such as protections of inherent liberty and rights. However, at their core, they are attempts to solve the practical problem of formulating effective foreign policy in a world where both private information and public consent are necessary.

In the following sections, I provide a tour of a few meaningful institutional innovations and their consequences. We will see common patterns in each of the three cases, involving the world's first freedom of information law, a mechanism to discuss national security secrets with the press, and a potent legislative committee formed during the US Civil War. First, the leaders were faced with significant skepticism and distrust that threatened to hamper national security policy. Second, a group of elites attempted to create new institutions and rules that limited, in different ways, the power of the executive to subsequently increase the public's confidence. Third, in these early examples, there were significant problems with the mechanisms used to restrain executive excesses that would later spur improvements. We will see that the foundation of the modern national security oversight apparatus rests on these historical innovations and others like them.

His Majesty's Gracious Ordinance Relating to Freedom of Writing and of the Press, 1766

Partisan distrust and skepticism immobilized Sweden in the mid-1700s. The kingdom of Sweden, which included modern Sweden and Finland, had a titular monarch but was fundamentally governed by a Senate that was responsible to the Swedish Diet. A group known as the Hats had controlled the Diet for decades. But in 1760, they began to lose significant support and were challenged by a faction known as the Caps, on the grounds that the Diet had "systematic and deep corruption."[8] In fact, foreign powers had been purchasing votes in the Diet, and censorship was commonplace. Indeed, by law the foreign policy of Sweden and all foreign policy documents could not be published under legal penalty in Sweden.[9] This secrecy and rumors of payoffs at the hands of the English, French, and Russians fueled distrust and eventually led to the fall of the Hats from power in 1765.

In that year the Caps took power, but they faced a precarious international political situation. They were under pressure from Russia and were split between allying with France or England. Further, the range of foreign policy goals that Sweden should aspire to was up for debate. The Hats had been arguing that a restoration of Sweden as a European great power was necessary and believed that an alliance with France was crucial. The Caps, on the other hand, believed that more modest foreign policy goals should be attempted, and they suggested a smaller-scale alliance with England and accommodation with Russia.[10]

Faced with this split in opinion, the new Cap majority pushed a substantial legislative innovation. The Caps had been prodding the Hats to release more information on government affairs when they were in opposition. As it was the Caps turn to rule, they saw a chance to flip state censorship on its head. A group of new Diet members under the significant influence of Anders Chydenius, a priest and member of the Riksdag, argued that the Hats, now in opposition, would not trust their judgment unless government documents were guaranteed to be published, thus reducing the possibility of clandestine corruption. These ideas were eventually formulated into the 1766 Swedish freedom of information law, "His Majesty's Gracious Ordinance Relating to Freedom of Writing and of the Press, 1766." Manninen argues that publicizing documents and speeches "was considered necessary for gaining general confidence and deflecting suspicions."[11] Thus, the Caps attempted to open up their deliberations and publicize government documents. Exceptions for decency and military means were included and broadened over time, but the principle of combating secrecy, corruption, and suspicion with information took another step forward in 1766. Chydenius wrote in his notes the very kernel of this innovation: "The freedom of a nation does not consist in the sovereign estates acting as they will, but in that the light of the nation binds their hands so that they cannot act in a biased manner."[12] Sweden had lived through centralization and censorship paralyzing the state. The power to repress and hide wrongdoing enervated rather than energized the Hats despite their grand foreign policy designs. In response, Chydenius and the Caps pushed for scrutiny and publicly available information.

The world's first freedom of information law was far from optimal. For example, it failed to protect speech that did not appear in print and allowed the Council of State considerable opacity. Further, the act itself ceased being law due to a coup d'état 6 years after its passage. Despite that setback, the ideal in various guises continues to appear in Swedish politics. In fact, Sweden's current freedom of information law is an amended version of this three-century-old innovation.[13] Further, the public right to eventually access government information has spread to dozens of democracies today, as we will see in Chapter 8.[14]

A Cabinet Order to His Danish Chancellery, 1770

While Sweden's 1766 innovation pertained to public access to government documents as well as protecting some limited opinions in print, it continued to ban all criticism of government. However, only a few years later, another experiment in the Kingdom of Denmark, which controlled not only Denmark, but Norway and the Duchy of Schleswig-Holstein, temporarily removed political censorship. One of the most important components of modern press freedom is the ability to criticize the political leadership. However, that ability had been severely constrained in practice around the world for the previous century. Under English law, for example, criticizing the monarch or government was outlawed. Further, the truth of the statement was not a defense.[15] Denmark at the time had a similar regime of political censorship under a succession of reigns up to King Fredrick V and through to King Christian VII, who ascended to the throne in 1766.

In the mid-1700s, Denmark had managed to remain neutral in the Seven Years' War but was disorganized domestically. Fredrick V was an alcoholic and ineffective. His ministers, particularly Johann Hartwig Ernst von Bernstorff, faced considerable domestic opposition when Fredrick V passed. Bernstorff was criticized for his foreign policy moves in allying with France and then attempting to exchange that alliance for ties with Russia.[16] King Christian VII was mentally ill, and through a series of intrigues, Johann Friedrich Struensee, the King's personal physician, gained de facto political power.

Struensee had little support outside of the King's trust. In fact, he was German, did not speak Danish, and in his grasping for power had alienated most of the ruling elite. In response to his precarious position, Struensee implemented a dizzying number of reforms and was heavily influenced by the work of Voltaire and Rousseau on government and liberal ideas.[17] The most groundbreaking change that Struensee, with Christian VII's signature, was able to implement was the removal of all censorship in Denmark–Norway. The order read, in part, "we have decided to permit in our kingdoms and lands in general an unlimited freedom of the press of such a form, that from now on no one shall be required and obliged to submit books and writings that he wants to bring to the press to the previously required censorship and approval."[18] The reasons given for the order were:

we are fully convinced that it is as harmful to the impartial search for truth as it is to the discovery of obsolete errors and prejudices, if upright patriots, zealous for the common good and what is genuinely best for their fellow citizens, because they are frightened by reputation, orders and preconceived opinion, are hindered from being free to write according to their insight, conscience, and conviction, attacking abuses and uncovering prejudices.[19]

Power reports that "this decree, needless to say, caused quite a sensation, and by no means only in Denmark–Norway."[20] In response, no less a thinker than Voltaire wrote a public letter praising the law.[21]

The law did not prove as successful as Struensee had hoped, however. The opening up of the media led to an onslaught of criticism of Struensee, since he was foreign and had many political enemies. It became known, in fact, that Struensee was having an affair with the Queen. With these revelations, Struensee's extreme press freedom law, in unshackling criticism, was doomed to be short-lived. The light of transparency proved to be too much for the doctor. By fall of 1772, he had reinstated some forms of censorship. At the same time, Struensee's enemies organized a force to arrest Struensee, the Queen, and several associates. Struensee was drawn and quartered, and the Queen was exiled.

However, the press freedom law did not expire with Struensee. The norm in Europe at the time was to allow censors to stop publications from being read by the public before being printed, a process known as prior restraint. Denmark did not reinstate this form of prior censorship after Struensee's execution.[22] Further, after a coup in 1784 brought a new group, (including a wiser Bernstorff) to power, reforms both informal and formal in 1784, 1785, and 1788 reopened the press and the government to the potential for criticism.[23] The protection of the press spread to America with the Virginia Declaration of Rights in 1776, the Habsburg Empire in 1781 with an act by Joseph II, and France in 1790 with the Declaration of the Rights of Man.[24]

Struensee's added exemptions are also mirrored in its legal offspring. In the United States, the First Amendment rights have been circumscribed for "the rights of others ... and by the demands of national security and public decency."[25] Many laws are based on the UN Declaration of Human Rights, which includes limitations for "public order."[26]

The Joint Committee on the Conduct of the War, 1861

Similar to the distrust and unrest that was faced by the Caps and Struensee, US President Lincoln suffered inter-party gridlock bisected with intra-party distrust as his term began. In fact, in 1856 trust and civil discourse between pro-slavery Democrats and anti-slavery Republicans reached a dramatic nadir when, on the Senate floor, Republican Senator Charles Sumner was attacked with a cane and beaten into an unconscious state by Democratic Representative Preston Brooks after giving a fiery anti-slavery speech. Not only was Brooks not censured for the incident, although fellow Representative Laurence Keitt was censured for pulling out a pistol on the Senate floor to stop others from intervening, but after he resigned, he was immediately reelected and reportedly sent dozens of new canes from constituents and admirers around the South. Even during the war, opposition Democrats complained that Lincoln "was making a selfish and corrupt use of his power."[27]

Within his party, several influential Republicans doubted Lincoln's ability and motivations in the war.[28] In July 1861, a delegation of fellow Republicans that differed with Lincoln over emancipation and how to execute the Civil War came to the White House. Ohio Republican Ben Wade denounced Lincoln as "incompetent or treacherous."[29] Another Republican critic of Lincoln, Zacharia Chandler of Michigan, described Lincoln as "timid, vacillating and inefficient" and "as unstable as water."[30] Later in 1864, Wade would offer the appraisal that Lincoln's "stupid willfulness cost this nation more than a hundred thousand men."[31] It was into this political environment that Lincoln was attempting to raise sufficient public consent for his policies to win the Civil War.

Matters early in the rebellion did not help matters. In the face of northern overconfidence, Lincoln's forces had to beat a disorganized retreat at Bull Run. Soon after, defeats at Wilson's Creek and Balls Bluff increased the dissatisfaction. While the cleavage between North and South was drawing blood, the trilateral split among Democrats, Lincoln Republicans, and the Radical Republican wing led by Wade began to take on ominous tones. Some argued that the military's "nationalism in which West Point took such pride was actually larded heavily with pro-Southern sentiment."[32] Tap notes: "Suspicions about disloyalty, discontent on the slavery issue, and frustration with the state of military affairs came to a head when the 37th Congress convened in early December 1861."[33]

In response to defeat and what many in Congress saw as failed policy, several members of the legislature, particularly Republican opponents of Lincoln such as Chandler and Wade, proposed creating a committee that could oversee the executive's prosecution of the war. Thus, a debate was engaged in about creating a joint congressional investigative committee. While there was some disagreement on its particulars, the idea had broad appeal. In fact, as the debate opened, the idea grew from a narrow investigation into only Bulls Run and Balls Bluff to a call for an investigation into all defeats and finally into a remit to investigate "all aspects of the war." The committee was also voted the power to subpoena "persons and papers." The resolution was accepted by a wide bipartisan margin, with a vote of 33–3 in the Senate. In the end, all three groups largely supported the creation of the Joint Committee on the Conduct of the War (CCW). In exclaiming his support for the creation of the committee, Senator James Grimes of Iowa stated, "Let the country know what are the facts." Fessenden supported this point when he added, "We must satisfy the people of this country that things go on well."[34]

While the idea of a congressional investigative committee was by no means new, even on military affairs, the remit of the CCW was unique. For example, the 1792 congressional investigation into General Arthur St. Clair's battle with Native American forces was analyzed to ascertain whether public funds had been misused. Andrew Jackson's Florida adventure was investigated in 1818. However, these previous attempts at oversight were specific and short-lived affairs. The CCW was given a broad mandate that would allow the committee to act, for a time, as if it were a standing committee tasked with overseeing a whole department of the executive. This is how committees are now tasked in legislatures around the world, but in 1861 the idea was novel. Most important, the goal of the committee was not necessarily legislative. The role was investigative and to publicize facts and analysis that would not otherwise have seen the light of day.[35]

The committee's investigation of the details of contracts and procurement turned up significant waste and corruption. For example, the committee found problems with the naval artillery being purchased. This led to a more expensive weapon, but with increased reliability, being put into service.[36] Similarly, the committee found a system of payoffs and patronage was at work in the planning of a line of light-draught vessels based on the success of John Ericsson's *Monitor*. Further, corruption of public funds was uncovered as part of an investigation into government contracts for ice.[37] Eric McKitrick believed that the committee, as part of the democratic governance of the war effort, helped win the Civil War for the North.[38] He argues that since there is always opposition to war, as there was in both the North and the South, it is important to provide mechanisms for the opposition to oversee and scrutinize the leadership's actions. At the same time, McKitrick argues that this scrutiny keeps leaders from straying in corrupt directions.[39]

Counterbalancing these improvements, the CCW had significant flaws. The work of the committee was highly partisan, and the role of the Democratic minority was undervalued. These limitations illuminated the fact that committee investigations on national security issues worked best after an event, such as a battle, procurement, or negotiation. It is difficult to prosecute potential abuse before something has happened. More problematic was the committee's attempt to drive policy in real time. Attempts to pick generals and strategy were almost uniformly counterproductive and have contributed to the historical impression that the committee was a failure overall.[40]

The legislature and executive have distinct comparative advantages. Steering through turbulence with an obstructed view takes significant resources to manage, and even then, it can lead to calamity. The executive during the Civil War had thousands of times more resources to devote to intelligence and judging military strategy as compared to the Congress and the CCW. When the legislative committee pretended to be the executive, they usually fell short.[41]

The committee was on much firmer ground when it scrutinized past actions, motives, and contracts. In these cases, the committee could in fact "[l]et the country know what are the facts," as opposed to simplistic opinions on immediate policy directions. Unlike an executive who might have an interest in inefficient contracts with cronies or minimizing casualties before an election, the CCW had an incentive and the means to uncover and publicize these foibles. While the executive was designed appropriately to fight a war, it could also fail in its goals specifically because of its centralization and power. A strong executive can act with speed, dispatch, and determination, but it lacks credibility. Opposition partisans and even members of an executive's party may doubt whether the leader is using the tools of national security in the best interest of the public. In this case the Radical Republicans and Democrats both had significant doubts about Lincoln. The CCW began to show that the legislature had an important role to play in guiding an executive to stay on course.[42] Through independent investigation, information revelation, and publication, the committee increased the confidence of many of these doubters.[43]

Both the positive and negative lessons from the experiment with the CCW informed future institutional innovations. During World War II, the Truman Committee mirrored the retrospective methods employed by the CCW while attempting to learn from and avoid partisan excess, with Truman likening his version of congressional oversight to a "benevolent policeman."[44] After the war, Truman's Committee was made permanent, and it became a model for further innovations in the 1970s such as the congressional committees on intelligence.[45]

OVERSIGHT RIGHT UNDER OUR NOSES

George Orwell once said, "To see what is in front of one's nose needs a constant struggle."[46] These first rudimentary innovations provide the clues to how national security oversight works to marry executive secrecy and extra-executive oversight in some, but not all, democracies today. The modern progeny of the Swedish Freedom of Information Law, the Danish Press Freedom edict, and the Committee on the Conduct of the War are much more elaborate in their rules, systems, and effects. In some ways this is like comparing the first wooden frame airplane design to an F-22 Raptor. The capabilities, materials, and technologies involved are thoroughly distinct. However, the blueprint of the former helped us get to the latter. While the specifics have undoubtably changed, evolving from short-lived edicts with no enforcement mechanism to an elected legislative committee with subpoena power and research staffs, the lofty goal of combining private information and public mobilization into effective foreign policy remains constant.

Like with other innovations and technologies, forces can be mastered that improve performance over time. Modern national security oversight in democracies leverages two political forces that were not well understood previously. First, the possibility of low-cost oversight relies on the dynamics of transparency costs. As I have argued, the ability to keep national security secrets is extremely valuable; however, each individual bit of secret information tends to lose its security value over time. This means that information can be publicized retrospectively much more cheaply than in the heat of the moment. One lesson that the Truman Committee learned from Wade's Committee on the Conduct of the War[47] is that legislative powers worked better in retrospect than they did in prospect. Or to be more precise, retrospective investigation changes the prospective course of a leader more effectively than micromanaging the war effort from outside the executive. Further, the expectation of future oversight has immediate beneficial consequences. Oversight that attempts to publicize immediate information will be counterproductive. On the other hand, retrospective accountability, due to decaying transparency costs of previously secret information, induces fewer alarms.

Second, extra-executive bodies that do not rely on the president or prime minister for legitimacy and political power are the only reliable engines of oversight. There is no guarantee that an executive and even members of the executive's political clique will commit to significant investigations of themselves and publicize wrongdoing. Struensee tried to undo his own law in reaction to press criticism of his policies and personal life.

In Chapter 5, I argued that the potential for abuse can cast a shadow on public consent and lead to underinvestment. A reverse, and more productive, inter-temporal relationship is also possible. The light of expected future oversight can illuminate the way for present executive decisions and public consent as leaders and citizens calculate what is in their best interests.

The tragedy of the secrecy dilemma is that leaders need public consent to execute security-enhancing policies, but the potential for abuse may lead to the withholding of that consent. If oversight is selectively turned on and off through executive control of the process, the public cannot be confident that abuse will be revealed; without revelation, abuse cannot be punished. It is only if non-executive actors have access to the tools and spotlights of oversight that public confidence is likely to be increased.

Modern oversight mechanisms include strong protections for press freedom, minority representation on legislative committees, and balanced freedom of information law exemptions for national security information. These engines of oversight reside outside of the executive, allowing legislators, the press, or members of the public to churn through national security policy evaluations and publicize non-security-generating policy paid for with public funds. While this places them at arm's length from the classified information that resides within the executive, it also means that they can operate with more independence. In the next section we will explore the benefits and limitations of transparency cost deflation and oversight institutions in more detail.

TRANSPARENCY COSTS AND OPPORTUNITIES
FOR OVERSIGHT

The first clue to unraveling the riddle of democratic foreign policy success lies in understanding the dynamics of transparency costs and how this can open the way for the partial restoration of accountability at a reasonable foreign policy price in democracies. I have argued that immediate national security secrecy is crucial for foreign policy effectiveness. Anticipating, deceiving, and suppressing the capabilities of other competitors, as we have seen, has been the difference between supremacy in times of war (War in the Pacific, Operation Mincemeat, and Operation Overlord) and peace (the Washington Naval Conference and Cold War stealth program) as well as swinging the nuclear balance toward Moscow (Fuch's spying) and then back to Washington (keeping the Teller–Ulam discovery secret).

However, this is not the end of the story. The value of these secrets, while high for a time, deflates. Instead of turning our attention from one international crisis to the next around the globe, if we fix our glare in one place even after international attention has rolled elsewhere, we can see that individual bundles of secrets lose their value over time. Take, for example, the use by American forces of Japanese codes during the Washington Naval Conference. If this secret had gotten out during the negotiations, not only would the codes have been changed but the arms control conference would have collapsed in outrage. However, after the conference was over and time went by, the Japanese switched codes anyway. Further, the context that made the negotiations so important—that is, attempts to control a costly naval arms race—became less important as war began to rumble in Europe. When the successful US spying operation was made public by a former US codebreaker in a widely read book, *The American Black Chamber*, it enthralled Japanese attention but had little foreign policy impact.[48]

More generally, transparency costs decline as sources die or are removed from harm's way, the strategic situation changes, or an enemy learns the information by other means. The location and strength of the D-Day invasion, the falsity of the Operation Mincemeat papers, the breaking of the Enigma and Purple codes, and the camera lens used in U-2 aircraft were all valuable secrets when operationally necessary, but their revelation costs declined over time. The feints involved in Operations Overlord and Mincemeat were useful for the element of surprise as well as in the subsequent weeks as enemy forces were tied down waiting on phantom units. However, after the footholds were secured, the enemy learned that they had been deceived. Keeping information relating to the specific planning, motives, and execution of these operations secret became less important after the context evolved. Transparency cost deflation can be highly uneven across bits of information, of course. The exact location of the first D-Day attack was of enormous value on Monday, June 5, 1944, but was of little relevance by Wednesday of that week.[49] The plans for a sophisticated nuclear device or the ingredients to the radar-absorbing paint on stealth planes continue to remain precious secrets for the states that have this information.

The Cuban Missile Crisis is one high-profile illustration of dynamic transparency costs over time. We can think about four principal secrets that were highly valuable to the United States at the beginning of the crisis: Colonel Penkosky's information and identity, the U-2 photographic evidence, the value Washington ascribed to the US Jupiter missiles in Turkey, and Washington's ability and motivation to invade Cuba.[50] Over the course of the crisis and after, each of these secrets lost its value. First, the USSR learned of Colonel Penkosky's role in spying during the crisis, and he was captured before Kennedy's announcement of the blockade. Second, the United States announced the U-2 photographic evidence in a live address by the President on October 15, 1962, and it showed more detailed information at the UN days later. In the first week of the crisis, Washington moved troops to the southeastern United States under Operation Ortsac,[51] and this was monitored by the Soviet Union.[52] The value the United States placed on the Jupiter missiles was unknown until the missiles were actually removed in April 1963. More consistently opaque were the United States' intentions toward

Cuba, which remained opaque to the USSR through to the Ceinfuegos submarine crisis and after. Six years after the Cuban Missile Crisis, Robert F. Kennedy published a detailed book about the incident.[53] While this might be a selective telling of the political tale, transparency costs were low at this point.[54]

Transparency Cost Deflation

Drawing on this intuition about the value of specific secrets—that they lose their potency over time—we can think about what that means for a more realistic number of secrets involved in a given crisis or operation. To do this, we can simulate relative transparency costs over time for many secrets (1000 bits of information). In the simulation, each secret receives a randomly drawn value from a uniform distribution on the $(0, 1)$ interval.[55] Then at each time point, the specific threat of information may quickly lose value with probability p,[56] due to a source moving out of danger, a battle ending, or a rival learning information anyway. What we are interested in is the changing expected value of transparency over time.[57] Thus we can think about the revelation of secrets as a grab bag, from which one can randomly sample. The average value is the expected transparency costs of any drawn sample at a given time. This is analogous to the way an investigation operates. It cannot simply dump all the secrets out of the executive (then sum up the costs). Instead it selectively samples the secrets and attempts to understand the underlying programs and decisions.[58] The mean transparency cost for this information is a smooth decreasing function over time. Figure 6.1 plots 1000 of these bits of information (thin black lines), as well as the aggregate mean transparency cost function (gray dashed line). Therefore, even though specific conflicts or intelligence operations may produce an array of information, the expected value of the transparency costs decline over time. This is particularly important because given the capacity for secrecy, a legislator, for example, may not be able to accurately estimate the transparency costs of a particular bit of information.[59]

The fact that secrets tend to lose their value over time opens up a partial solution to the tension between national security classification and accountability. While secrecy and transparency on a given issue cannot coexist simultaneously, they can take turns. Immediate secrecy within international crises, weapons programs, and negotiations can be vigorously protected with the very institutions we have seen democracies utilize around the world in Chapter 3: classification powers and penalties for divulging national security secrets. Yet, since the secrets submerged in the capacity for secrecy lose their national security value over time, retrospective oversight is possible at a much lower cost than would occur with immediate monitoring of foreign policy issues in democracies. Further, since

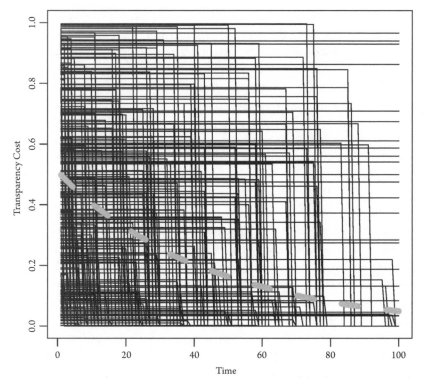

Figure 6.1 The value of simulated secrets (black), and the average transparency cost over time (gray).

investigating national secrecy information takes time, this delay is practical as well as relatively efficient due to deflating transparency costs.

We must keep in mind, however, that secrets do not jump out into public view on their own. Information that is classified stays undercover unless forcibly excavated from the national security vaults. Not only does this excavation take time, but it can be greatly facilitated with institutional tools and rules. In the next section, we will explore how some democracies have engineered oversight institutions to allow for efficient retrospective investigations and the publication of foreign policy facts ex post. In other democracies, where competent tools for oversight are lacking, secrets and abuses are more likely to be buried out of public view.

THE INSTITUTIONS OF RETROSPECTIVE OVERSIGHT

As noted earlier, all democracies have a capacity for secrecy. What is less well appreciated is that some democracies, but not others, currently maintain a set of institutions that take advantage of the relative deflation of national security transparency costs over time. From the meager beginnings outlined above, innovations have taken root, unevenly around the world, that allow accountability and invest national security oversight powers in extra-executive bodies.

These innovations take advantage of the fact that retrospective oversight allows the executive immediate secrecy to carry out national security policies that anticipate, deceive, and suppress the capabilities of rivals, but also empowers citizens, the press, and legislature to investigate and publicize previously classified information to uncover abuses. In this way, the comparative advantages of the executive and extra-executive institutions such as the legislature and press can be utilized.

Specifically, the United Nations and several non-governmental organizations have laid out best practices of oversight of national security.[60] These guidelines summarize three sets of institutional oversight tools that have been usefully applied to revealing national-security-relevant information to the public ex post in some democracies. The accountability tools, in their modern form, include codified legislative committees tasked with overseeing national security, balanced freedom of information law exemptions for security policy, and press freedoms that explicitly apply to national security information. These institutions are complementary but conceptually distinct from more general democratic institutions such as free and fair elections. While all democracies must have free and fair elections to be counted as democratic, not all democracies have national security oversight institutions that allow for retrospective accountability. It is important to keep in mind that these modern engines of oversight continue to be imperfect and in need of tinkering and at times re-engineering, but they deserve significantly more attention than they have received from IR scholars and policy analysis to date.

Legislative Committees and Specific National Security Oversight Powers

Most obviously, effective legislative oversight on national security issues increases the probability that the public will learn relevant information, over time. This relies on the legislature's ability to investigate, deliberate, and publicize foreign policy facts and opinions that may run counter to the information emanating from the executive. To adequately fulfill this role within national security policy, the experts have suggested (1) standing committees on national security issues with membership rules such that legislators and staffers can gain experience and knowledge concerning executive foreign policy decisions, (2) the power to hear and possibly compel written or oral testimony, (3) the opportunity to publicize both a majority and a minority report to increase the diversity of information and opinions released, and (4) adequate staff to process information and investigate executive claims.[61] Note that these powers, to be relevant for the current analysis, must not be limited to domestic or nonsecurity issues. While the legislatures in Greece and Italy fail to plug their holes in democratic oversight of national security, the lawmaking bodies in the United States and the Netherlands include sophisticated sets of retrospective oversight tools including most of the tools listed above.[62] Examples of effective legislative oversight can be found in the United States with the Church Committee and in Norway with the Lund Commission and in detailed reports from the Intelligence and Security Services Review Committee (CTIVD).[63] A detailed analysis of the post hoc versus real-time powers of parliamentary oversight of intelligence information in Europe shows that while 15 parliaments had severe restrictions on legislators' access to real-time intelligence, even if they were serving on an intelligence-relevant committee, the rules in eight of the countries allowed much greater access to past operations, budgets, or information.[64]

The Breadth and Scope of Freedom of Information Laws

Apart from relying on the legislature, citizens and watchdog groups themselves may be able to access national-security-relevant information. Freedom of information (FOI) laws in many countries supply the right to directly query the government over a number of issues and expect to receive substantive feedback while also exempting to varying degrees national-security-relevant information. As noted above, all freedom of information laws include explicit exemptions for national security information. However, all exceptions are not created equal. The least stringent exemption from the public point of view is one where a balance test is used. For example, Australia, Belgium, Moldova, and New Zealand currently use a balance test to decide whether the public value of releasing information is worth the potential security risk.[65] As we have seen, this bar gets easier to clear as transparency costs decline. The absence of other impediments to the release of government information also improves the national security relevance of varying FOI laws. These include implementing the law across all executive functions, not requiring citizens to prove a legal interest in the information for which they are asking, and not charging expensive fees. Each trait varies across time and space in democracies. Between 1972 and 2002 the United States included a relatively useful set of FOI tools in comparison to many democracies, with low fees, a harm exception, and no interest test. After 2002, the United States FOI was limited through a stricter interpretation of the harm exceptions. The documents at the National Security Archive, at George Washington

University, are a testament to the usefulness of FOI laws to publicize previously classified information. That organization purports to have published over one million pages of previously secret documents, many of which are available in searchable form to the public. They also publish briefs on documents that they have uncovered from a range of national security topics, from what the Nixon administration knew about the Indian nuclear program[66] to new information on the Iran–Contra affairs.[67,68] Although more recent, the UK has begun compiling FOI requested documents at the national archive for public viewing in person or online.[69]

Press Freedom Protections

Finally, the press may be legally empowered to investigate and publicize information concerning national security policy. A free press is one that has the ability to probe national-security-relevant stories unimpeded by major legal, political, or economic obstacles. Legal and political traits that can either aid or impede press freedom include (1) the absence of de jure government censorship and prior restraint, (2) the protection of freedom of expression and publication, including shield laws for sources, and (3) a lack of political intimidation from the government or government allies leading to de facto censorship. Issues of secrecy, censorship, and penalties for divulging classified information often decrease the effectiveness of press freedom on national security issues. While classification schemes simultaneously reduce the ability of journalists to investigate national security facts and provide material punishments for publication of relevant facts, some democracies protect press and public publication more strongly than others. The Netherlands has continued a tradition since the 1920s of open channels of public communication and a limitation on media censorship. Similar protections of free speech even on national security grounds have been present, although inconsistently, in Poland and more recently in Costa Rica.[70] These include an absence of official pressure and repression.[71] In the United States, the possibility of retrospective national security transparency was evident during the publication of the Pentagon Papers.[72]

These three processes work together, as both complements and substitutes, to increase the ex post national security knowledge of the electorate in some democracies.[73] Legislative oversight that cannot be broadcast to the public through the press is far less effective. Facts released by either the press or a legislative body that cannot be independently verified through a freedom of information request may be less persuasive. For example, the Israeli Knesset's Foreign Affairs and Defense Committee oversees the media censorship regime. Similarly, the national-security-related data from freedom of information requests have been presented at congressional hearings in the United States, which are then reported in the press.[74] Together, these institutions have the ability to provide the public with richer information than what they would have available in the absence of these extra-executive powers, although with a lag.

Making It Hurt: Position, Party, Policy, and Reputation

The oversight institutions discussed in the previous section have the ability to supply the information that makes holding a leader accountable for abuse or rewarding a leader for competent policy possible. Free and fair elections are the most obvious democratic dunking booths for leaders and parties. However, leaders are unlikely to be removed from their official positions if the public is unaware of their malfeasance or incompetence.

The two sides of accountability are, in essence, similar to concepts that IR scholars have long been familiar with: deterrence and compellence. The public would like to deter a leader from manipulating information and policy at public cost, but at the same time would like to support security-enhancing investments. While the capacity for secrecy leads to worries of abuse and underinvestment, the expectation of retrospective information may redress underinvestment. However, just like in the nuclear deterrence literature, the ability of the public to get what they want relies upon their ability to credibly hurt a leader. Conditional pain is part of the process. If the public knows that abuse is less likely, because it is being partially deterred, it are more likely to consent to executive initiatives.

Yet the effectiveness of accountability relies upon the public having levers accessible, even knowing previously classified information, to punish a leader retrospectively. If a leader can get away relatively unscathed—or, worse, the benefits of corruption are greater than any costs the public can place on a corrupt leader—deterrence will fail despite oversight institutions, and the public has no reason to be compelled to support an executive. In turn, this means we must look at what leaders care about. If the public can target items of value to a leader, then retrospective accountability is possible.

I suggest that there are four categories of political goods that a leader generally cares about. Further, each political good can be hit by the public in retrospect, but some targets are more available than others. These goods are political positions, parties, policies, and reputation.

First, the processes of elections and impeachment directly threaten a leader's political position of power. Assuming that leaders care about political power is common across comparative and international relations research.[75] Further, we have examples of this lever of power being employed, as when the government of Rajiv Ghandi lost power in 1989 after the Bofors AB scandal came to light and was investigated by a joint parliamentary committee.[76]

On the other hand, the limitation of relying solely on elections and impeachment for leadership punishment is that information may not be available until after a leader is already out of power or is not up for reelection again. For example, the most wide-ranging investigation to date of the role intelligence played in the political decision to initiate the Iraq War was the Phase II report by the Senate Select Committee on Intelligence (SSCI). This report was not delivered until June 5, 2008, almost 5 years after the war and 7 months after George W. Bush was already out of office.[77] Allegations about intelligence of the Gulf of Tonkin incident in the early phases of the Vietnam conflict took years to become public.[78] Additionally, impeachment is difficult to achieve due to potential party cohesion, electoral rules, and its reliance on a legislative body to act rather than the public.[79]

However, Laver and Shepsle[80] and Goemans and Choizza[81] have both made strong cases that leaders care about more than simply staying in office. Laver and Shepsle argue that politicians have strong preferences for both their party and policies.[82] Therefore, even if a corrupt leader has already announced he or she is not running for reelection or is already out of office, the public can back alternative parties and positions that will damage the political prospects of the leader's faction or dismantle legislative achievements that the previous executive cares about. For example, Tony Blair in the United Kingdom faced a rare backbench revolt over University Fees after his party became increasingly unhappy with his role in the lead-up to the Iraq War.[83] In the United States, President Nixon's domestic agenda came to a halt during the disclosures about Watergate and COINTELPRO. Revelations in France of arms deals with Angola in the 1990s and the Rainbow Warrior attack each had similar domestic policy costs.[84]

Further, political punishment of a leader via that leader's political party or preferred policy positions are more easily targeted in retrospect, as compared to direct personal electoral defeat. While President Bush was not up for reelection after the Phase II report on Iraq was made public, many Republicans faced electoral headwinds in 2008 in his stead. In the November 2008 election, the Democrats took the White House and both Houses of Congress. Commentator Ross Douthat, a correspondent for the *Atlantic* at the time, noted just before the 2008 elections that the Iraq war was "exerting a downward pull on the Republican brand."[85] Moreover, a retrospective on opinion polling of Republican positions on Iraq in 2008 and 2012 concluded that "[t]he exit polls from the 2008 and 2012 elections showed how thoroughly the Iraq War had destroyed the GOP edge over the Democrats on national security and foreign policy."[86] If leaders care about their parties and policies, this is a potential soft spot where retrospective punishment can be effective even after a leader is out of office or beyond the trajectory of elections.

Goemans[87] continues along this path and suggests that leaders care about their post-office fate. While his work contrasts exile and execution as potential post-office punishment, it is not a great leap to believe that post-office rewards may also matter to leaders. Thus, a final and more diffuse political good that an executive might value is his or her reputation and legacy. There is considerable evidence at least in the US context that leaders think about how history will judge them. Biographer Robert Caro has said that President Johnson was focused on the Great Society being his legacy but saw that slipping away as the body count rose in Vietnam.[88] Similarly, US President Bush often compared his presidency to that of Truman and suggested, "You never know what your history is going to be like until long after you're gone."[89]

Therefore, if executives value their party, policies, post-office fate and reputations, even long-term retrospective oversight on the order of decades may be a useful part of the domestic accountability story. Leaders might have greater fear of the ballot box than of a Harvard historian, but that does not mean they ignore party, position, and legacy considerations altogether.[90] Ultimately, the question of whether retrospective accountability can be effective on national security issues will be an empirical question. To explore and test this, we need to understand the consequences of effective oversight in democracies, which is the subject of the next chapter.

The Consequences of National Security Oversight in Democracies

Retrospective oversight on national security, if effective, reroutes the circuits of liberal IR theory with a model of foreign policy that balances the necessity of secrecy[1] with the benefits of democratic accountability. This new perspective avoids assuming that democracies either do not or cannot keep secrets. Further, unlike critiques of liberal theory that assert that secrecy fully negates the usefulness of accountability, the theory explored herein emphasizes the importance of domestic national security institutions that have previously been ignored.

Elections cannot ensure public accountability for the misuse of policy, due to either incompetence or corruption, without information supplied by extra-executive sources that do not have an incentive to hide, lie about, or only selectively reveal what they know. Lacking accountability, the public has reason to distrust the executive and to withhold consent for investments and policy priorities. To judge the usefulness of this contribution, relative to other perspectives, we need to understand the unique observable implications of oversight theory.

There are several likely benefits for democracies that are institutionally able to counterbalance national security secrecy with retrospective oversight institutions. These involve the ability to increase public support for foreign policy initiatives and the ability to both raise money for defense and reduce the overpayment for defense. Ultimately, through this continued public support and investment in security, the formation of effective foreign policy should result, if transparency costs do not cancel out these benefits. At the most basic level, these oversight mechanisms work with executive classification to empower executives in democracies to wield private information, rather than collapsing under the weight of distrust and potential abuse. Retrospective oversight uniquely provides executives with disincentives to abuse the capacity for secrecy, and in turn this increases public confidence that their ballots, bucks, and sometimes blood are fueling foreign policy success.

ABUSE CONTINUES, ABATED: THE PARADOX OF PERFECT NATIONAL SECURITY OVERSIGHT

It is important to keep in mind that despite the usefulness of national security oversight, it is not a Rhadamanthine cure to the problem of potential foreign policy abuse. As I show in the Appendix formally, if a legislature or public would commit to investigating all foreign policy decisions without any failures, executives would indeed have little to no incentive to abuse secrecy. Yet, as the public and legislature would then know that the executive was effectively deterred from abuse, there would be no incentive to continue paying the costs to investigate. Since investigation is costly, in terms of both time and the risk of revealing some secrets that may have residual value, without an expectation of discovering corruption or incompetence, there is no reason to investigate. Coming full circle, the leader then knows that investigation is not in the interests of the public or legislature, and hence abuse or covering up incompetence becomes more attractive again and is not deterred.

These expectations mean that perfect foreign policy oversight is a paradox. Due to nonzero investigation and transparency costs, there is no reason to investigate if there is no chance of uncovering abuse. Further, if there is no reason to investigate, there is no added disincentive for a leader to avoid policies that are suboptimal to the public.

However, although some abuse continues, and in fact is necessary for oversight to be practicable, retrospective oversight can still *reduce* these nonsecurity motives. There are a range of strategies available to a legislature that can rationally deter an executive from most, but not all, abuse. For example, a legislature or public can commit to investigating a certain percentage of foreign policy actions or a subset of international contexts, without specifying exactly which actions or issues a priori. This means that an executive thinking about promoting a policy that will improve his election chances at public cost is faced with the possibility, but not the certainty, of investigation and punishment. A rational response by that leader is to mix in private interest with public security-providing policies. The more accurate the oversight, the lower the content of corruption and incompetence within foreign policy.

In addition, oversight will always have some costs to potential overseers, in the form of transparency costs, the maintenance of legislative committee staffs and archives, and opportunity costs. The lower the expected costs of oversight, the greater the likely oversight activity and thus the deterrence of abuse.[2] If a committee has the means to easily gather information and expertise, a freedom of information law does not include large out-of-pocket costs to the interested member of the public, and the press does not fear significant punishments for revealing evidence of abuse, an executive will have less confidence that he or she can get away with corruption or allowing incompetence without being discovered.

We should be clear up front about the promise and limitations of national security oversight. The paradox of investigation and abuse stands; misuse can be reduced, but it cannot be zeroed out. Yet, this reduction in abuse means that skeptical members of the public, while not certain that a policy is in the public interest, have less distrust than they would without the threat of retrospective oversight hanging over the executive. There is a reinforcing relationship connecting the potential for abuse, imperfect oversight, and public consent. We do not get back a full and open marketplace of ideas, but oversight does help to provide incentives for less abuse and better public policy, since incompetence and corruption are more likely to be revealed. Oversight can reassure the public both that the uses of the capacity for secrecy are worth the potential abuses and that investments in security are more likely to pay off in the form of public security.

PUBLIC SKEPTICISM AND CRISES

The first hypothesized consequence of effective retrospective national security oversight should be greater, on average, public opinion behind an executive's dramatic foreign policy decisions. There is a long literature on the rally effect in international relations providing evidence that the public becomes more supportive of a leader during times of military crisis. Many have assumed that the rally effect is an irrational patriotic response by the public. In fact, several realist critics of democracy have pointed out that the rally effect undercuts accountability, since a leader can count on reflexive foreign policy support.[3] In contrast to this interpretation, a focus on retrospective accountability in democracies suggests that in some cases the rally effect might be a rational response to new information. The public knows that a leader holds private information on threats around the world. If that leader can be retrospectively punished for policy malfeasance, there is less reason to be skeptical that a dramatic foreign policy action by the president, for example, is in the public interest. In this way, ex post partial accountability can lead to a priori support for a leader that would not exist otherwise.

If a leader launches a military attack on an enemy, the public may be split between two perspectives. First, some members of the public, particularly members of the opposition, may believe that the leader is using foreign policy for partisan gain, and they will not support the decision. Alternatively, others may believe that the executive knows something that they do not about the international situation and support the decision. Without national security oversight, a sincere leader has no way, short of publicizing costly secrets that may not be credible anyway, of signaling to the doubtful members of the public that the attack is in the national interest. Skeptical members of the public remain skeptical because the incentives are such that a leader can benefit from foreign policy if it is either in the national interest or in his or her private interest. Thus, action does not signal to the public that a potentially costly international skirmish has public security benefits.

However, if retrospective oversight institutions hold sway on national security issues, the public can be more certain a priori that any foreign policy corruption will be punished ex post. For example, any leader that is faced with the prospect of a powerful legislative investigation, protected press inquiries, and broad freedom of information requests will need to think twice before promoting a policy that is not in the public interest. While that leader might be able to dupe the public temporarily, eventually an intrepid reporter or legislator may alert the public. Knowing this is a possibility, opposition partisans, when they do see a leader push for a robust and costly foreign policy action, will be more certain that the action is in the public interest. Under the farsighted but effective gaze of oversight, a leader's incentives are shifted. Private gains from policy might be counterbalanced by investigation and subsequent electoral, partisan, policy, or legacy costs. In Chapter 9 we will explore this hypothesized relationship empirically in the United States, the United Kingdom, and France.

Hypothesis 1 Increases in public support for foreign policy actions by an executive should be greater with high national security oversight, as compared to democracies with low oversight.

INVESTMENT AND MODERATE OVERSIGHT

A second potential consequence of national security oversight is that executives should be able to mobilize greater resources for the military and national defense as compared to democracies that lack oversight. As noted earlier, in democracies that lack retrospective information institutions, the potential for foreign policy corruption undercuts support for raising money. The public has no reason to believe that a proposed military budget increase is in the national interest as opposed to a leader's private political interests. In contrast, legislators and the public who are more confident that they will have access to retrospective investigative tools can also be more sure that an executive's proposed military budget is not packed with nonsecurity funding.

The example of Costa Rica usefully explicates how polarization and distrust without oversight can paralyze a country's ability to mobilize resources, as well as how innovative improvements in oversight can remobilize spending. After controversial elections in 1948, a rebel group took up arms under Jose Figueres Ferrer. The resulting skirmishes escalated to a civil war killing more than 2000 people. In the wake of the civil war, distrust of the security forces in the state swelled, since they had been used for repression and to centralize political power. The new government, under Figueres Ferrer, disbanded the military entirely to "protect" democracy. Literally, public distrust and skepticism sapped the executive's ability to mobilize resources for the military to the point that the military budget was near zero. However, over time, Costa Rica has built a free press, a moderate freedom of information law, and legislative oversight that has helped support national defense through a security, culture, and education line item in the budget, as well as train a national guard and troops that can be mobilized for peacekeeping operations.[4] Costa Rica has moved from the total collapse of a military to a credible local presence.[5]

It is also true that these oversight tools cannot rid a country of foreign policy corruption and waste. For example, in Costa Rica, by 2005, three former presidents were being charged with secretly accepting bribes and kickbacks from foreign relations.[6] Instead of pure publicly beneficial policy, imperfect oversight allows a leader to push through private interest projects mixed in with spending that efficiently provides national security. This complicates the comparison across democracies. States with very little to no press and legislative oversight as well as weak freedom of information laws should have difficulty raising money for defense, since the public has little insurance that corruption would not pay on the part of the leader. It is at moderate levels of oversight, alternatively, where raising military dollars should be the easiest. Legislative rules rely on a threshold of votes, usually 50%, to pass a budget. This means that only a limited number of skeptics need to be convinced that oversight is either forthcoming or unnecessary to raise funds. A moderate amount of oversight may provide this type of push toward support for higher spending. Yet, because oversight is only moderate, an executive can place nonpublic security spending in the budget and have a relatively good shot at benefiting from it. Thus, we need to keep in mind, as the paradox of perfect oversight makes clear, that some military spending will involve corruption and waste. When oversight is functionally blind, the military budget is likely to be anemic, and thus the level of corrupt spending also will be low. However, at moderate levels of oversight, skepticism may be reduced enough to get the budget passed, but the leader and his cronies still have the ability to fold in nonsecurity projects in the budget and get away with it. It is only when retrospective oversight is further strengthened that the nonsecurity/corrupt spending can be deterred. The public and legislature must have significant tools at their disposal to reduce overspending.

The way to think about this is that oversight has two opposing but unequal effects on spending. The first is a mobilizing effect, where the expectation of oversight reduces the probability of large-scale corruption and thus increases support for military spending. The second is a constraining effect, where a leader who might prefer to add private interest spending to the military budget is deterred because oversight will punish some proportion of that spending. At low to moderate levels of oversight, the mobilizing effect is likely to be much stronger than the constraining effect. The public know that some military spending is needed for security even if they do not believe the dire threat scenarios that a leader might spin. Further, they know that some nonsecurity spending is inevitably going to be part of the military appropriations process. As one analyst put it in the 1980s, "If you are serious about retaining defense programs, you must plan to fund the waste along with the substance or you will end up cutting the substance along with the waste."[7] Going from moderate to low levels of oversight, the public are willing to support higher levels of military spending because they believe that the mix of security to nonsecurity spending is worth the investment. However, because oversight is so weak, leaders can still top up military spending with pet projects and get away with it a reasonable proportion of the time. A formal description of this process is included in the Appendix for those that are interested in the math behind this intuition.

Hypothesis 2 Democracies with moderate national security oversight will bear higher military defense burdens than democracies with low national security oversight.

CONSTRAINING CORRUPTION AND OVERSPENDING

A third consequence of oversight is related to the strengthening of the constraining effect. To appreciate the arc of oversight, let's take a step back. In countries with little to no oversight over national security policy we expect less mobilization of funds, as the public remains skeptical that military spending would be used for private rather than public gains. In these cases the possibility of corruption stunts mobilization, sometimes dramatically as in Costa Rica in 1949. As we move up to moderate levels of oversight, some corruption is now effectively constrained, and this can effectively convince the public to support military spending at a higher level than they would without any oversight. For example, large-ticket and obvious corruption can now be detected and punished at least intermittently. Since the price of security now has limits, although it remains high, the executive can offer a military budget that includes some security spending but with an additional tranche of nonsecurity spending packed in. This nonsecurity portion of the budget will likely be as big as the executive can get away with,[8] but it will ensure that the public still thinks it is worth it to pay the bill.[9] The public, in supporting this military spending, now is paying for some nonsecurity spending. This results in overspending on the military, relative to what would be optimal given the security situation of a state. Therefore, at moderate levels of national security oversight, the public is mobilized to pay a high price for security, but the executive is still able to extract private nonsecurity funding as part of the bargain.[10]

On the other hand, at high levels of oversight—where freedom of information laws are widely applicable to national security information, and where intelligence committees exist with the power to subpoena witnesses and issue minority reports—the constraining effect pushes out more and more of the corrupt spending. This occurs because as oversight becomes more accurate and sure, the probability of a leader being able to get away with nonsecurity spending is lower. This means leaders are more and more deterred from pushing overstuffed and overpriced military budgets on the public. While the nonsecurity spending never fully vanishes,[11] it should lessen above a certain threshold of oversight.

Thus, as oversight becomes increasingly strong, the constraining effect can begin to, at least theoretically, dominate the mobilization effect. To see this, imagine a stylized example where a legislature is working with supremely powerful retrospective information tools at the same time that the press can broadcast details and freedom of information requests are processed with speed. Thus, we are at a very high level of oversight. Additionally, assume that the executive has private information about what the true price of security is at the time. In this context an executive can think about promoting four types of budgets. The first would be a bare-minimum military proposal that would be sure to gain public support but might legitimately cost the country security in the future by failing to prepare it for threats that have been discerned through private intelligence. The second budget is similar to the first but spends closer to, but still less than, the optimal level. Two other alternatives spend more than what is necessary. The third proposal includes small contracts to political cronies that raise the public price tag by a small amount that is hidden among thousands of programs. The final proposal includes large-scale nonsecurity spending that significantly raises the price tag over and above what would be publicly optimal.

In this stylized example, when strong oversight powers are present, the first two proposals are not attractive since they leave the country vulnerable and provide no private political goods for the leader. A leader would only choose the lowest budget figure if he or she were forced to do so by severe public skepticism. The latter two, more expensive proposals are better for the leader. They both provide security while simultaneously raising money for personal, partisan, or other nonpublic ends. In isolation, the executive would prefer the largest-ticket budget. However, oversight makes this very unattractive, since that level of corruption is highly likely to be discovered and punished. On the other hand, proposing military spending with a few hidden political riders attached is both attractive and practical. Oversight institutions cannot investigate every policy decision and dollar; we have seen that paradox before. Therefore, after some threshold is reached, oversight begins to incrementally constrain spending back toward optimal spending levels.

Figure 7.1 sketches out the hypothesized relationship between national security oversight strength (on the x-axis) and expected military spending (on the y-axis). The dashed line represents the estimated optimal spending level that may be known through intelligence information to the executive but not the public. We can think of this dashed line as the true price that security should cost the public if there were no need for national security secrecy. At the very lowest levels

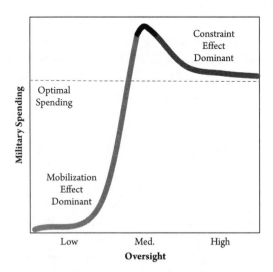

Figure 7.1 The nonlinear relationship between oversight institutions and predicted military spending.

of oversight, it is difficult to mobilize the public and elites to support a budget, and thus spending is very low. This is where Costa Rica in 1949 would fit. As oversight institutions are strengthened and we move to the right on the graph, however, the public becomes more receptive to spending. Specifically, the public is quickly willing to pay a larger defense bill to avoid potential insecurity as long as there is some insurance that the expected overspending will be less painful than continuing to underfund defense. In this region, increasing oversight has the net effect of mobilizing support. For a leader, there is a peak at which you have just enough oversight to convince the public that nonsecurity spending will be less costly than denying funding and thus having insecurity, but not too much oversight such that the nonsecurity spending will trigger excessive penalties in the future.

After this peak, as we continue to move to the right and increase the glare of oversight in the national security rearview mirror, penalties for nonsecurity funding begin to bite into leaders' own private benefits. Spending is already above the optimal spending needed to provide public security, and leaders are less and less likely to be able to mislead the public—and get away with it—such that the security situation necessitates overspending. Thus constraints are placed on nonsecurity funding as oversight increases and spending levels are expected to decrease. After a certain point, the constraining effect of oversight reduces military spending back toward—but never quite reaching—the underlying cost of security. In total, we expect to find empirically in later chapters a nonlinear relationship between national security oversight strength and military spending that mirrors Figure 7.1.

> *Hypothesis 3* Democracies with high national security oversight will bear lower military defense burdens than will democracies with moderate national security oversight, but they will have higher military defense burdens than will democracies with low national security oversight.

RELATIVE FOREIGN POLICY EFFECTIVENESS

A final and important consequence of national security oversight in democracies is relative foreign policy success. One of the puzzles that motivated this study was how democracies seemed to be able to survive and thrive in the international system despite the ostensible requirement of secrecy and mobilization. Retrospective national security oversight helps to explain why some democratic systems are able to compete internationally at a high level.

Two components of democratic foreign policy success must be a capacity for secrecy and public consent. As Chapters 2 and 3 argued, secrecy aids the foreign policy ability of states. Further, Chapters 4 and 5 illustrated that without further innovations, the potential for abuse can reduce investments and public support and lead to insecurity. This should manifest itself in lower rates of foreign policy success, as we saw occurred in France in the early twentieth century and in the United States in 1974.

On the other hand, with retrospective oversight, executives are armed with immediate secrecy and greater public consent. Leaders are then able to harness the powers of anticipation, deception, and capability suppression through immediate secrecy, without the relative drag of consistent distrust and skepticism of those democracies that lack oversight.

Figure 7.2 presents a schematic of how national security oversight improves the foreign policy ability of democracies. Immediate secrecy continues to enhance foreign policy ability in these democracies, but oversight institutions increase the expectation that abuse will be revealed. This leads to greater public confidence that policies, even those based on secret intelligence, will serve a public benefit and thus will have public support. Over time, this investment, the mobilizing effect of oversight, should increase foreign policy success, relative to those democracies that lack oversight. This occurs because the theory specifies that spending should be invested, at least partially, on security-enhancing capabilities. The benefits of oversight, in terms of secrecy and public consent, are hypothesized to lead to greater foreign policy ability.[12] This view of crisis outcomes is distinct from the role that success and victory played in the thin marketplace of ideas. In that framework, defeat was punished in all democracies, and

Figure 7.2 How ex post oversight can increase a priori foreign policy ability.

the foreign policy ability of a state was ignored. Here, I am arguing that oversight increases the foreign policy ability of states through increasing public consent without inducing excessive transparency costs, and this ability leads to success or failure.

> *Hypothesis 4* Democracies with high national security oversight should have improved foreign policy ability and win more of their international disputes than will democracies with low national security oversight.

This discussion extends the democratic effectiveness arguments of Reiter and Stam and others.[13] Since not all democracies maintain effective national security oversight institutions, not all democracies should be able to project effective foreign policy. I argue that it is oversight, coupled with elections, that drives effectiveness for democracies, since it allows for secrecy and public consent. Elections without information is not a path toward accountability, only Madison's fear of farce and tragedy. Oversight, if present, should reassure the public that investments are more likely to be used for security, without the release of potentially valuable information to the public and a potential enemy. Therefore, we should see democracies with oversight winning more of their international disputes, all else being equal, as compared to democracies that lack oversight.

In the next section, I illustrate the uses of oversight for increasing public consent and investments by peering further ahead at the oversight trajectories of France after World War I and the United States after a series of institutional adjustments in the mid-1970s. What we see is that without institutional innovations, France continued to falter on the international stage. On the contrary, institutional changes in the United States raised oversight to above-average levels, with a strengthened freedom of information law and permanent intelligence committees. There were uses and abuses of secrecy in both cases, but while France collapsed behind the Maginot Line under the weight of foreign policy pressure, the United States invested in a portfolio of programs that, while likely inefficient, helped propel the United States toward the end of the Cold War.

COMPARING OVERSIGHT IN FRANCE
AND THE UNITED STATES

From the Dreyfus Affair to the end of World War I, oversight functions in France were not improved. No legislative changes were passed to focus more specifically on intelligence oversight, and there was no freedom of information law in France until 1978.[14] Instead, the Statistics Section was shut down and bureaucratic fixes within the executive were attempted. While the legislature did have interpellation powers, there was no ability to subpoena witnesses, call hearings to publicize previously classified information, or present minority reports. Committees also did not have access to intelligence information or significant investigative staff.[15]

The situation was quite different in the United States. After the revelations of Watergate and abuses of the capacity for secrecy, several institutional innovations were made to reinforce national security oversight institutions. The ability of the public to retrospectively access national-security-relevant information was significantly strengthened when the previously very weak 1966 US Freedom of Information Law[16] was amended. The original 1966 act had given the executive broad powers to exclude national security information from the law, by merely claiming that the information was related to "national security." The Privacy Act of 1974, which was passed when Congress overrode President Ford's veto, changed this nearly absolute exemption to include the provision that to be exempted from release, if requested, publication of the information would have to harm US interest. In addition, the law included a non-executive review of claims of secrecy.

Equally important were changes in legislative committee structure. While bills in 1946 and 1970 had support for committees overseeing foreign policy, intelligence received considerably less oversight.[17] The specific national-security-relevant functions of the committees were strengthened in 1975 with the creation of the Church and Pike Committees that eventually led to specialized House and Senate committees on intelligence that more efficiently allocated staff to the task. Oversight in the United States still had significant blind spots, even in the rearview mirror. The United States continued to lack a provision to balance the harm versus the public benefit of releasing national security information in its freedom of information regime, and it also had no means for minorities to initiate hearings or issue reports in legislative committees.

Thus, while France remained on the low end of democratic oversight of national security from the turn of the century through 1940, the United States in the 1970s moved toward a nonnegligible probability that foreign policy information would in time be publicized and investigated.[18]

The divergence in institutional paths in Paris and Washington allows us to trace out not only whether public support and subsequent foreign policy success match the predictions of oversight theory, but also whether the hypothesized processes are in evidence. Given low oversight, we would expect continued distrust and skepticism in France, as well as underinvestment in security-enhancing policies.

In the United States, with above-average but moderate and imperfect oversight, we should expect to see three related dynamics. First, the abuse of secrecy should continue, despite oversight, as suggested by the paradox of perfect oversight. Relatedly, we should also be able, from the vantage point of history, to see some uses for the capacity for secrecy. Second, the probability of abuse, while nonzero, should be constrained by the fear of future oversight, such that we should see evidence that members of the executive were aware that they could face penalties if they attempted to deceive the public about the costs and benefits of investments and policies. This is the constraining effect. Third, abuse should be rare enough that public support is raised even for costly policies whose benefits may be ambiguous. This is the mobilization effect. Together, these three processes in the United States should lead to high spending levels that include some waste and a residue of abuse, but ultimately significant success as they combine the benefits of the capacity for secrecy with public consent.

FRANCE: TO THE MAGINOT LINE, BUT NOT BEYOND

Both historians and contemporaneous observers agree that distrust between the public and the military, as well as polarization on national security issues, continued after World War I in France. This lack of mutual trust between the leadership and the public manifested itself when the government refused for years to release casualty figures on the war and charges of "political manipulation" and "cover-ups" were leveled by the opposition.[19] Bloch in 1940 argued that foreign policy in France in the inter-war years was riven with "party bias and base political ambitions"[20] as well as worries about cover-ups and profiteering.[21] All of this led to "an attitude of skepticism to all propaganda."[22]

This distrust of the executive and skepticism of foreign policy announcements manifested itself most centrally in debate about how to effectively deter future threats from Berlin. Those that wanted to keep France under arms and continue to be in a position to occupy parts of German territory if reparations payments were not made were decried as "warmongers" who wanted to spur France toward costly and needless "adventures," such as those that led to World War I.[23] On the left, politicians that argued for a quick reduction in arms and overtures to foster a democratic Germany could gain public support for their proposed decreases in arms spending, but not significant cooperative steps with Germany.[24]

This polarization of opinion arose to international attention in 1922. While Premier Briand was negotiating a possible reduction in German reparations payments, with the goal of trying to increase London's commitment to the Anglo-French alliance, the Foreign Minister and several deputies met in Paris to publicly repudiate this position. Upon returning to Paris during the middle of negotiations, Briand was accused of "betraying France."[25] In the chamber, after calling a pause to negotiations while back in France, he stated, "[A] statesman . . . expects to be fired on by other countries but not by his own."[26] Briand then resigned, stating, "I never knew what it was like to row in the galleys of the King, but I now know what it is like to row in the galleys of the Republic, and I do not want to continue this toil any longer."[27]

Neither side of the debate—either those that supported increased cooperation with Germany or those that supported greater investments in the military—could secure sufficient consent for its initiatives to push a coherent portfolio of policies. After Briand stepped down, Poincaré formed a government that leaned toward confrontation. Yet, even when proponents of increased payments to officers and investment in arms, such as Minister of War Lefevre, attempted to publicize intelligence estimates of the German threat, they failed to raise enough support.[28]

Putting the Breaks on Effective Code

The security services themselves were inhibited by worries of potential abuse. Despite decades having passed since the cover-ups and abuses of the Dreyfus Affair, Porch reports "that there was residual distrust of the secret services dating from the Dreyfus Affair."[29] Administrative changes were made after World War I that "scaled down" both operations and training for code-breakers.[30] One insider later wrote that "the Service de Renseignements was a slightly mysterious organization whose necessity was reluctantly acknowledged, but whose initiatives, it was feared, could cause problems."[31]

These potential "problems" led to a "dysfunctional" arrangement of intelligence services that were split up into several separate offices to reduce their threat and crucially refusing to invest in greater intelligence capabilities.[32] During the inter-war years, great technological leaps were being made in machine-aided encryption, as the world entered an era of "industrial-scale" code-breaking and code-keeping that required significant investments to be successful.[33] Bletchley Park is an exemplar of the potential payoffs for this scale of investment and innovation. The Germans had made a serious step forward in code-keeping with the Enigma machine, whose design was based on a commercially available model from the early 1920s, but with significant added complexities.

The French were aware of the necessity of increasing cryptographic security for their communications while at the same time building their ability to break such codes from other governments and particularly Berlin. In fact, the French Army ordnance section tried to create a prototype given their awareness of the vast potential of the devices. However, two related obstacles derailed the French move toward an Enigma-like device. The first obstacle was a lack of trained personnel to take up the designs suggested by the ordnance section. Low pay and layoffs after the war had depleted the knowledge base in the government intelligence sector. Those agents that were qualified to design and improve on the prototype device were overworked and did not have time for this forward-thinking project.[34] This lack of trained personnel could have been overcome with an investment in a modern, for the time, cryptographic office as was being developed in Germany, Britain, and Poland. Thus the second obstacle involved "financial and political constraints" that were imposed by Parliament that made it impossible to find money to invest in this infrastructure. The French Enigma prototype was abandoned, despite general agreement of its potential use in the future. Work did not stop on machine-aided code-keeping systems. However, the impediments to a modern code-keeping system meant that as the drums of war grew louder in the late 1930s, France was at a relative disadvantage. Porch writes that "when the [French] army did develop an automatic encoding system based on perforated paper, it was dropped because it would require a specialized corp of trained cryptographers," and this investment was beyond the consent of the French public and political leadership.[35] In addition, while France had a robust network of spies, many were paid quite lowly sums, and they failed to routinely provide radios to their spies in Germany to transmit information on the developing war situation, as other countries had done.[36]

Too Little Consent, Too Late Investments

This lack of public consent, along with the inability of the government to increase support for potentially security-enhancing policies, led to underinvestment on several other fronts. By the time Germany began to rearm and remilitarize the Rhineland, Paris had fallen behind in training, air power, and anti-tank weapons.[37] France reduced military service commitments to 18 months and then to 1 year in 1928, due to "overwhelming political pressure."[38] When arguments were raised to have two-year service requirements in the 1930s, this was deemed "political unacceptable."[39] Officers continued to be paid less than other civil servants and comparable personnel in other states, yet Parliament refused to support raising salaries. This continued to hinder recruitment.[40] Expenditures for artillery and the air force were also neglected "even to the point where orders fell below the minimum necessary for economical mass production."[41] During the 1930s, the French military was "struggling to maintain itself as a fighting force."[42] In fact, as before World War I, the army during the inter-war years tended not to ask for large investments, and the Senate and deputies did not push for more, anticipating unmovable opposition.[43] In 1936 when the Popular Front and Leon Blum attempted to raise military funding and supply the Republican side in the Spanish Civil War, a backlash ensued, and the government fell the next year.

Even from 1938 to 1940, as the threat from Germany became increasingly obvious, distrust of the leadership was rampant. Around Paris, opposition politicians posted signs that read in part, "People of France, you are being deceived! A cunning trap has been set . . . to make war inevitable."[44] Polarization led another unity government proposed by Blum to fall that year in one month.[45] The next government led by Daladier attempted to centralize power by postponing elections and proroguing Parliament and asking for significant discretion to deal with emerging crises.[46] However, when Daladier attempted and failed to organize intervention in the Winter War in Finland, his government fell. The Reynaud government rose on the eve of war with a vote of 268 in favor and 267 either voting against or abstaining, hardly a unified political front.[47]

Historians have argued whether the cause of French defeat in 1940 was primarily lack of morale or an intelligence failure.[48] What is striking upon reflection is that these potential explanations are at least partial complements to an explanation involving the secrecy dilemma in the French Third Republic. There was indeed a lack of support for more robust initiatives, for both war and peace. However, this was not laziness or "decadence," but an offshoot of significant distrust and skepticism. When the dangers of the strategic situation accelerated for France in the late 1930s, indeed production accelerated. Yet, this did not erase years of underinvestment in the air force, tank battalions, and professional infantry, as well as underinvestment in crucial training for personnel across the services. Jackson writes, "In 1936 the army still only possessed 27 B tanks. Once these tanks did start coming on stream there was precious little time for training before they were thrown into battle."[49] The training of a professional army, air force, and security service was also put off until the eve of war.[50]

While the failure to identify the German advance through the Ardennes in 1940 and the overestimates of German forces awaiting the main French thrust through Belgium were clear intelligence failures, these might have proved less consequential if France had had greater room for error with improved preparations. Quite explicitly, it was not lack of intelligence on the rising German threat that led France to be materially unprepared for war in the late 1930s and early 1940s. Paul Reynaud argued before Parliament in March 1935 that the French army needed to be mechanized and investments made in a professional military with training to match new technologies. Yet, just as with Lefevre's warnings before, these "proposals got nowhere," not because the arguments were deemed to be faulty, but because it was viewed as politically infeasible.[51] There was a recognition of the German problem for France, but no effective solution could garner enough public consent. As Porch declares on the subject, "It was not that French politicians ignored intelligence. Au contraire, they pondered it to the point of paralysis."[52] Politicians came to the conclusion that there was a lack of political will to match the "costs of confronting" Berlin.[53] Even more directly, where intelligence was lacking, in the timing and location of the German attack on France, the lack of investment in code-breaking and keeping did not help.

This lack of preparation left France in a position where an attack "threatened to fall on troops who were far from battle-hardened, whose tanks and planes had yet to come on-line, who were not yet formed into armored divisions and drilled in the intricacies of modern mobile operations."[54] It was known within the military leadership that French forces were "short of antitank and antiaircraft weapons, combat aircraft, and independent tank divisions."[55] The lack of airpower was consequential for both operational effectiveness and intelligence. The Luftwaffe's air superiority provided air cover for the advancing Germans while French air reconnaissance of the Ardennes region was scant as the French thrust into what amounted to a trap in Belgium.[56]

Cement Instead of Soldiers

The one exception to this lack of investment, the construction of the Maginot Line, proves the rule. Spending on personnel or offensive weapons was unpopular specifically because those that distrusted the government were worried that they were not necessary for security and instead would be used for "adventurous" moves and "over-hasty engagements."[57] However, an armament program that was purely defensive and had a much lower likelihood of being abused by a distrusted military could draw support. This was the lure of a system of fixed defensive fortifications. One historian writes:

> France had no stomach for adventurous military strategies. The fortifications signified that France was a status quo power; what it had, it would hold. Nothing more. This ensured that the fortifications would be acceptable to French taxpayers and to international opinion. Indeed, the defenses were the only new military burden that the war-weary French would agree to assume.[58]

In fact, this is how the series of fortifications were sold to the public; General Louis Maurin in 1935 stated:

> How can anyone believe that we are still thinking of an offensive when we have spent billions on setting up a fortified barrier? Would we be so mad as to march out in front of this barrier on the way to some kind of adventure.[59]

Of course, going beyond the line of fortifications was indeed in French battle plans. This was later formalized in secret tank battle orders.[60] Alexander concludes: "The French were, knowingly, playing to the gallery in their presentation of the fortifications program." He went on to suggest that the process was politicized rather than targeted at investing in security.[61]

At the time, the weaknesses of the fortifications were well known in the military and political hierarchies. First, Minister Andre Maginot, for whom the wall was named,[62] had been briefed that an effective system of fortifications would be too costly and that the fortifications that were being built would be undermanned.[63] Second, the fortifications did not protect France from an invasion through Belgium or in the North. This vulnerability was discussed in the High Command, particularly after Belgium withdrew from its alliance commitments with France in 1936, but never sufficiently solved. Only weaker and ineffective fortifications were added in the Northern sector.[64] Later events would prove these weaknesses, as the Maginot Line was driven around not only once, during the German occupation, but two more times, during the Allied advance and again during the German counteroffensive.

However, it is important to understand that in the political context of distrust and polarization, the money appropriated for the Maginot Line could not have been shifted to more immediate military needs. Alexander argues convincingly that as Hitler was coming to power and accelerating his demands "it was impossible for French military chiefs to choose between concrete and cavalry tanks, between barbed wire and bombers."[65] Skepticism took the form of concluding that the military could not be trusted with more than the minimal war materiel, only concrete. Thus, the Maginot Line became a "shield that protected their country not only from its traditional enemy, but from the consequences of their own unwillingness to make greater military sacrifices."[66]

The defeat of France in 1940 was made more probable by the lack of planning and efficient investment in the security services, military training, and capital over the inter-war years. French codes were being read by the Germans during the early stages of the war, and air superiority allowed the Luftwaffe to monitor the unfolding situation.[67] Even as the German threat became more obvious and the procurement of tanks and airplanes accelerated after 1938, there was not enough time to get the war materiel to the front.[68] In any case, training and battle plans taking advantage of these late-arriving assets were even further behind. After occupying France and its war production facilities, the Germans had hundreds of planes waiting for them, ready for use against the Allies.[69] In 1940, Bloch summarized the way a lack of information led to insecurity and eventually to occupation.

Our system of government demands the participation of the masses. The destiny of the People is in their own hands, and I see no reason for believing that they are not perfectly capable of choosing rightly. But what effort had been made to supply them with that minimum of clear and definite information without which no rational conduct is possible? To that question, the answer is 'None'. In no way did our so-called democratic system so singlely fail. That particular dereliction of duty constituted the most heinous crime.[70]

While Bloch may have undervalued transparency costs, he rightly identified the necessity of public consent in democracies to invest in security. The French defeat was both an intelligence failure and an example of lack of investments, particularly before 1938, to prepare for rising threats. The case of the United States in the late 1970s provides a different and more hopeful dynamic for democratic foreign policy success, although not without instructive abuses and inefficiencies.

THE UNITED STATES: TO THE END OF THE COLD WAR AND BEYOND

As the Cold War continued into the late 1970s and the early 1980s, the United States was faced with a similar dilemma of how to invest in security, as compared to France. While it was a consensus view that the Soviet Union continued to be a serious threat, how to best respond to Moscow's capabilities, and at what cost, was highly contentious. As we will see, there were disagreements about arms control, defensive weapons, and modernization, as in France. There were also worries about potential abuse and deception by the executive in the United States, as had hampered security in France. Yet, the dynamic in the United States, after investing in improving oversight institutions, was quite different. In this section, I highlight uses and abuses of secrecy during this time, as well as how national security oversight, through both constraining and mobilizing effects, helps to explain why the United States mounted a large military build-up in the 1980s, in juxtaposition to French underinvestment. As hypothesized, this build-up included overspending, waste, and abuse, but it also included investments in security that paid off in surviving the Cold War and the impressive military display in the 1991 Gulf War.

In the late 1970s, in the wake of Watergate and Vietnam, these successes were not predicted. Many commentators on US national security policy made explicit forecasts that, without changes, the United States might suffer the same inaction and costs that plagued Europe in the inter-war years. Eugene Rostow typified this warning when he stated, "Since the final bitter phases of the Vietnam War, our governments have been reacting with the same fear, passivity, and inadequacy which characterized British and American policy so fatally in the 1930s and British policy before 1914."[71] Rostow and others pushed for greater arms build-ups and military modernization. Many of these worries scuttled ratification of the SALT II treaty that US President Carter had negotiated.[72]

As the 1980 election approached, President Carter and his challenger Ronald Reagan argued for significantly increased investments in national security. Reagan's set of proposals, which went beyond the spending increases that Carter had initiated, included floating a 600-ship Navy, flying stealth fighters and new supersonic bombers, burying M-X missiles in hardened silos, and, most controversially, imagining a missile defense system under the Strategic Defense Initiative.[73] The price tag for these investments was steep and would need to be paid by the public and consented to by Congress. The plan was to spend almost $1.5 trillion from 1981 to 1986.[74] However, this number did not include other planned security-related programs run out of the CIA.[75]

After Reagan won the election, defense officials continued to argue for greater spending with warnings of the inter-war fate of Europe. Defense Secretary Casper Weinberger argued that the United States was now in a position that "was much like that of the 1930s, when Hitler was building the German war machine and Churchill was the lone voice calling for rearmament."[76] The administration argued that there would soon be a "window of vulnerability" for the United States, and that the USSR now had several capabilities that were superior to those of the United States. As evidence, the administration asserted that the USSR had "out-invested us by eighty or ninety percent in the last few years."[77]

Many of these proposals, and their concern for Soviet capabilities, were at least partially related to intelligence that the United States had collected, but that was unknown to the public. One important source of information on Soviet capabilities, which was kept secret during the 1980s, was known as Farewell. Farewell was Vladimir Vetrov, who rose to be the KGB officer in charge of evaluating espionage on the Line X, which was the Soviet term for technical intelligence. This gave him access to an enormous trove of information on the Soviet program.[78]

In 1980, Vetrov offered to provide the French with information on Soviet espionage in the West.[79] When Francois Mitterrand took power in 1981, he shared the Farewell dossier with Reagan and then the CIA. Through this information, it became clear to the leadership in Washington that Moscow had successfully infiltrated technology companies throughout the United States and Europe. As one insider put it, "[the information] made clear that the Soviets had been running their R&D on the back of the West for years. Given the massive transfer of technology in radars, computers, machine tools, and semiconductors from the United States to the USSR, the Pentagon had been in an arms race with itself."[80]

Vetrov passed on Moscow's military technology "shopping" list, which in turn pointed to vulnerabilities that might be exploited. Instead of arresting the Soviet informants immediately, the CIA and other European intelligence agencies worked to provide not only incorrect information through these unsuspecting informants but, more important, sabotaged code and infrastructure. This program reportedly culminated in a large explosion in the trans-Siberian pipeline, according to a recent book by Thomas Reed.[81] This was a useful deception emanating from the United States' capacity for secrecy.

The Potential for Abuse

However, the informational advantage of the executive did not lead to automatic support of Reagan's policies or forecast of Soviet threats. Many of the specific proposals faced a background of distrust and skepticism, not dissimilar to the political rhetoric of inter-war France. Opposition positions ranged from suggesting that the administration was overselling the Soviet threat[82] to others that went as far as to accuse the administration of "fearmongering and McCarthyite Red-baiting" meant to deceive the public.[83] Congressional critics of the budget increases, including Republican Senator Durenberger and the Democrats for Defense group, argued that the budget was too high and was filled with waste.[84]

Specific programs that involved a potential first-use capability drew intense criticism. Opposition to the M-X program suggested that the missiles were a waste or would be used by the Reagan administration as a first-strike capability.[85] Fitzgerald writes:

> The MX decision was the first strategic initiative the administration had taken, but the reaction was hostile. In congressional hearings defense experts testified that the missile would be burned to cinders if the Soviets targeted it in a first strike. Critics argued that, given its vulnerability in a fixed silo, it could only be used as a first-strike or a launch-on-warning weapon. Pointing out that the decision did nothing to close the window of vulnerability, a *Washington Post* reporter asked whether that window was going to disappear in the way that the missile gap disappeared after the Kennedy campaign in 1960. A *New York Times* editorial suggested that it might be better if the administration forgot the MX and simply drilled more holes in the missile fields to make the Russians think we had more missiles.[86]

This skepticism was felt inside the White House, where there were worries that the entire M-X missile program was going to be canceled. As the discussion about funding M-X continued, a *Washington Post* article appeared with an administration source quoted as saying, "Our duty now is to minimize further damage to the President."[87]

Similarly, in 1983 when President Reagan announced what would become his Strategic Defense Initiative (SDI), it was immediately met by skeptical voices in government and the scientific community. The day after the president announced the initiative, Senator Edward Kennedy called it "misleading Red Scare tactics and reckless 'Star Wars' schemes."[88] Fitzgerald reports that those who were skeptical of SDI, not only in Congress, but also within the Pentagon, estimated that the initiative was a "hare-brained scheme" and "would not only be an enormous waste of resources but would signal a US breakout from the ABM Treaty, thereby causing all kinds of havoc in US–Soviet relations."[89] While SDI was doubted by many in the scientific community, it was being pushed by other powerful voices including Edward Teller. An article in *Time Magazine* suggested that SDI was "partly a political ploy to change the context of the debate over defense spending."[90]

This skepticism was not without some merit. The usefulness of the M-X missile depended on its ability to survive a first strike. This survivability, in turn, depended on what was known about Soviet missile capabilities, and particularly the circular error probability of missile systems.[91] Information on this was classified. In fact, evidence on the capabilities of the United States' own Minuteman and M-X missiles was classified.[92] The ambiguities around SDI were even greater, as tests and technologies were also highly guarded secrets.[93]

Oversight and Abuse

Counterbalancing this skepticism was the threat of meaningful oversight by Congress and the press publishing any scandals that came to light. As noted, Congress had greater tools for oversight than were available in the early 1970s.[94] Just in the first two years of the Reagan administration, the Senate Select Committee on Intelligence investigated Arm Control programs and monitoring of Soviet compliance, Intermediate Nuclear Forces, MX basing, and more generally the costs of defections and failed counterintelligence policies. Other committees worked with the intelligence committees to hold their own hearings on related topics.[95] Over the next years, SDI also was investigated in the House and the Senate.[96]

Yet, contemporaneous oversight of programs and proposals was limited. Program details were often classified, and even when they were shared with committees, the members could not pass the information along due to transparency costs. Senator John Warner expressed some of this frustration in hearings on Soviet capabilities in 1985: "In many years of receiving classified testimony from these gentlemen and their colleagues, I have been frustrated by our inability to share the facts about the Soviet strategic force build-up with the American people."[97]

Retrospective oversight was more successful and was better able to work in concert with other information institutions such as the Freedom of Information Act and the press. For example, the House Select Committee on Intelligence had hearings related to CIA involvement in the Wilson/Terpil affair, which had been building for several years.[98] Press reports around this time further broadened the revelations.[99]

However, the Iran–Contra Affair was the high-profile example of this dynamic between potential abuse and imperfect oversight. The scandal involved selling arms to Iran, via Israel, and transferring the proceeds to Contras in Nicaragua. While the original leak of the Iranian side of the interactions happened in a Lebanese paper, this merely lit a larger fuse of revelations in Washington. The facts and decision-chain in the Iran–Contra scandal were investigated and at least partially uncovered by the Senate Select Committee on Intelligence, the Tower Commission, which was led by a former senator and chairman of the Senate Armed Services Committee, and special investigative committees in the House and the Senate. An independent council was also assigned to investigate.[100]

This oversight was not insignificant. Congressional hearings and investigations led to the declassification of cabinet meeting minutes to the public and other detailed information that normally would have been classified for a much longer period of time.[101] The hearings for the first time publicized the mechanisms, known as the "the Enterprise," that were used to secretly fund the Contras and how that was connected to the Iran deals.[102] Hearings led National Security Advisor John Poindexter to admit that the cover-up was not for national security but to avoid "significant political embarrassment."[103]

The collection of this information allowed Congress to release a report on November 18, 1987, that found ""secrecy, deception and disdain for the law" in the administration's actions.[104] The report read, in part, that agents of the executive, and most specifically Oliver North and John Poindexter, "lied repeatedly to Congress and to the American people about the Contra covert action and Iran arms sales" and also "altered and destroyed official documents."[105]

The Iran–Contra example shows, not surprisingly in light of the paradox of perfect oversight, that some abuse is still possible, and is even probable when faced with investigative institutions such as the United States had deployed. The details of the investigations, and particularly the way the committee struggled with how to balance transparency costs with what information to relay to the public, underscored the imperfections and incompleteness of oversight. Many of the members of the special committees investigating the scandal echoed the frustration of John Warner quoted earlier.[106]

Normally, there are enough checks and balances within the governmental framework that such anomalies are detected and corrected early on. In the national security area, however, where secrecy is necessarily a tool of the trade, there is a greater potential that secrecy will neutralize the normal checks and balances of government. This was clearly demonstrated in the Iran-Contra Affair.[107]

A supplemental view by Bill McCollum in the report stated the difficulties of investigating national security policy because "simple public disclosure of classified information can be just as damaging to our national security as selling secrets to the enemy."[108] Some committee members even had a paper by John Norton Moore inserted into an appendix which explained the difficulty of national security oversight as follows: "Intelligence oversight, however, is not like oversight of the social security program or the Department of the Agriculture that can proceed fully in the open. Rather, it must respect the requisite secrecy of the intelligence process."[109]

A small example is emblematic of the present but partial, oversight in this case. In discussions about the Iran–Contra Affair both in the report and in the hearings, many country names were replaced with numbers to avoid transparency costs. These numbers ranged from 1 to 16. However, only 8 out of the 16 were publicly revealed.[110]

All told, the Iran–Contra hearings and revelations led to costs for the Reagan White House. Many point out that Reagan avoided impeachment, but he did pay a political cost in declining approval, months of lost time on his legislative agenda, and more difficulty in getting approval for aid to the Contras in the future.[111] This was not the same price extracted for the Watergate abuses, but the evidence of abuse and incompetence was also thinner. If oversight on the Iran–Contra Affair got an average grade,[112] this is consistent with moderate oversight, and surely better than French oversight of abuse, particularly during the Dreyfus Affair.

The Constraining Effect of Oversight

Moreover, one important component of oversight is that those in the executive that might abuse the capacity for secrecy should worry about that abuse being revealed after the fact. The evidence in the Iran–Contra hearings and insider accounts available today suggest that there was an awareness that oversight might happen and lead to political costs. The Iran–Contra money scheme was designed to avoid congressional oversight, although this was ultimately unsuccessful.[113] It is likely that the program would have been much bigger without the worry of congressional investigations.

There is also evidence that the White House was concerned about the revelation of waste and deception in their weapons program proposals. The President was warned that on programs such as the M-X, the B-2, and SDI, waste or overpromising on capabilities would lead to sanctions and political difficulties.[114] In reaction to debates about hiding the potential uses of the M-X from the Soviets and the public, while discussing arms control agreements, Schultz warned that "when the US Congress picks up this inconsistency, it hurts our appropriations."[115] Similarly, John Whitehead, who was Deputy Secretary of State, noted in a meeting with the President on March 25, 1986, that a decision under consideration to fund obsolete equipment mainly for symbolic purposes would eventually be met with legislative penalties and that "Congressional reaction on the defense budget would present severe problems and these options would further handicap us on the Hill."[116] Baker and others in the administration were particularly worried about inflating the capabilities of SDI. They forecasted that eventually Congress would learn of the more limited capabilities and that this would lead to "disillusionment." He suggested, particularly on SDI, that the administration should not "describe hypothetical outcomes as if they were virtual accomplishments," because "this form of salesmanship . . . sometimes created unfortunate mood swings in the Congress" and led to decreased funding.[117]

Another series of events during the mid-1980s illustrates the interaction between potential deception and oversight. Since 1976, a system of tests known as Homing Overlay Experiments (HOEs) were run to try and expand technologies for ballistic missile defense. The HOE design was such that a surplus Minuteman I missile was fitted with an intercepter that had steel rods that extended around the nose-cone like an imposing pinwheel. A year after the 1983 announcement by Reagan that he was seeking funding and support for SDI, including both laser and kinetic interception technologies, a test named HOE-4 was prepared. In fact, this test occurred prior to a key vote on funding for the SDI-related programs in Congress for the next fiscal year. The public and press could not monitor the test, since it occurred over the Pacific Ocean. In fact, the Defense Department had difficulty tracking the experiment.[118] However, the day after the test, it was announced that HOE-4 was a success, and in testimony before Congress on April 5, 1985, a representative declared that the United States "hit a bullet with a bullet for the first time."[119]

There were doubts about the veracity of this success in the press and among skeptics of the program. Skeptics believed that "the manipulation of 'Star Wars' tests was part of a deception campaign, intended to fool the Soviet Union, that overstepped its bounds and wound up misleading Congress about the progress of the missile-defense program."[120]

In fact, rumors of potential deception operations continued through the early 1990s. According to a GAO report conducted for the Senate Governmental Affairs Committee in July 1994, the HOE-4 test was not a deception. However, the first two tests, HOE-1 and HOE-2, did have a deception element. The faux-warhead had an explosive planted inside that was to detonate if the kill vehicle was close enough to appear to hit the target but missed. Parts of this device were still in the HOE-4 test, but the deception program had been abandoned earlier for fears of being discovered.[121] Thus, deception was discovered through retrospective oversight (for HOE-1 and HOE-2), but additional deception operations (for HOE-3 and HOE-4) were trimmed for fear of the cost of their being revealed.

The Mobilizing Effect of Oversight

The Reagan era of defense spending fits the model of a country with moderately accurate oversight quite well because the constraints did not collapse funding. Despite skepticism, scandal, and public moves by Gorbachev to signal deescalation, a sufficient proportion of the public consented to not only investing in SDI programs, but also investing in Intermediate Nuclear Forces in Europe, the MX missile, aircraft such as the B-1 and B-2 bombers, the A-10, and the F-117A, as well as Ohio-class submarines and Nimitz-class Carriers and the Bradley Fighting Vehicle. Public support for increased defense spending was high and broad after the 1980 election and helped to persuade Congress to pass the large budgets.[122]

Although many of the proposed programs were scaled back—the Navy did not reach 600 ships, and SDI investments were cut over time—significant funding and investments had public consent. Opponents did not block the mobilization of the potentially provocative deployment of nuclear missiles in Europe,[123] and the funding and eventual deployment of the M-X missile was passed,[124] as was funding for SDI in 1985, in no small part because there was not greater skepticism of the early tests.[125] While there were doubts and hearings about the Bradley vehicles and the usefulness of the testing procedures used to validate their performance, the army improved the survivability of the platform.[126]

The military spending packages that Reagan promoted needed Democratic support to pass. Without public support from some opposition partisans, it would have been unlikely that Congress would have been persuaded to pass the large budgets in the early 1980s.[127] The M-X missile vote on May 24 in the House was representative of this necessity. Democrat Les Aspin, Chairman of the House Armed Services Committee, helped support the program, and it passed 239 to 186.[128] Similarly, ratification of the INF treaty was accomplished with crucial Democratic votes and the support of Robert Byrd, the Democratic Majority Leader at the time.

Moreover, as the reaction to the INF treaty made clear, the public was not blindly bellicose during this period. The cooperative agreement was widely popular and enhanced Reagan's approval.[129] Thus, the President was able to tack toward cooperation without fear of being upended at home as Briand had been in France. As with the military build-ups, there were skeptical voices to be overcome. Democrats worried that once the INF was ratified, a "broad interpretation" by the administration might render it moot. Republicans fretted that the limitations included would infringe on support for SDI and other initiatives.[130] Yet, these concerns were not debilitating. Movements toward further strategic arms reductions continued into the Bush administration.

Comparing Investments and Outcomes

We can compare US investments just before and after the oversight innovations in the 1970s, as well to inter-war French investments. First, the Ford administration faced significant skepticism not only on the investments in Cyprus in the wake of scandals, but also across the defense budget. The distrust from the revelations of the domestic spying and Watergate led to cuts in defense programs across the board, in real terms. Despite vociferous arguments from Ford and Secretary of Defense James Schlesinger, Congress refused to consent to even keep the budget constant, once adjusted for inflation.[131] The inability of the late Nixon and early Ford administrations to overcome skepticism about defense spending led to deep disagreements in the White House as to whether it was even politically prudent to ask for military increases in the run-up to the 1976 election.[132] Eventually these disagreements led to Schlesinger being fired due, at least in part, to his going public with his opinion that military spending was inadequate during this period. After being fired, Schlesinger shot back at Ford, "The military establishment cannot live on rhetoric and sentiment."[133] These debates helped to confirm what one commentator called "an essential fact of American political life in the immediate post-Watergate era: the executive branch . . . had lost much of its authority and power . . . [and] [t]his . . . had immediate consequences for the efforts towards renewing American foreign policy in the fall of 1974."[134]

Of course, this was not the end of the story. In the United States, this distrust was met by innovations in national security oversight institutions. Several commentators make the case that improvements in retrospective evaluation of intelligence and foreign policy in the United States were crucial to continued investments in security over the next decade. One report notes that "[a]ccording to former Senate Intelligence Committee staffers, within three years of establishing the Senate Committee, its staff and members pushed for an increase in the budget for the Intelligence Community after concluding that the existing budget and budget requests were insufficient for ongoing intelligence efforts."[135] Loch Johnson concludes that the innovations diverted suspicions into an "uneasy partnership" between the legislature and the executive.[136]

Oversight was far from perfect, and as we have seen there were abuses[137]; but there is also evidence of the benefits of the mobilizing and constraining effects of oversight, as compared to the process of distrust and underinvestment in France. The United States was able to keep secrets, such as about Farewell and missile capabilities, but at the same time enjoy support for investments in security. If the spending had all been waste and corruption, it is unlikely that the Cold War would have ended up the way it did. More revealingly, many of the weapons systems purchased and deployed in the Reagan arms build-up, including the F-117, the A-10, and the Bradley fighting vehicle, performed well in the 1991 Gulf War.[138] The USS Theodore Roosevelt, a Nimitz-class aircraft carrier whose first weld was completed by Casper Weinberger, launched the most sorties during the conflict.[139] Many of these investments spur successes even today. For example, as mentioned, stealth technology was utilized in a previously secret helicopter in the operation to kill Osama bin Laden. Without the public reassurance of oversight, mobilizing this renewed challenge to the USSR might have collapsed into greater skepticism as occurred in the French case.

A second comparison, between the Maginot Line and SDI, is also instructive for understanding the process of public support for security investments. Both programs appeared defensive to the public, and thus were less prone to abuse. These properties increased their relative popularity. However, both had significant vulnerabilities in isolation. The Maginot Line was revealed to be ineffective in World War II, and SDI to this day has failed to live up to early promises. In debates about the threat of SDI within the USSR, Andrei Sakharov explicitly compared SDI to the French concrete defense system. He argued that SDI "would never be militarily effective against a well-armed opponent; rather, it would be a kind of 'Maginot line in space,'" expensive and vulnerable to countermeasures. It would not serve as a population defense, or as a shield behind which a first strike could be launched, because it could be easily defeated.[140]

Yet, there are two key differences in the US and French cases once we zoom out from the Maginot Line and SDI. First, the Maginot Line stood alone for much of the inter-wars years as the only significant French national security investment, while SDI was only one of many investments. Had SDI been funded, but not stealth technology, carriers, and precision-guided munitions, the Cold War might have turned out differently, and the 1991 Gulf War may also have been less of a definitive victory. The United States was able to go far beyond just investing in SDI because the public would support it.

Second, the United States was able to keep specific strategic defense capabilities secrets. For comparison, Germany knew quite well what the Maginot Line entailed and even built mock fortifications for training.[141] US investments created significant uncertainty in Moscow, not unlike that produced by Project Azorian. Reed controversially argues that strategic uncertainty about what the United States could achieve in SDI and related programs, particularly targeting the high-technology sector that the Farewell dossier revealed to be a Soviet weakness, "was a key contributor to the Soviet collapse."[142] However, regardless of the controversial topic of whether specifically SDI may have contributed to the end of the Cold War,[143] keeping the secrets of stealth technology and other advanced strategic capabilities from the USSR created a strategic situation that increased Soviet incentives for arms control[144] and allowed the United States to negotiate from a position of strength.[145] As Historian John Lewis Gaddis concludes, "What is apparent is that the United States began to challenge the Soviet Union during the first half of the 1980s in a manner unprecedented since the early Cold War. That state soon exhausted itself and expired."[146] The ability to mobilize spending and avoid collapsing into continued skepticism and underinvestment was crucial to that challenge.

In the next section, I re-explore some potential objections from alternative theories. Both liberal theorists and their critics have made important contributions to understanding the rally effect, military spending, and crisis success. Comparing the prediction of oversight theory to these alternatives illustrates what is new in the theory, as well as what to look for in empirical tests of oversight theory in Part IV of the book.

ALTERNATIVES TO OVERSIGHT THEORY

As discussed in Chapters 2 and 4, there are a few perspectives that would expect very different empirical relationships between oversight and public support, spending, and success in crises, respectively. These alternative perspectives are important because they serve both as contrasts and as guides. They are contrasts because the alternative assumptions and predictions about foreign policy and domestic institutions frame the relative contribution of oversight theory. It could be the case that democratic oversight is useful, but only at the margins. Without a point of comparison, we risk mistaking anecdotal molehills for empirical mountains.

Alternative theories also serve as guides because they help us understand what predictions are novel and which duplicate preexisting hypotheses. For example, if two theories of meteorology both successfully predicted rain on a given day, we don't know which theory helped us bring an umbrella to the office. On the other hand, if we have an idea that predicts snow, while another theory predicts sunshine, the subsequent presence of snowmen supports one idea more clearly than the other. If we are going to try to probe the empirical usefulness of retrospective oversight in democracies in relation to alternatives, we need to find predictions that are in competition with those other theories. Here I briefly explicate three additional perspectives that would challenge the relatively sanguine predictions on oversight in the previous section.

Democratic Irrelevantists

One alternative perspective is that of the democratic irrelevantists. Associated with Kenneth Waltz and Michael Desch, this set of ideas suggests that domestic political institutions should have little bearing on international politics. This is because all states seek security and any leader that chooses to wander from the production of public security is likely to be attacked or exploited by other states.

According to this perspective, public opinion gives leaders the room to maneuver that they need, even in democracies.[147] Thus, with domestic politics out of the way, raw power and strategic interaction between unitary states are the true drivers of international relations, not oversight.

If the assumptions and arguments of democratic irrelevantists usefully summarize the fundamentals of international relations,we should not see any systematic difference in support, military spending, or effectiveness when comparing democracies with and without oversight. The public, regardless of domestic institutions, should support the leadership in crises. Likewise, military spending will rise and fall with international threats, not in response to fears of oversight. Finally, since leaders are assumed to be able to generate sufficient public consent at will while maintaining secrecy, domestic oversight institutions should not further enhance these ingredients of success.

Democratic Doubters

An even more extreme alternative is put forward in the research of Schweller and Ripsman.[148] These democracy doubters find democratic institutions and oversight far from irrelevant. Instead, they believe that by allowing the public to withdraw its consent from foreign policy and fail to contribute to foreign policy, democratic freedoms and rights exacerbate rather than solve problems. For example, Downes[149] argues that domestic political concerns in the United States specifically led to the quagmire of Vietnam. Schweller suggests that highly nationalist fascist governments are more efficient war machines than are disarmed or bumbling democracies.[150] This perspective sees the need to centralize power in the executive and reduce accountability, where oversight theory suggests the opposite—that is, that extra-executive constraints, in the form of retrospective transparency and accountability, are necessary in a democracy to raise support, military spending, and foreign policy success.

From the doubters' perspective, national security oversight institutions such as strong freedom of information laws, press freedoms, and legislative committee powers should be at the heart of democratic incompetence. The greater the oversight, the worse the public meddling and problems. National security oversight in democracies should lead to greater partisan polarization, less military spending, and less foreign policy ability as compared to democracies that eschew costly and problematic oversight. This provides a stark contrast for oversight theory.

Liberal Electioneers

Another alternative argument has been put forward by the liberal IR thinkers reviewed in Chapter 2. Here the argument is not that democracies and non-democracies are identical, nor that democracy is dangerous, but instead that oversight is redundant. In the frameworks of Reiter and Stam,[151] Reiter,[151] Schultz,[152] Bueno de Mesquita et al.,[153] and others,[154] regular, free, and fair elections with a large electorate for both the executive and the legislature ensures accountability on both domestic and foreign policy.

While I have argued extensively that national security secrecy obfuscates the information necessary for accountability, one counterargument is that sufficient information exists to solve for any unknowns. National security secrecy may be shallow enough, according to this alternative perspective, to allow accountability without the bells and whistles of oversight. One might think about this as a game of Sudoku or KenKen. There are unknowns when you look at the puzzle, but the information revealed is sufficient to solve for those unknowns.[155] If the marketplace of ideas is already thick across all democracies, such that elections can successfully punish corrupt or incompetent leaders on foreign policy as on domestic issues, then specific retrospective national security oversight institutions are unnecessary. The public is already protected from executive corruption, and we should see that public mobilization, military spending, and foreign policy success do not covary with oversight institutions. This constellation of predictions, when compared to the oversight perspective, is similar to the democratic irrelevantist position but stems from a distinct set of assumptions. Further, liberal electioneers differ markedly from democratic irrelevantists on the relative usefulness of democracy versus other forms of government. However, comparing democracies with non-democracies lies outside the scope of this project.

For the current enterprise, the important contrast is that electioneers would expect that oversight institutions should not increase support and foreign policy ability or lead to the hypothesized changes in militarized spending patterns. If the secrecy dilemma is ignorable, so too would be the suggested solution. On the other hand, if we see evidence that these oversight institutions have some of their hypothesized effects, this increases our confidence that a focus on the secrecy dilemma and potential solutions is useful.[156]

Table 7-1 provides a brief comparison across the different perspectives. The predictions from the retrospective oversight perspective do not duplicate any of

Table 7-1. TABLE OF EMPIRICAL HYPOTHESES FROM OVERSIGHT THEORY AND
THREE OTHER PERSPECTIVES

THE PREDICTED EFFECT OF OVERSIGHT ON:

	Public Support	Spending	Ability
Oversight Theory	Higher	Higher but nonlinear	Highest with oversight
Democracy Irreleventists	No difference	No difference	No difference
Democracy Doubters	Lower with oversight	Lower with oversight	Lowest with oversight
Liberal Electioneers	No difference	No difference with oversight, but lower for democracies	No difference with oversight, but higher for democracies

the alternative perspectives. Further, the tests for support, spending, and ability complement each other and can allow us to learn more about the underlying process of democratic foreign policy. If oversight raises support and spending, but not foreign policy ability, this would be inconsistent with oversight theory, but instead might imply that democracies with oversight are prone to support-ing non-security-enhancing policies. Similarly, if oversight strength leads to an expected linear increase in spending; this might suggest that the mobilizing ef-fect of oversight is greater than the constraining version given the current state of oversight institutions.

CONCLUSION

Together, Chapters 6 and 7 have presented a partial solution to the dilemma of national security secrecy in democracies. I suggest that through transparency, cost deflation, and institutional tools to reveal previously secret information, retrospective oversight is possible. My perspective challenges the liberal assump-tion of automatic and omnipresent transparency, since it seems to redact a good deal of theoretical argumentation, historical information, and practical evidence. On the other hand, just like in renovating a house, it is possible to change the structure of the argument, and even shift load-bearing assumptions (if careful), without the whole edifice falling down. Critics might believe that secrecy and ex-ecutive centralization destabilize liberal arguments. However, to the contrary, I argue that if the capacity for secrecy is incorporated in previous theories of accountability, a more stable liberal theory of democratic foreign policy can emerge when the empirical dust settles.

What are the reasons to pursue this remodeling of liberal theories? First, there is historical precedent. From at least 1766 to the present day, elites and the public have been tinkering with ways to allow executives the necessary freedom of movement on national security while engineering some semblance of accountability. Second, previous work has failed to account for dynamic transparency costs. As a specific secret loses its potency over time, it can be transmitted to the public, framing the possibility of retrospective oversight. Neglecting this tendency has created the false appearance of a zero-sum trade-off between secrecy and accountability. Third, when we turn from the history books to the legislatures in democracies around the world currently, we see, in places, the structures of retrospective accountability and oversight at work. Legislative oversight committees, freedom of information laws, and press freedoms are arrayed unequally around the globe, providing ex post information on national security information to citizens—information that was previously classified.

While the proposed solution is necessarily partial, because costly oversight would not occur if the probability of corruption or incompetence were zero, novel empirical predictions emerge from this theoretical structure. Oversight institutions should decrease partisan skepticism of dramatic foreign policy, help raise money for defense while simultaneously constraining overspending, and ultimately increase a democracy's probability of foreign policy success.

While the cases of France and the United States have illustrated the secrecy dilemma and the proposed solution with moderate oversight, in the next chapters I investigate whether these predictions stand up to the pressure of systematic empirical scrutiny or whether they collapse in the shadow of more convincing explanations. I have suggested that oversight and accountability are not simply values in and of themselves, but practical problem-solving devices for democracy. One does not need to value accountability for its own sake, because it makes the provision of public security and successful policy more likely. It is to the task of testing the usefulness of national security oversight that I turn in the next section.

PART IV

The Evidence

A View of National Security Oversight Institutions

Having traversed the deep necessity of national security secrecy (Part I) and public consent for international security issues (Part II), we emerged with a partial solution to this tension between secrecy and accountability on national security issues (Part III). I argued in the last two chapters that declining transparency costs allow for the possibility of oversight over the use and abuse of executive secrecy, retrospectively. However, it was pointed out that specific institutions were necessary to plug the gaps left in accountability by national security secrecy and that these institutions are likely to be present in some democracies and not others.

We are now in a position to explore whether the variation in retrospective national security oversight institutions explains important parts of how the world works. Specifically, we are looking for clues—empirical fingerprints—that oversight institutions are of practical use, on average, to democracies. The three places we are looking for these fingerprints are in support for an executive during crises, military spending patterns, and the foreign policy ability of democracies as evidenced in overall success in disputes. Do they increase public support for military actions? Do oversight institutions systematically mobilize and subsequently constrain military spending? Finally, do they improve the foreign policy ability of states that maintain them?

Yet, to open these investigations we need to find out which democracies have had robust national security oversight and which have not, over time. One might think at first glance that this information is already available. For example, we have measures that tell us that the United States was more democratic than Brazil in 1990.[1] Further, these systematic measures of aggregated democracy, like the Polity score[2] or the global Freedom House "Freedom in the World" summary scores,[3] provide indicators over several dimensions of democracy, including executive recruitment and constraints, that are then aggregated into an index for each country in a given year. The problem with using these conventional measures of democracy to understand national security oversight is that they fail to account for the specific national security loopholes that exist in democracies and, more important, the retrospective institutions that we are currently interested in evaluating.[4]

Several countries provide extant examples of the divergence between these aggregate democracy scores, focused as they are on measuring domestic-centric electoral competition, versus national-security-specific institutions. In the mid-1990s, Greece received the highest possible democracy score in the Polity dataset. By that measure, Greece was an exemplary democracy in every way and in the same category as the United States and Sweden. However, the Greek Parliament, despite having the power to investigate and call for evidence from the executive on domestic issues, is explicitly limited in its national security oversight powers. Ireland also receives consistently high Polity and Freedom House scores but lacks significant oversight specifically on national security issues. For example, the Dáil has no committee or subcommittee tasked with overseeing the security sector, unlike many democratic counterparts.[5] The defense committee in the German Bundestag meets in secret and out of public view. In fact, even the meeting place for the Bundestag's defense committee is supposed to be a state secret. This is in contrast to procedures for the Food, Agriculture, and Consumer Protection and other domestic-focused committees in Germany. While an active press has a long history in Israel, national security secrets there can be guarded by a military censor who has the power to restrain publication of certain facts.[6] Thus we would be left with our own information deficit if we relied on aggregate, domestically focused democracy measures.

SPII-ING ON DEMOCRACIES

To fill this lacuna in our understanding of democratic accountability on national security policy, I have collected information on the strength of specific extra-executive tools that could be used by the legislature, public, or press to investigate national security policy. As discussed in Chapter 7, I used the research by the Geneva Center for the Democratic Control of the Armed Forces to select salient dimensions of oversight that could be measured systematically across time and space. The data have been coded from 1972 to 2006 for all democracies around the world.[7] These powers are coded from an analysis of a state's specific national security oversight powers in legislative committee tools, freedom of information laws, and civil liberties. I refer to this catalog of information as the Security Policy Information Institutions (SPII) dataset and use it to create an index, supplying a numerical measure from 0 to 1, where higher values represent greater oversight powers. This is the first time that a consistent cross-national and cross-time catalog of this information has been collected.

Matching the discussion above, national security oversight is coded as stronger for states where legislatures have standing national-security-focused committees with the ability to compel testimony (both written and oral), present minority reports, and publicize findings and that have their own staff. Similarly, national security oversight is higher in states with freedom of information laws that include a balance test for information released on national security matters and do not exclude public access with excessive fees or on technicalities.[8] Also, laws that limit the government's ability to censor public and journalistic investigations and publications raise the probability of national security oversight.

In the case of national-security-relevant legislative rules and freedom of information laws, no previously existing systematic data source existed. Therefore, historical research was undertaken to identify, in the period under study, what tools were present across cases in each year. For freedom of information laws, this was aided by the work of Banisar,[9] who includes summaries of national security exemptions of existing and previous freedom of information laws, links to existing laws, and the dates when these laws were passed and implemented.[10] For legislative oversight a series of publications from the Inter-parliamentary Union,[11] in addition to articles on their online Web database PARLINE,[12] were used to code legislative investigation effectiveness on national security. Additional works such as the volumes of Kurian[13] and Doring,[14] as well as country and region-based studies collected at the Geneva Centre for the Democratic Control of the Armed Forces, were also particularly useful. In almost all cases, the websites for particular legislatures included committee lists, rules, and histories that were consulted.[15]

For free speech components of the index, I utilize the preexisting data on civil liberties from Freedom House. These data represent the level of "freedom of expression, assembly, association, education and religion" in a country in a given year.[16] The raw civil liberties score runs from 1 to 7, where 1 represents the greatest freedom of expression. This raw measure is rescaled and reversed to the interval $(0, 1)$ such that 0 represents the lowest category of civil liberties and 1 the highest. This matches the coding of the other indicators. These three indicators are then averaged to create the SPII index. The range of the SPII index is meaningful. Numbers close to 0 mean that the democracy is missing most or all tools for oversight. A score near 1 implies that the state has the full complement of tools that are coded.

Two Examples: Canada and Denmark

To better explain how the national security oversight index was created, I will outline here the steps for two specific examples. For each state, I first collected data on the specific committee oversight powers and freedom of information laws and also used the recoded Freedom House civil liberties scale as described above. With legislative oversight, I recorded whether a state had an elected legislature with a committee tasked with investigating national-security-relevant policies of the executive. This information was recorded as a yes (1) when a standing permanent committee was present, as partial if the legislature did have a select nonpermanent committee (.5), or no (0) when no committee existed. Next, I coded whether this committee could take evidence (1 for yes, 0 for no, .5 for oral but not written, and .25 if additional limits were present), as well as whether the committee could subpoena witnesses (1 for yes, 0 for no, .5 for yes, but limited, and .25 if the limits extended explicitly to the executive). I also included information on whether the committee could issue public reports as well as minority reports (1 for yes, 0 for no in both cases) and whether the committee had their own research staff (1 for yes, .25 for no). I aggregated these indicators into a legislative oversight score by summing the committee presence, evidence, subpoena, and public and minority report scores, dividing by the number of indicators (5), and then multiplying that by the score for staffing. The idea is that each of the powers is additive and of equal weight[17] but relies on staffing to carry out effective oversight.[18]

To code freedom of information laws, I was interested in whether the country had a law guaranteeing access to government information and whether this law had been implemented. If not, this component was coded as a zero for that year. If a freedom of information law had been passed, I checked what the exemption status was for national security information and whether the balance or harm test was used. A balance test law was coded as a 1, a harm test as .75, and a full exemption as .25.[19] Next, I checked for whether fees or an interest test were used to reduce access to information. In either case, the resulting index was lowered by .25. Therefore the freedom of information index was a product of the score for the exemption times the score for limits on access. These two components, each ranging theoretically from 0 to 1, together with the rescaled civil liberties score (explained above), were averaged to produce the national security oversight index.

In 1999, Canada had a standing committee on national defense and a standing committee on Foreign Affairs and international development in the House of Commons (1). These committees had significant oversight powers and could take evidence (1), subpoena witnesses (1), report publicly (1), and issue minority reports (1).[20] The committees also had adequate staffs (1).[21] This aggregates to a legislative score of 1. On freedom of information, Canada began implementation of their freedom of information law (the 1983 Access to Information Act) in 1983. This law included a full exemption (.25) and does not include an interest test or charge fees. Therefore the Canadian freedom of information score is .25 for 1999. Since Freedom House gives Canada a score of 1 out of 7, this is scaled to 1, and it results in a national security oversight index of $(1 + .25 + 1)/3 = .75$.

In comparison, the legislature in Denmark, the Folketinget, has a standing foreign affairs and defense committee that has limits on both the evidence and witnesses that can be called. While public and minority reports are allowed, staffs are limited.[22] This leads to a legislative score of .2.[23] Denmark's freedom of information score is identical to Canada's after the 1985 Access to Public Administration Files Act, and thus is .25. The civil liberties score for Denmark is 1, however, so this leads to a national security oversight index of $(.2 + .25 + 1)/3 = .48$ in 1999.

Note that changes do occur in the data for countries over time. For example, in the Canadian scores, the House of Commons previously had restrictions on committee powers to initiate investigations (.5) and issue public and minority reports (0,0).[24] Further, staffing was reported as a problem in starting investigations.[25] This led to a legislative oversight score in 1986 for Canada of .125, for an aggregate national security oversight score of $(.125 + .25 + 1)/3 = .46$ before 1990.[26] Similarly, South Korea's national security oversight score jumped from .28 to .61 after the passing of the Act on Information Disclosure by Public Agencies (No. 5242).[27] India's national security oversight rose in 1993 after the Lok Sabha strengthened committee evidence-gathering and oversight of the executive in defense and other fields.[28] As we will see below, the aggregate trend in oversight over time is particularly striking.

EXPLORING THE PATTERNS OF OVERSIGHT

Now that we have for the first time a measure of which countries have national security oversight capabilities and which do not, we can begin to explore the over-time, geographic, and institutional patterns of retrospective national security accountability. First, we can track whether the average strength of oversight has increased or not over time. If the development of oversight follows the patterns of other institutional innovations, like competitive elections, we might expect stronger oversight in later years.[29] Alternatively, we could see a pattern of weakening oversight if executives or other elites have found ways to block or cripple oversight over time, or if the institutions have proven to be more costly than beneficial. It will be particularly interesting to look at the specific trends in legislative powers, freedom of information laws, and civil liberties and how they might differ from each other. Geographically, we are interested in whether oversight is clustered within a specific region or dispersed around the globe. We can also look for patterns of diffusion. For example, has oversight tended to spill into neighboring countries over time? Although a systematic analysis of these diffusion patterns is beyond the scope of this chapter, we can compare regional snapshots of national security oversight across time. Finally, we are interested in whether the measure of oversight is not simply a proxy for higher levels of democracy. Thus, we want to ensure that even within democracy categories there is variation in oversight capabilities.

Oversight Over Time

Figure 8.1 presents information on the strength of national security oversight institutions from 1972 to 2006 for strong democracies.[30] The plot first has separate indices so we can track changes over time across average legislative oversight powers (LOP), freedom of information laws (FOI), and press freedoms as measured by civil liberties (CL).[31] Here we see that, starting in 1972, strong civil liberties were relatively well established, but legislative oversight and freedom of information laws were not. Instead, dramatic, though incomplete, changes have taken place in legislatures and in freedom of information laws. The average legislative oversight powers in strong democracies doubled from .2 to .4 from 1972 to 2006, and freedom of information law powers on national security increased by over sixfold over the same time period, from .04 to .27. This mirrors the perspective in other work that oversight of national security has been growing over this period.[32] While there has been a flattening of the trend in legislative national security oversight powers over the last 5 years, the same change is not evident here in civil liberties or freedom of information laws.

Legislative oversight powers began to rise swiftly in the early to mid-1980s and saw a large increase between 1985 and 1988. This occurred mostly in Europe with Belgium, the Netherlands, and Denmark improving their oversight capabilities during this time. Freedom of information laws remained rarer during this time period, but these retrospective powers grew steadily stronger, on average, over time. Two relatively sharp increases in oversight occurred in the early 1980s and late 1990s. Overall, when we look at the average of all these national security oversight powers each year (the thickest line), we see a modest increasing trend, and that trend has been led by changes in freedom of information and legislative oversight powers.[33]

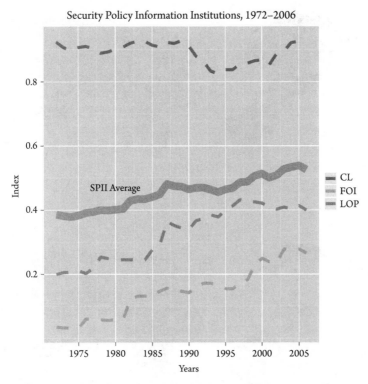

Figure 8.1 Graph of press freedom, freedom of information, and legislative oversight powers and the average Security Policy Information Institutions, 1972–2006.

When we look beyond the averages, we see that the upward push of oversight has not been relegated solely to older democracies. Croatia has among the strongest mechanisms for defense oversight currently, with an expert intelligence committee complementing elected parliamentary defense committee powers and a freedom of information law with limited exemptions. On the other hand, Ireland, Greece, Turkey, and the United Kingdom have had low to middling oversight, particularly in their legislatures. In fact, Ireland and Turkey have been singled out in recent NGO and IGO reports for lacking oversight over national security intelligence.[34]

Oversight Around the Globe

A complementary picture of oversight emerges if we look at snapshots of oversight around the globe for all states. Figure 8.2 presents two such pictures of oversight, one in 1975 and the other in 2005. White represents stronger

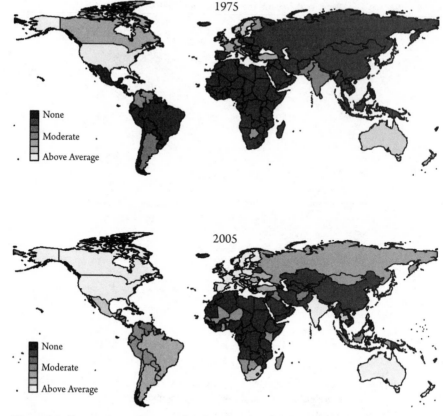

Figure 8.2 Comparison of geographic distribution of oversight institutions in 1975 and 2005. Lighter is greater oversight.

oversight,[35] and varying shades of gray represent middle values, with lighter grays measuring greater oversight. Black illustrates no oversight (less than .01 on the scale).[36]

The 1975 map illustrates the dimness of oversight at the time. While in 1975 the United States had a freedom of information law and some meaningful legislative oversight in the form of national security committees empowered to instigate executive actions and information, most other countries lacked moderate oversight. Next door, even Canada had weaker oversight. Additionally, much of Europe was quite literally in the dark. France, Italy, Spain,[37] and the United Kingdom lacked both effective committee powers on national security policy and freedom of information laws. While Norway and Sweden had maintained, and continue to maintain, some meaningful powers, Finland and Denmark wielded weaker national-security-relevant investigative powers. Other regions from Latin America to Asia also broadly lacked oversight, with important exceptions. For

example, Colombia and Venezuela in Latin America and Botswana in Africa had
some oversight, but mainly related to civil liberties, not freedom of information
laws or parliamentary oversight.

By 2005, large changes could be seen not only in Western and Eastern Europe but also in Latin America, with more limited improvements in Africa, the
Middle East, and Asia. In Europe, stronger oversight had taken hold in the Netherlands, Denmark, Sweden, Norway, Germany, and France, although still with
limitations in the latter two cases. Portugal, Ireland, Turkey, and Greece continued to lag behind. In the Western Hemisphere, Canada, Costa Rica, Chile, Brazil,
and Argentina had increased retrospective national security. There was also some
movement in India and South Africa. While we do see geographic patterns of national security accountability institutions, oversight is not limited to one region.
In fact, from Japan though Israel to the United States, and from Sweden to South
Africa, examples of stronger oversight are arrayed on each continent.

Regional Trends Over Time

Despite the regional disparities in levels of effective retrospective oversight institutions around the world, there is a clear commonality apparent when we take a
different angle in analyzing these measures. Figure 8.3 plots the annual distribution of oversight institutions for each region over time.[38] As in Figure 8.2, darker
colors represent less oversight whereas lighter colors represent more effective

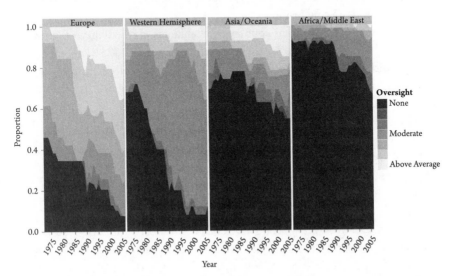

Figure 8.3 Graphs of the regional trends in oversight institutions, 1972–2006. Lighter
is greater oversight.

oversight. In each plot, the gray areas track the middle values of oversight.[39] Thus, in the Western Hemisphere (the first panel in Figure 8.3), the year 1972 saw slightly less than 70% of countries with no oversight. Approximately 5% of countries in the region had strong oversight.[40] By 2006, only 10% of countries in the Western Hemisphere had no oversight and the percentage representing the strongest oversight category had grown to that same percentage. Importantly, each region saw a decline not only in the lowest levels of oversight, but in the weaker oversight institutions (darker colors). Put another way, the lighter colors near the top of each of the regional plots have been growing steadily from 1972 to 2006. There is a consistent trend in increasing oversight across each region.

However, regions still differ as to their relative distributions of oversight. The Asia/Oceania region, in 2006, has a similar distribution of oversight institutions as compared to the Western Hemisphere in the early 1980s. The distribution in the Middle East and Africa subset[41] in 2006 is similar to the Asia/Oceania portfolio of security oversight institutions in the early 1970s. This suggests that security policy institutions, particularly newer innovations like permanent national-security-relevant legislative committees and freedom of information laws, might diffuse locally more readily than across the globe. While there are exceptions to this rule—for example, Australia and Chile[42]—it supports Tobler's first law of geography that "[e]verything is related to everything else, but near things are more related than distant things."[43] It remains to be seen whether countries in Africa and the Middle East will continue on the oversight trajectory of that followed in Europe and the Western Hemisphere. This is a question we will return to in the conclusion.

We can see the constituent country-level changes in oversight in Figure 8.4. This plot[44] arrays countries by their oversight scores in 1975 (left) and 2005 (right), and connects the scores by a line. The lines are colored gray if they are increasing, and they are colored black if they are decreasing or flat. While many countries had dips and rises in between these times, this figure focuses on the overall 30-year trend for each country. Several important facets of national security oversight are apparent from this view. First, the general upward trend in national security oversight is apparent, as there are many more gray lines than black lines. In fact, there are dramatic risers like the Netherlands, New Zealand, Canada, and Israel.[45] India is a particularly interesting case. It moved from having the least amount of national security oversight in 1975 of all democracies,[46] due to anemic legislative oversight and a lack of a freedom of information law and restrictions on the press, to a score in the top half of democracies in 2005, with the passing of the 2003 Freedom of Information Law as well as strengthened oversight in 1993. In fact, while India had borrowed the United Kingdom's Official

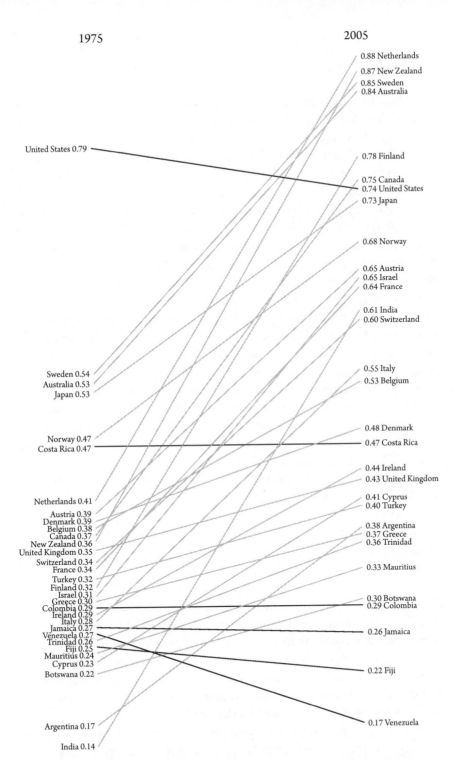

Figure 8.4 A slopegraph of the changes in national security oversight from 1975 to 2005 in specific countries, with SPII scores next to the country names. Countries with identical or very close values moved upward or downward to improve readability.

Secrets Act at independence, by 2005 it had leapfrogged London in national security oversight.

Second, the plot places the US increases in oversight in the mid-1970s in context. Oversight in Washington was increased from the low levels of other democracies to moderate/above-average levels, as discussed in Chapter 7. However, there was significant room for improvement. By 2005, other countries had stronger oversight institutions. Using the security policy information institution index, six countries (the Netherlands, New Zealand, Sweden, Australia, Finland, and Canada) had more effective national security oversight as compared to the United States by 2005. While some of this is caused by the illumination of these countries' oversight laws, the United States' score also dropped slightly with the 2002 narrowing of who can utilize the freedom of information statutes in the United States.[47]

Third, along with the United States, there are a few countries that have not been propelled toward greater oversight. Costa Rica, which had the highest oversight score in Central and Latin America in 1975, and Colombia did not improve over the 30 years.[48] Jamaica, Fiji, and Venezuela each had less oversight in 2005 than in 1975. Venezuela had the largest drop in the sample over this period of time due to restrictions on civil liberties and press freedoms.

The chart also shows several countries that, while improving their oversight, have not kept pace with other countries. These include Denmark, which lags behind other Scandinavian countries, the United Kingdom,[49] Greece, Turkey, and Ireland.[50] While the trend is generally upward as we can see from the map and regional plots, there is a great deal of democratic diversity when it comes to national security oversight powers.

OVERSIGHT AND LEVELS OF DEMOCRACY

The relationship between the more general notion of democracy and the national security oversight institutions index is also of interest. Primarily, we want to be sure that there is variation in national security oversight and that it does not simply re-create the democratic wheel. I utilize the Polity score to measure democracy, which takes into account constraints on the executive, regulation of participation, and the openness and competitiveness of executive recruitment. I define democracies as those countries that score a 6 or above on the aggregate Polity 2 scale,[51] which is a summary measure across these various facets of democracy. The pairwise correlation between the oversight strength index (SPII) and the Polity democracy score for democracies is only .57. This is meaningful, but by no means suggestive that the two measures are identical.

In fact, there is considerable variation within each category of democracy. The Polity measure only takes on integer values 6 to 10. Table 8-1 shows how oversight scores are arrayed within and across each specific level of democracy, as measured by the Polity project, from 6 to 10. The second column provides the name and oversight score for a representative low, middle, and high country based on the SPII scores in 2006. The third column provides a graph of the density of the oversight score for all the countries and includes all years where data are available, 1972 to 2006, that have a specific polity score (e.g., 6 in the first row). The height of the shaded area at a specific horizontal coordinate in the density plots represents how frequent specific values of oversight (on the x-axis) are within this category of Polity. The higher the colored area, the more frequent those values of oversight within that level of democracy. For example, we can see in the first row that while Burundi, Malawi, and Russia each had a score of 6 according to Polity in 2006, they had different SPII scores, with Russia's almost three times that of Burundi. Further, we can see from the density plot in the top row that while most of the SPII scores are toward the low end, there are a few that creep to the middle of the scale. The next three rows down tell a similar story. While the distribution of oversight creeps to the right as we step down the rows (and become more democratic), the overlap between the oversight scores is substantial. While Ukraine, for example, has a democracy score two points lower than that of Comoros, it was twice the oversight index. We further see, as represented by the spreading out of the shaded portions of the distributions, that the spread of oversight increases as we move to more democratic levels (9 and 10). The final row aggregates the densities for each of the previous rows, so the overlap between oversight scores across levels of democracy can be compared. Here we see that while the central tendency of oversight grows as democracy increases, there are many exceptions to the rule. In fact, the variance in oversight grows also. Thus, far from being redundant, this measure of security policy information institutions contains information that is not encoded in the underlying aggregated democracy measure for these cases.

CONCLUSION

With this information in hand, we can now move on to answering the question: Do these oversight institutions, on average, help or hinder foreign policy for democracies on the dimensions of support, spending, and foreign policy ability? Moving forward there are several hypotheses we will be investigating. First, did increases in national security oversight institutions raise support for a leader when they became involved in international crises, on average? Second, comparing democracies from around the world, does increasing oversight from low to

Table 8-1. TABLE OF POLITY DEMOCRACY SCORE (≥ 6) AND THE SECURITY POLICY INFORMATION INSTITUTIONS (SPII) INDEX[a]

Polity Score	Examples in 2006 (SPII) High, Middle, Low	Distribution of Oversight Score
6	Burundi (.11), Malawi (.22), Russia (.31)	
7	Lebanon (.17), Ukraine (.34), Turkey (.41)	
8	Senegal (.22), Brazil (.36), South Korea (.61)	
9	Comoros (.17), Estonia (.46), Croatia (.72)	
10	Mongolia (.28), Poland (.63), Netherlands (.88)	
All		

[a] The first column gives the Polity score, the second column gives examples of SPII scores for each democracy score, and the final column presents the density of the SPII scores conditional on each democracy score. The final row illustrates the overlap between the densities.

moderate levels increase the ability of an executive to raise money for military spending, as expected? As argued earlier, these first two questions are related to the mobilizing effect of retrospective oversight. If the public know that a leader can get away with less, but nonzero, waste and corruption, they are more likely to support action and spending. Third, I expect that moving to highly effective oversight, with strong freedom of information laws, press freedoms, or legislative powers, will begin to decrease military spending as compared to states with moderate oversight. This occurs because as oversight grows stronger, more and more corruption is pushed out of the procurement process. Finally, we will look at whether the ability to hold private information while maintaing public consent pays off during international crises. Do democracies with oversight win more of their conflicts as compared to democracies that lack oversight? In the next chapter, we turn to uncovering the empirical purchase of national security oversight for democracy.

Revealing Evidence: Support, Spending, and Success

The next sections provide three sets of tests to probe whether facts on the ground are consistent with the new predictions from retrospective oversight theory. The first examination explores whether oversight institutions—such as freedom of information laws, press freedoms, and civil liberties—together increase public support for an executive's foreign policy during crises, as argued. This is accomplished by analyzing whether the rally-'round-the-flag effect—the public's proclivity to increase its support for an executive—varies with the probability of retrospective oversight. Specifically, we can compare the size of the rally effect, on average, in the United States and France both before and after changes in security policy information institutions, as well as comparing those changes to the rally effect in the United Kingdom, where no significant changes have taken place according to these measures. We should find that both France and the United States have larger public rallies after they reinforce oversight, in 1978 and 1974, respectively, and that the rally in the United Kingdom remains relatively unchanged after a superficial alternation in parliamentary committee powers in 1979, which did not increase retrospective national security oversight. While previous research has treated the rally as either consistently reflexive or purely a product of the size of the conflict, we will see that this new cross-time and cross-national comparison lends considerable support to the mobilizing effect of oversight.

The second set of tests builds on the first. While public opinion is a useful measure of the mobilization of opinion, it does not tell us about the price the public is paying for whatever national security they are receiving. This is important because oversight is expected not only to mobilize the public, but also to constrain executive corruption, as explained in Chapters 6 and 7. The price paid in each country, in terms of military spending, is one place where we should be able to observe both the mobilizing and constraining effects. Without any hope of oversight, military spending in democracies is likely to be very low, on average, as a proportion of GDP. Even a leader that partially reveals information in an attempt to increase support for more spending can be faulted for what remains classified. The public have reason to doubt that they are going to get a worthwhile return for each dollar they invest. Lower benefits and higher costs might be covered up.

However, as oversight increases, the public become more sure that big-ticket corruption is going to be retrospectively exposed and punished and thus is less likely to happen. This means that they are willing to support more military spending—even though it will involve overspending on their part with the surplus going to a leader's private goals. Support is now acceptable to the public because it is better than underspending in these circumstances. Thus, we should see oversight institutions not only mobilizing public support, as in the previous hypothesis, but also increasing military spending as we move from low to middle levels of oversight. This occurs because the mobilizing effect of oversight is stronger than the constraining effect at low initial values of oversight.

As oversight gets stronger, there is less and less room for private-interest spending in the military budget without it being retrospectively revealed. This means that as we move from middling to strong oversight, we should see military spending decline as a proportion of GDP. This is because the increased oversight is squeezing out some of the excess dollars that an executive would have charged the public for security but is unable to, given the increasing probability of being caught and punished. Indeed, while previous research has suggested that democracies have greater constraints on military spending than dictatorships, this ignored the diversity in military spending across democracies.

From 1972 to 2006, there is consistent evidence that national security oversight has an asymmetric inverted U-shaped relationship with the defense burden in a country. Increasing oversight from low levels has the net effect of mobilizing more spending, allowing more security spending, but also more overspending on nonsecurity goods for the executive. As oversight continues to grow toward stronger and more accurate oversight, the spending on security remains, but the excess costs to the public of abuses and non-security-enhancing policies decrease. This is evidence for the hypothesized constraining effect. It also appears that the constraining effect may be weaker than the mobilizing effect of oversight institutions.

Finally, the third set of investigations offers a view of the payoff for national security oversight. I have argued that both national security secrecy and retrospective accountability are important components of foreign policy effectiveness of democracies. Secrecy allows states to anticipate, deceive, and suppress the capabilities of a potential rival. Yet, these gains disappear in the haze of the secrecy dilemma if sufficient public consent is not present. Retrospective accountability for executive action allows the public to trust that secrecy is being used, on balance, for public ends: supporting the mobilization of resources to execute a policy. In this section I explore whether, indeed, democracies that maintain national security oversight institutions have higher foreign policy abilities, ceteris paribus, as compared to democracies that lack these institutions. I show that, indeed, not only do they win more of their disputes, but they also are able to kill greater numbers of enemy combatants during disputes. This final set of tests compares the foreign policy behavior of these democracies to that of autocracies.

In none of these investigations do I assume that oversight is the only driving force behind support, spending, or success. But, the combined evidence suggests that oversight institutions and retrospective accountability not only support the values that are synonymous with democracy, including liberties and the availability of information, but also are practical innovations that improve foreign policy. Retrospective oversight over national security policy is not a drag on foreign policy, because it fuels public support, increases spending relative to low levels of oversight, and produces greater effectiveness.

SUPPORT

One of the central debates in international relations dissects what role the public plays in foreign policy and world politics. In fact, it is in observing the patterns in public reactions to executive actions that we should be able to begin to explore whether the facts of international politics are consistent with the theory of retrospective oversight offered here. Contemporary liberal theories of international politics assume that the public has continual access to foreign policy information and uses that information to actively constrain overzealous foreign policy in democracies.[1] Theoretical models building on this public accountability assumption suggest that where leaders face institutional checks and balances from effective legislatures and regular elections, foreign policy action is likely to be more effective at communicating intentions.[2] For example, the fact that the public was perceived to be both unwilling to endure Soviet missiles in Cuba and likely to electorally punish any leader that ignored their preferences increased the credibility of US threats and the effectiveness of the Cuban blockade.[3]

However, as was summarized in Chapter 3, realist critics argue that the empirical record is not uniformly consistent with the public accountability assumption. Specifically, critics have pointed to an exposed chink in the liberal argument. These scholars suggest that the systematic spikes in public approval for a leader during international conflicts—known as the rally-'round-the-flag effect[4]—imply that public preferences are at best functionally irrelevant to the efficient formulation of international policies and at worst a wayward guide to foreign policy. Further, the dominant theoretical models of the rally effect, relying as they do on social–psychological principals, treat public opinion as reflexive. This provides further support for these realist claims of an emotional, rather than a rational, public.[5] Since, the argument goes, the public automatically rallies to the side of a leader in an international crisis, there is no reason to expect leaders to be held accountable for their policies or for those leaders to pander to citizens' preferences.[6] In this view, US decisions during the Cuban Missile Crisis were not limited by public preferences, since the public was going to reflexively rally in response to the increased Soviet threat anyway. These emotional reactions highlight the public's lack of knowledge and interest in the realities of world politics.[7] As a result, citizen preferences are hypothesized to be poor guides to rational and effective policy. Morgenthau summarizes the argument when he states that "good foreign policy cannot from the outset count upon the support of a public opinion whose preferences are emotional rather than rational."[8] Instead, national executives should lead, rather than follow, these emotional and malleable public preferences. To critics of liberal IR theories, deferring to the public on questions of international relations and foreign policy would be like letting the sheep herd the shepherds.

There are several reasons that we need to take this particular criticism of the public's role in foreign policy seriously. First, given the extreme information asymmetries that exist on national security issues, the opportunity for an elite-driven theory of action has some attraction. More substantively, however, the theory considered here relies upon the public to play a role in punishing leaders if they are caught—and that is in many places a big if—using national security tools toward nonpublic goals. A reflexive public that supported a leader by default when national security crises were announced, regardless of underlying motives, would stop accountability before it started. If the public can be easily blindly led by elites, then they can be misled.[9]

On the other hand, while evidence of the public supporting a leader may at first glance appear to undercut the possibility of public accountability on national security policy, upon further scrutiny the opposite is true. It may be the case, and in this chapter I reveal that the historical record is consistent with this idea, that the prospects of retrospective accountability foster the prospects for increased immediate support during an international conflict.

Hypotheses: From Oversight to Public Support

As we have seen in the preceding chapters, a leader's foreign policy decisions are calculated within a dynamic context of both secrecy and, in some places, retrospective oversight. Even in democratic states like the United States and France, these institutions include mechanisms for the centralization and concentration of foreign policy information in the executive. Classification is carried out through legal confidentiality clauses, penalties for endangering the nation (treason), and executive privilege. It has been generally acknowledged that information centralization and concentration mechanisms are executive powers necessary for implementing and formulating consistent and effective foreign policy. Quite simply, policies that involve anticipation, deception, and capability suppression require the executive to have private information.[10]

At the same time, institutions that protect and accelerate post hoc information revelation and contingent leadership punishment help to create the atmosphere in which rallying is a rational response to foreign policy action. When the public is weighing its reaction to an executive's foreign policy initiatives or statements, it takes into account the likely motives of the leadership. If the current crisis provides the leadership with an institutionally constituted opportunity to politically manipulate foreign policy for private gain, through information control, and no counterbalancing incentive to avoid abuses of foreign policy power exists, the public is likely to be skeptical of foreign policy moves. This tendency will vary from crisis to crisis based on the prior beliefs of members of the public, but without retrospective oversight, all else being equal, there is little reason to decrease one's skepticism of a leader during a crisis. On the other hand, situations that provide an active disincentive to mislead the public—in the form of ex post revelation and punishment for nonsecurity motives—increase the probability of a public rally, even in the face of limited contemporaneous information. The post hoc revelation of abuses of power and opportunity to punish any abuses, with both the public and the leadership's common knowledge, supplies just such an incentive. For example, in 1998, when President Clinton ordered the bombing of Al Qaeda sites while being investigated during the Lewinsky scandal, there was significant skepticism. Yet, when New York Times journalist Frank Bruni interviewed people about whether they believed the President would divert attention from the scandal and get away from it, thus mirroring the movie Wag the Dog that had recently been released, they pushed back. Several even suggested that while they did not trust the President, he would have to be a "dimwit."

Republican Representative Bob Ney went so far as to say, "I don't think the President would be foolish enough to do a 'Wag the Dog.' "[11]

In short, some institutional arrangements and situations lend themselves to elites credibly signaling foreign policy needs to the public because leaders are vulnerable to punishment if they abuse their temporary informational advantage. Where Reagan suggested the mantra "trust but verify," retrospective oversight follows a similar principal: the likelier the verification, the greater the trust. This variation leads to several potentially observable patterns in rally behavior in democracies. Most important, we should see that, on average, a country that meaningfully increases its foreign policy oversight should garner a larger rally effect after the increase in oversight, as compared to before. Countries that have low oversight and remain so may see sporadic rallies when the situation appears unlikely to be privately motivated (e.g., when they are attacked[12]). Yet on average, little or no increase in support is likely, since the leader has little institutional means to signal the sincerity of his or her actions.

Alternative Explanations

The expectation that greater national security oversight will, on average, increase public support for military action and dramatic foreign policy moves by a leader is in contrast to several alternative viewpoints. Specifically, those that believe that domestic institutions such as freedom of information laws, legislative committee structures, and press freedoms are irrelevant would predict that there should be no systematic difference in public support for a leader after a change

Table 9-1. TABLE OF EMPIRICAL HYPOTHESES FROM OVERSIGHT THEORY AND THREE OTHER PERSPECTIVES

THE PREDICTED EFFECT OF OVERSIGHT ON:

	Public Support	Spending	Ability
Oversight Theory	Higher	Higher but nonlinear	Highest with oversight
Democracy Irrelevantists	No difference	No difference	No difference
Democracy Doubters	Lower with oversight	Lower with oversight	Lowest with oversight
Liberal Electioneers	No difference	No difference with oversight, but lower for democracies	No difference with oversight, but higher for democracies

in domestic retrospective constraints. On this score, even some liberals would agree. For example, it would be reasonable to argue that, until proven otherwise, domestic elections are enough to instill accountability. Thus, specific oversight institutions should not be important, since democracy is enough. Finally, democracy doubters, who fret about the foreign policy viability of accountable systems where the uninformed public has a say in international relations decisions, would aver that the creation of greater opportunities for the public to interfere with elite-led policies causes support to erode over time. In this view, opposition will deadlock policy as the public's tantrums for accountability delay the necessary secrecy, speed, and consideration for success. These predictions are compared in the first column of Table 9-1.

RESEARCH DESIGN

In order to analyze the variation in the rally, I exploit the fact that we have public opinion data on support for leaders as crises arise in France, the United States, and the United Kingdom. Further, in two of these cases we have changes in national security oversight institutions. Figure 9.1 plots the changes for France, the United States, and the United Kingdom from 1960 to 2005. The solid red line is the overall security policy information institutions score (which ranges from 0 to 1), while the dashed lines are the subcomponents, as explained in the previous chapter: civil liberties (CL), freedom of information laws (FOI), and legislative oversight powers (LOP). In 1978 France implemented a new freedom of information law that includes meaningful oversight powers, including a harm-test exemption with no limiting interest test or prohibitive

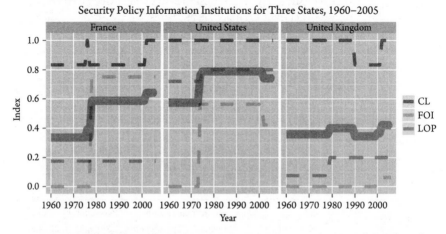

Figure 9.1 Security policy information institutions in France, the United States, and the United Kingdom, 1960–2005.

fees. In the United States, an early and ineffective 1966 Freedom of Information Act, which did not cover national security information, was significantly strengthened in 1974. Also in 1975 the Church and Pike Committees were set up; these eventually evolved into permanent committees. This led to jumps in national security oversight (thick gray line) in these two countries that can be seen in Figure 9.1. In contrast, during this time, the United Kingdom did not institute any meaningful oversight. While select committees were given some increased powers in 1979, including the ability to issue public reports and interview witnesses, they remained very weak—they did not have adequate staff or allow for minority reports and continued to have significant restrictions on the types of evidence and information the committees had access to. Later, the implementation of the 1999 Freedom of Information Act in the United Kingdom was delayed and marred by a strong exemption for national security information.

Another non-change in the United Kingdom, from the perspective of extra-executive oversight and national security accountability, is the 1994 creation of the Intelligence and Security Committee. The change did not register on the legislative index and thus the security policy information index for very good reasons. First, the committee is not legislative/parliamentary. It is a committee that is set up to report to the prime minister and cannot divulge information without the prime minister's approval. In fact, no lines of communication exist between the committee and the legislature save going through the prime minister. Second, the committee lacks the ability to collect some specific forms of evidence and has a limited remit on collecting information from the Ministry of Defense.[13] We can also check, below, whether this change had a substantive impact on raising public support during crises or not.

This information allows us to test whether in France and the United States the public was more likely to support the executive after the increases in national security oversight, as compared to before. Further, the UK case can act as a control or placebo group. By the logic of oversight theory, because the 1979 legislative reorganization did little to enhance national security accountability, it should have little effect across the post-1979 time period. This is important, because a skeptical reader might argue that across all democracies the rally effect is larger in the 1980s than in the 1960s and 1970s. Therefore showing that a greater percentage of the public increased their support for a leader after these changes, as compared to before, would only be measuring a preexisting tendency. If no measurable change occurs in the United Kingdom, this is less likely to be a problem. Additionally, we can specifically analyze the changes in public support during crises over time in each case. It might be the case that the rally effect begins to increase before the imposition of a new national security oversight regime. If that were the case, it would be less plausible to attribute the changes to the new institutional rules.

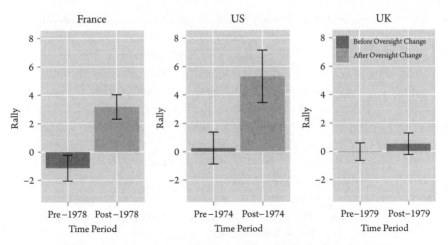

Figure 9.2 The average change in public support for a leader before changes in oversight laws (darker) and after (lighter). The black bars represent two standard errors around the mean. The UK is the control case with no change in oversight during this time.

Figure 9.2 presents the average rally effect for each country before (darker) and after (lighter) their respective jumps in oversight (1974 in the United States and 1978 in France). The y-axis is the change in public approval after a crisis begins, compared to where it was prior to the crisis.[14] In the United Kingdom, the change is assumed to be in 1979; however, this is not hypothesized to be a meaningful increase in oversight, so both bars are dark to illustrate the contrast with the other states. The black bars represent the 90% confidence intervals for the expected rally effects within the period. We can see that as expected, both France and the United States have a larger average rally effect after their national security oversight powers increase. Additionally, these changes are highly unlikely to be a product of chance[15]; In the United Kingdom, while the average rally did increase marginally in the post-1979 time period, this change could have very easily happened by chance.[16] Additionally, even this insubstantial increase is a function of the Falklands War, where Argentina attacked territory claimed by the United Kingdom. So while it is possible that some of the increase in the rally effect pre–post SPII change in France and the United States is not explained by institutional changes, much of it is still consistent with the mobilizing benefits of oversight.

The pre–post analysis in Figure 9.2 is useful, but since we are simply grouping changes in presidential approval during a crisis by period, a great deal of nuance could be missed. Specifically, it could be the case that the increase in the rally effects in France and the United States could have started before the institutional changes were implemented. This would undercut the evidence. To look at this, I plot a smoothed representation of the trends in the rally effect in each country over time in Figure 9.3. The vertical lines represent the changes, the dark curve

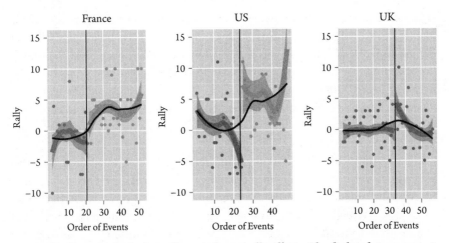

Figure 9.3 **Loess smooth plots of pre- and post-rally effects. The darker dots represent rallies before the change in oversight laws, the lighter dots after. The darker and lighter lines respectively represent the Loess smooth plots fit only to the period before or after the changes. The thin black lines are Loess smooth plots fit to the whole data for each country.**

illustrates the trend of the rally effect for pre-change crises, and the lighter curve illustrates the smoothed trend after the changes. Again, the United Kingdom is colored darker across the 1979 divide. Specifically the dark and light curves, along with their confidence intervals (which are similarly shaded), only fit the data pre and post. The thin black line presents the trend across all of the rally events ignoring the institutional change.[17] In France we see that the overall trend was for the rally effect to decline prior to the 1978 changes. The public then tended to respond more favorably to the crisis, increasing their support, after 1978. A similar, but more dramatic, pattern is illustrated in the United States.[18] The black line shows that oversight was generally decreasing in the United States prior to the 1974 changes in oversight strength, but then increased. The difference between the prior trend (darker) and the posterior trend (lighter) illustrates that there is little evidence that the rally event increase predated the 1974 institutional changes. For comparison, in the United Kingdom, we see in the black line little to no effect for the 1979 intervention. While there is a slight rise just after 1979, this is the Falklands War pulling the average up temporarily before it falls back down to pre-1979 levels.

While cross-national differences are more tenuous—for example, comparing the size of the rally effect in the United States versus that in the United Kingdom—the differential sizes are in the direction of those expected when looking at the underlying oversight institutions. While the United States has the strongest oversight institutions, it has the largest rally, with France in the middle and the United Kingdom last, when looking at the post-change periods.[19]

The tables of the regression results and several alternative analyses with these data are provided in the data analysis appendix. There I also investigate whether signals from the United Nations, as argued by Chapman and Reiter,[20] continue to be a predictor of rally behavior (they do) and whether they cancel out the effect of oversight institutions (they do not). Finally, I test whether bipartisan signals reduce the evidence for the relationship between oversight and support. The results are consistent with the findings presented here, and in fact are more dramatic in several instances.

The results strongly support the relationship between retrospective oversight—with its ability to constrain executive corruption of foreign policy—and public mobilization and support, which can be undercut due to secrecy and mistrust. Increasing oversight raises the support that a leader receives during intense international crises. We saw evidence of this in the United States and France and were able to compare it to the UK case where no change in the rally effect was expected, given the superficial changes in oversight institutions.[21]

SPENDING

Next, it would be useful to empirically illuminate evidence not only of the mobilization effect of national security oversight, but also of the constraints placed on an executive. The preceding evidence on the rally effect assumed that more accurate retrospective verification of executive motives would constrain leaders from greater malfeasance. To dig deeper into the usefulness of national security oversight, we can turn to the problem of military spending in democracies. Fordham and Walker argue that liberal theory suggests that democracies will spend less on the military as compared to non-democracies, because the public, in footing the bill for defense, will not want to pay for expensive policies and in particular for non-security-generating programs.[22] Indeed, they find useful evidence that democracies do spend less than autocracies. Figure 9.4 illustrates this fact, where the distribution of spending as a proportion of GDP (logged) is pushed toward higher values for full autocracies (darker) as compared to democracies (lighter).[23]

Fordham and Walker's well-crafted research opens a related question for the present study. They specifically and consciously left unanswered the question of whether the difference in public spending was a positive or negative development for these democracies. For example, they explicitly do not take a stand as to whether democracies or autocracies are the ones that are over- or under-spending on defense on average. This gets to the heart of many critiques of democratic facilities for national security, as we had discussed in Chapter 3. If democracies cannot raise the necessary funds to defend themselves, then they

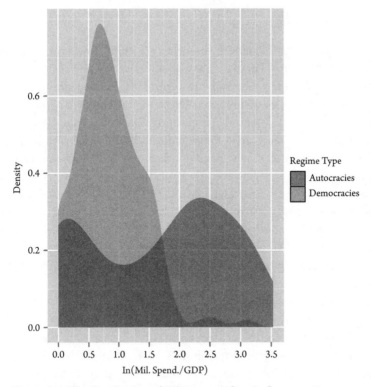

Figure 9.4 The distribution of military spending in democracies (lighter) and autocracies (darker).

are unlikely to be effective on the international stage. On the other hand, if autocracies are overspending on defense, which seems most likely given the lack of constraints on executives in those places and their ability to use repression to mobilize funds, then democracies may be spending appropriately.

Even in this rosier scenario, where spending is not uniformly deficient in democracies, there is more to the problem. In the data that Fordham and Walker utilize in their analysis, there is extreme variation across spending levels in democracies. We can see this here in Figure 9.4. While this may be simply a result of tough or peaceful neighborhoods, it might also suggest that some democracies still might be underspending on defense, with others overspending. We will need to look beyond the binary democracy/non-democracy distinction to make progress on this question.

Additionally, the work of Fordham and Walker hints at where to look for evidence of constraints on the executive misuse of national security policy even in democracies. If the autocratic leader's lack of constraints shows up in the defense burden for which the public (over)pays, then the hypothesized mechanisms may be evident, but less dramatically within democracies across distinct levels of national security oversight.

Hypotheses: From Oversight to (Not) Overspending

To see this, we can mathematically model a very simple world that connects the strength (or lack thereof) of oversight with military spending. I will give a verbal outline here, and the formal proofs are available in the Appendix. Imagine that there are only two types of military budgets: high spending, as a percentage of the total economy in a state, and low spending. The public would like to support high spending when necessary—for example, to deter or deal with an oncoming crisis—but otherwise want low spending when times are more quiescent. Given national security secrecy, however, the executive is at an informational advantage and thus knows whether high spending or low spending is called for. The executive, seeing this information, gets to make an offer to the public, of either a high or a low military budget, and the public can either support or oppose that budget. There is also an overseer, a legislative oversight committee, that can decide to retrospectively investigate the spending decisions of a leader, if they are supported.

The incentives are such that an executive, if he believes the public will support a high military budget, will offer that budget, even if he knows, secretly, that security can be had for the low-budget cost. This is because the leader is able to pocket the surplus nonsecurity spending. The executive always has an incentive to reach for the high military budget, if it will be supported. At the same time, the executive would like to avoid having his budget voted down, as this wastes time and resources and has domestic reputational costs.

Additionally, the public has some skin in the game. Investing in security at the optimal level—high when it is a crisis, low when it is not—provides security. Underinvesting in security, by supporting a low budget when a crisis is brewing, comes with a cost. The public will suffer this insecurity cost in the form of economic hardship as uncertainty increases, high costs later, direct military defeat, or loss of an international stake that they value. This stake could be territory or some other foreign policy good. Overinvesting in security, by supporting a high budget when there is no crisis, is simply a waste of resources for the public, since they do not benefit from the excess paid for security.

The question then becomes, How can the public be confident that when a leader offers a high military budget, it is worth paying? It turns out that without oversight, this is not possible. Since the executive has an incentive to proffer a high military budget regardless of the state of the world (crisis or no crisis), seeing a high military budget does not provide the public with any information on the underlying threat level. This means that in times of peace, when the public is unlikely to have a strong belief that a crisis is coming and high spending is necessary, the leader knows that high spending will not be supported. Further, from the executive's point of view, this lack of support for high spending does not depend on the secret information he has about the actual threat level. Thus, lacking oversight, we expect spending to be low in times without obvious crisis and immediate crisis.[24]

However, if we add moderate amounts of oversight to the mix, we generate different equilibrium behavior. When freedom of information laws lower the barrier to accessing past national security facts and committees have adequate staffs and powers, the overseers have a greater incentive and ability to probe and publicize budgets that might include excess spending. This means that an executive contemplating promoting overspending might be deterred. Even more important, the public now sees that an executive has a disincentive to offer higher spending when it is not public-justified. This means that in offering a higher proposed budget, a leader is bearing a potential cost—being caught, if it is overspending. This increases the public's belief that the spending is necessary.[25] Now the paradox of perfect oversight is still operable. The legislature/overseers does/do not always investigate high spending; they play a mixed strategy of sometimes overseeing and other times not. In response, the executive always offers high spending when it is necessary, but this is mixed in with some overspending and some appropriate low spending. In fact, the executive now has the ability to create a portfolio of military spending over time[26] that threads the needle between maximizing the overspending he or she can get away with while still being worth the cost of being caught with some positive probability and not triggering the public to withdraw their support from high spending because the corruption is too great. With moderate oversight the public is mobilized, and thus the executive is able to collect extra dollars, but not so many as to trigger opposition. This spending level will be more than optimal because a high budget is offered with probability 1 when it is needed by the public, but also in times when it is not needed.[27] This means that moving from low to moderate oversight levels increases the expected military spending in a state from lower than adequate levels to higher than adequate levels. So far, this is consistent with the mobilization effect of oversight, stemming from the underlying threat of revealing corruption.

Interestingly, as we increase oversight further, we can finally see the constraining effect of oversight come to the forefront empirically. At moderate, but still low, levels of oversight, leaders do not have too much to fear from oversight. They can still get away with quite a bit of overspending, pocketing the excess. However, if we increase the powers of retrospective oversight further—moving from a harm test to a balance test, for example, on freedom of information law exemptions or increasing the types of evidence a legislative committee is allowed to require as part of an investigation—the incentives for the executive are altered for a second time. Now, compared to the case of moderate oversight, overspending is more likely to be revealed and punished. This means that the executive must scale back corruption; however, it never disappears, since perfect oversight is a paradox.

Putting this story together suggests a nonlinear relationship between military spending and national security oversight strength during times of peace. Moving from low to moderate levels of oversight is predicted to increase spending, as the public is more confident that high spending is not a waste. In fact, this spending should be higher than would be optimal if the exigencies of secrecy were not present. As we move toward even more effective oversight, the public remains mobilized to support the military budget, but the leader now is increasingly forced to pare back excess spending, lowering the expected military budget closer to efficient spending (high when a crisis, low when not).

Alternative Theories

In addition, we need to compare several relevant alternative theories alongside oversight to weight their relative explanatory powers. These predictions are summarized in Table 9-2, specifically along the gray central column. The first, and simplest, is that democracy, oversight mechanisms, and other domestic institutions are simply window dressing and that the real power politics of international relations is played necessarily the same way by all leaders. If this were the case, then we would not see systematic differences between either (a) autocracies and democracies or (b) democracies with and without oversight. Any difference that did result would be a product of international circumstances.

The second relevant theory, from the democracy doubters, is related to the insights of neoclassical realism: that national security oversight, to the extent that it exists in a country, acts as an impractical check on foreign policy. This implies that national security oversight does not have a mobilizing effect, but only limits

Table 9-2. TABLE OF EMPIRICAL HYPOTHESES FROM OVERSIGHT THEORY AND THREE OTHER PERSPECTIVES

THE PREDICTED EFFECT OF OVERSIGHT ON:

	Public Support	Spending	Ability
Oversight Theory	Higher	Higher but nonlinear	Highest with oversight
Democracy Irreleventists	No difference	No difference	No difference
Democracy Doubters	Lower with oversight	Lower with oversight	Lowest with oversight
Liberal Electioneers	No difference	No difference with oversight, but lower for democracies	No difference with oversight, but higher for democracies

necessary military spending. We can analyze this hypothesis by checking for two empirical fingerprints. First, there should be a monotonic and declining relationship between oversight and military spending, such that as we increase oversight, spending declines. Additionally, countries with high oversight should have anemic military spending. Thus the predicted level of spending and the trend are important, for comparison. While defining in any given country at a specific time what the optimal spending level for that country would be is challenging, given national security secrecy, on average, we have several guidelines that will help us compare.

Third, liberal electioneers argue that conventional notions of democracy, taking the form of competitive elections, are sufficient to constrain executives and reduce military spending. If this were the case, then specific oversight institutions such as those measured by the SPII index would not add much to our understanding of military spending patterns around the world. We can analyze this idea by measuring the strength of electoral competition—a combination of party regulations, executive recruitment, and executive constraints on non-national security matters—and checking whether military spending varies with democracy as opposed to oversight. Thus, the specific expectation would be that democracy itself would be negatively correlated with military spending, as shown by Fordham and Walker, but that oversight would have no meaningful relationship with spending after we accounted for the underlying effect of democracy.

These predictions are in contrast to the hypotheses drawn for analyzing national security oversight, specifically that there will be an inverted and reversed J-shaped relationship between oversight and spending, where increasing low levels of oversight mobilize more spending, but increasing moderate to high levels of oversight decreases spending. Additionally, the lowest-spending democracies should be the states that lack meaningful oversight, the highest-spending ones should be in the countries that have moderate levels of oversight, and those states with the strongest oversight should have adequate, although not excessive, spending levels.

Research Design

To test these predictions, I have a measure of a country's military burden, calculated as military spending divided by total GDP in a country.[28] Oversight is measured by the SPII index, and democracy is determined using the Polity score. I also measure several other concepts that have been shown to increase or decrease military spending. These include the number of countries that the state borders, the spending levels in international rivals, whether the country has nuclear weapons or not, whether there is an ongoing militarized dispute or war, the population of a state, and whether the state is a major power. I also include the military spending of all neighboring states in a spatial analysis of military spending. As in the previous section, the details of these variables and the analyses are included in the Appendix.

Additionally, I collected this information for several subsets of countries to probe the limits of the oversight. The first subset of countries we are interested in are members of the Organization of Economic Co-operation and Development. These are all developed economies that have functional accountability structures on domestic issues. This allows us to focus our comparison on some similar units and then explore whether oversight makes a difference in their spending levels. The second subset are strong democracies. These are states that score the highest on the aggregate Polity score, as described in the previous chapter. Again, this allows us to examine, holding democracy constant, whether oversight can explain the remaining variation in military spending and whether the relationship is as expected. The final subset includes all countries that score above a 6 on the Polity scale. While this is a very diverse group, it allows us to expand our exploration to a greater number of countries and linearly control for the variation in democracy across levels.

It will also be important to get our bearing on what very high and very low military spending looks like. Luckily, on this score we have some external guidance. Most famously, NATO has a long-standing goal for member states to devote 2% of GDP to military spending. While some might argue that this is too high, since NATO is a military alliance, and indeed many member states do not spend this every year, it does provide one goal post. Also, a study for the World Bank, done by Knight et al., (1996) suggests that, on average, spending of about 1.9% was a useful goal for countries. They argued that while spending would be higher in some places due to threats and lower elsewhere due to a lack of external challenges, 1.9% was a useful middle ground. This guidance suggests that across many countries, over decades, underspending will be significantly less than this figure while overspending will be more. To be clear, this is not an expectation of healthy spending in any one country at a given point in time. Instead, it is useful to calibrate our interpretation of the distribution of the spending data and estimated effects. If we have a statistical model, for example, that predicts for a group of states that their spending will on average be 6% over the long run, that is quite high. This prediction will be a summary, and the model itself will predict, as we will see, that some states will be above this while others will be below. Similarly, finding that democracies with very strong national security oversight are only spending .25% on defense is unlikely to be evidence of optimal spending; instead it is likely to be underspending. This would provide evidence for the democracy doubters on this score.[29] Using around 1.9% as a goal post sets up very specific expectations for the national security oversight theory to meet. Spending with low oversight should be significantly below 1.9%, rise to above 1.9%, on average, due to the mixing of security and nonsecurity spending, and then decline back toward 1.9%.[30]

Findings

Using these data, we can first see that repressive autocracies tend to spend more on their military than democracies, as Fordham and Walker find, but that there are a great diversity of military spending investments across democracies. Figure 9.4 illustrates the distribution of military spending for repressive autocracies (darker)[31] and democracies (lighter).[32] The height on the y-axis measures how often we see values of specific spending intervals. The x-axis measures the log of military spending as a proportion of GDP.[33] In fact, the median spending for democracies is 1.2%, and for fully repressive autocracies it is 5.7% of GDP.[34]

We are now going to zoom into the lighter area in Figure 9.4 and explore the systematic variation among democracies. To do this, we can look at first the focused OECD group of democracies and then all full democracies and their specific oversight scores. The distribution of spending, conditional on oversight strength, is presented in Figure 9.5 for the OECD group. The gray boxplots show the central tendencies and range of spending as we move up the oversight scale.[35] The white line within the gray box is the median. The edges of the gray boxes illuminate the 25th and 75th percentiles, while the gray lines that extend upward or downward are drawn to show the inter-quartile range.[36] The swooping line is a locally weighted regression estimate of the underlying SPII data and related military spending. This supplies a very flexible curve that can bend up or down at many points to fit the underlying patterns in the sample. The horizontal line is drawn at the transformed value of spending at 1.9%, the World Bank suggestion. I use this as an approximate guideline to calibrate our interpretations. Finally, the notches on the x- and y-axes represent the values in the sample. What we see is that, as predicted, military spending rises from low values (.4 on the logged scale here represents spending slightly less than .5% on the military) to higher values (1.2 on the logged scale represents over 2.3% spent on the military) and finally falls back to moderate values of spending (1.05 represents just over 1.8% spending). Figure 9.6 presents these same results for full democracies.[37] Again a similar pattern is apparent, with the expected nonlinear pattern of rising and then falling spending as we move from the lowest values of oversight to the highest. This pattern is an average across greater variability, as one can see from the boxplots. To place these graphs in perspective, Jamaica, Luxembourg, Iceland, and

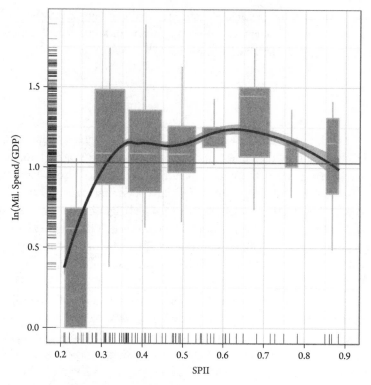

Figure 9.5 The distribution of military spending across oversight strength in OECD countries.

Mongolia all have very low oversight scores for national security and very low military spending despite being full democracies by the Polity definition. The United Kingdom and Greece, as well as Sweden in the 1980s, have middling oversight scores but have spending near the top of all full democracies. Finally, the Netherlands and Australia have oversight scores near .8, which places them near the end of the curve, and have spending around 1.9% of GDP.

We can further disaggregate the patterns in the OECD countries and democracies by looking at the Cold War and post–Cold War periods separately, as well as plotting states with higher and lower external threats. This could help us illuminate whether the nonlinear relationship is conditional on a particular time-period or external threat environment. Figure 9.7 separates the data for OECD countries into the Cold War (pre-1989) and post–Cold War (1989 or after) cases. While, on average, spending was high in the Cold War period, this did little to alter the mobilizing and constraining trajectories of oversight. Instead of changing the fundamental relationship between oversight and spending, the upside-down J-curve is shifted downward in the post–Cold War period. Figure 9.8 repeats the same analysis for all democracies and evinces the same supportive evidence.

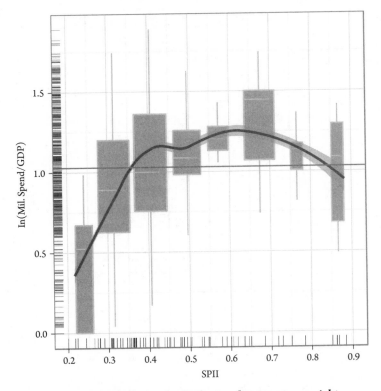

Figure 9.6 The distribution of military spending across oversight strength in fully democratic countries.

Likewise, we can look at whether the curvilinear relationship between oversight and spending is conditional on a lack of external threat. Figure 9.9 separates the observations into years where specific states faced an external rival or were involved in a militarized interstate dispute and years when states faced few threats and, thus, no external rival or dispute in a given year.[38] Again, while the spending levels are, on average, higher, when external threats weigh more heavily, the nonlinear relationship remains. It should be noted that across each of these plots there is nothing forcing the smoothed Loess line to curve upward and then down, and this curve is simply tracking the weighted average of the spending observations as we sweep from left to right.

To further explore the relationship between oversight and military spending, I estimate two types of models that allow us to control for other variables that may alter our inferences here. The first set of models assumes that the curvilinear relationship can be summarized with quadratic terms in a linear model.[39] The second set of models relaxes this assumption and allows the relationship to smoothly bend upward or downward several times conditional on the data. Specifically, these are generalized additive models (GAMs) using cross-validation to

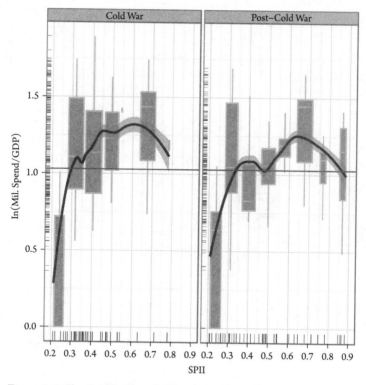

Figure 9.7 The distribution of military spending across oversight
strength in OECD countries during the Cold War and after the Cold
War.

select the smoothness of the function.[40] In each case, we can now introduce our
battery of other control variables, including the number of countries the state
borders, the spending levels in international rivals, whether the country has nuclear weapons or not, whether there is an ongoing militarized dispute or war, the
population of a state, and whether the state is a major power. I ran these results
on three data subsets: OECD countries, all full democracies, and then a broader
subset of all democracies that score about a 6 on the Polity score. The results
from the quadratic and GAM models across different specifications are available
in the online supplementary material. Here I want to summarize graphically the
results predicting military spending.

What we find is that across 14 different model specifications, in every case, the
curvilinear specification between linking oversight with military spending fits the
data better than either a linear fit or a model that ignores oversight. Additionally, in each case, the models predict that at low values of oversight, increasing
retrospective accountability institutions increases military spending, while moving from middling to strong oversight powers reduces military spending. This

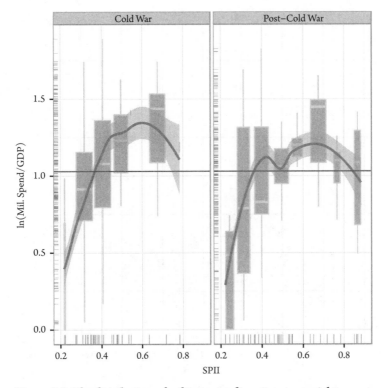

Figure 9.8 The distribution of military spending across oversight strength in fully democratic countries during the Cold War and after the Cold War.

is as predicted. The best fitting models[41] to the data were the generalized additive models that allowed a flexible fit, although even the quadratic models fit in every case better than a linear fit or a fit that ignored national security oversight. Figures 9.10, 9.11, and 9.12 plot the best-fitting GAM to samples of all full democracies, OECD countries, and a broader category of democracy. Specifically, these are predictions from the model for an average country across the many dimensions. Each of these models controls for several other variables, including militarized disputes, rival spending, and the number of borders a state has. The horizontal line again highlights the World Bank guidance for spending. The pattern of overmobilization of resources and then declining back toward the target is apparent.

The evidence strongly supports the nuances suggested by oversight theory. While I do find limited evidence that higher democracy scores lower spending, national security oversight remains an important predictor in the face of this intermittent effect.[42] Additionally, the evidence is not consistent with the idea, proffered by democracy irreleventists, that national security oversight and accountability are sideshows. This means that we now have tangible evidence on

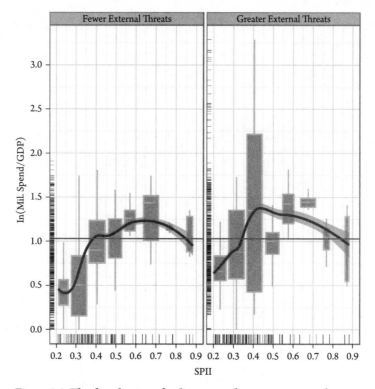

Figure 9.9 The distribution of military spending across oversight strength in democratic countries with and without external threats.

military spending. Not only does oversight increase public support, but it also has mobilizing and constraining effects on spending.

One limitation of this section has been that, even with World Bank or NATO guidance on what average military spending should be for a state, it is difficult to say which states are overspending and which are underspending. To probe this further, we are going to have to turn from the inputs of foreign policy, public support, and military spending and turn to an analysis of the outputs of the foreign policy process, most notably, foreign policy success.

SUCCESS

A dual focus on secrecy and mobilization leads to the hypothesis that the foreign policy ability of democracies with national security oversight institutions should be, ceteris paribus, higher than that of democracies that lack these types of institutions. While this seems to be a simple comparison, the task of measurement is significantly complicated by the fact that foreign policy ability is a latent trait.

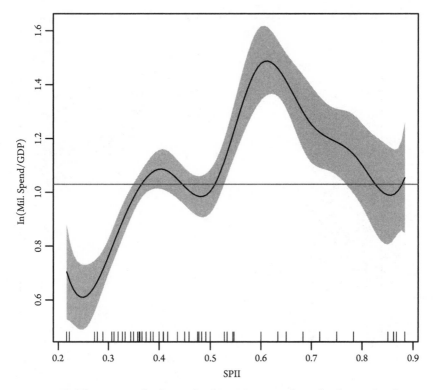

Figure 9.10 The estimated relationship between oversight and military spending from a GAM fit to the sample of full democracies.

States have strong incentives to hide and misreport their foreign policy ability for strategic reasons, so as to shield vulnerabilities, unleash surprises, or bluff. Further, while historical measures of military and economic capabilities are available, they quantify only one piece of foreign policy effectiveness. In 1990, the USSR remained the second strongest state in the world according to the Correlates of War material capabilities data, but it was internally divided and in the throes of dissolution.

However, there are times when we receive signals as to the relative foreign policy ability of states. As eloquently put by Kenneth Waltz when discussing the distribution of international power, "Like a flash of lightning, crises reveal the landscape's real features"[43] During disputes, armies mobilize and threats are made, bluffs are called, and military preparations peak. In 1967, while Egypt had four times the aggregate military capabilities of Israel,[44] Israel had a mobilized population, valuable strategic intelligence, and a successful plan. The resulting conflict illuminated the effectiveness gap at the time, in Israel's favor.[45] Dispute outcomes provide a snapshot of the

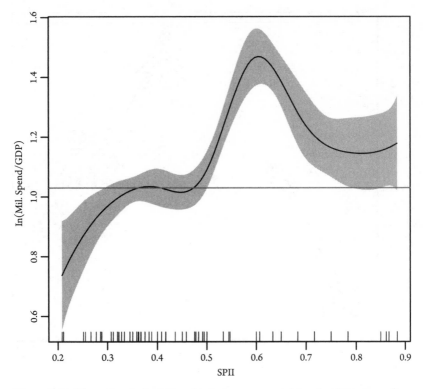

Figure 9.11 The estimated relationship between oversight and military spending from a GAM fit to the sample of OECD countries.

relative ability of states. It is also possible that more specific battlefield outcomes such as net fatalities can provide analogous pictures of a state's ability.

Hypothesis: From Oversight to Success

These clues can provide another crucial test of the effects of oversight in democracies. If retrospective oversight allows for public mobilization as well as necessary national security secrecy, and military spending is more efficient rather than wasteful or anemic, then these processes should pay off during international crises. Oversight should illuminate greater foreign policy success for the democracies that have it. Those that lack oversight should be mired in costly problems: either they must sacrifice secrecy to try and convince a skeptical public to support a policy (and the public may not believe them even then) or they may underinvest and underprepare for conflicts, knowing that increased spending will be unpopular. Each of these suboptimal interactions between the executive, legislature, and public at large has foreign policy costs. But are they apparent in

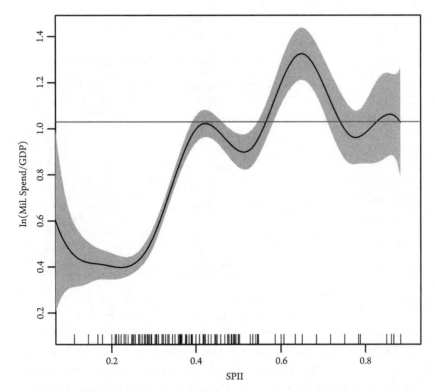

Figure 9.12 **The estimated relationship between oversight and military spending from a GAM fit to the sample of all democracies.**

the data to the extent that we can see a measurable increase in the foreign policy ability of democracies with oversight, as opposed to those without them?

Alternative Hypotheses

Looking at the eventual foreign policy success of states provides crucial distinctions between oversight theory and other perspectives, particularly democracy doubters. One could argue that the foreign policy inputs of public support and military spending are tangential to their ultimate use in international politics. Thus, even if one were persuaded that oversight led to greater citizen support in crisis and more efficient funding levels for security, the possibility would remain that those resources are not effectively marshaled on the battlefield or negotiating table. Specifically, democracy doubters would argue that these oversight institutions, by increasing the constraints on the executive and forcing executives to balance the public's perspective in their decision-making, should render inferior policy, as compared to democracies that lack these institutions as well as

Table 9-3. TABLE OF EMPIRICAL HYPOTHESES FROM OVERSIGHT THEORY AND
THREE OTHER PERSPECTIVES

THE PREDICTED EFFECT OF OVERSIGHT ON:

	Public Support	Spending	Ability
Oversight Theory	Higher	Higher but nonlinear	Highest with oversight
Democracy Irreleventists	No difference	No difference	No difference
Democracy Doubters	Lower with oversight	Lower with oversight	Lowest with oversight
Liberal Electioneers	No difference	No difference with oversight, but lower for democracies	No difference with oversight, but higher for democracies

non-democracies. Waltz and other democracy irreleventists might counter that these institutions are meaningless and that to survive, all states, with or without security policy information institutions, will wriggle free from these loose institutional bonds and enter the fray on equal footing. If that were the case, we would not expect oversight to be correlated with foreign policy success. Finally, liberal arguments that do not recognize the distinctions between national security policy and domestic policy may argue that open elections and accountability foster equal benefits for all democracies, regardless of oversight. The distinction with the democracy irrelevantists is that democracies should all have approximately equal success, but all should be more effective on average than corrupt non-democracies. Table 9-3 presents these alternative predictions on foreign policy ability in the last column.

Research Design

To analyze the relative success of various institutional frameworks, we will need to model how foreign policy ability is related to observable indicators of foreign policy effectiveness. This can be accomplished in what are known as Bradley–Terry models,[46] which analyze competition between units and estimate the underlying ability of the units from the eventual successes. This framework is needed because while we observe success or failure in a specific dispute, we do not directly observe the latent foreign policy abilities of states; we must instead estimate them from what is available. Importantly, we can look at the outcomes of disputes as probabilistic projections of the differences between the abilities of the states competing within them. If the United States competes against Haiti repeatedly and has a higher latent foreign policy ability, then we should expect Washington to win a disproportionate share of these competitions. Specifically, we can investigate whether states that have strong oversight institutions tend to have higher latent foreign policy abilities and, thus, greater probabilities of winning disputes, all else being equal. The Bradley–Terry framework is explained in the Appendix, along with the specific Bayesian ordered Bradley–Terry model that I utilize for the analysis here.

I measure foreign policy success using the dyadic militarized dispute data, version 2.0, as collected by Zeev Maoz.[47] This allows us to measure not only when states competed with each other, but also which, if any, state was victorious.[48] As an alternative measure, I use net enemy fatalities in the disputes.[49] This is an interval level measurement, where in most cases we do not know the exact fatalities count, but we do know the net fatalities within a specific interval.[50] I use all democracies with a Polity score greater than 6 for this analysis.

Additionally, I control for the major power status of a state; the material capabilities of a state including demographic, military, and economic components; the strength of external rivals; and the number of disputes that a state is involved in, for a given year. Within a dispute, I measure whether there is a first-mover advantage and whether force was used. Finally, I include a variable marking whether the United States was involved in the dispute, since the role of the United States might sway democratic victories.

Findings

The results of three specifications of the structured Bayesian ordered Bradley–Terry model of winning an interstate dispute, as described in the Appendix, provide strong confirmatory evidence of the usefulness of oversight. Far from being a burden, these models estimate that oversight increases the foreign policy ability of states and increases the chances for success. The following results plot the added benefit of having strong oversight for democracies as compared to democracies with weak oversight. The estimates are presented as distributions, because the effect is estimated and uncertain. I summarize these distributions in the text using highest posterior density (HPD) intervals. These display the most likely range of the estimates given a specific proportion of the probability mass.

Over several different specifications, the parameter representing national security oversight institutions is positive, suggesting that democracies with greater oversight have an increased probability of winning their international disputes, as compared to democracies with few institutional mechanisms for national security oversight. Figure 9.13 plots the posterior distribution of the oversight institutions coefficient for the four models. The first model includes only the

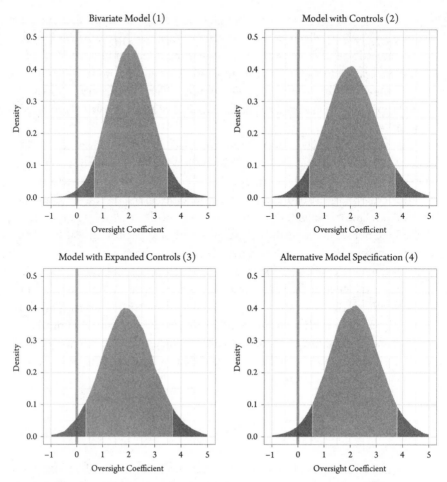

Figure 9.13 The posterior density of the national security oversight institution coefficient across the four difference specifications of the Bayesian ordered Bradley–Terry model. The lighter area indicates the density within the 90% HPD intervals, and the darker area represents the posterior probability mass that lies outside this range.

national security oversight institutions index. This provides some evidence on the aggregate effect of oversight institutions on ability without separating out the effects of large capabilities and other potential factors. The second adds the structural controls such as material capabilities, major power status, external threat burden, and other ongoing militarized disputes. The third model adds the intra-crisis variables, who moved first, whether asymmetric force was present, and whether the United States was involved, as described above. Consistently, the changes in the specification do not substantively alter the mean or spread of the posterior estimate for oversight institutions. In models 1 and 2, there is less than a 0.023 and 0.026 probability, respectively, that the effect of oversight institutions on conflict outcomes is zero or less. In model 3, this probability rises only slightly to 0.06. Thus, given the data and priors, there are posterior probabilities of 0.977, 0.974, and 0.94, depending on the specification, that the effect of oversight institutions on foreign policy ability is greater than zero. The fourth model, which includes a subset of covariates, illustrates the same pattern.

Substantively, we are interested in how the underlying probability of victory changes as we increase national security oversight institutions. This is explored in Figure 9.14, which plots the posterior probability of a democratic state with

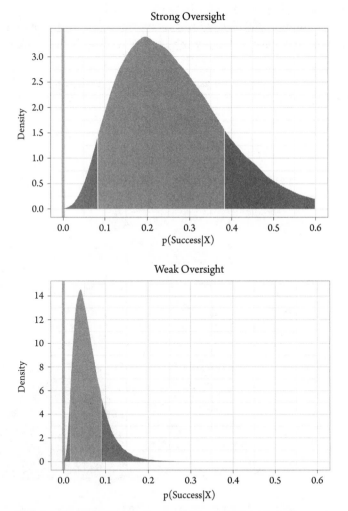

Figure 9.14 The estimated posterior probability of winning a dispute for a democracy with strong oversight (**top panel**) and a democracy that lacks oversight (**bottom panel**). The light gray area represents the area within the 90% HPD intervals.

strong oversight (top) and a democratic state lacking oversight (bottom) winning a dispute against a non-democracy while enjoying a capability advantage.[51] Figure 9.15 represents the estimated difference between these two scenarios. A democracy with strong oversight institutions is estimated to have a 20% chance of winning such an encounter, with a 90% highest posterior interval of $(0.07, 0.37)$ as compared to a 5% estimated posterior probability of victory for a democracy with no oversight advantage.[52] Moving from an institutional setting that lacks oversight to one with strong oversight is estimated to increase the probability of a foreign policy victory by .15 with a 90% HPD of $(0.03, 0.33)$ in absolute terms and by 400% in relative risk terms. These results are consistent with the hypothesis that oversight institutions, through retrospective rather than simultaneous public accountability in national security policy, uniquely allow

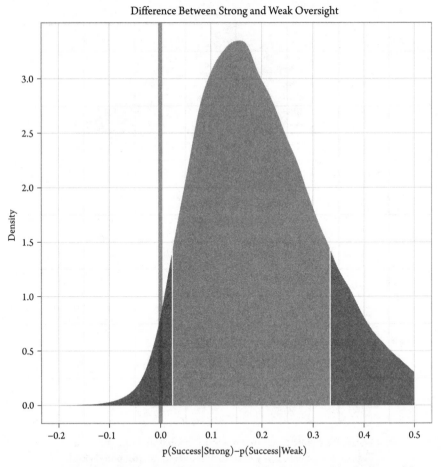

Difference Between Strong and Weak Oversight

p(Success|Strong)−p(Success|Weak)

Figure 9.15 Plot illustrating the difference between the posterior distributions of the scenarios depicted in Figure 9.14. The light area represents 90% HPD interval.

democracies to accrue foreign policy benefits from both private information and public mobilization. Democracies that fail to maintain these oversight institutions are less likely to win their foreign policy disputes. Interestingly, the effect does not decline noticeably as measures of capabilities are included.[53]

To probe the plausibility of this finding further and reveal some additional information about the mechanisms, I conducted a battery of alternative tests. Moving away from the complexity of the Bayesian ordered Bradley–Terry models, Figure 9.16 plots the crises where democracies were targeted by other states

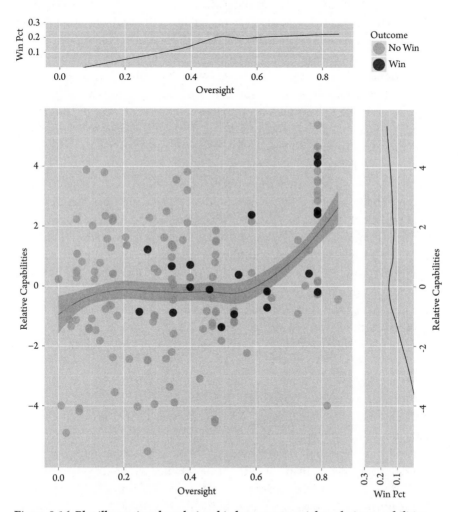

Figure 9.16 Plot illustrating the relationship between oversight, relative capabilities, and the percentage of wins in crises where a democracy was targeted by another state. The larger middle plot includes a Loess curve, with black dots indicating wins. The two corner plots (top left and bottom right) include Loess curves of how the percentage of observations that are wins rises as oversight and military capabilities increase.

by the oversight institutions of the democracy and the relative capabilities of the opponents. If oversight weakened a democracy and left it unprepared for future crises, then we should see evidence in this plot that other states are taking advantage of the situation. Instead, we see the opposite; that is, democracies with stronger oversight institutions tend to find themselves, when targeted in crisis, with more favorable material capability balances. This relationship is indicated by the upward Loess smoothed line, and it suggests that oversight might be useful, as predicted, to prepare democracies for future conflict. The marginal plots in this figure track the percentage of crisis wins as oversight increases (on top) and as relative capabilities increase (on the right). Both lines slope upward as expected. The three plots together, in the light of the previous findings, suggest that democracies with oversight are able to put themselves in relatively more secure international situations, even when targeted by other states.[54]

In a second reanalysis of the success of oversight, I used net fatalities in disputes as an alternative measure of dispute outcomes.[55] These results are particularly useful because one could argue that the higher average win percentages for democracies with oversight are a function of democracies avoiding the tough, but necessary, fights. Perhaps democracies with oversight are really wimps that only win in low-stakes crises. If this were true, we should see oversight leading to lower ability when we switch our indicator of winning from the crisis outcome to the net fatalities in a dispute. Yet, in this interval regression version of the BOB-T model the results remained consistent with the foreign policy efficacy of oversight institutions with the posterior probability that the national security oversight coefficient is greater than zero being .98. Figure 9.17 plots the posterior distribution of the estimated effect of increasing the national security oversight index from its minimum to its maximum. This suggests that increasing the strength of oversight institutions from 0 to .8 (approximately equal to the Netherlands in 2000) leads to an expected increase in net enemy fatalities of 234 with a 90% HPD of (95, 374).[56] Oversight increases not only the probability of a positive outcome of a dispute, but also the expected relative damage a state can do during a crisis to its competitors.

Three other robustness checks were conducted. First, I dropped all cases where force was not used by both sides. If it were the case that democracies with oversight were only winning inconsequential crises that were not worth fighting about, then perhaps the other side was not trying. Therefore we can subset the analysis to those crises where some effort is put forth by both sides. On the other hand, if oversight theory is useful, despite the reduction in sample size, the effectiveness of oversight institutions should remain stable in militarized crises, since it is in these cases that the benefits of secrecy and mobilization are manifest. When a BOB-T model was estimated using only disputes where force was used, the mean of the posterior distribution for the national security

Difference in Expected Net Enemy Fatalities (Strong – Weak)

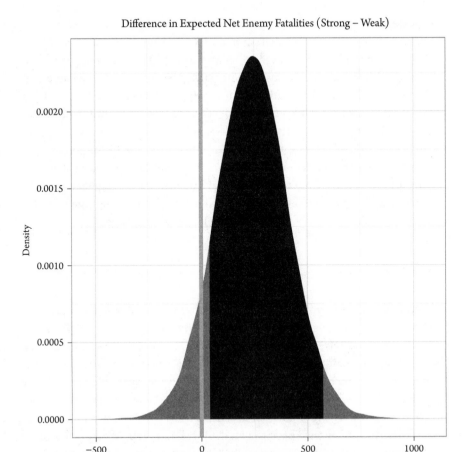

Figure 9.17 **The posterior expected value of additional net enemy fatalities (enemy fatalities minus own fatalities) for a democracy with oversight versus a democracy without oversight over national security policy from the interval regression version of the Bradley–Terry model.** The area within the 90% HPD interval is shaded black, while the area outside of the interval is shaded gray.

oversight coefficient was 2.34, with a standard deviation of 1.32 and a 90% HPD of (.66, 3.99). Therefore the posterior inferences we draw from all disputes and only militarized disputes are substantively similar.[57] Second, I removed all cases where the United States was involved in the dispute. In this case the influence of oversight institutions was moderately reduced with a posterior mean of 1.60, a standard deviation of 1.19, and a 90% HPD of (.009, 3.06). In the force and non–United States subset analyses the posterior probability that the national security oversight coefficient is greater than zero was .96 and .91, respectively.

   In the final robustness check, I controlled for the Polity democracy score. In this case, not only did the effect of oversight institutions remain stable, where the posterior parameter mean was 2.11 with a 90% HPD of (0.49, 3.69) and a prior probability that the oversight parameter was greater than zero equal to 95%, but also the partial effect of the democracy score on the probability of a state winning a dispute was inconclusive. The parameter for democracy had a posterior mean and standard deviation of –0.16 with an 80% HPD of (–0.12, 0.06). Thus, the posterior probability mass for the Polity democracy score was centered on zero, while the mass for the national security oversight index was positive. This evidence is consistent with the inference that oversight institutions are important components of democratic success, mirroring the results illustrated in Figure 9.14. One should not make the mistake of inferring that higher overall democracy scores are inconsequential for foreign policy ability, since the spread of the posterior distribution of the effect of the Polity score is large.[58]

CONCLUSION

The most important implication from these findings is that not all democracies logically follow the single path to accountability that was illuminated by Immanuel Kant and retread within current liberal international relations theory. While all states, democracies, and non-democracies alike keep national security secrets, some democracies retrospectively patch these accountability holes, while others do not. Democracies that include balanced national security exceptions in freedom of information laws, an absence of censorship and prior restraint, and legislative committees specifically tasked with oversight of national security with tangible investigative powers should have greater accountability on national security issues as compared to democracies that lack these tools.

This chapter has continued the argument that these distinct oversight institutions have significant national-security-relevant ramifications. They uniquely allow for keeping national security secrets from potential enemies and competitors (and necessarily the public) while allowing retrospective accountability if that secrecy is abused for nonsecurity motives. Democracies that lack the retrospective institutional apparatus to credibly signal whether public support or increased defense spending is necessary for security are hypothesized to systematically have smaller public rallies during crises, underinvest in security at the extreme, and be less successful in the field of international disputes. Conversely, those democracies that maintain a triumvirate of strong security policy oversight institutions, while unable to erase all executive foreign policy corruption, can simultaneously increase public mobilization, minimize corruption, ensure that necessary defense spending is supported, and foster greater foreign policy ability. The liberal logic of domestic institutional accountability should be conditional on specific national security oversight institutions that fill the informational gaps left by national executive classification powers.

The empirical evidence presented herein is consistent with the importance of understanding specific national security oversight institutions. I find that oversight increased public support during a foreign policy crisis in the United States and France only after oversight institutions were strengthened. In the United Kingdom, during a time when only superficial changes were made to their oversight system, no meaningful increase in public support during crises was detected. This supports the findings of Colaresi[59] that the rally-round-the-flag effect is consistent with a reasonable, rather than irrational and emotional, public that, instead of reflexively supporting an executive, reacts systematically to institutionally altered executive preferences. Similarly, we saw that national security oversight both mobilized and constrained the price the public paid for the military. In very low oversight democracies, such as Ireland in the 1970s, spending tends to be very low, while moderate oversight generates greater spending than necessary. In fact, among democracies, the non-great powers that spend the most have moderate oversight. It is only at stronger oversight levels that overspending on defense is reduced, however imperfectly. The data the from 1970s to the 2000s illustrated this pattern, as spending rose at first, with increasing oversight, and surpassed aggregate spending guidance from NATO and the World Bank and then fell back toward these guideposts as oversight increased. This supports other work—for example, that of Colaresi[60]—that presented evidence that increased investment in the military, relative to democracies that lack oversight on international issues, purchases a greater public return on that investment in terms of economic growth. Further, we see that these high oversight states, on average, win more of their disputes and have more beneficial capability ratios when force is used.

Thus, the empirical purchase of these distinct institutional tools simultaneously supports recent work on domestic institutions and foreign policy outputs by Bueno de Mesquita et al.[61] and Guisinger and Smith[62] while refining the specific constellation of rules that support retrospective accountability. Transparency on national security issues is treated distinctly in democracies due to classification of information, and thus national security oversight is a necessary complement to democratic elections for accountability on foreign policy.

Finally, a paradox has emerged within liberal theory that the introduction of retrospective oversight helps to resolve. While Fordham and Walker[63] have found that democracies tend to spend less on their militaries, there are relatively robust findings that democracies also tend to win more of their wars.[64] Some theorists have suggested that this merely indicates that democracies choose low-cost wars and bob and weave to avoid potentially costly conflicts. However, this explanation begs the question of how democracies are able to avoid being taken advantage of by other states. If all democracies chronically underspend on security, other states should be able to exploit this in the international arena.

Democracies could be targeted for their weakness, or face deteriorating security because they are unwilling to face up to costly, yet overall beneficial, fights.

This is not what we see in the empirical record. Instead, the implications of these findings suggest two important lessons. First, ignoring the ability-enhancing effects of national security oversight is a mistake. Democracies on average do not appear to be weak or pushed around because many are fueled by both secrecy—to anticipate, deceive, and suppress the capabilities of enemies—and consent, in the form of public support and adequate military spending. Second, when the foreign policy benefits of democracy have been extolled, less attention than is necessary has been paid to the diversity across democracies. For example, the work of Fordham and Walker, Schultz, Reiter and Stam, and others highlighting democratic efficiency and effectiveness as compared to autocratic states is useful and supported, in part, by the findings herein. However, the important caveat is that these previous works have averaged across democracies. While some are effective foreign policy players on the international scene, others are less so, and looking at oversight institutions helps us to appreciate the distinction.

PART V

Conclusion

Implications and Innovations

This book has sought to highlight the necessary tension between national security secrecy and public accountability in democracies, a tension that has often been hidden from view in theorizing about democratic foreign policy to date. On the one hand, researchers have exalted the benefits of accountability while assuming adequate democratic transparency across both domestic and foreign policy issues—hushing up secrecy. On the other hand, critics of liberal international relations theory have pointed out the usefulness of secrecy in national security policy but then assumed that public consent will be achieved in democracies even without accountability. These assumptions have both hidden, from different perspectives, the secrecy dilemma in democracies.

In response to this contemporary debate, I have argued that not only is the capacity for executive secrecy necessary for foreign policy effectiveness, but it does not obviate the necessity for public consent in democracies. In fact, instead of assuming away the capability of an executive to keep national security secrets or the ability of the public to dissent from policies, this work has been an attempt to grapple with the implication of transparency costs, and thus the capacity for secrecy, directly for public consent. How can citizens be assured by the executive that a given policy proposal will increase public security, relative to other alternatives, instead of being a product of incompetence or corruption? This is the secrecy dilemma in democracies.

The answer to this question is much more difficult when there are legitimate public uses for secrecy on national security issues. On domestic issues the failure to be transparent is itself usually evidence of covering up something embarrassing. Yet, if a national security advisor states that a specific policy by the executive has reduced the number of terrorist attacks in a country but cannot reveal the details, the claim of secrecy is plausible. Revealing information on the policy could, in theory, have transparency costs as enemies learned better how to attack vulnerabilities. The uses of secrecy for anticipation, deception, and capability suppression justify providing the executive with the capacity to keep national security secrets.

However, the nature of information is such that once you allow an executive to select what content is secret, the public cannot vet what content is classified. Secrets can be kept and guarded to deceive an enemy and increase net security efficiently, or information can be covered up to deceive the public about the relative costs and benefits of preferred policies or incompetence of a leader. The capacity for secrecy has uses, but then necessarily also has potential abuses. The national security advisor might be selectively revealing information on the counterterrorism policy and using official secrecy to hide mistakes. The same capacity that covered up the incompetence and corruption of the Dreyfus Affair helped keep the French 75-mm gun secret. Tools of counterintelligence in the United States aided Project Azorian, but also were abused in Watergate and other programs.

The potential abuse of the capacity to keep secrets has consequences for public consent. Specifically, in cases where the public already is not sufficiently persuaded of the merits of policy, an executive will have a difficult time convincing the public to offer support. Counter-terrorism policies might be doubted and shut down based on public skepticism and the inability of leaders to convince the public that abuse of the program is being kept secret. In France, skepticism and distrust led many to resist raising military service requirements and investing in heavy artillery. Similarly, US President Ford was unable to convince Congress in 1974 that withdrawing support for Turkey would lead to unnecessary costs with regard to US security and the ability to monitor the USSR. In both these cases, underinvestment led to costs to the public. Further, in both cases, the executive attempted to partially reveal previously secret information to convince the public, to little avail.

The secrecy dilemma in democracies such as the United States and France is not theoretical, and it highlights the dual necessity of public consent and the capacity for secrecy in democracies. Keeping secrets is useful, but without public consent, intelligence on its own cannot stop a German offensive or provide funds to an ally. The public must supply the ballots, bucks, and blood for foreign policy. Sometimes the problem is eased by a clumsy enemy that rattles its sword so the public can hear, as did Germany in the Agadir crisis. Yet, even if identifying the source of the threat is uncontroversial, the dilemma returns in working out the details of how to meet that threat. There was a consensus in Washington during the Cold War that the USSR was a threat, but that did not forestall significant disagreements about arms control agreements and military modernization programs.

Thus, in a democracy, centralizing information and national security activity within an executive, without mechanisms for accountability, sows doubts, not effectiveness. The greater the ability of a leader to use national security tools for his own benefit and get away with it, the less credible will be that executive's message that his policies are indeed in the public's interest. This is Madison's farce and tragedy, discussed in Chapter 3, coming to the forefront. The public is stuck with a risky gamble: support a policy, pay the bill, and hope some security accrues, or withhold support and funds, crossing your fingers that the insecurity costs are not substantial.

When pitched as a battle between secrecy and transparency, on national security grounds, the capacity for secrecy seems to hold a strategically sound position. However, one can hardly stop here. For in practice, democracies keep secrets and seem to be effective, as argued by Reiter and Stam, Lake, and Schultz. The problem is that, in assuming a single trade-off between national-security-enhancing secrecy on one side and the public's right to information, civil liberties, political representation, and accountability on the other, the complex and important dynamics of transparency costs and the value of secrecy have been flattened into a single dimension. One can see this clearly in the top plot in Figure 10.1. If one has

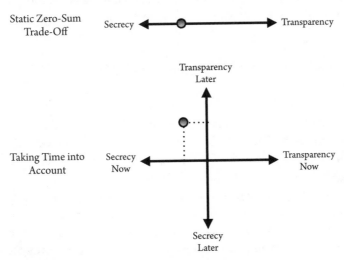

Figure 10.1 A comparison of one-dimensional thinking on national security secrecy and transparency (top) and the role that time plays in resolving the secrecy dilemma (bottom).

to choose between national security secrecy and transparency—graphically, this would be a choice of where to place the gray dot in the top panel—then there is necessarily a trade-off: more transparency means less secrecy.[1] This framework implies that the necessities of secrecy and accountability—of which transparency is a central component—are not complementary and cannot simultaneously increase foreign policy effectiveness for democracies. Looking at the problem in this way, one must conclude that something has to give, and more often than not it is transparency and accountability.[2]

IMPLICATIONS AND INNOVATIONS

Recognizing the secrecy dilemma leads to several important implications. In fact, some of the central debates in emerging and mature democracies around the world relate to the costs and benefits of expanding executive powers (e.g., domestic surveillance, detention without charges, torture, extraordinary rendition, and drone strikes), relative to extra-executive institutions, on national security policy. These questions, being debated in capitals including Tunis, London, Washington, and Warsaw, can benefit from a careful reanalysis in light of the reflections herein on transparency, the paradox of executive power, and the mobilizing and constraining effects of oversight. I have argued that no perfect solution is attainable on international oversight due to nonzero investigation costs. However, since some places are more adept than others at limiting corruption, generating public consensus for policies, and executing effective foreign policy, it would be folly to ignore these lessons and innovations going forward.

Implication 1: The Secrecy Dilemma Leaks Out

Discussions about recent leaks in the United States have brought one-dimensional thinking on secrecy and accountability to the surface. When WikiLeaks released a trove of US diplomatic cables, the leaker Chelsea Manning and WikiLeaks founder Julian Assange were accused by some of being traitors and harming security. Max Boot wrote that "it seems that they have no respect for the secrecy that must accompany successful diplomacy." He continued on to describe WikiLeaks as "disreputable" and "sleazy" and to characterize reporting of the leaks by major newspapers as "journalism as pure vandalism."[3] Others take the opposite position and hail leaks as preserving democracy. Roy Greenslade argued, "Aren't we in the job of ferreting out secrets so that our readers—the voters—can know what their elected governments are doing in their name? Isn't it therefore better that we can, at last, get at them?"[4]

Recent revelations by Edward Snowden have stirred similar disagreements. Democratic Senator and Chair of the Senate Select Committee on Intelligence Dianne Feinstein accused Snowden of treason.[5] Law scholar Geoffrey Stone wrote that, based on the information he had, "Snowden is neither a hero nor a traitor, but is most certainly a criminal who deserves serious punishment."[6] Former Republican Presidential candidate and Representative Ron Paul, on the other hand, suggested that "[w]e should be thankful" for the information being publicized, and he was joined in his praise of Snowden by Julian Assange and others.[7]

In this one-dimensional paradigm, if secrecy is useful to security, anything that reveals previously secret information must harm security. On the other side, if secrecy is abusive to accountability, those that reveal information aid accountability and thus democracy. Arguments like this ping back and forth across partisan divides, newsrooms, servers, and the corridors of governments. Yet, they miss several fundamental points. First, for those that trumpet the necessity of information for accountability, ignoring transparency costs is neither practical nor convincing. The capacity to keep secrets exists in all democracies, and the legitimate uses of secrecy make this unlikely to change. Daniel Patrick Moynihan, who was the chair of a commission investigating secrecy after the end of the Cold War, wrote in 1997 that "[s]ecrecy is for losers" and "[i]t is time to dismantle government secrecy."[8] Yet, the capacity for secrecy has not been dismantled in the intervening 17 years. In 2009, when questions were raised about torture, a Gallup poll found that, among those following the news, the CIA had higher approval than the President and both parties in Congress.[9] Former US Foreign Service Officer Jordan Stancil argues this "is a false debate, because in cases where safety is truly threatened, it's obvious that openness must be curtailed, as it always has been ever since the First Continental Congress met in secret in 1774."[10]

However, the opposing calls to embrace secrecy ignore the potential for its abuse and the distrust this can cause. In his defense of NSA spying programs in 2013, President Obama admitted that the program has enormous potential for abuse.[11] Geoffrey Stone similarly concedes in his accusations against Snowden that

> Now, this is not to say that there might not be situations in which it would be in the national interest for certain classified information to be disclosed to the public. It is easy to think of situations in which the decision to classify certain information is misguided, corrupt and dangerous to the nation. In some situations the information may be classified not to protect the national security, but to protect public officials from exposure. Perhaps they have acted foolishly, callously, unlawfully or unconstitutionally. Perhaps it

is important for the American people to know what their representatives are doing—even though the information is classified.[12]

A June 2013 poll, taken in the wake of the revelation of the NSA spying programs, found that 77% of Republicans and 69% of independents did not approve of the way President Obama was handling government surveillance.[13] While other polls found less dramatic numbers, it is clear that worries about potential abuse are significantly more than marginal concerns.

Therefore, both of these perspectives fail to appreciate the secrecy dilemma by only embracing one side: secrecy or transparency. As a result, they miss the opportunity for common ground and practical solutions. This leads to implication 2.

Implication 2: Oversight Needs Time

Many immediate secrets are indeed valuable, but that importance declines over time. Sources are moved out of harm's way, contexts change, or competitors learn the information from other sources. Erwin Griswold, who was the Solicitor General in the Johnson and Nixon administrations and argued the case for the Pentagon Papers to remain secret before the Supreme Court to protect national security, in 1989 wrote, "I have never seen any trace of a threat to the national security from the publication [of the Pentagon Papers]." He explained that it was because "there is very rarely any real risk to current national security from the publication of facts relating to transactions in the past, even the fairly recent past. This is the lesson of the Pentagon Papers experience."[14]

These deflating transparency costs open up the possibility of revealing national security information post hoc. Thus, we have a second dimension emerge out of the first in the bottom plot of Figure 10.1. Information can be released to the public or kept secret at a specific time. Now there is not necessarily a one-to-one trade-off between secrecy and accountability. In fact, as the circle on this graph illustrates, it is possible to have offsetting hedges. Concurrent information is more likely to be secret; however, over time this shifts toward transparency. One can move the trajectory of the information vertically without altering immediate secrecy.

Thinking about the problem in this way suggests the potential for at least a partial solution to the democratic secrecy dilemma. However, the tools must be present to dig up previously secret information. Reasonable expectations of retrospective accountability on the part of the executive, as well as investigations of potentially embarrassing secrets, are far from automatic. Executive classification in many ways is typified by Churchill's description of Russian policies: they involve "a riddle, wrapped in a mystery inside an enigma."[15] Yet democracies have engineered several institutional keys available to imperfectly unlock public accountability. These include the reinforcing tools of national-security-relevant legislative oversight powers, freedom of information acts, and speech and press freedoms. These institutions increase the probability of post hoc investigation and revelation of wrongdoing by the executive and thus, in turn, limit executive misuse of national security. Indeed, the early prototypes of modern oversight institutions were test flown in Sweden with the first freedom of information law, in Denmark with novel press freedoms, and in the United States during the Civil War with a mercurial committee investigating the conflict. Like in many test flights, there were faults, problems, and even disasters. Adjustments were and continue to be necessary.

Yet there are traces even in these early experiments in oversight of the later and more developed technologies that have allowed Seymour Hersh's stories on Vietnam, the dramatic committee investigation by the Security Intelligence Review Committee in Canada of extraordinary rendition and the Maher Arar case, and the Stortinget's Intelligence Oversight Committee's (EOS) investigation into the Treholt case.[16] Oversight during the Reagan years helped to maintain public consent through a large arms build-up, and minimize the skepticism and distrust that paralyzed France into underinvestment.

As we have seen, effective national security oversight is arrayed unequally around the world. This allowed us to probe the empirical effects of varying levels of national security oversight for democracies. Specifically, we found that, as expected, democracies that had strong oversight institutions were able to raise greater public support during crises, have more military spending than those states that lacked oversight while controlling overspending, and demonstrate greater foreign policy efficacy as measured by winning international disputes. These empirical regularities were argued to be the product of an executive's inability to marshal public support consistently across diverse contexts without institutions that subject decisions to a high probability of retrospective oversight. Additionally, executives under regimes of moderate oversight have the ability to generate support, but without the effective constraints on spending. Thus, the highest spending democracies were found to be those with only moderate amounts of oversight. Together, the evidence corroborates the importance of oversight across democracies and the usefulness of tracking the diversity of retrospective information institutions.

Implication 3: A Unitary Executive Is a Solitary One

The uses of not only secrecy, but also public consent provide important lessons for debates about the role of the executive. In both the United States and the

United Kingdom after 2001 and through to 2012, there was a strong push to expand executive powers. One clear proponent of expanding executive powers in both academic and policy arguments is John Yoo. When he was an attorney at the Justice Department in the White House, the *Wall Street Journal* reported that he wrote an influential memo that read, in part, "The centralization of authority in the president alone is particularly crucial in matters of national defense, war, and foreign policy, where a unitary executive can evaluate threats, consider policy choices and mobilize national resources with a speed and energy that is far superior to any other branch."[17] This centralization of authority in the United States was carried out in the Patriot Act, passed in 2001, in the wake of the 9/11 attacks, as well as during the creation of the Department of Homeland Security and increased use of wiretaps. In the United Kingdom, the centripetal forces set off by having an ally attacked in 2001 and later suffering the 7/7 London bombings induced the Blair government to pass the Anti-Terrorism, Crime and Security Act of 2001 and the Prevention of Terrorism Act of 2005, allowing the government to seize assets, detain suspects for up to 14 days (in 2001), and then raise that time to 28 days (in 2006) without charge.[18] Critics in both countries have pointed to their worries about threats to civil liberties in these countries.[19]

What both supporters and critics of strengthening executive powers miss is that there are significant practical problems with maximizing executive national security powers. In Yoo's original memo he writes specifically about "mobilization of resources," as well as speed and energy. Thinkers from James Hamilton to Sissela Bok have agreed that executives have unique abilities regarding speed of decision and executing national security policy (and they would add secrecy), but this is not mobilization.[20] In fact, the paradox of executive power over time renders the arguments of executive proponents counterproductive to their stated ends. An executive must rely on political and public support in a democracy to execute policy. The captain still needs a crew, as well as someone to finance the ship of state.

Let's imagine an all-powerful executive, unchecked on national security matters by other institutions such as the legislature, legal protections for civil liberties, press freedoms, and the availability of government institutions. Now some intelligence crosses this leader's desk that a security risk is building and will take a large investment of capital to prepare for and potentially head off. However, revealing the information raises the cost of preparing for the threat. For example, terrorists or an enemy nation can change operational details but still carry out the plan, and in the process the source of information is compromised. In this situation, the executive needs to vaguely alert the public, as well as opinion and legislative elites, that increased spending is necessary. But why should those extra-executive leaders believe that this spending is indeed in the public interest? Further, if someone had a negative opinion of the leader previously, what can the leader do to convince that skeptical member of the public to put their differences aside and support greater action and investment in security? Since there is no extra-executive force looking over the leader's shoulder, even retrospectively, signaling a crisis is not credible. From the public's point of view, asking for greater military spending in response to a vague but secret threat assessment could be a response to an actual threat (in which case they want to support investing in security) but could also simply be an executive money and power grab (in which case they do not want to support paying for corruption). The lack of institutional oversight deprives the executive of the chance to constructively increase public consent. A strong, unchecked, unitary executive in a democracy is a solitary one; deprived of the tools of accountability, mobilization will suffer. In fact, as we have seen, the public increases their support for a leader less, and sometimes not at all, when oversight is largely absent.

We can agree that the executive has an important role to play in national security policy, but the details of the role matter. Secrecy, speed, and dispatch are all benefits of the executive. In fact, ignoring the comparative advantage of executive institutions, several democracies in inter-war Europe imbued legislatures with extremely strong immediate national security powers. The outcome of this Sejm-ocracy[21] was either inaction and gridlock as in Lithuania or the use of extralegal mandates to negotiate and steer foreign policy as done by Jozef Pilsudski in Poland. Yet, the energy that executives are supposed to distribute toward security must be generated by the public, in the form of political support (or they lose control of the ship), spending (or they cannot afford a mast and cannons for the ship), and military service (or there is no crew). Since an executive cannot credibly commit to using resources for the public good without oversight, citizens are less likely to generate the heat and light that animates policy.

In both the United States and the United Kingdom, the 2003 Iraq War illuminated large partisan gaps in support for a large-scale conflict. In fact, in the United States, the partisan gap in support for the Iraq War in 2006 was far larger than that same gap at any time during the Vietnam War by some accounts. During Vietnam, the difference between the proportion of Republicans versus Democrats that viewed the war as a mistake was never greater than 18%.[22] In 2006 during the Iraq War, the gap in one poll was 50%.[23] Interestingly, according to recent research, before increases in executive power in the United States, partisan differences, even including regarding Vietnam, were rare and smaller in scope.[24] Perhaps the United Kingdom is an even clearer illustration. From late 2002 to early 2003, Tony Blair was attempting to rally support for military action in Iraq. He stated in September 2002 that "the assessed intelligence has established beyond doubt" that a military response was necessary. The public, in turn, was very skeptical of whether this military action would increase UK security. In fact, only 33% of the Prime Minister's own party supported military action.[25] The lack of support remained for much of the conflict and inhibited planning and preparations.[26]

Apart from the moral reasons to object to breaches of civil liberties, there are significant practical long-run security problems with reducing accountability. The greater the powers of executives to abuse policy for personal or partisan gain without getting caught, the fewer resources and support they are likely to be trusted with. The ability of the public to access information and judge policy, retrospectively, is paramount in unwinding this paradox. This suggests that if executive powers are increased, based on either new circumstances (e.g., a terrorist attack) or changing technology (e.g., government storage of exabytes of data on the public), oversight must keep step, or the changes are less likely to be effective.

Implication 4: Oversight Must Run a Red Queen's Race

Related to the last implication, we must remember that oversight is not only a competitive enterprise, but also one run on changing ground. In this respect, the overlapping arcs of oversight and executive actions resemble the Red Queen's Race from *Through the Looking-Glass*. In this part of the story, Alice and the Red Queen race each other by running as fast as they can, but never moving forward. As the Queen states, "here, you see, it takes all the running you can do, to keep in the same place. If you want to get somewhere else, you must run at least twice as fast as that!" At a basic level, oversight is a competition between an executive attempting to utilize policy to get the best outcomes possible for him- or herself or a party and the public attempting to head off corruption and catch wrongdoing. But just as oversight can evolve in this race, from pieces of parchment in Denmark to expert committees reporting to the Stortinget in Oslo, so too can executive strategies and techniques for potentially avoiding detection. While avoiding public revelations might have been relatively simple in places without oversight institutions, even nontrivial oversight can be avoided, as the revelations of the Church and Pike Committees in the United States, the McDonald Commission in Canada, and the Lund Commission in Norway make clear.[27]

Yet, even in places with very strong oversight, deterring corruption and cover-ups is difficult. As I have argued previously, not only is perfect oversight a paradox, but additionally the rules of oversight institutions are themselves not secret from the executive. This means that the executive can watch and learn what might be caught and adapt. For example, in the 1960s the intelligence community in the United States began using the idea of plausible deniability to shield the president from punishment if controversial covert actions were revealed. The Church Committee found that " 'plausible denial' . . . [was used] to mask decisions of the president and his senior staff members."[28] The Hughes–Ryan Act of 1974 was the legislature's reaction to this loophole in accountability. It stated that the president must sign off in writing on important intelligence actions.[29]

Even then, the executive appeared to adapt and dodge. In the Iran–Contra affair in the United States, the legislature specifically articulated constraints on providing assistance to the Contras who were working against the pro-USSR Nicaraguan government. Interspersed with hearings and testimony, the relevant funding resolution for fiscal year 1985 read, in part, "no funds available to the Central Intelligence Agency, the Department of Defense or any other agency or entity of the United States involved in intelligence activities may be obligated or expended for the purpose . . . of supporting, directly or indirectly, military or paramilitary operation in Nicaragua."[30] To avoid this roadblock, members of the Reagan administration decided to use National Security Council money that was not listed among the agencies in the language passed. When this was discovered, the administration altered a scheme that was aimed at having Israel provide missiles to an Iranian-backed group that had promised upon receipt to attempt to gain the release of seven American hostages. The United States would then re-supply the Israelis and receive a payment. It is that payment, which would be off the books, that was targeted at supplying the Contras. Soon the plan shifted to the United States directly supplying elements in the Iranian army, with the proceeds being funneled to the Contras in Nicaragua.

A leak to a Lebanese newspaper and the crashing of a supply plane in Nicaragua set the US press and Congress toward investigating what was happening.[31] While oversight had progressed since COINTELPRO and Watergate, the executive as an institution had evolved to attempt to deflect some of this scrutiny. In his testimony, Vice Admiral Poindexter admitted, "I made a deliberate decision not to ask the President, so that I could insulate him from the decision and provide some future deniability for the President if it ever leaked out."[32] Similar attempts to dodge oversight were seen in the AB Bofors scandal in India and the 1999 arms trade scandal for the ANC in South Africa. The most direct analog might be the French sinking of the Rainbow Warrior in a New Zealand dock. In an action honestly titled Operation Satanique, the DSGE set out to scuttle the craft before it could disturb a scheduled French nuclear test; Francois Mitterrand denied ordering the covert sinking, although several lower-level administration officials resigned during the ensuing scandal. The use of the DSGE in this case was specifically targeted at avoiding domestic implications of the action.[33] Since the executive has the ability to blunt oversight at times, finding new places and ways to hide information, the same ability needs to be present for information revelation institutions to maximize their effectiveness.

In addition to strategies to dodge eventual oversight, technological advances make oversight more daunting if they fail to keep up. For example, in the United Kingdom, where weak freedom of information statutes and legislative oversight make accessing information on national security difficult, both citizens and the prime minister's Intelligence Security Committee (ISC) have had trouble understanding the scope of GCHQ[34] surveillance. In addition, asymmetric operational and technical information enabled MI5 to provide what turned out to be inaccurate evidence to the Intelligence and Security Committee of Parliament about the 7/7 bombings and the practice of rendition.[35] This was also the case in the United States with the NSA wire-tapping scandal. In these cases, the technological sophistication and sheer volume of information are far beyond the investigative expertise of most citizens and legislative committee staffers that are trained as historians or lawyers. How are experts in laws written when landline telephones and even telegraphs were state of the art going to keep up with data mining approaches to Internet and mobile device surveillance and collection at an ever increasing scale?

The answer is to innovate oversight, in turn. Some countries over the last few years have incorporated significant innovations, particularly in supplementing legislative committee powers. Specifically, Belgium, Croatia, Norway, Sweden, and the Netherlands have joined Canada in creating expert oversight bodies to complement a regular national security committee.[36] Table 10-1 presents

Table 10-1. TABLE OF EXPERT AND HYBRID COMMITTEES TASKED WITH REPORTING ON NATIONAL SECURITY MATTERS TO PARLIAMENT LISTING THE NAME, THE BREADTH OF NATIONAL SECURITY MANDATE, WHETHER THE COMMITTEE REPORTS TO PARLIAMENT AS OPPOSED TO THE EXECUTIVE, AND THE MEMBERSHIP

Country	Committee Name	Mandate	Reporting	Membership
Belgium	Standing Intelligence Agencies Review Committee	Broad	Yes	Non-elected experts
Croatia	Council for Civilian Scrutiny of Security and Intelligence Agencies	Broad	Yes	Non-elected experts
Canada	Security Intelligence Review Committee	Broad	Yes	Expert
Netherlands	Review Committee on the Intelligence and Security Services	Broad	Yes	Non-elected experts
Norway	Parliamentary Intelligence Oversight Committee	Broad	Yes	Non-elected experts
Sweden	The Commission on Security and Integrity	Moderate	Yes	Hybrid

some information on these innovations. These committees can be either all non-elected officials, as in Canada, or a hybrid committee that brings together experts in different fields with legislators, as in Sweden. This is in contrast to committees such as the House Permanent Select Committee on Intelligence in the United States that are made up of elected officials. These extra-parliamentary bodies' main benefit is that they can provide expert advice on national security matters directly to parliamentarians. These bodies can also potentially hire staff with significant technical know-how and can be thought of as national-security-targeted Accountability Offices. This expertise is necessary because citizen and legislative oversight from elected politicians, while important, is limited in time and expertise.[37] These committees, if used in conjunction with a legislative oversight committee with substantial powers of retrospective information revelation, can significantly lower the costs of investigation and thus increase the chances that corruption is exposed ex post.[38] Improved oversight, in turn, should deter corruption a priori in some cases and raise citizen trust on average. While the jury is still out on the marginal effect of these expert bodies, the Belgian Standing Intelligence Review Committee's review of extraordinary rendition from 2005 to 2007 has received considerable attention. Additionally, the committee took the unique step of ensuring that its reports were published in English for the first time so that citizens and politicians in other countries could have access to its data.[39] The stated reason was that experts have defined rendition as a transnational problem that would require significant coordination between legislatures. Countries that are mired in partisan polarization over national security issues might look to these models to increase executive credibility on secrecy-scorched topics.

Some activists have been tempted to believe that recent leaks, and in particular the large-scale WikiLeaks document dumps, can provide adequate oversight for the public. *Guardian* journalists David Leigh and Luke Harding suggested that we have seen "the end of secrecy in the old-fashioned, Cold War–era sense."[40] Yet, this assumption appears to be sorely mistaken. Personal drives have changed the scale of leaking from page-by-page drips to gigabyte waves, but at the same time, governments have developed the ability to collect a virtual "tsunami" of even greater peta- and exabytes of data.[41] The largest WikiLeaks release, the State Department cables, of which only a fraction were classified as secret, have been estimated to be approximately 2 gigabytes of data. Alasdair Roberts writes that "[b]y comparison, it has been estimated that the outgoing Bush White House transferred 77 terabytes of data to the National Archives in 2009 alone." That does not include any of the secrets classified in other agencies such as the NSA, CIA, or Pentagon. Roberts continues, "None of this is an argument for complacency about government secrecy. Precisely because of the scale and importance of the national security apparatus, it ought to be subjected to close scrutiny. Existing oversight mechanisms such as freedom of information laws and declassification policies are inadequate and should be strengthened."[42] In the wake of the Snowden leaks in the United States, 65% of the public supported eventually having public hearings on the topic. One commentator noted, "[W]e appear to be inclined to give the government the benefit of the doubt, while wishing we had more information," and explained that the government response has been " 'we're doing all we can.' Time will tell if those responses are adequate."[43] The Red Queen's race continues.

Implication 5: Failure Is the Mother of Invention

As we saw in the early examples of oversight, the first freedom of information laws and constraints on executive national security powers were born out of partisan distrust and fear of private interest policy. This has continued today. One thing about the states that have significant oversight institutions is that they are born out of perceptions of skepticism. In the United States, both the strengthening of the Freedom of Information Act and significant changes in legislative oversight followed revelations about Watergate, COINTELPRO, and doubts about the Vietnam War. Increased oversight in Norway followed the revelation from the Lund Commission, and SIRC was built after the McDonald Commission in Canada uncovered significant abuse of secrecy powers by the Royal Canadian Mounted Police. In Belgium, while investigations in the late 1980s and early 1990s did not uncover significant problems with the intelligence services, a series of bombings coupled with distrust between the Dutch-and French-speaking portions of the countries raised skepticism about how national security powers were being wielded. A former advisor to the Belgian oversight committee noted that "[n]umerous rumours and accusations then circulated concerning the working of the police services and the intelligence services . . . and gave rise to a good deal of criticism." She went on to state that in this context of distrust, "there was a need for external supervision of these services." This led to the Permanent Committee for Control of the Intelligence Services, which augmented the powers of several permanent national security committees and committees of inquiry at the time. One key to the system was that "these members are answerable to Parliament" and report to Parliament. Given the empirical evidence that these institutions increase public support during crises and raise sufficient military funds to be effective but constrain overspending, the changes seem justified.[44]

The question then remains of whether countries such as the United States and the United Kingdom, after the Iraq War and with continued partisan bickering, will re-energize their oversight mechanisms. There have been some positive green shoots in the United Kingdom. For example, there has been a wide-ranging and important debate on the limitations of the Intelligence and Security Committee. The current chairman, Malcolm Rifkind, has stated his support for turning the body into a parliamentary committee with significant retrospective investigative powers. Many of these suggestions made their way into the government's Green Paper on Justice and Security, which yielded the Justice and Security Bill that was passed in April 2013. While several of the ideas in the bill relating to secrecy in judicial trials are controversial, increasing oversight in light of the Iraq War and worries about the United Kingdom's role in extraordinary rendition has prospects. MP Rifkind noted during the debate on increasing the ISC powers and making it a parliamentary oversight committee that "[o]ur responsibility is to provide retrospective oversight, and the Government appears in principle to have accepted that, as we are dealing with matters of significant national interest . . . the principle is of profound importance."[45]

In the United States, however, there has been little movement to improve and innovate on national security oversight. Upon being sworn in as President, Barak Obama stated, "I don't believe that anybody is above the law. On the other hand, I also have a belief that we need to look forward as opposed to looking backwards . . . . My orientation is going to be to move forward." But as Dawn Johnsen, previously a nominee to head the Office of Legal Council, stated, "We must avoid any temptation simply to move on. We must instead be honest with ourselves and the world as we condemn our nation's past transgressions . . . . Our constitutional democracy cannot survive with a government shrouded in secrecy, nor can our nation's honor be restored without full disclosure." One reason that Johnsen was withdrawn as nominee for Office of Legal Council was that she supported the retrospective investigation of national security policy on Iraq. The costs of failing to look back were further emphasized by Jonathan Turley, a law professor at George Washington University, when he stated that the lack of retrospective investigation in the United States was "very worrisome."

From the perspective of this work, and the evidence herein, it is not surprising that an executive resists vigorously investigating national security. What is slightly more surprising is the lack of legislative activity on this issue. While hearings on Iraq and particularly pre-war intelligence did occur, they have not spurred any changes in tightening oversight and increasing executive credibility. Regardless of this choice, the implication for the future is that future conflicts that may seem ambiguous to the public—for example, a preemptive strike on a country that may be developing nuclear weapons—may continue to draw support from only the president's party. In fact, despite the relatively low cost to the American public, the intervention in Libya generated significantly different perspectives from Republicans and Democrats, with a 34-percentage-point gap between Democrats approving of how Obama handled the crisis (64%) and Republicans approving (30%). Again, this partisan divide dwarfs those in other contexts.[46] In earlier polls, overall only 30% of the public saw a clear national security goal in the conflict for the benefit of the United States.[47] These types of divides and distrust of the executive do not augur well for generating consent and public support into the future without improvements in oversight powers for the legislature, public, and press. The case of France in the inter-war years should remind us that innovation in oversight is not automatic and that simply reorganizing the executive is likely to be insufficient.

Implication 6: Accountability is Codependent

I have spent much of this book arguing that democratic accountability is more than simply competitive elections. For without information, these elections cannot hold a leader to account. This is particularly important in the sealed-off realm of national security policy. I believe this has been a useful corrective to a great deal of influential and important work on the domestic political institutional effect of democracy on foreign policy. These works assumed, either explicitly in their theorizing or implicitly in their evidence and measures, that democratic accountability was not issue-specific and that crucial foreign policy information such as the expected costs and benefits of a specific executive action was just as likely to become public as the analogous information on a domestic policy. This beggars belief given the prevalence of secrecy laws in democracies around the world and rules explicitly allowing executives the capacity to keep national security secrets. I then set out to amend rather than attack this logic of domestic accountability and its importance for understanding foreign policy support, strength, and success. Specifically, I constructed and then subsequently found support for a theory that suggests democratic accountability institutions—such as competitive elections—need to be supplemented by oversight institutions. If retrospective oversight is lacking, then democracies will be unlikely to consistently match mobilization to security needs. On the other hand, significant oversight provides the tools for success that explains why democracies, while remaining partially cloaked in secrecy, have been able to exist and expand in the international system but avoid the extreme excesses and waste that have plagued repressive dictatorships.

However, just as the effectiveness of elections in creating public accountability on national security issues depends on information and oversight institutions, so too does the effectiveness of oversight institutions hinge on competitive and meaningful elections. Some recent scholarship has warned about a worrying trend toward illiberal democracies. These are states that have some of the trappings of democracies—for example, they hold regular elections—but fall far short of the liberal standards that most OECD countries would hold. Thus, these elections might be rigged, gerrymandered, or subtly altered through implicit threats and favors. Illiberalism is not a disease that only affects transitioning countries. Even some relatively mature democracies as of late have begun to succumb to symptoms of declining competition and accountability. Most notable, Hungary serves as a warning on this score. From 1990 through 2010, Hungary was awarded the highest value on the Polity democracy scale.[48] Additionally, from 1992 to 2006, Budapest built a useful set of national security oversight institutions. These included a Freedom of Information Act with a harm test, and an extra-executive body to apply a public-interest test to national security information. Also, the committee on national security had significant powers, was headed by a member of the opposition, had access to evidence on previous intelligence operations, and could report publicly on its findings. These are a strong set of tools. However, on January 1, 2012, a new constitution, put forward by Prime Minister Viktor Orban and his Fidesz party, came into effect. This constitution and its concomitant changes altered the electoral map and increased censorship powers.[49] The changes have been investigated by the European Parliament's Civil Liberties Committee.[50] Even if several oversight functions continue, the ability to hold incumbents to account will be significantly lower. While maintaining a less impressive array of oversight institutions, Russia has also significantly decreased its accountability through elections, seeing a decline from 6 to 4 on the democracy scale during this time.

These cases serve as a useful reminder that the argument about oversight complements, rather than competes with, preexisting liberal explanations of democratic foreign policy. Oversight theory adds another layer onto accountability that, for the first time, explains democratic success on the international stage, without having to assume away national security secrecy. While the omnipresence of national security secrecy in democracies has been a point of theoretical vulnerability,[51] retrospective oversight institutions help to reinforce the liberal IR theory's flank. However, without accountability institutions such as competitive elections, oversight itself is exposed to criticism of being mere words without action. While the evidence provided here buttresses the joint significance of elections and information, more research on these topics is called for, particularly at the boundary points in marginal democracies.[52] In addition, recent research has suggested that the same logic of executives innovating to evade accountability may be present in the choice of repressive organizations.[53]

Looking Back: From Private Information to Public Consent

Kenneth Schultz's last sentence in one of the most influential works of contemporary systematic international relations research reads in part, "... if democracies want to enjoy the benefits of their institutions while minimizing the liabilities, the answer lies not in circumventing debate or suppressing dissent but in building true consensus." It is understanding both the problems and progress in how democracies can build consent that has been in large measure the charge of this project. As Gaubatz[54] has shown, a consensus over national security policies, particularly costly ones such as wars, is rare and often hardwon across democracies. In fact, building consensus, at its core, means changing citizens, minds, moving them from being skeptical of a specific policy to being supportive. To date, we have been left with little guidance about how democracies across the globe have been able to do this in the face of the exigencies of executive information asymmetries and public information deficits. In fact the lack of scrutiny that had been given to secrecy in democracies conjures up Sir Michael Howard's comments on the United Kingdom in 1986, when he stated, "So far as official government policy is concerned . . . enemy agents are found under gooseberry bushes and intelligence is brought by storks." Further, this important gap has led some scholars to doubt that the public has a productive role to play in foreign policy or whether democracies are really distinct types of states from autocracies when on the world stage.

Perhaps some of this doubt results from the notion that only democracies are forced to trade off secrecy and effectiveness for luxury goods such as civil rights and competitive elections. This notion has been fostered from talk show green rooms to government green papers. For example, in 2004, the British Home Office published a discussion paper entitled "Counter-Terrorism Powers: Reconciling Security and Liberty in an Open Society" that begins by stating "liberty may be exploited by those supporting, aiding or engaging in terrorism," and concludes that rights can get in the way of providing security, which is "the first duty of Government."[55,56] In 2006, future Conservative PM David Cameron stated in a speech in London that "[t]he fundamental challenge, then, is to strike the right balance between security and liberty. But it's hard—extremely hard—to make that crucial judgment: How much freedom should we forego in order to be safe?"[57] The USA Patriot Act, which increased executive powers in the United States, is an acronym for "United and Strengthening America by Providing Appropriate Tools Required to Intercept and Obstruct Terrorism." Author Geoffrey Stone has written that "[t]he war on terrorism has posed fundamental questions about the appropriate balance between individual liberty and national security."[58] These statements suggest that freedoms and rights necessarily reduce security.

I believe the arguments in this book reframe the debate about how to secure a democracy with both private information and public consent. There is indeed a secrecy dilemma for democracies. However, there are also partial solutions being practiced around the globe. Neither the metaphor of balance nor the specific identification of the poles—as security and civil liberty—is particularly helpful or accurate. For in the metaphor, it is taken for granted that allowing the executive greater surveillance powers, a freer hand for drone strikes, or the ability to detain citizens indefinitely automatically procures the public greater security. This is akin to assuming that if you provide the executive with greater military spending, then you are automatically more safe. But this should not be taken for granted.

There is significant evidence that unchecked executives, at the extreme in nondemocratic circumstances, feel no consistent and undeviating compunction to secure the state and avoid personal or partisan gain.[59] The trade-off, to the extent one exists, is between executive secrecy and private information and broader information revelation, which includes civil liberties as one component; and even here, the dimension of time allows for coexistence. Political debates need to be had about the mechanisms to both empower an executive to act and constrain that action toward the public interest. There are plenty of details to grapple and tinker with. We must remember Madison's worry that "the management of foreign relations appears to be the most susceptible of abuse, of all the trusts committed to a government," but reflect with the confidence that over the last 200 years, significant strides are in evidence. Oversight, although imperfect, helps to make the world safe for democracies and to make democracies safe for the world.

Appendix: Formal Models, Data, and Statistical Results

FORMAL MODELS

In this section I present two related formal models of the interaction between a leader and the public. In the first, retrospective oversight is modeled as a probabilistic lottery. In the second, I add endogenous oversight to the model, allowing an overseer to choose to oversee or not when foreign policy action is costly. The models reinforce each other, because the first, while simplistic, allows us to focus on the key interactions, and the second illustrates that an oversight lottery does indeed arise under many conditions even when the choice to oversee or not is endogenous. These models formally illustrate the logic of the mobilizing and constraining effects of retrospective security policy information institutions as discussed in the main text.[1]

Exogenous Oversight and Public Support

The structure of the first game is as follows:

1. Nature chooses an international crisis situation. This is revealed to the agent (the president) but not the principal (the public). The principal has belief $p \in (0, 1)$ about whether the specific situation is one where action will accrue private benefits to the agent (β) or the complementary belief $(1 - p)$ that action in this case will provide a benefit to all (θ).
2. The agent chooses action α or $\neg\alpha$.[2]

3. The game ends with the status quo if $\neg\alpha$ is chosen. The payoffs are then $(0, 0)$.
4. If the agent acts (α), the principal chooses whether to support (s) the action or not (o).
   a. Support leads to payoffs $(\beta - (p(\nu|\alpha) \times \phi), -\gamma)$ in a β-world and $(\theta, \theta - \gamma)$ in a θ-world. γ includes both the cost of the action and an information extraction cost. $p(\nu|\alpha)$ represents the probability that the principal will be able to verify that the action was not in its interest, where $p(\nu|\alpha) \in (0, 1)$. ϕ measures the level of punishment that an agent can incur if verification occurs. β measures the private benefits and θ indicates the public benefits.
   b. Oppose leads to payoffs (τ_a, τ_p).

For simplicity, we can define $\epsilon = p(\nu|\alpha) \times \phi$. The costs γ and ϕ are constrained to be greater than zero, as are the benefits β and θ. Further, $\theta > \gamma$, constraining the game to model crisis situations where the potential benefit to the national interest/security of the state is strictly greater than the costs incurred in a θ-world.[3] Finally, $\tau_i < 0$, where opposition is costly for the principal and the agent. The game[4] is similar to many principal–agent models with incomplete information, where the principal is at a potential informational disadvantage.[5] I analyze the game using perfect Bayesian equilibria (PBE) as the solution concept. The idea is that players (in this case the principal) update their beliefs about the game according to Bayes' rule.

Proposition 1 In situations where $\beta - \epsilon > 0$, no pure separating equilibrium exists.

The proof is included below, but the intuition is easily grasped. In situations where retrospective information diffusion and conditional punishment are unlikely, foreign policy action does not convey information to the public. Since $\theta > 0$, the agent will prefer α to $\neg\alpha$ if the anticipated probability of support from the principal is sufficiently high. However, the converse is true if opposition is the principal's likely strategy ($\because \tau_p < 0$). When the outcome (β, α, S) is better than the status quo for the agent ($\beta - \epsilon > 0$), the incentives for a β-crisis are similar to the incentives in the θ-case. Both crisis situations supply the agent with an incentive to act (α) when the anticipated probability of support from the principal is high enough. Similarly, both types have an incentive to avoid being opposed, since $\tau_a < 0$. If the principal is skeptical enough to prefer opposition to support, then both crisis types will lead an agent to avoid α. If the principal is trusting enough (i.e., p is sufficiently low), both types of agents can take advantage of that and offer α. For the principal, support strictly dominates oppose when $p < \frac{-\tau_p + (\theta - \gamma)}{\theta}$. Significantly, seeing α or $\neg\alpha$ does not supply the principal with information on the crisis situation. The two pure strategy pooling equilibria under these conditions are $(\neg\alpha, \neg\alpha, O)$ if $p > \frac{-\tau_p + (\theta - \gamma)}{\theta}$ and are (α, α, S) if $p < \frac{-\tau_p + (\theta - \gamma)}{\theta}$.[6] A separating equilibrium does not exist because the agent's incentives are similar in both cases.

These pooling equilibria have significant implications for the interaction between foreign policy and public opinion in the United States. When post hoc information diffusion and contingent leadership punishment are unlikely ($\because \epsilon < \beta$)—for example, due to poor legislative oversight, weak freedom of information and incomplete press freedom—either the principal can be taken advantage of, given β and a low enough p, or an agent can fail to garner principal support, given θ and a high enough p. Here, policy action and support depend to a large extent on prior beliefs, and these beliefs are not updated based on action. Therefore, action does not credibly signal an international threat.

Proposition 2 When $\tau_a < \beta - \epsilon < 0$, a separating equilibrium exists where α is chosen only in a θ-situation, and the principal supports that action.

In crisis situations where principals are sufficiently confident that they can recognize and punish agents for acting in the private interest ($\because \beta - \epsilon < 0$), only a θ-situation will lead an agent to offer α. Agents in β-situations do not offer α since they prefer the status quo ($\because 0 > \beta - \epsilon$). Conversely, θ-situations do present an incentive for α over $\neg\alpha$ ($\because \theta > 0$). The specific situations that allow for post hoc verification and punishment, by raising ϵ, create the conditions for an informative signal to principals that the situation is one of national rather than private interests. Knowing this, principals can update their beliefs $(p|\alpha)$ about the crisis situation and judge that support rather than opposition is their best strategy. Under these key conditions, skepticism leads to not inaction $(\neg\alpha)$ but rather both action and support. When principals see a signal, they can be confident that the situation calls for action in the national interest. Active checks on the president as the foreign policy agent, through an active press following a hot story or an opposition-controlled legislature, can both reduce private-interest action (that solely in the private interest of the agent) and induce principal support (due to the informative signal).

Additional Proofs

Here I explore two perfect Bayesian equilibria in the principal agent game, given the constraints:

$$\beta > 0$$
$$\epsilon \geq 0$$
$$\tau_i < 0$$
$$\theta > 0 > \gamma$$
$$\theta - \gamma > 0$$
$$p \in (0, 1)$$

Proof of Proposition 1

When $\beta - \epsilon > 0$, at the last stage of the game, P plays support (S) if

$$EU_p(S) > EU_p(O)$$
$$p - \gamma + (1 - p)(\theta - \gamma) > \tau_p$$
$$p < \frac{-\tau_p + (\theta - \gamma)}{\theta}$$

We can define

$$\hbar = \frac{-\tau_p + (\theta - \gamma)}{\theta}$$

When $p < \hbar$, A_β will play α if

$$EU_A(\alpha|S, \beta) > EU_A(\neg\alpha|S, \beta), \qquad \beta - \epsilon > 0$$

As long as these are true, A_β plays α.

Similarly, when $p < \hbar$, A_θ will play α if

$$EU_A(\alpha|S, \theta) > EU_A(\neg\alpha|S, \theta), \qquad \theta > 0$$

This is true by definition. Using Bayes' rule, P's posterior beliefs remain unchanged:

$$\frac{p \times 1}{(p \times 1) + (1 - p) \times (1)} = p$$

Therefore, the triple (α, α, S) describes a perfect Bayesian equilibrium when $p < \hbar$ and $\beta - \epsilon > 0$. A_β chooses α, A_θ chooses α, and P chooses support.

On the other hand, when $p > \hbar$, P's best strategy is to oppose. Knowing that, A_β will only play α if

$$EU_A(\alpha|O, \beta) > EU_A(\neg\alpha|O, \beta), \qquad \tau_a > 0$$

Since this is never true by definition, A_β plays $\neg\alpha$.

Similarly, A_θ will only play α if

$$EU_A(\alpha|O,\theta) > EU_A(\neg\alpha|O,\theta), \qquad \tau_a > 0$$

Again, this cannot be true.

Note that $p > \hbar$ can only be true if $|\tau_p| < |\gamma|$. If the cost of opposition is greater than the cost of α, then $\hbar > 1, \therefore p \not> \hbar$.

Using Bayes' rule, P's posterior beliefs remain unchanged:

$$\frac{p \times 1}{(p \times 1) + ((1-p) \times (1))} = p$$

Therefore, the triple $(\neg\alpha, \neg\alpha, O)$ describes a perfect Bayesian equilibrium when $p > \hbar$ and $\beta - \epsilon > 0$. A_β chooses α, A_θ chooses α, and P chooses support.

With the above constraints, a separating equilibrium $(\neg\alpha, \alpha, S)$ does not exist. If it is in P's interest to play S, both θ and β situations will lead to α, because

$$EU_A(\alpha|S,\beta) > EU_A(\neg\alpha|S,\beta), \qquad \beta - \epsilon > 0$$

as described above.

Proof of Proposition 2

When $\beta - \epsilon < \tau_a < 0$, we can still use the cut point $\hbar$ to differentiate P's choice.

If $p < \hbar$, P's best strategy would be to support. However, now A_β and A_θ have differing incentives.

A_β will play α if

$$EU_A(\alpha|S,\beta) > EU_A(\neg\alpha|S,\beta), \beta - \epsilon > 0$$

which is now false. Therefore, A_β will play $\neg\alpha$.

A_θ will play α if

$$EU_A(\alpha|S,\theta) > EU_A(\neg\alpha|S,\theta), \theta > 0$$

which is always true. Therefore, A_θ will play α. This new information allows P to update her posterior belief, with

$$\frac{p \times 0}{(p \times 0) + ((1-p) \times (1))} = 0$$

Thus, a separating equilibrium is expressed by the triple $(\neg\alpha, \alpha, S)$, when $\beta - \epsilon < \tau_a < 0$ and $|\tau_p| < |\gamma|$.

A Formal Model of Spending with Endogenous Oversight

The setup of the second game is as follows[7]:

1. Nature (N) defines the security environment whereby the price of optimal public security in a state $(\dot{P})$ is either expensive $(\dot{P} = \gamma)$ or cheap $(\dot{P} = \alpha)$.[8] This is revealed to the executive but not the public or the legislature. The public and legislature have prior belief $p \in (0, 1)$ that $\dot{P} = \alpha$ and corresponding belief $(1 - p)$ that $\dot{P} = \gamma$. For convenience I define $\gamma = \gamma^* + \alpha$, where $\gamma \gg \alpha \geq 0$.

2. The executive chooses a military budget $(\hat{\gamma})$ of either γ or α. Thus, α is a nominal investment value that is uncontroversial and maintains the status quo, given $\dot{P} = \alpha$, but does not improve on it. $\hat{\gamma} = \alpha$ leads to payoffs $(-\theta, -\theta, -\theta)|(\dot{P} = \gamma)$ and $(0, 0, 0)|(\dot{P} = \alpha)$. The nominal spending α is zeroed out by the small benefits of maintenance.[9] $\theta > 0$ and represents the public economic stakes of the military investment when national security is threatened. This economic return can be lost by underspending or can be collected by optimal spending $|\dot{P} = \gamma$.

3. If $\hat{\gamma} = \gamma$, the public chooses to support (s) or oppose (o) the proposed budget. Opposition leads to payoffs $(-\theta, -\theta - \tau, -\theta - \tau)|(\dot{P} = \gamma)$ and $(0, 0, 0)|(\dot{P} = \alpha)$.

4. If the public chooses support, the legislature then chooses whether or not to investigate $(I, \sim I)$, and $\sim I$ leads to payoffs $(\theta, \theta - \gamma, \theta - \gamma)|(\dot{P} = \gamma)$ and $(\gamma, -\gamma, -\gamma)|(\dot{P} = \alpha)$. I leads to payoffs $(\theta, \theta - \gamma, \theta - \gamma - \lambda)|(\dot{P} = \gamma)$ and $(\gamma - \phi, -\gamma, -\gamma + \xi - \lambda)|(\dot{P} = \alpha)$. ξ and λ represent the benefits and costs, respectively, of investigation to the legislature. ϕ is the penalty suffered by the executive for being investigated conditional on overspending, $\hat{\gamma} > \dot{P}$.

Therefore, γ represents the private leadership benefit an executive would receive if he could mobilize support for overspending when security was inexpensive. The information asymmetry between the executive and the other players involves $\dot{P}$, the optimal level of spending, not the actual spending, which is represented in $\hat{\gamma}$ and is observed by all players.[10] I apply the constraints that $2\theta > \gamma$, such that the investment in security yields a positive net return to the public when $\dot{P} = \gamma$, and $\phi > \gamma$; thus the revelation of overspending could be costly to a leader if revealed. τ is assumed to be the cost of opposition generally. Since we are dealing with democratic states this is assumed to be zero. Future generalizations of this game could explore nonzero values. I use perfect Bayesian equilibria as the solution concept. This involves finding sets of strategies that are simultaneously best replies to the other players' strategies and consistent with rational beliefs[11] on the equilibrium path. Proofs of the following propositions can be found below.

Insecurity Costs and Democracies Without Oversight

In a democracy where national security oversight is prohibitively costly ($\xi < \lambda$), a set of equilibria are described in Proposition 1 for the second model.

Proposition 1 When $1-p < \gamma/2\theta$ and $\xi < \lambda$, all equilibria include the strategy o.

All equilibria with $1 - p < \gamma/2\theta$ and $\xi < \lambda$ resemble problems of adverse selection. In theories of principal–agent relations, adverse selection is the process by which socially suboptimal outcomes or even market collapse can occur under conditions of asymmetric information. Akerlof's[12] seminal article on markets and information proved that if a seller had more information than the buyer about the quality of the good and there were no means of quality verification for the buyer, then high-quality goods would be priced out of the market. In extreme forms of the game, no goods were traded in equilibrium.

Just as a buyer might fail to purchase a quality used car because the incentive exists for the seller to over-hype the car's virtues, in this equilibrium asymmetric information and potential private leadership benefits lead the public to oppose any high spending that is offered.[13] While the executive cannot extort private benefits in this equilibrium, the public underspends on the military and pays the insecurity cost $-\theta$, failing to pay γ even when $\dot{P} = \gamma$. Suboptimal security policy results from the asymmetric information environment. Regardless of what the executive does, the public opposes increased military spending. This leads to the public failing to reap the security benefits θ, which could have been purchased at cost $\gamma < \theta$, but instead net $-\theta$, where $|-\theta| > \gamma$.

The low oversight equilibrium would be expected in democracies that lack national security oversight institutions. If $\xi < \lambda$, the costs of national security oversight are greater than the benefits to the legislature. Further, when the prior public belief that security is expensive is low relative to the ratio of costs and benefits, specifically $1 - p < \gamma/2\theta$, the public does not view the potential benefits of supporting expensive spending a priori as worth the risks.[14]

This set of equilibria mirrors many criticisms of excessive sloth in democratic foreign policy. For example, Morgenthau[15] and Herring[16] have chastised the United States for a lack of public support for war preparations leading up to World War II, while Kennan[17] laments that the United States is chronically late in marshaling its defenses. More generally, others[18] believe that each of the three democratic great powers during the inter-war years undermobilized given external threat conditions. Berend[19] extends the same argument to the underspending of fledgling democracies in Central and Eastern Europe. Without freedom of information laws or even formal legislative oversight of national security matters during this time, the executive held secrets, but the public and representatives had little confidence in successfully investigating national security policy decisions. In the United States, the Dolittle report in 1954 noted that secrecy made mobilizing the public difficult on national security matters.[20] Further, Johnson[21] notes the lack of staffing and lack of quality oversight before the legislative reorganization acts.

Imperfect but Informative National Security Oversight in Democracies

To explore the logically consistent behaviors of actors in democracies with retrospective national security information institutions, we can solve the model when $\xi > \lambda$. In this case, it is now less costly for the legislature to investigate potentially private-interest executive foreign policy, and there is an explicit net benefit for the legislature when they uncover the executive overspending on defense. One might expect that there would be a pure strategy separating equilibrium, mirroring game 1, whereby the threat of legislative oversight and punishment deters an executive from asking for $\hat{\gamma} = \gamma$ when the optimal spending given the state of the world is $\dot{P} = \alpha$. However, this is not the case, as stated in Proposition 2 for the second formal model.

Proposition 2 When $\lambda > 0$, no pure strategy separating equilibrium exists that includes the strategy vector $(\hat{\gamma} = \gamma | \dot{P} = \gamma, \hat{\gamma} = \alpha | \dot{P} = \alpha, s, I)$.

While the formal conditional impossibility proof is included below, the intuition behind it is straightforward. Suppose that the legislature announced that it was investigating for certain. This would mean that the executive would only proffer $\hat{\gamma} = \gamma | \dot{P} = \gamma$. Knowing this, the legislature would be able to update their beliefs about the world,

$$prob(\dot{P} = \alpha | \hat{\gamma} = \gamma)$$

$$= \frac{prob(\hat{\gamma} = \gamma | \dot{P} = \alpha) \times p}{(prob(\hat{\gamma} = \gamma | \dot{P} = \alpha) \times p) + (prob(\hat{\gamma} = \gamma | \dot{P} = \gamma) \times (1-p))}$$

$$= \frac{0 \times p}{(0 \times p) + (1 \times (1-p))} = 0$$

The legislature would only investigate if $EU(I) > EU(\sim I)$, which is only true when $\hat{p} > \lambda/\xi$. Given the updated belief $\hat{p} = 0$ and the nonzero constraint on λ, this condition can never be met. Since the legislature knows for certain $(\hat{p} = 0)$ that an expensive military budget signals a threatening international situation, they do not waste their resources investigating. Thus, a potential publicly optimal pure separating equilibrium does not exist. If national security oversight is costly, it is going to be imperfect. This is the paradox of perfect oversight.

Instead, there exists a partial separating equilibrium, such that the legislature investigates foreign policy decisions imperfectly and the executive always asks for γ when security is expensive, but still attempts to cheat $(\hat{\gamma} = \gamma | \dot{\mathcal{P}} = \alpha)$ with nonzero probability. In this equilibrium, the public supports the proposed budget. This equilibrium only exists when $\xi > \lambda$.

Proposition 3 When $\lambda/\xi < min(p, 1 - \gamma/2\theta)$, a mixed-strategy equilibria exists with $(\hat{\gamma} = \gamma | \dot{\mathcal{P}} = \gamma, g(\hat{\gamma} = \gamma | \dot{\mathcal{P}} = \alpha), s, \sigma(I))$.

Here, the legislature investigates with probability $\sigma(I)$ and the executive always asks for $\hat{\gamma} = \gamma | \dot{\mathcal{P}} = \gamma$ and $\hat{\gamma} = \gamma | \dot{\mathcal{P}} = \alpha$ only with probability $g(\hat{\gamma} = \gamma | \dot{\mathcal{P}} = \alpha)$. Specifically, $\sigma(I) = \gamma/\phi$ and $g(\hat{\gamma} = \gamma | \dot{\mathcal{P}} = \alpha) = (1 - p)\lambda/p(\xi - \lambda)$. In this equilibrium the public supports the proposed budget as long as $\lambda/\xi < 1 - \gamma/2\theta$. This is true even when $p > 1 - \gamma/2\theta$ because the public is able to learn something about the state of the world from the executive's actions.

Therefore, in the partial separating equilibrium, information is uniquely exchanged between the executive and public about the state of the world through the executive's action. The public moves from p, their prior, to $p|(\hat{\gamma} = \gamma) = \lambda/\xi$. For all cases where $p > 1 - \gamma/2\theta$, such that the public's unconditional prior would have led to opposition, this equilibrium generates support through oversight. Within the partial separating equilibrium, the imperfect legislative oversight, exercised with positive probability $0 > \sigma(I) < 1$, is enough to mobilize the public in situations where they were originally skeptical. For new and emerging threats, this will be crucial. While still allowing some private interest policy, $0 < g(\hat{\gamma} = \gamma | \dot{\mathcal{P}} = \alpha) < 1$, the public consent problems are solved. In the equilibrium the joint conditional probability of observing the executive ask for an accurate military budget and the public supporting that choice when the external situation is threatening, $prob((\hat{\gamma} = \gamma, s) | \dot{\mathcal{P}} = \gamma)$, equals 1. However, the executive also asks for, and receives support for, overspending with positive probability.

Corollary 1 Executive overspending is reduced in the partial separating equilibrium expressed in Proposition 3 as $\xi \rightarrow \infty$ or $\lambda \rightarrow 0$, $\because$ $\lim_{\xi \rightarrow \infty} (1 - p)\lambda/p(\xi - \lambda) = 0$ and $\lim_{\lambda \rightarrow 0} (1 - p)\lambda/p(\xi - \lambda) = 0$.

The model also delineates the conditions that decrease the probability of private interest foreign policy in equilibrium. As stated in Corollary 1, as the benefits (costs) of legislative investigation grow (shrink), the probability of overspending ($\hat{\gamma} > \dot{P}$) decreases toward zero. Thus, national security oversight institutions that allow for sufficient punishment $\phi > \gamma$ of executive malfeasance and net legislative rewards for scrutiny ($\xi > \lambda$) increase public mobilization as well as reduce military overspending. A similar interpretation is that if the accuracy of oversight increases as the costs are lowered, smaller and smaller deviations from optimality could be potentially detected, and thus deterred.

In the partial separating equilibrium we would expect leaders within democracies to have both a nonzero probability of private interest foreign policy and a positive probability of retrospective investigation. Chapter 4 provided exemplars of oversight institutions uncovering abuses previously shrouded in secrecy.[22]

Additional Proofs

Proof of Proposition 1

Define q as the probability of the public supporting and σ_I as the probability of investigation. Suppose $\sigma_I = 0$. Then the executive would choose $\hat{\gamma} = \gamma | \dot{P} = \alpha$ when $EU(\hat{\gamma} = \gamma | \dot{P} = \alpha) > EU(\hat{\gamma} = \alpha | \dot{P} = 0)$. This will be true when $q(\gamma) + (1 - q)(0) > 0$, which is to say $q > 0$. Similarly, the executive would choose $\hat{\gamma} = \gamma | \dot{P} = \gamma$ when $EU(\hat{\gamma} = \gamma | \dot{P} = \gamma) > EU(\hat{\gamma} = \alpha | \dot{P} = \gamma)$. This is true when $q(\theta) + (1 - q)(-\theta) > -\theta$, which is to say $q > 0$. Therefore, if there is positive probability of support and zero probability of investigation, the executive prefers to play $\hat{\gamma} = \gamma$ for both states of the world. When $q = \sigma_I = 0$, the executive is indifferent between $\hat{\gamma} = \alpha$ and $\hat{\gamma} = \gamma$ and the eventual spending is at low levels, regardless.

The public will support $\hat{\gamma} = \gamma$ when $EU(s) > EU(o)$. This is true when $(1 - p)(\theta - \gamma) + p(-\gamma) > (1 - p)(-\theta - \tau) + p(-\tau)$; solving for p yields $p < 1 + (\tau - \gamma)/2\theta$. Seeing $\hat{\gamma} = \gamma$, when $q > 0$, the public cannot update their prior belief, p, that $\dot{P} = \alpha$. Using Bayes' rule, $prob(\dot{P} = \alpha | \hat{\gamma} = \gamma) = 1 \times p/1 \times p + (1 - p) \times 1 = p$.

The legislature will investigate when $EU(I) > EU(\sim I)$. This inequality will be satisfied when $(1 - p)(\theta - \gamma - \lambda) + p(-\gamma + \xi - \lambda) > (1 - p)(\theta - \gamma) + p(-\gamma)$. Solving for p yields $p > \lambda/\xi$.

When $\lambda > \xi, p < (\lambda/\xi) \forall p$. When $\sigma_I = 0$ and $q > 0$, the legislature cannot update p, $prob(\dot{P} = \alpha | \hat{\gamma} = \gamma) = (1 \times p)/(1 \times p + (1 - p) \times 1) = p$.

Given the preceding, if we reintroduce $\tau > -2\theta(1 - p) + \gamma$ and $\lambda > \xi$, we have the PBE from Proposition 1 with the strategy set ($\hat{\gamma} = \gamma | \dot{P} = \gamma, \hat{\gamma} =$

$\gamma|\dot{P} = \alpha, s, \sim I)$. Note that when $\tau > \gamma$, $\tau > -2\theta(1 - p) + \gamma$ is always true, since $\theta > 0$ and $p \in (0, 1)$. $\tau = 0$ is simply a special case.

Therefore, when $\tau < -2\theta(1-p)+\gamma$ and $\lambda > \xi$, we have the array of PBE from Proposition 2 which includes o. The public here prefers to oppose any action. There is nothing the executive can do about this. The executive has a dominant strategy regardless of the state of the world if there is any positive probability of support. If the public plays support with any positive probability, the executive will offer $\hat{\gamma} = \gamma$. Knowing that, the public fails to update prior belief p since $p|(\hat{\gamma} = \gamma) = (1 \times p)/(1 \times p + (1 + p) \times 1) = p$.

Given this lack of updating, the public's decision to support or oppose is unaffected by the executive's budget. Thus, there is no equilibrium with $\tau < -2\theta(1 - p) + \gamma$ and $\lambda > \xi$ where the public plays support. Here, $\dot{P} = \gamma$ does not generate defense spending and the public plays o while the executive is indifferent to offering $\hat{\gamma} = \gamma$ or not in either state of the world. With $\tau = 0$, we thus have the condition on Proposition 1, $1 - p > \gamma/ - 2\theta$, which is simply the above inequality solved for $1 - p$.

Proof of Proposition 2

If $q = 1$, the executive will prefer to $\hat{\gamma} = \gamma|\dot{P} = \alpha$ when $EU(\hat{\gamma} = \gamma|\dot{P} = \alpha)$ $> EU(\hat{\gamma} = \alpha|\dot{P} = \alpha)$ solving for σ_I, $\sigma_I < \gamma/\phi$. Note that if $\gamma > \phi$, $\sigma_I < (\gamma/\phi)\forall\sigma_I$. When $\dot{P} = \gamma$, the executive's payoff does not depend on investigation. $EU(\hat{\gamma} = \gamma|\dot{P} = \gamma) > EU(\hat{\gamma} = \alpha|\dot{P} = \gamma)$, which is equal to $2\theta > 0$.

Recall that the legislature will investigate when $p > \lambda/\xi$. For the pure strategy separating equilibrium $(\hat{\gamma} = \gamma|\dot{P} = \gamma, \hat{\gamma} = \alpha|\dot{P} = \alpha, s, I)$ to exist, both $\sigma_I < \frac{\gamma}{\phi}$ and $p|(\hat{\gamma} = \gamma) > \lambda/\xi$ must hold. In this proposed equilibrium, $\sigma_I = 1 \not< \gamma/\phi$ when $\phi > \gamma$. Further, $p|(\hat{\gamma} = \gamma) = 0 \not> \lambda/\xi$ $\therefore$, $p|(\hat{\gamma} = \gamma) = (p \times 0)/(p \times 0 + (p + 1) \times 1) = 0$. This is true for all nonzero λ. Since neither condition is fulfilled, the equilibrium does not exist, as specified in Proposition 2.

Proof of Proposition 3 and Corollary 1

Given $\xi > \lambda$, $\tau = 0$, $\phi > \gamma$, an equilibrium with mixed strategies for the executive and legislature will exist when the legislature can play I with some positive probability $\sigma_I < 1$, and the executive will play $\hat{\gamma} = \gamma|\dot{P} = \alpha$ with probability g. This can only happen if the legislature can make the executive indifferent such that $EU(\hat{\gamma} = \gamma|\dot{P} = \alpha) = EU(\hat{\gamma} = \alpha|\dot{P} = \alpha)$. Solving for σ_I, $\sigma_I = \gamma/\phi$.

Therefore, when $\phi > \gamma$, it is possible for the legislature to fulfill this condition.

As before, $EU(\hat{\gamma} = \gamma | \dot{P} = \gamma) > EU(\hat{\gamma} = 0 | \dot{P} = \gamma)$ when $q > 0$.

In turn, the executive needs to play $\hat{\gamma} = \gamma | \dot{P} = \alpha$ with probability $0 < g < 1$ such that the legislature is indifferent to investigation. This is, $EU(I) = EU(\sim I)$, $p|(\hat{\gamma} = \gamma) = \frac{\lambda}{\xi} = gp/(gp + 1 - p) = \lambda/\xi$. Solving for g, we obtain $g = (1 - p)\lambda/p(\xi - \lambda)$.

Such a $g \in (0, 1)$ exists as long as $p > \frac{\lambda}{\xi}$.

Knowing this, the public would update their prior belief p to $p|(\hat{\gamma} = \gamma) = \lambda/\xi$. When $\lambda/\xi < 1 - \gamma/2\theta$ and $p > \lambda/\xi$, the public plays support, the legislature investigates with probability σ_I, and the executive always asks for $\hat{\gamma} = \gamma | \dot{P} = \gamma$ and asks for $\hat{\gamma} = \gamma | \dot{P} = \alpha$ with probability g. This defines the partial separating equilibrium in Proposition 3.

It follows from Proposition 5 that in the partial separating equilibrium the probability of overspending g, such that $\hat{\gamma} = \gamma | \dot{P} = \alpha$, is described by the function $(1 - p)\lambda/p(\xi - \lambda)$. The probability of overspending decreases as ξ, the conditional benefits of investigation, rises:

$$\lim_{\xi \to \infty} \frac{(1 - p)\lambda}{p(\xi - \lambda)} = \frac{\lim_{\xi \to \infty}((1 - p)\lambda)}{\lim_{\xi \to \infty}(p(\xi - \lambda))} = \frac{(1 - p)\lambda}{p(\infty - \gamma)} = 0$$

Similarly, the probability of overspending decreases to zero as λ, the unconditional costs of investigation, falls toward zero.

$$\lim_{\lambda \to 0} \frac{(1 - p)\lambda}{p(\xi - \lambda)} = \frac{\lim_{\lambda \to 0}((1 - p)\lambda)}{\lim_{\lambda \to 0}(p(\xi - \lambda))} = \frac{(1 - p) \times 0}{p(\xi - 0)} = 0$$

This explains the curvilinear relationship between oversight and spending. For low values of oversight (see Proposition 1), spending increases. From moderate to high values of oversight, oversight begins to constrain spending (see Proposition 3 and Corollary 1).

EMPIRICAL ANALYSES

Support

The data for changes in public support across the three countries come from Reiter and Chapman for the United States, Lai and Reiter for the United Kingdom, and Conley for France.[23]

Here I present the regression tables of several analyses comparing the pre–post oversight changes and rally behavior. Tables A-1 and A-2 present results for the United States over several specifications. The coefficients come from OLS regression with robust standard errors.[24]

Table A-1. REGRESSION RESULTS FOR THE UNITED STATES PREDICTING THE
RALLY-EFFECT SIZE PRE AND POST OVERSIGHT CHANGES[a]

Variable	MODEL 1 Coefficient	SE	MODEL 2 Coefficient	SE	MODEL 3 Coefficient	SE
Intercept	0.25	1.32	−0.36	5.75	−0.82	4.74
Post oversight change	5.10	1.87	5.48	2.03	8.17	3.34
Lagged level of opinion			0.01	0.09	0.03	0.79
Time until election			0.05	0.10		
Time in office			−0.46	0.49		
UN authorization					12.57	3.14
Trend					−0.19	0.12

[a]The *n*-size is 48 for each model.

Table A-2. REGRESSION RESULTS, WITH ADDITIONAL CONTROLS, FOR THE UNITED
STATES PREDICTING THE RALLY-EFFECT SIZE PRE AND POST OVERSIGHT CHANGES[a]

Variable	MODEL 4 Coefficient	SE
Intercept	7.71	5.56
Post oversight change	13.85	4.80
Lagged level of opinion	0.05	0.11
Bipartisan support	1.54	1.60
Presidential statement	2.37	1.46
Time until election	0.012	0.06
New York Times coverage	1.43	1.18
Business confidence	0.024	0.026
Revisionist or originator	3.01	1.58
Hostility level	2.26	1.29
Major power opponent	3.46	1.68
Allies	0.10	0.14
Ongoing war	5.04	2.31
UN authorization	2.81	3.37
UN action	1.43	0.95
Regional organization	1.82	3.25
Order of severity	2.92	1.20
Trend	0.48	0.14
Afghanistan	23.55	4.61

[a]The *n*-size is 48 for each model.

Thus one can see that the coefficient for oversight change is positive and more than twice the standard error across each specification. Other specifications, including taking out the 2001 outliers for the United States, do not alter our inference. To further improve our confidence in the results, I finally utilize the controls from Chapman and Reiter (2004, model 1, p. 900). These results are again consistent with the hypothesis and are presented below.

The analogous results for France are included in Table A-3.

Again, these results support the idea that increased oversight led to a greater rally effect. This is the case even when we take out the unpopular case of Algeria before the oversight change.

In the UK case, there is no statistical evidence of a nonrandom difference between the pre- and post-1979 time periods, as expected. The regression results are supplied in Table A-4. The coefficient for this time period is never significant at the .05 level and is small in absolute value. Model 3 probes whether the Falklands War was significantly different from other rally events; there is little evidence for this in the current specification. I also ran these same specifications using prime ministerial satisfaction with similar inference. Additionally, I included a dummy variable marking the post-1994 existence of the ISC committee in the United Kingdom. While this committee was very weak, it also could be conceived of as a placebo. The results were similar. However, it is important to note that a failure to reject a null hypothesis does not supply evidence that the true effect is actually zero.

Spending

To test the relative spending levels of democracies with and without national security oversight institutions, we are interested in modeling democratic military

Table A-3. REGRESSION RESULTS FOR FRANCE PREDICTING THE RALLY-EFFECT SIZE PRE AND POST OVERSIGHT CHANGES[a]

Variable	MODEL 1		MODEL 2		MODEL 3	
	Coefficient	SE	Coefficient	SE	Coefficient	SE
Intercept	−1.14	0.86	1.85	4.88	0.40	4.75
Post oversight change	4.22	1.15	3.28	1.58	3.39	1.53
Lagged level of opinion			−0.07	0.07	−0.03	0.07
Time until election			−0.23	2.36	−0.04	2.28
Time in office			0.32	0.42	0.24	0.40
Algeria					−8.40	4.76

[a]The *n*-size is 47 for each model.

Table A-4. REGRESSION RESULTS FOR THE UNITED KINGDOM PREDICTING THE
RALLY-EFFECT SIZE PRE AND POST OVERSIGHT CHANGES[a]

Variable	MODEL 1 Coefficient	SE	MODEL 2 Coefficient	SE	MODEL 3 Coefficient	SE
Intercept	−0.03	0.55	10.81	2.68	11.27	4.19
Post-1979	0.55	0.84	1.42	1.79	1.90	1.74
Lagged level of opinion			−0.24	0.06	−0.20	0.07
Time until election			2.23	1.33	2.07	1.34
Time in office			−0.41	0.32	−0.61	0.34
Trend					−0.41	0.50
By election					−1.43	0.78
Falklands					2.29	1.95

[a]The *n*-size is 57 for each model.

spending, y^D, as a function of national security oversight institutions as well as the other observable indicators that may raise or lower military spending.[25] y^D is a vector of y_o stacked with $y_{\sim o}$ for all years only for democracies. The elements of vector y^D can be indexed by state i and year t for convenience. One immediate inferential problem is the potential for the value of military spending in one state to influence, possibly at a later date, the military spending of another state. It is conceivable that the correlation between spending levels across states may occur indirectly and thus be controlled for by other observable factors, such as rivalry, major power status, or alliance ties. However, theories of deterrence as well as the security dilemma suggest that greater military spending by one state is likely to spur greater military spending for neighbors.[26] While the theoretical expectation of spatial interdependence is usually assumed away conditional on observed covariates, Goldsmith[27] explicitly finds spatial patterns in the underlying military expenditure data.[28] I parameterize the effect of neighbor spending using a spatial lag of the form $\rho W_t^{d,w} L y_t^w$, where y_t^w is a vector of military spending scores for the world in time t, with length j equal to the number of states.[29] $W_t^{d,w}$ is an $i \times j$ row-standardized weights matrix,[30] ρ is the parameter describing the covariance between a state's spending and that of its neighbors, and L is the lag operator. The product $W^{d,w} L y^w$ yields a weighted average of military spending by neighbors.[31]

Of course, states could be reacting not only to the spending decisions of neighbors, but through other types of international relations also. Therefore, I code the sum of a state's rivals' spending in the variable *Rival spending* and the sum of a state's allies' spending as *Ally spending*.[32]

I also control for several additional variables that past work has found to be robust predictors of military spending.[33] These include the number of borders a state shares with another state and whether a civil war or international crisis is ongoing. The greater the number of distinct borders a state maintains with other states, the greater the potential demand for defense spending.[34] The variables *borders* is equal to the log of the number of borders a state maintains, plus 1. Similarly, civil wars and international crises are likely to raise military spending as the state attempts to overcome these threats. The variable *civil war* is coded as present or absent from the Correlates of War Civil War dataset.[35] The variable *crisis* is coded as present or absent according to the International Crisis Behavior Project data.[36] I code the potential shift in perceived systemic threat after the end of the Cold War as measured with a dichotomous variable *post–Cold War*, taking the value of 1 after 1990 and 0 before. Each variable in this set, potentially in addition to ally and rival spending, is observable to the public and provides different priors (p) on the necessity of expensive military spending, and therefore they offer alternative opportunities for deciphering actual threat levels.

There is also an argument in the literature that small states and non-nuclear states may free-ride on the spending of larger and more powerful states' spending.[37] To measure this effect, I include a variable *population* that controls for the log of population size,[38] along with the variable *nuclear*, which is coded as a 1 when states possess nuclear weapons according to Jo and Gartzke.[39] Additionally, I code the variable *major power* as a 1 if a state was a major power according to the Correlates of War operationalization of the term[40] and 0 otherwise.[41]

As noted above, one inferential problem is differentiating the effect of national security oversight institutions from other possible distinctions among democracies. These include different levels of democratization on the Polity score, whether elections are being held in a given year, and whether the system of government is presidential or parliamentary.[42] Therefore I code the variable *democracy* that is a continuous measure of democracy from the Polity democracy score. Additional results are available in the online supplementary information.

Success

In this section I present the methodological details of the analysis of foreign policy success found in the main text. These are from Colaresi (2012). I also include a series of non-Bayesian estimates for comparison.

A Bayesian Ordered Bradley–Terry Model of Foreign Policy Ability

Let each state i at some time t have foreign policy ability λ_{it}. In a dyadic foreign policy crisis, where y_{ijt} indexes the outcomes of a particular dispute for state i

against state j at time t, the propensity for a winning outcome for state i will be a function of the difference between state i's ability and the opponent state j's abilities at time t, where $j \neq i$, and some stochastic component ϵ_{ijt}.[43]

The mapping from the latent abilities to a measured outcome y_{ijt} would be

$$y_{ijt} = \begin{cases} Lose & \text{if } \lambda_i - \lambda_j \leq \epsilon_{ijk} \\ Win & \text{if } \lambda_i - \lambda_j > \epsilon_{ijt} \end{cases}$$

This implies that

$$\begin{aligned} P(y_{ijt} = Win) &= Pr(\lambda_i - \lambda_j > \epsilon_{ijk}) \\ &= F(\lambda_i - \lambda_j) \end{aligned} \tag{A.1}$$

and

$$\begin{aligned} P(y_{ijt} = Lose) &= Pr(\lambda_i - \lambda_j \leq \epsilon_{ijk}) \\ &= 1 - F(\lambda_i - \lambda_j) \end{aligned}$$

where $F(\cdot)$ is a cdf that maps the difference in abilities to the associated probabilities.

The discussion in the previous section suggests that the abilities of each democratic state will vary, among other things, with the oversight institutions present in that state. If we drop the time subscript for clarity and let the observed institutional traits of state i be R_i and let those other observed traits that affect ability, such as material military capabilities, be C_i, then we can express the ability of democracy i as

$$\lambda_i = \beta_R R_i + \beta_C C_i + \epsilon_i \tag{A.2}$$

The β-terms represent potentially nonscalar linear weights that link the observed traits to the outcome of interest,[44] and ϵ_i represents the unmeasured portion of state foreign policy ability.

Substituting (A.2) into (A.1) yields

$$P(y_{ij}t = Win) = F(\beta_R(R_i - R_j) + \beta_C(C_i - C_j) + \epsilon_i - \epsilon_j)$$

In this formulation, β weights that are positive increase a state's ability and thus the probability of a win, all else being equal.

This formulation is similar to the well-known structured Bradley–Terry model for paired comparisons that has been used to analyze the abilities of sports teams,[45] journal citation patterns,[46] and animal behavior.[47,48] For present purposes there are two additional complications. The first can be seen in the additive random effect terms (ϵ_i and ϵ_j) for each country in the dispute. Ignoring these disturbances, as has been done in the past,[49] assumes that the observed covariates measure state ability without error. This would seem unlikely, a priori. The inclusion of the random effect allows us to look at the posterior distribution of the variance of the ability parameters for democracies and non-democracies. The second complication is that all international conflicts do not end in a victory for one side or the other. In fact, international draws are the modal category for militarized interstate disputes. Therefore, our unobserved latent abilities will result in wins, draw, or loses. As previously suggested by Tutz,[50] we can handle ties in Bradley–Terry models by adding a threshold,[51] $\tau > 0$, to model the difficulty of generating a win for either side. Thus, we can reexpress y_{ijt} as the observed index of state i losing, drawing, or winning a dispute as

$$y_{ijt} = \begin{cases} Lose & \text{if } \lambda_i - \lambda_j + \epsilon_{ijt} < -\tau \\ Draw & \text{if } \tau > \lambda_i - \lambda_j + \epsilon_{ijt} > -\tau \\ Win & \text{if } \lambda_i - \lambda_j + \epsilon_{ijt} > \tau \end{cases}$$

leading to

$$\begin{aligned} P(y_{ijt} = Lose) &= Pr(\lambda_i - \lambda_j + \epsilon_{ijt} \leq -\tau) \\ &= F(-\tau - (\lambda_i - \lambda_j)) \end{aligned}$$

$$\begin{aligned} P(y_{ijt} = Draw) &= Pr(\tau > \lambda_i - \lambda_j + \epsilon_{ijt} > -\tau) \\ &= F(\tau - (\lambda_i - \lambda_j)) - F(-\tau - (\lambda_i - \lambda_j)) \end{aligned}$$

and

$$\begin{aligned} P(y_{ijt} = Win) &= Pr(\lambda_i - \lambda_j + \epsilon_{ijt} > \tau) \\ &= 1 - F(\tau - (\lambda_i - \lambda_j)) \end{aligned}$$

Substituting (A.2) into the above equations produces

$$\begin{aligned} P(y_{ijt} = Loss) &= F(-\tau - \beta_R(R_i - R_j) - \beta_C(C_i - C_j) - \epsilon_i + \epsilon_j) \\ P(y_{ijt} = Draw) &= F(\tau - \beta_R(R_i - R_j) - \beta_C(C_i - C_j) - \epsilon_i + \epsilon_j) \\ &\quad - F(-\tau - \beta_R(R_i - R_j) - \beta_C(C_i - C_j) - \epsilon_i + \epsilon_j) \\ P(y_{ijt} = Win) &= 1 - F(\tau - \beta_R(R_i - R_j) - \beta_C(C_i - C_j) - \epsilon_i + \epsilon_j) \end{aligned}$$

This model can be estimated within a Bayesian framework by selecting an inverse link function for $F(\cdot)$ and placing priors on the unobserved parameters. Specifically, I replace $F(\cdot)$ with the inverse logistic function[52] and use the following prior specification, where β is a vector of coefficients and ϵ is a stacking of the random effects:

$$\beta \sim \mathcal{N}(0, 1 \times 10^{-8})$$
$$\epsilon \sim \mathcal{N}(0, v^2)$$
$$\tau \sim |\mathcal{N}(0, .01)|$$
$$v \sim \mathcal{U}(0, 10)$$

The priors on β are diffuse and contain little information,[53] and the prior on τ is a Half Normal distribution.[54] I will refer to this model as a Bayesian ordered Bradley–Terry model (BOB-T) for brevity.[55] This model allows us to compute the probability of a democratic state winning a dispute against another state, depending on their national-security-relevant oversight institutions and other observable traits.

Further, the framework is flexible enough to accommodate more nuanced indicators of relative abilities between states, such as the difference between state i's and state j's fatalities in a dispute. For the measurement of net fatalities, we can define $F(\cdot)$ now as the normal cdf and include the observed thresholds for the fatality intervals.[56] This type of analysis is analogous to inferring abilities from point differentials in sports and is similar to interval regression with two additive random effects.[57] The interval-level BOB-T model to estimate state abilities from net fatalities data takes the form

$$P(Y \in (-\infty, \tau_1)) = \Phi[(\tau_1 - \beta_R(R_i - R_j) - \beta_C(C_i - C_j) - \epsilon_i + \epsilon_j)/\sigma]$$
$$P(Y \in (\tau_1, \tau_2)) = \Phi[(\tau_2 - \beta_R(R_i - R_j) - \beta_C(C_i - C_j) - \epsilon_i + \epsilon_j)/\sigma]$$
$$- \Phi[(\tau_1 - \beta_R(R_i - R_j) - \beta_C(C_i - C_j) - \epsilon_i + \epsilon_j)/\sigma]$$
$$\vdots$$
$$P(Y \in (\tau_k, \infty)) = 1 - \Phi[(\tau_k - \beta_R(R_i - R_j) - \beta_C(C_i - C_j) - \epsilon_i + \epsilon_j)/\sigma]$$

where in this case the τ_k thresholds are observed quantities that represent the borders between categories, and σ represents[58] the variance of unobserved net fatalities measured as intervals. This interval-level BOB-T model allows us to compute the expected number of net fatalities, $E(Y)$ or y^*, as $\beta_R(R_i - R_j) -$

$\beta_C(C_i - C_j)$, since the coefficients are estimated on the underlying metric of the observed intervals, in this case net fatalities.

I also measure[59] several other variables whose absence might confound or inflate the relationship between the national security oversight institutions index and foreign policy ability.[60] I weigh a state's prestige and status by including whether a state is a major power or not.[61] To control for the material strength of a state, I measure the natural log of each state's capabilities in the dispute.[62] Additionally, dispute outcomes may be linked to opponents that are not already involved in the dispute. For example, a state facing a strong external threat, such as Israel, from one or many rivals may find foreign policy success more difficult to achieve. Therefore, I control for the strength of a country's external rivals.[63] I also record both the number of disputes in which a state becomes initially involved in each year and the time since the last dispute between the pair of disputants. Even a major power like the United States cannot simultaneously start and easily win multiple disputes. Further, recent crises between the same disputants might signal a conflict that is difficult to resolve and unlikely to lead to victory on either side.

Within a dispute, I measure the potential for first-mover advantage by including whether a state both moves first[64] and is an originator of the dispute rather than a joiner, per the MID data. Similarly, the potential for an asymmetric effort in a dispute should be evident if one state is using force in a dispute but the other state is not. Therefore, I coded a variable marking whether a state was using force[65] and whether the United States was involved in the dispute, since the role of the United States might sway outcomes toward more democratic victories.[66]

The model results were computed using JAGS 2.0[67] running the Gibbs sampler for 505,000 iterations, discarding the first 5000 runs and then keeping every 10th run for posterior inference on the 50,000 remaining samples. This chain passes the run-length criterion of Heidelberger and Welch.[68] A smaller pilot run that was discarded was analyzed using the Raftery and Lewis[69] diagnostic and suggested that this length of run would be more than adequate for posterior inference.

Table A-5 presents the results from four specifications of the BOB-T models with different control variables in each. The posterior distributions of the coefficients are shown in the paper.

Table A-6 presents the results from two additional specifications of the BOB-T models. The first column includes only militarized interstate disputes where at least one side used force. The second column drops all disputes that involved the United States. The results, which are discussed in the body of the main text, remain consistent across these specifications.

Table A-5. Results from Four BOB-T Model Specifications Predicting the Outcome of Disputes Involving at Least One Democracy

	Model 1, Mean (SD)	Model 2, Mean (SD)	Model 3, Mean (SD)	Model 4, Mean (SD)
National Security Oversight	2.06 (0.86)	2.04 (0.99)	1.97 (1.01)	2.15 (0.99)
Capabilities		-0.01 (0.17)	0.09 (0.18)	0.12 (0.14)
Major Power		-0.17 (0.19)	-0.14 (0.19)	
External Threat		0.11 (0.59)	0.30 (0.64)	-0.15 (0.20)
Other MIDs		-0.33 (0.25)	-0.45 (0.27)	-0.39 (0.26)
Force			1.60 (0.39)	1.54 (0.39)
Dispute Initiator			-0.85 (0.25)	-0.82 (0.24)
Time Since Last Dispute		-0.01 (0.03)	-0.02 (0.04)	-0.03 (0.03)
Number of Previous Disputes		0.03 (0.04)	0.05 (0.04)	
Number of Previous Losses		-0.41 (0.41)	-0.39 (0.44)	
$\mu_1 - \mu_2$	0.58 (0.29)	0.64 (0.31)	0.72 (0.33)	0.69 (0.32)
ϵ_1	0.35 (0.27)	0.44 (0.30)	0.52 (0.34)	0.49 (0.32)
ϵ_2	0.92 (0.29)	0.98 (0.33)	1.00 (0.36)	1.01 (0.32)
τ	3.73 (0.29)	3.40 (0.32)	4.33 (0.37)	4.24 (0.36)

Table A-6. Results from Two Additional BOB-T Model Specifications Predicting the Outcome of Disputes Involving at Least One Democracy[a]

	Use of Force, Mean (SD)	Non-US Cases, Mean (SD)
National Security Oversight	2.73 (1.45)	3.13 (2.11)
Capabilities	-0.05 (0.21)	0.08 (0.30)
Major Power	-0.23 (0.26)	-0.66 (0.54)
External Threat	0.46 (0.89)	0.04 (1.19)
Other MIDs	-0.25 (0.34)	-0.43 (0.49)
Time Since Last Dispute	0.07 (0.05)	0.15 (0.08)
Number of Previous Disputes	0.07 (0.06)	0.12 (0.09)
Number of Previous Losses	-0.30 (0.61)	-0.58 (0.76)
$\mu_1 - \mu_2$	0.46 (0.29)	0.25 (0.31)
ϵ_1	1.14 (0.62)	1.68 (0.81)
ϵ_2	0.96 (0.44)	1.64 (0.56)
τ	4.17 (0.48)	5.03 (0.78)

[a]The first specification includes only those crises where at least one side used force. The second specification excludes cases where the United States was an actor.

THE RANDOM EFFECTS

Figure A.1 plots the estimated variances of ϵ_1 and ϵ_2, which are the random effect terms in the state-ability equations for democracies and non-democracies, respectively.[70] We can see that the probability mass is pushed away from zero in both cases, especially in the non-democratic cases. It is important to note that these random effect terms do have a moderate influence on the posterior parameter estimates in the model. I ran similar BOB-T models with and without the random effect terms and found that the uncertainty estimates around the coefficients shrank by approximately 23% when the random effect terms were omitted. Given the strong prior reasons for expecting unmeasured heterogeneity in foreign policy ability, these results suggest that the inclusion of the random effect terms is useful and aids in avoiding overconfidence in the results and providing conservative estimates for posterior inference.

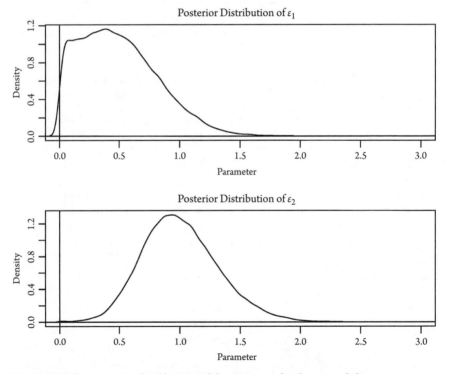

Figure A.1 The posterior distribution of the variances for the state-ability random-effect terms from model 2. The variance of ϵ_1 represents unmeasured heterogeneity for democratic states, and the variance of ϵ_2 represents unmeasured heterogeneity for non-democratic opponents.

PLOTS OF THE POSTERIOR DISTRIBUTION OF THE CONTROL VARIABLES

Figures A.2 and A.3 show plots of the posterior distribution of the control variables. Having a capability advantage is estimated to give a state a small increase in the probability of victory, although this is estimated imprecisely. In model 4, when major power status is omitted, the estimate for capabilities increases in size and precision. Major power states are less likely to win a dispute, possibly measuring their tendency to compromise in any given conflagration to maintain the regional or global status quo. Both being involved in other militarized disputes simultaneously and facing powerful rivals are estimated to reduce the probability of victory for a state, although the posterior distribution for the effect of multiple simultaneous MIDs has far greater probability mass below zero. It is important to note that the posterior probability that the four coefficients that measure the relationships between crises in model 4 are simultaneously equal to zero is less

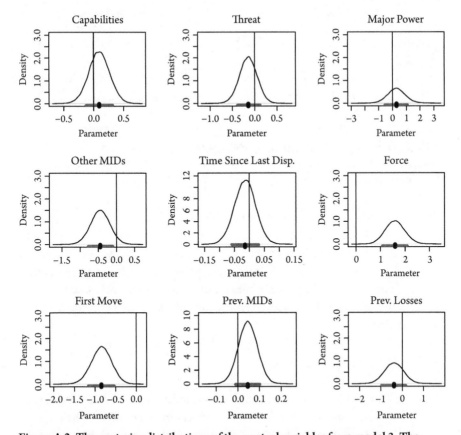

Figure A.2 The posterior distributions of the control variables from model 3. The horizontal lines near the x-axis represent 80% HPD intervals, and the black dots are means.

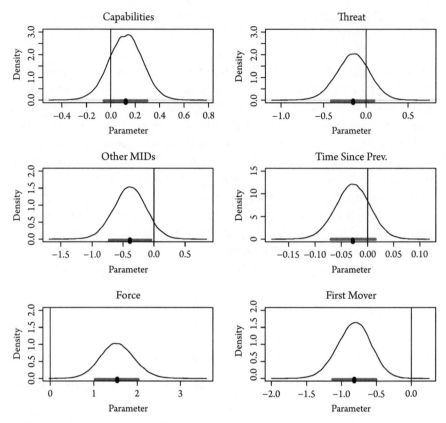

Figure A.3 The posterior distribution of the additional control variables from model 4. The horizontal lines near the x-axis represent 80% HPD intervals, and the black dots are means.

than 85%. This suggests that these variables do aid in measuring the ways in which disputes may be related to each other over space and time. Specifically, while the finding is sensitive to specification, I find that being simultaneously involved in multiple disputes decreases the probability of that state winning a dispute. I present here the posterior distributions for the control variable parameters for model 3 (which includes the most controls) and model 4 (which is more parsimonious).

NON-BAYESIAN MODELS

Table A-7 presents the results from four specifications of ordered logit models. These models assume that the random effect terms are zero.[71] These results provide even more confident support for the theory in terms of the ratio of the coefficients to the standard errors for the national security oversight coefficients. However, because these models zero out the specification uncertainty in the

Table A-7. RESULTS FROM FOUR ORDERED LOGIT MODEL SPECIFICATIONS
PREDICTING THE OUTCOME OF DISPUTES INVOLVING AT LEAST ONE DEMOCRACY

	Model 1 Coefficient (SE)	Model 2 Coefficient (SE)	Model 3 Coefficient (SE)	Model 4 Coefficient (SE)
National Security Oversight	2.17 (0.64)	1.71 (0.72)	1.60 (0.71)	1.93 (0.69)
Capabilities		0.03 (0.14)	0.13 (0.14)	0.26 (0.10)
Major Power		0.51 (0.42)	0.65 (0.44)	
External Threat		−0.20 (0.15)	−0.17 (0.15)	−0.18 (0.15)
Other MIDs		−0.38 (0.21)	−0.42 (0.21)	−0.42 (0.22)
Force			1.40 (0.36)	1.32 (0.34)
Dispute Initiator			−0.67 (0.22)	−0.70 (0.22)
Time Since Last Dispute		−0.02 (0.03)	−0.03 (0.03)	−0.04 (0.03)
Number of Previous Disputes		0.03 (0.03)	0.02 (0.03)	
Number of Previous Losses		−0.25 (0.35)	−0.23 (0.35)	
$\mu_1 - \mu_2$	0.58 (0.18)	0.58 (0.18)	−0.44 (0.42)	−0.41 (0.36)
τ	3.25 (0.19)	3.37 (0.21)	3.64 (0.24)	3.57 (0.23)
AIC	330.8	334.7	319.13	317.2
Brant test χ^2(df)	0.3(1)	10.2(8)	11.7(10)	8.8(7)

ability equations, I believe the BOB-T estimates are more consistent with the specified theory. I present these results for comparison and to illustrate how the BOB-T estimates are conservative in juxtaposition. The last row presents the χ^2 values from Brant tests of the parallel regression assumption. In each specification we fail to reject the null hypothesis that the parallel regression assumption holds at the .10 level.[72]

An interval-level BOB-T model, with observed cut points, is used to estimate state abilities from net fatalities data. The justification and results for this estimation strategy are discussed in the text. The interval-level BOB-T model takes the form

$$P(Y \in (-\infty, \tau_1)) = \Phi[(\tau_1 - \mu_1 - \mu_2 - \beta_R(R_i - R_j) - \beta_C(C_i - C_j)$$
$$- \epsilon_i + \epsilon_j)/\sigma]$$

$$P(Y \in (\tau_1, \tau_2)) = \Phi[(\tau_2 - \mu_1 - \mu_2 - \beta_R(R_i - R_j) - \beta_C(C_i - C_j)$$
$$- \epsilon_i + \epsilon_j)/\sigma]$$
$$- \Phi[(\tau_1 - \mu_1 - \mu_2 - \beta_R(R_i - R_j) - \beta_C(C_i - C_j)$$
$$- \epsilon_i + \epsilon_j)/\sigma]$$

$$\vdots$$

$$P(Y \in (\tau_k, \infty)) = 1 - \Phi[(\tau_k - \mu_1 - \mu_2 - \beta_R(R_i - R_j) - \beta_C(C_i - C_j)$$
$$- \epsilon_i + \epsilon_j)/\sigma]$$

where in this case the τ_k thresholds are observed quantities that represent the borders between categories (the range in number of net fatalities), and σ represents[73] the variance of unobserved net fatalities. This is akin to an ordered probit model where the threshold parameters are known and therefore the intercept and variance of the errors are identified quantities that can be estimated from the data. This interval level BOB-T model allows us to compute the expected number of net fatalities, $E(Y)$ or y^*, as $\beta_R(R_i - R_j) - \beta_C(C_i - C_j)$, since the coefficients are estimated on the underlying metric of the observed intervals, in this case net fatalities. The dependent variable is coded using the cut points $(-749, -225, -75, -24, 0, 24, 75, 225, 749)$. This means that a democracy killing 100 more enemy troops than it loses itself would be placed in the 75 to 225 category. Conversely, a democracy that lost 300 more troops than it killed in the enemy ranks would be placed in the -749 to -225 category. While precise point estimates for fatalities were unavailable in a large majority of the cases, a consistent range within this coding, particularly with the help of the MID and Dyadic MID data, was possible. These results are presented in Table A-8.

Changing the Oversight Index

In this section I detail results from tests that explore whether one specific aspect of the national security oversight measure is driving the results. Specifically, it may be the case that press freedom is the only significant component of the index,

Table A-8. RESULTS FROM AN INTERVAL-LEVEL BOB-T MODEL PREDICTING THE NET FATALITY LEVELS BETWEEN DISPUTANTS[a]

	Fatalities, Mean (SD)
National Security Oversight	103.2 (56.1)
Capabilities	−6.3 (7.5)
Major Power	29.2 (31.2)
US Actor	−53.4 (76.3)
Previous Disputes	0.4 (2.5)
Previous Losses	−29.4 (23.6)
$\mu_1 - \mu_2$	14.3 (11.2)
ϵ_1	42.0 (22.7)
ϵ_2	18.1 (11.9)
σ	96.9 (5.5)

[a]Positive values reflect higher fatalities for non-democracies, and negative values reflect higher fatalities for the democratic member of the dyad.

and when this is dropped from the calculation of national security oversight, the results change substantially. I ran three additional BOB-T models, each with a new measure of national security oversight that dropped each component one at a time. As can be seen in the plots in Figure A.4, there is still a consistent pattern of evidence linking each two-component index to increased foreign policy ability. The results do not appear to be driven solely by press freedom, since when we measure national security oversight solely with regard to legislative oversight powers and freedom of information laws, these institutions continue to increase the estimated foreign policy ability of democracies. Additionally, in a non-Bayesian context, we cannot reject the null hypothesis that the coefficients are the same across all three models.[74] Figure A.4 illustrates the effect of the oversight index when we drop each component, one at a time. The top plot represents the effect of oversight on foreign policy ability using only legislative

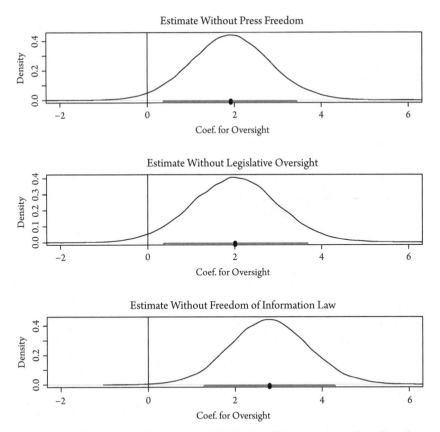

Figure A.4 The posterior distribution of the national security oversight index when each component is dropped in succession. The horizontal lines near the x-axis represent 90% HPD intervals, and the black dots are the posterior means.

oversight and freedom of information laws, thus dropping press freedom from the computation. The estimated posterior mean effect is 1.9 with over 98% posterior probability of the parameter being greater than zero, thus increasing foreign policy ability. The middle panel drops legislative oversight from the computation and only uses press freedom and freedom of information laws, yielding a posterior mean of 2.0 with greater than 97% posterior probability of the parameter being greater than zero. Finally, the bottom panel illustrates the same pattern, with freedom of information laws being dropped. This results in an estimated posterior mean of 2.7 and greater than 99% posterior probability of increasing foreign policy ability for democracies.[75]

CHAPTER 1

1. See the Second Addendum in particular Kant 1957.
2. See "On Publicity," p. 315, in Bentham 1843.
3. See letter to Jefferson of May 13, 1798, in *The Papers of James Madison*, Vol. 17, p. 130.
4. See Thompson 1999.
5. For examples, see Chapters 12 and 13 in Bok 1989.
6. I compare Lake 1992, Reiter and Stam 2002, and Desch 2002 in Chapter 3.
7. See, for example, "Journalism that Knows No Shame" by Max Boot, November 28, 2010, *Commentary Magazine*, available at http://www.commentarymagazine.com/blogs/index.php/boot/382682; and "Edward Snowden: 'Hero or Traitor'" by Geoffrey Stone, *Huffington Post*, available at http://www.huffingtonpost.com/geoffrey-r-stone/edward-snowden-hero-or-tr_b_3418939.html.
8. See, for example, "Why Do Editors Committed to Press Freedom Attack Wikileaks?" by Roy Greenslade, *The Guardian*, November 28, 2010, available at guardiannews.com/media/greenslade/2010/nov/28/wikileaks-national-newspapers; and "Edward Snowden Hailed as Hero, Accused of Treason—As It Happened" by Paul Owen and Tom McCarthy, *The Guardian*, June 10, 2013, available at http://www.guardian.co.uk/world/blog/2013/jun/10/edward-snowden-revealed-as-nsa-whistleblower-reaction-live.
9. Fledman 1997, p. 100.
10. Schoenfeld 2010, p. 259. He calls this "the public's right not to know."
11. Quoted in Johnson 2007, p. xv.
12. Additionally, basing consent on shared party identity with a leader, or perceived trust, and not on information about a particular case opens the public to manipulation. Trust may be abused, particularly if veiled within the confines of national security secrecy. For example, if a leader knows that a public will support policies, even when the facts are classified, then that executive might be tempted to use policy for private nonsecurity rather than public security ends. This incentive itself might give members of the public pause in supporting a leader's national

security policy, and especially those that are predisposed toward skepticism of the executive. This is a major theme of Chapters 5 and 6.

13. See Johnson 2006, as well as Johnson 1997.

14. Chapter 6 more fully develops this argument and example.

15. Chapter 2 lays out evidence for this claim.

16. There is some secrecy on nonsecurity issues, of course. In fact, the capacity for secrecy is likely to be granted whenever there are legitimate public transparency costs. On a large majority of nonsecurity issues, claims of secrecy will be taken as a hint of wrongdoing because there are fewer coherent reasons for public transparency costs; see Bok 1989. However, information on pending financial transactions and police investigations are two other examples of areas with justifiable secrecy due to public transparency costs that are beyond the scope of this work.

17. See, for example, Mitchell, Gates, and Hegre 1999.

18. Evidence of this is offered in the Appendix.

19. For counterpoints to these arguments see Desch 2002; Downes 2009.

20. See "The First Domino: Nixon and the Pentagon Papers" by Jordan Moran, Presidential Recordings Program, Miller Center, University of Virginia, available at http://whitehousetapes.net/exhibit/first-domino-nixon-and-pentagon-papers.

21. See Press Briefing by Press Secretary Jay Carney, June 6, 2013, available at http://www.whitehouse.gov/the-press-office/2013/06/10/press-briefing-press-secretary-jay-carney-6102013.

22. What is now USC 952, Title 18, which criminalizes leaking signal intelligence information, was passed in direct response to Yardley's revelation of previously secret information in 1933. His place in the NSA hall of honor can be found at http://www.nsa.gov/about/cryptologic_heritage/hall_of_honor/1999/yardley.shtml. Yardley is discussed in more detail in Chapters 3.

23. "Information Security Oversight Office Report to the President 2013," Information Security Oversight Office, Washington, DC. Note that the number of documents classified is itself classified, as one classification decision might apply to many documents. I use decisions conservatively here.

24. Ninety-five million secrets in a year, divided by 365 days a year, yields an average rate of 260,274 secrets per day. The leaks I refer to are the Iraqi and Afghan war logs and the Snowden leaks, for a document count of 391,832 + 91,731 + 58,000 = 541,563; see "N.S.A. Able to Foil Basic Safeguards of Privacy on Web" by Nicole Perlroth, Jeff Larson, and Scott Shane, New York Times, September 5, 2013. The number of documents actually revealed to the public is much less than this. The calculation conservatively equates a classification decision with a document; see "Information Security Oversight Office Report to the President 2013," Information Security Oversight Office, Washington, DC.

25. I return to these examples in Chapters 4 and 10.

26. See the discussion in Chapter 4.

27. In one of what will be many hall-of-mirror-type examples, Peter Wright, a former scientist for MI5 in the United Kingdom, suggests that Penkovsky was actually a Soviet plant. The evidence for this, however, is circumstantial and does not change the role of the information he revealed during the Cuban Missile Crisis. See the discussion in Chapter 4.

28. This is discussed in Chapter 3. The Berlin Airlift also depended crucially on the USSR underestimating the operational airlift capabilities of the United States and the United Kingdom. See the discussion in Zubok and Pleshakov 1996, pp. 48–50.

29. This success played a crucial role in Israeli advances in the Six Day War.

30. "Attack on bin Laden Used Stealthy Helicopter that Had Been a Secret" by Christopher Drew, *New York Times*, May 5, 2011, http://www.nytimes.com/2011/05/06/world/asia/06helicopter.html.

31. See Kennedy 1969. The spy was apprehended during the crisis, as discussed by Suvorov 1984. See the discusion of this case in Chapter 3 for more details.

32. This capacity, as well as its justification, is discussed extensively in later chapters.

33. In Chapter 5, I describe how the same secrecy apparatus that carried out Project Azorian, where intelligence was collected from a sunk Soviet submarine undercover of a scientific mission, simultaneously provided equipment and personnel for the operations that culminated in Watergate.

34. Knightley 2004, p. 75. These examples, and particularly the Dreyfus Affair, are discussed in more depth in Chapters 4 and 5.

35. See discusion of the incentives for abuse in Chapter 4.

36. See Reiter and Stam 2002, Bueno de Mesquita et al. 2003, and Huth and Allee 2003.

37. See the useful discussion in Reiter and Stam 2002, pp. 6, 145.

38. In Chapter 3 I discuss the assumption of available information in liberal international relations theories.

39. See "Obama Says Phone Spying Not Abused, Will Continue" by Eileen Sullivan and Pete Yost, Associated Press, August 9, 2013, available at http://bigstory.ap.org/article/obama-new-oversight-no-change-spying-power.

40. These are discussed in Chapters 3, 4, and 6, respectively.

41. "Still Dangerous After All These Years," *The Economist*, August 6, 2013, available at http://www.economist.com/blogs/democracyinamerica/2013/08/al-qaeda.

42. See the discussion in Knightley 2004, pp. 358–389. See also the discussion in Chapter 4.

43. For example, see "Claim on 'Attacks Thwarted' by NSA Spreads Despite Lack of Evidence," by Justin Elliott and Theodoric Meyer, ProPublica, available at http://www.propublica.org/article/claim-on-attacks-thwarted-by-nsa-spreads-despite-lack-of-evidence, where the quote is in response to the Obama administration's suggestion that over 50 potential threats have been diverted by a combination of surveillance programs.

44. Kennan 1951, p. 62. However, as I discuss in Chapter 5, critics of democratic transparency make the mistake of assuming that the public will follow leadership policies despite knowing that deception is possible, and even probable, without accountability.

45. The costs did not decline to zero immediately, particularly in the case of the D-Day landing. See the discussion in Chapter 4.

46. Chapter 7 argues that leaders are likely to care about more than simply remaining in office and also discusses the limitations of the solution if leaders do not value their legacy, their policies, or their party.

47.   I do not view incompetence as a fixed trait either in leaders or in organizations, as such leaders can be given incentives to avoid mistakes and also replace mistake-inducing bureacratic incentives or rules.

48.   Reiter and Stam 2002; Schultz 2001; Lake 1992.

49.   See, for example, Waltz 1967, p. 272, and the discussion in Rosato 2003, p. 599.

50.   Further, Colaresi 2007 illustrates that the variation in the rally effect over 50 years in the United States ebbs and flows with the probability of ex post oversight, as expected.

51.   This debate is discussed in Chapter 3.

52.   See Fearon 1995 for a seminal contribution and Reiter 2003.

53.   For example, in Fearon 1994.

54.   See, for example, Brooke and Hislop 2006.

55.   The extremely useful Born and Leigh 2008 is an example. While the chapters contain country studies that are rich and evocative, less attention is paid to cross-national comparisons and systematic patterns across democracies.

56.   I return to some suggestion in Chapter 10.

57.   See "NSA Director Firmly Defends Surveillance Efforts" by David Sanger and Thom Shanker, *New York Times*, October 12, 2013, available at http://www.nytimes.com/2013/10/13/us/nsa-director-gives-firm-and-broad-defense-of-surveillance-efforts.html?_r=0, as well as the opinion piece by three US senators: "End the NSA Dragnet, Now" by Ron Wyden, Mark Udall, and Martin Heinrich, *New York Times*, November 25, 2013, available at http://www.nytimes.com/2013/11/26/opinion/end-the-nsa-dragnet-now.html. In a sign of hope, several prominent Internet companies called for greater "Oversight and Accountability"; however, they failed to include suggestions for improved legislative oversight, press freedoms, or freedom of information laws. See "Global Government Surveillance Reform," available at http://reformgovernmentsurveillance.com.

58.   Where statistical and formal mathematical tools are used, these are explained in footnotes and appendices, as noted in the main text of the chapters.

59.   See Reiter and Stam 2002.

CHAPTER 2

1.   Huntington 1993.

2.   See Desch 2002 for a summary.

3.   Suggesting that democracies are less likely to fight each other. See Russett and Oneal 2000.

4.   Reiter and Stam 2002.

5.   Schultz 2001.

6.   Huth and Allee 2003.

7.   See Schultz 2001, Bueno de Mesquita et al. 2003, Huth and Allee 2003, and Reiter and Stam 2002.

8.   Desch 2002, Schuessler 2010, and Downes 2009.

9.   We can define fully efficient and effective foreign policy as an outcome that pays net public security benefits above all available policy alternatives. In practice, it will be more helpful to think of efficient and effective foreign policy as an

outcome that approximates full efficiency but may not necessarily maximize net pubic security benefits in all cases.

10. Reiter and Stam 2002, p. 7.

11. See, for example, Russett and Oneal 2000.

12. See Leeds 1999 for a summary and empirical analysis of democratic cooperation. It should be noted that the normative argument of pacific relations between democracies does not necessarily lead to a hypothesis that democracies formulate effective foreign policy toward autocratic states. Many argue that friendly relations between democracies and the formation of the League of Nations provided a false sense of security for France, Great Britain, and others during the inter-war years; see Reynolds 2000.

13. See Reiter and Stam 2002.

14. For supportive evidence of the role of democratic norms on foreign policy see Russett 1993, Russett and Oneal 2000, and Reiter and Stam 2002, Chapter 3. For skeptical viewpoints, see Schultz 2001 and Bueno de Mesquita et al. 2003, p. 219. Another critique of the normative arguments behind democratic effectiveness can be found in Desch 2002, pp. 60–61.

15. Reiter and Stam 2002, p. 5.

16. Montinola and Jackman 2002; Rasmusen and Ramseyer 1994; Freille, Haque, and Kneller 2005; Chowdhury 2004.

17. Rose-Ackerman 1978; Shleifer and Vishny 1993; Schultz 2001.

18. See Schultz 2001, Bueno de Mesquita et al. 2003, Huth and Allee 2003, and Reiter and Stam 2002.

19. Russett 1993; Russett and Oneal 2000, as well as Bueno de Mesquita et al. 2003; Schultz 2001.

20. As we will see, Kant includes caveats for secrecy in other work; Mahon 2009.

21. Kant 1957, pp. 12–13.

22. Russett 1993, pp. 38–39.

23. Bueno de Mesquita and Lalman 1992, p. 45.

24. Doyle 1997, p. 280.

25. Lake 1992, pp. 28–29

26. Schultz 2001, pp. 13–19. For a nuanced discussion of the Kantian assumption see Gaubatz 1999, pp. 10–11 and 148–151.

27. Bueno de Mesquita et al. 2003.

28. Lake 1992, pp. 28–29.

29. Lake 1992, p. 25.

30. Lake 1992, p. 26. Information is one term in the accountability equation for Lake, along with the ability to punish the executive if the information received indicates that excessive rents are being taken. These involve voting or exiting the political system, as described in the previous paragraph.

31. Lake 1992, pp. 25–28.

32. Lake 1992, p. 29.

33. Lake 1992, p. 28.

34. Lake 1992, pp. 28–30. Similarly, Schultz and Weingast 1998 argue that domestic liberal democratic institutions allow for identical domestic and foreign policy benefits related to sovereign debt.

35. Schultz 2001.

36. Schultz 2001, p. 58.

37. Schultz 2001, p. 58.

38. Schultz 2001, p. 62.

39. Schultz 2001, pp. 58–59.

40. Schultz 2001, pp. 59–65. Specifically, his argument is that since opposition parties can rotate into office, members of a current opposition party might have been previously in government. When they were in government, he assumes, they had significant access to classified information. This is discussed below.

41. Ikenberry 2000, p. 76. One partial exception to the consistent use of the democratic transparency assumption is in the work of Helen Milner, see Milner 1997, p. 21. She notes that an executive often has access to more and deeper information than a legislature. However, Milner's subsequent theory assumes that interest groups are fully informed, which assumes away the issue of national security classification. However, this does hint at the power of extra-executive institutions, about which we will have much more to say.

42. Reiter and Stam 2002.

43. See Reiter and Stam 2002, pp. 6, 145.

44. Reiter and Stam 2002, p. 23.

45. The one difference discussed between domestic and national security policy is covert action and the possibility for secrecy; see Reiter and Stam 2002, p. 7. I discuss this in depth below.

46. Reiter and Stam 2002, p. 11; see also p. 146.

47. Reiter and Stam 2002, p. 11. They mainly discuss these benefits as deriving from more accurate estimates of the probability of victory (pp. 23–25), although it could also be the case that better estimates of the value of specific policies' net costs/benefits are available to the public.

48. Reiter and Stam 2002, pp. 19–22.

49. Russett and Oneal 2000.

50. Fordham and Walker 2005.

51. Martin 2000; Schultz 2001.

52. Reiter and Stam 2002.

53. Russett and Oneal 2001.

54. See Desch 2002, Schuessler 2010, Downes 2009, and Rosato 2003, for example, as discussed below.

55. These are not the only lines of attack on the notion that democracies are more effective in foreign policy as compared to autocracies. However, as discussed below, these are central to the mechanism of public accountability, which is of interest here.

56. Johnson 1997; Gibbs 1995; Forsythe 1992.

57. Almond 1956, pp. 371–378, and de Tocqueville, Mayer (ed.), and Lawrence (trans.) 2007 (1835), p. 243.

58. See below. A potential mutation of this critique is that transparency costs are greater than accountability benefits for democracies. In the following chapters, I suggest why there is not necessarily a one-to-one trade-off between these costs and benefits of accountability.

59. Desch 2002.
60. Schuessler 2010.
61. Downes 2009.
62. There are other criticisms of specific war-fighting efficiency arguments in Reiter and Stam 2002 pertaining to legitimacy, troop morale, and leadership. Desch 2002, for example, makes the case that soldiers and democratic militaries are "effective in spite, not because, of the nature of their political systems . . . . Rather than liberalism pervading the militaries, it is most often the case that the armed forces are a distinct and isolated caste, particularly in democratic societies" (p. 61). These sets of arguments are tangential here, except for the fact that perceived legitimacy, and thus the will to fight, might be a function of accountability.
63. Desch 2002, p. 42, emphasis added.
64. Schuessler 2010, p. 143.
65. Schuessler 2010, p. 133 and footnote 1.
66. Schuessler 2010, p. 134.
67. Downes 2009.
68. Downes 2009, p. 44.
69. See, for example, Kaufmann 2004.
70. The more limited claim that leaders in democracies may be electorally punished for losing a war, even if the war has net public benefits, is less compromised by this criticism, although the public still needs to be able to define victory independently of executive information and self-serving motives. Retreating to this thin version of information in a democracy, however, has its own weaknesses. This is discussed below.
71. Bueno de Mesquita et al. 2003, Appendix.
72. Debs and Goemans (2010) make an identical assumption.
73. Schultz 2001, p. 62. Note that this is an assumption about extra-executive actors. Anyone contesting for power needs access to this information, since they must be able to judge whether a threat is actually supported by the public or not if carried through. For this to be meaningful, however, the public itself must be able to know whether the costs are less than the benefits of pressing an issue. If the public does not know this, as a threat is unfolding, the opposition does not have an incentive to oppose a noncredible threat, since they would not be receiving domestic support for this signal of opposition. Put another way, if a leader can convince the public that they should be resolved over a given issue (their costs are lower than the benefits), then a democratic threat toward an enemy is no more credible than a non-democratic threat. The democratic credibility advantage is a function of the leader suffering audience costs, costs that are signaled by an opposition taking advantage of leadership bluffing. When the public cannot identify clearly the costs and benefits of that policy (threaten or not), the signal dissolves. This explains why Schultz goes to such lengths to defend transparency.
74. Schultz 2001, p. 62.
75. Schultz 2001, pp. 62–63.
76. Schultz 2001, p. 64.
77. Legislative oversight powers will be analyzed in depth in Chapter 6. Schultz also adds that party organizations help competition by amplifying messages and

providing research on public opinion. However, the party apparatus is not argued to be able to pry information out of the executive.

78. Schultz 2001, p. 63.
79. See Colaresi 2007 and Colaresi, Rasler, and Thompson 2007 for an exploration of rivalries and rivalry processes.
80. See, for example, Tap 1998, Maney 1998, Reynolds 2000, and Thorp 2011.
81. See, for example, Johnson 1997 for a convincing justification and discussion of the literature.
82. Available at http://www.npr.org/documents/2005/dec/rockefeller.pdf.
83. The theme of the timing of information revelation will be discussed further in Chapter 6.
84. Footnote 16.
85. Reiter and Stam 2002.
86. Forsythe 1992.
87. Reiter and Stam 2002, p. 160.
88. Reiter and Stam 2002, p. 161.
89. There are some practical limits on secrecy; for example, if the public already knows a fact, it can itself be a secret. This is discussed below.
90. At least not systematically. While we forget, we cannot intentionally forget.
91. Some individuals might be allowed to check a specific secret, but then they themselves are bound by classification laws. The issue of trust is dealt with in more depth in Chapters 4 and 5.
92. Gibbs 1995 and Forsythe 1992.
93. Reiter and Stam 2002, pp. 159–163, and Reiter 2012.
94. See below, as well as Johnson 1997; Holt 2004.
95. In later work, Reiter (2012 2011) has suggested that secrecy is a mixed blessing. Sometimes keeping something secret has helped military actions, other times it has hindered. However, even in this analysis, secrecy is treated as something that can be turned on or off in a given situation. For this to be true, the capacity for secrecy must exist in democracies. A completely transparent marketplace of ideas would zero out or severely limit this capacity, not just the quantity of secrets; however, there may be limits, as we will have a chance to discuss at length in this chapter.
96. Although the uncertainty around this estimate might be lower in democracies with a robust free press and marketplace of ideas, this is not necessary for the theory.
97. Kissinger 2000 and Shlaim 2001.
98. See Leeds et al. 2002 and Maoz 2000.
99. In fact, the logic of offering concessions to lower net costs was the explict policy justification used by Lord Landsdowne in the United Kingdom during the late nineteenth and early twentieth century to avoid conflicts that might be won in the short term but would have significant opportunity costs to the United Kingdom. See Reynolds 2000, pp. 68–73.
100. For a discussion of Egypt's role in the Yemen War see Heikal 1973, as well as Shlaim 2001.
101. Chen 2001.

102. See Fisher 2003 for one useful commentary.

103. Counterfactuals make that translation even murkier. France lost the opening stages of World War II quite dramatically, but that does not mean that it was not worth fighting. While they could have been better prepared and managed, it is difficult to argue that immediate surrender would have been more beneficial in the long run. Without the immediate combat and post-occupation resistance, US and UK aid as well as the success of the eventual liberation might have been delayed or even forestalled.

104. See Reiter 2011, esp. p. 22.

105. See Reiter 2011, p. 28.

106. Reiter and Stam 2002, p. 21.

107. Reiter and Stam 2002, p. 21.

108. This argument is theoretical, not empirical. Victory and defeat can be useful measures to test theories of foreign policy ability.

109. At least without any additional institutional machinery, as discussed in Chapter 6.

CHAPTER 3

1. However, in Chapter 6 a qualified version of democratic transparency will be discusssed and developed.

2. Of course, the list would include many others. I am using these four theorists as examples due to their importance to liberal IR thought and, as we will see, their worry about the role of secrecy in democracies.

3. See p. 208; also see footnote 4 in the present chapter.

4. In this, these theorists were not alone. Schumpeter, in his tome on democratic competition, noted that transparency had its limits, particularly in foreign policy. He noted that the executive often was able to mislead the public to avoid direct and immediate accountability "to the point of resorting to secret diplomacy and lying about intentions and commitments" (Schumpeter 1947, location 6315).

5. Kant 1983, p. 381.

6. In *Perpetual Peace*, Kant includes a "Second Supplement" to his articles for perpetual peace entitled "[A] Secret Article for Securing Perpetual Peace." There he argues that nations could justly keep secret that they took advice from philosophers, since this would be unpopular and potentially embarrassing (Kant 1983). Interpretations of this article vary (see Mahon 2003 and Bennington 2011).

7. Kant 1979, p. 55.

8. See Mahon 2009, pp. 21 and 31, and Ellis 2005, p. 179.

9. Ellis 2005, p. 179.

10. Mill 2013, location 2312–2313.

11. Mill 2013, location 6275–6278.

12. Mill 2013, location 5212–5215.

13. Mill 2013, location 4181–4182.

14. Mill 2013, location 296.

15. Bentham 1843, p. 315, Vol. 2, Part 2.

16. Bentham 1843, p. 315, Vol. 2, Part 2.

17. Letter from James Madison to W. T. Barry, August 4, 1822, Writings 9: 103.
18. Letter to Jefferson of May 13, 1798, in *The Papers of James Madison*, Vol. 17, p. 130.
19. Madison, *Political Reflections*, p. 241
20. See Federalist Paper No. 10. Further, while Madison did not write Federalist Paper No. 64, he did not dissent from John Jay's assertion that "[i]t seldom happens in the negotiation of treaties of whatever nature, but that perfect secrecy and immediate dispatch are sometimes requisite. There are cases where the most useful intelligence may be obtained, if the persons possessing it can be relieved from apprehensions of discovery." In addition, there would be no dilemma between national security secrecy and accountability for Madison if there was no reason to have secrecy in the first place. If secrecy was never legitimate, then the capacity for secrecy would not be necessary, and further the keeping of a secret would be prima facie evidence of a policy that would not benefit the public.
21. Emma Rothschild, "Real, Pretended or Imaginary Dangers," *The New York Review of Books*, March 25, 2004, http://www.nybooks.com/articles/archives/2004/mar/25/real-pretended-or-imaginary-dangers/#fn19-250492562.
22. In fact, Madison's own presidency was threatened for a time in 1814 by a failure of both private information and adequate preparation. However, there is one possible answer from Madison's thoughts prior to this time, which we will discuss shortly. It could simply be that democracies are severely constrained and that these constraints are targeted at not necessarily stopping ill-advised policy or even advised policy—since the public would have to have access to information to make that distinction—but instead simply stopping most policies regardless of their ultimate and public unseen merits and costs. This will serve as a counter-hypothesis to be explored below. It is related to the thin version of the accountability argument discussed in the previous sections, whereby the public only punished non-victory as separated from the costs and benefits of various policies.
23. Prich 2000.
24. There are many different ways to organize the content of information that might or might not be justifiably classified. For example, one could analyze sources and methods of collection, military tactics, and diplomatic bottomlines; or technological versus organizational information. The point of this section is not to argue that specific types of secrets are more or less valuable than others. Instead, the point is that democracies having a capacity to keep secrets is reasonable and justifiable, *at least in some cases*. Therefore, once you have given the government the power to classify information, the public cannot directly check whether the information being classified is justifiably secret or not. Thus this section is an exploration of the benefits of the capacity for government secrecy in democracy, not an analysis of different types of secrets.
25. Letter from George Washington to Robert Hunter Morris, January 5, 1766.
26. Conventional aerial torpedoes needed to fire "100 feet deep into the water . . . Pearl Harbor's depth averages 42 feet" (see Gannon 2006, p. 19). The Japanese Thunder Fish (Type 91, modification 2) had wooden auxiliary fins so that they would dive only 35 feet deep. This example suggests how anticipation, deception,

and military capability advantages work together. The Japanese fleet trained extensively at Kyushu for the raid, and it knew that the depth would be sufficient. They had not only the technological capital but also the organization and strategy to put it to use (Gannon 2006, pp. 49–50). I thank an anonymous reviewer for pointing out this example.

27. Gannon 2006, p. 49.

28. It is possible that any one benefit is not in itself sufficient in a specific case to increase the chances of victory. For example, Stam 1996 (p. 153) finds that a surprise attack by the initiator has only a weak effect on the initiator's chance of victory. Similarly, Biddle 2004 presents evidence that simply having superior military technology does not in itself increase the probability of success, but successful cover and concealment for deception and operational planning (pp. 44–45, 60, 64–66) continue to be important. This suggests that the potential benefits of secrecy cannot be boiled down to any one of these specific functions. Moreover, as Chapter 5 makes clear in the cases of the Cyprus conflict and France before World War I, quality intelligence is only one part of the story of foreign policy success.

29. Porch 2003a.

30. Biddle 2004, p. 33.

31. Lupfer 1981, p. 67. Likewise, German military intelligence units and staff attempted to decipher Allied doctrine throughout the war, and one of the early German breakthroughs in thinking about "elastic defense" came about when the French were casual about publicizing a pamphlet about their lessons from previous battles. This pamphlet was found by the Germans, translated, and brought to the attention of the German hierarchy (p. 39). Similarly, as the German counterattack strategy was yielding results, the British worked to uncover its principles, finally capturing some documents in late 1917 that partially shed light on the problem (p. 35).

32. Biddle 2004 argues that successful technological innovation cannot be separated from organization innovations.

33. The possibility for private information to lead to war is explored more fully in Fearon 1995. See also Reiter 2011.

34. Tzu 2005, p. 163.

35. Parker 1993.

36. Prados 1995, p. 301.

37. Two islands in the Pacific (see Figure 3.1).

38. Lundstrom 2006.

39. Lundstrom 2006.

40. Bamford 1983.

41. Elsewhere within the crucible of war, codebreaking and anticipation proved their worth at Mortain, where the Allies were able to surround the Axis forces at Falaise, over Balaloe Island, allowing Admiral Yamamoto's plane to be shot down, as well as at the Battle of Alam el Halfa and El Alamein, where Montgomery had prior warning of Rommel's plan in both instances, just to name a few more examples (see Gannon 2001; Holt 2004).

42. Quoted in Yardley 2004 (1931), p. 313

43.   Yardley 2004 (1931), p. 313.

44.   This represented the warship tonnage of the respective navies. Specifically, they were set at 500,000 tons for the United States and the United Kingdom, 300,000 for Japan. The same treaty included a restriction of 175,000 tons for France and Italy.

45.   Schoenfeld 2010; Kahn 2004. The United States and the United Kingdom were victims of successful anticipation at Yalta at the hands of an ally. With their rooms bugged and Alger Hiss operating as a spy in the negotiation preparations, Stalin knew, for example, that the United States and United Kingdom, while preferring a democratic Poland, were willing to settle for some democratic elites to be included at the table; see Andrew and Mitrokhin 1999, p. 132.

46.   Rich and Janos 1996.

47.   Kennedy 1969.

48.   Schecter and Deriabin 1995.

49.   Scott 1999.

50.   Khrushchev 1970, p. 493.

51.   Correll 2005.

52.   Impunity here really is relative. The U-2 was a notoriously difficult plane to fly, particularly at lower altitudes and at landing; see Rich and Janos 1996.

53.   Kennedy 1969.

54.   Correll 2005.

55.   Suvorov 1984. However, all did not end well for Penkovsky. During the Cuban Missile Crisis, the USSR learned that it had a mole, from its own spy inside the United States. Thus, for his contribution to the eventual resolution of the crisis, Penkovsky was arrested on October 22, 1962, and then convicted of treason and executed. It should also be noted that the hall-of-mirrors aspects of intelligence and state secrets may obfuscate even Penkovsky's role here. Peter Wright, a British Intelligence analyst, has written that he believes Penkovsky was in fact a double agent (see Wright 1987). The balance of opinion in my reading of the case is against this interpretation, but given the necessities and realities of secrecy and deception, new information may come to light to change this interpretation. See Andrew and Gordiesky 1990 and Suvorov 1984 for descriptions of the available information.

56.   Frontius and Charles 1925, Book 1, p. 3.

57.   One form of deception that is common is bluffing, whereby one player feigns strength to induce another player to back down. I use the term "deception" here because it covers a broader range of cases and capabilities. The role of bluffing has taken on a central role in the debate concerning audience costs and democratic institutions. See Fearon 1994 and Snyder and Borghard 2011 for two sides of this discussion.

58.   Quoted in Macintyre 2011, p. 37.

59.   It is possible that MI5 got the idea for Operation Mincemeat from a memo written by subsequent James Bond author Ian Fleming, who was working in naval intelligence at the time. Fleming reportedly got the idea from an esoteric detective novel. The details in my retelling of the operation come from Macintyre 2011 and

Smyth 2010 as well as "Dead Man Floating: World War II's Oddest Operation,"
June 12, 2010, by Guy Raz, NPR.

60. A similar trick was experimented with in World War I in the Middle East and was
known as the Haversack Ruse (see Garfield 2007).

61. Macintyre 2011 explains that quality undergarments were highly difficult to procure due to rationing. However, someone of fictional Acting Major Martin's
rank would have them. A recently deceased Oxford don reportedly supplied the
needed equipment.

62. Macintyre 2011, p. 40.

63. Smyth 2010, p. 2.

64. Macintyre 2011, p. 296.

65. See Smyth 2010, pp. 1–5; Howard 1990, p. 89; and Macintyre 2011, p. 4.

66. Holt 2004, p. 56.

67. Holt 2004, p. 98.

68. Holt 2004, p. 591.

69. In many cases, the diffusion of information is what we want to happen to spur
invention and discovery. The discovery and mass production of penicillin was a
transnational process that crossed from the Middle East to France to England,
Belgium, and the United States (see Brown 2004). At each stop, information on
previous innovations was made public and allowed researchers in other countries
to spur further discoveries. On national security policy, there is a cost to this sharing process for the innovating state. While one country spends its time and energy
on creating a new offensive weapon, the other state can spend time refining a previous defensive weapon, for example. If the innovating state cannot keep secrets
and the other state can, then the secret state can instantly have a military edge by
generating a superior capability for defense while copying and thus having equal
offensive capabilities.

70. Rhodes 1995, p. 60.

71. My discussion of the US and Soviet research programs relies on Holloway 1996,
Rhodes 1995, Haynes, Klehr, and Alexander 2009, and Haynes and Klehr 1999.

72. Kuhn 1970, p. 206.

73. Haynes and Alexander 2009, pp. 60 and 143.

74. The United States created the Uranium Committee in 1939 to explore methods
for building an atomic bomb, partly in response to a letter that was cosigned by
Albert Einstein. This effort evolved into the Manhattan Project under the Army's
direction in 1942.

75. Haynes and Alexander 2009, pp. 59–61.

76. When using plutonium, the gun-type trigger design would not work because the
plutonium would then "fizzle" instead of exploding. This was solved with the "Fat
Man" design, encasing a sphere of plutonium in explosives triggered to squash the
plutonium within uniformly.

77. Rhodes 1995, p. 62.

78. While the USSR had a nuclear program before 1945, it was not vested with significant resources until after the atom bombs were used in Japan. Partly this was
due to Stalin's priorities, although the fevered pitch of Russia's war effort during

this time cannot be ignored as another central cause of the lackluster effort; see Rhodes 1995, pp. 62–71.

79. Rhodes 1995, pp. 360, 370–371.

80. Haynes, Klehr, and Alexander make the case that the 2 to 4 years the Soviets saved set the stage for a much more difficult Cold War environment for years to come; see Haynes, Klehr, and Alexander 2009, p. 62. Campbell and Radchenko make a similar claim; see Campbell and Radchenko 2008.

81. Of which they had an abundance; see Rhodes 1995.

82. Both steps were needed because the messages were coded and used a cypher.

83. Less well known is that Russia's isotope separation facilities located at Sverdlovsk-44 were constructed in an identical pattern to the analogous preexisting facilities at Oak Ridge; see Holloway 1996, p. 94, and Szasz 1992, p. 94.

84. One may wonder why the United States and United Kingdom were infiltrated to such an extent. See Haynes and Alexander 2009 for a discussion, but it is important to point out that the USSR and the United States were titular allies at the time that many of these spies began working on US soil.

85. The public record identifies Fuchs as the most valuable Soviet spy at the time. He was a scientist in Great Britain as the Manhattan Project was beginning and was brought to the United States as part of a British contingent of scientists. Fuchs was an extremely talented scientist and made what appear, in the limited public record, to be significant breakthroughs in the Manhattan Project, including the murky Fuchs–von Neumann patent, a classified patent potentially on implosions in the classical Super/hydrogen bomb design. Fuchs not only had access to the cutting-edge US puzzle-solvers at Los Alamos, but also solved significant puzzles himself. From Fuchs's confession under interrogation and other declassified evidence, we now know that Fuchs passed to the Soviet Union a detailed mock-up of the "Fat Man" bomb, the type dropped on Nagasaki and eventually copied into the Moscow's Joe-1. Even more problematic was his handing over to the Soviets in 1948 not only a detailed description of the US classical Super single-stage design, but also his own work on how an initiator for the blast would work (see Holloway 1996; Rhodes 1995; Szasz 1992; Haynes, Klehr, and Alexander 2009; Haynes and Klehr 1999). For this, Fuchs only served 9 years in prison due to the fact that technically the USSR was an ally at the time of the espionage.

86. Theodore Hall was a young physics prodigy that graduated from Harvard in 1944. Haynes et al. report that "[h]e was immediately recruited by the Manhattan Project and sent to Los Alamos" (see Haynes, Klehr, and Alexander 2009, p. 63). Hall was not recruited by Soviet intelligence, but volunteered his services to them, and was codenamed Mlad. He also passed significant intelligence on the workings of each Manhattan Project facility and methods of uranium separation (see Haynes, Klehr, and Alexander 2009, p. 115). In 1946, he was considered by Moscow to be one of the most important spies that the KGB operated in the United States. He was identified as a Soviet agent by the United States through the Venona intercepts in 1951, but was able to avoid prosecution due to the US attempts to keep Venona itself secret. He confirmed his spying when confronted in the 1990s after Venona became public.

87. The guilt of Ethel Rosenberg, as of this writing, is still murky and in need of further research. Evidence from the Venona project implicates her at the very least as being cognizant of the work of her husband (see Haynes and Klehr 1999, locations 4200–7052).

88. Koval's role is potentially important but has more uncertainty around it currently. The world learned about Koval's espionage and his potential importance in dramatic fashion. In November 2007, Russian President Vladimir Putin announced that he was awarding the honor of Hero of the Russian Federation to Zhorzh Abromovich Koval posthumously. Russian officials confirmed that Koval was a spy codenamed Delmar who was working for the GRU and provided the "recipe" for Joe-1. Delmar had gone undetected in the Venona intercepts both because the deciphering and decoding of the messages were extremely incomplete and because the GRU codes proved to be more difficult to break (see Haynes and Klehr 1999). Koval was born in Iowa to Belarussian parents, and he attended the University of Iowa for a time. In 1932, when he was 19 years old, his family moved to the Soviet Union. Some time before 1939 he was recruited and joined the GRU, and by 1940 he was disembarking from a tanker into San Francisco even though he no longer held a US passport. Eventually, Koval found himself, through a combination of luck and his intelligence, working for the Special Engineer Detachment, which was part of the covert Manhattan Project in 1944. He was first assigned to Oak Ridge, which was central to both the development of the original uranium weapon and the more recent, at the time, plutonium device. In his capacity as "health physics officer," Koval was given nearly unfettered access to the secrets at Oak Ridge. Further, he was able to learn, and pass on to the USSR, that the United States had found out that plutonium could not itself be used as an initiator due to its instability but that polonium would likely work. In 1945, Koval was transferred to a lab in Dayton, Ohio, where he learned more intimate and valuable details about materials used to initiate a blast, along with the practical methods needed to bring it to fruition. Koval passed these details on to Moscow (see Walsh 2009; Norris 2009). The US government became suspicious of Koval some time in the 1950s after he had already fled. Haynes et al. doubt Koval's importance and suggest that Putin's announcement was a stunt (see Haynes, Klehr, and Alexander 2009).

89. Haynes and Klehr 1999, locations 750–7052.

90. Haynes and Klehr 1999, locations 4515–7052.

91. We continue to learn about the extensive Soviet intelligence activities that were related to Project Enormoz. It should be noted that both the Venona transcripts and the KGB archive material that have come to light had dried up after 1949. Further allegations of Soviet atomic espionage into the 1950s are included in Reed and Stillman 2010.

92. Rhodes 1995, pp. 527–528 and Bernstein 2010.

93. More accurately: thousands of calculations.

94. Rhodes 1995; Bernstein 2010; Gorelik 2011.

95. However, there is still a major gap in our understanding of Soviet development of the hydogen bomb (see Haynes and Alexander 2009, Norris 2009, Reed and Stillman 2010, and Gorelik 2011).

96. Therefore, if a program explodes a bomb that yields 5 kilotons in 1949 but nothing in 1950, I continue to code their program as being able to produce a 5-kiloton blast in 1950. This metric is used merely as an illustration. It should be noted that by this measure the USSR would have been assumed to be well ahead in 1961 with the Tsar Bomba test despite the fact that the competition by that time was centering on guidance systems and deliverable systems.

97. These were the names of specific US nuclear tests as part of Operation Ivy and Operation Castle.

98. The Joe-4 blast could just as easily be included as a 6.4-megaton blast, instead of a 3.2-megaton blast. The scientist deliberately scaled back this test by a half. Again, as noted above, it remains an open case regarding how much help espionage was to the Soviets in the spring of 1954 to reach this point. This scaling back was also generally true of a number of US tests.

99. Haynes and Klehr 1999, locations 180–7052.

100. Haynes, Klehr, and Alexander 2009, p. 545.

101. The Obama–Lugar legislation, for example, is an attempt to stop proliferation.

102. "A Nuclear Standoff with Libya," *The Atlantic*, http://www.theatlantic.com/international/archive/2010/11/a-nuclear-standoff-with-libya/67076/, November 27, 2010.

103. See, for example, "Libyan Islamists Join al-Qaeda," *BBC*, November 3, 2007, http://news.bbc.co.uk/2/hi/7076604.stm, as well as "A Nuclear Standoff with Libya," *The Atlantic*, http://www.theatlantic.com/international/archive/2010/11/a-nuclear-standoff-with-libya/67076/, November 27, 2010.

104. Silverstein and Moag 2000, p. 74.

105. Ben Rich reports that the name was originally Skonk Works and was from a Li'l Abner cartoon that hit home to the engineers working at the secret operation set up by Clarence "Kelly" Johnson during World War II in a circus tent next to a chemical plant (see Rich and Janos 1996, pp. 111–112).

106. Crickmore 2004.

107. Bennis and Biederman 1998, pp. 138–139.

108. Rich and Janos 1996, p. 99, reports that crews would find the bodies of bats on the planes in the hangars.

109. Haynes and Alexander 2009, Chapter 7.

110. Haynes, Klehr, and Alexander 2009; Haynes and Klehr 1999.

111. See *Tri City Herald*, June 21, 1988, p. A10, "US Expels Top Soviet Air Attache for Spying" and *Washington Post*, June 21, 1986, "Soviet Attache Arrested, Will Be Expelled for Receiving Documents." Espionage in the Stealth program has happened since the Cold War ended, as the case of Noshir Gowadia exemplifies.

112. See "Security Awareness in the 1980's: Featured Articles from the *Security Awareness Bulletin*, 1981–1989," p. 4.

113. Silverstein and Moag 2000, p. 74.

114. These numbers are for the frontal RCS as planes have different RCS depending on the view. The sources of information come from various sources including issues of *Jane's Defense Weekly*, *Air Power Australia Analyses*, and globalsecurity.org, as well as Rich and Janos 1996.

115. This is not surprising, since the Su-27 was designed by the USSR in response to the F-15.

116. Unclassified sources suggest that the B-2 bomber had an even lower frontal RCS than the F-117A (see Richardson 1991).

117. The Sukhoi PAK FA, currently under development, will be a true stealth aircraft, by public accounts. A Chinese stealth fighter, the J-20, is also under development; see Christopher Bodeen, "Chinese Stealth Fighter Makes First Test Flight," *Washington Post*, January 11, 2011.

118. Rich and Janos 1996, p. 105.

119. See Desch 2002, Downes 2009, and Trachtenberg 2010.

120. I am not arguing that all democracies have the same number of secrets or relative scale of secrecy. Instead, what is crucial is that the capacity for an executive to use discretion to keep secrets exists. As the discussion below suggests, this capacity is widespread in democracies around the globe. A study of the scale of secrecy across democracies faces significant data collection difficulties, due to the very capacity for secrecy discussed here.

121. The latest of which as of this writing is EO 13526, signed by President Barack Obama in 2009. This difference can be overstated. While Sweden has statutory classification divisions between top secret and other information, what information goes where is often changed in practice out of public view; see Sweden country report, http://www.freedominfo.org/regions/europe/sweden/. This highlights the problems with the capacity for secrecy discussed above; content cannot be publicly monitored.

122. For a detailed discussion of this, see Rozell 2002. Yet even national-security-relevant committees in the United States can meet in closed session.

123. US Code Title 18, Chapter 47, p. 798.

124. A useful summary of secrecy laws and penalties in the United States can be found in Edgar and Schmidt 1973 and Elsea 2011.

125. As reported by the Information Security Oversight Office, "Cost Report for Fiscal Year 2008," available at www.archives.gov/isoo.

126. US Budget Summary for 2010 and prior years, http://www.gpoaccess.gov/usbudget/fy10/pdf/budget/, accessed on January 23, 2010.

127. See interview with Peter Galison and Robb Moss, quoted in Wesley Morris, "Where Does the Necessary Secrecy End?" *The Boston Globe*, September 19, 2008, available at http://www.boston.com/movies/display?display=movie&id=11656, accessed March 30, 2010.

128. The US ISOO reports that 368.4 million classification decisions have been made since 1980, while the WikiLeak tally is approximately 750,000 documents to date, counting the Iraq and Afghan War logs and the diplomatic cables.

129. Banisar 2004.

130. Vincent 1998.

131. The text can be found at http://www.helplinelaw.com/docs/THEOFFICIAL SECRETSACT, 1923, accessed January 20, 2010.

132. The text can be found at http://www.austlii.edu.au/au/legis/cth/consol_act/ca191482/, accessed January 20, 2010. Note that this secrecy also influences auditing institutions such as the Congressional Budget Office, the National Audit Bureau in Sweden, and the National Audit Office in the United Kingdom, since reports from these offices can be classified or information can be withheld from the audit, as was the case in the Bofors AB and various BAE scandals.

133. Of course, these facts can alter the interpretation of publicly available information.
134. However, there are a few exceptions to this, including central bank policies.
135. Interview aired July 13, 2003, on CNN's *Late Edition with Wolf Blitzer*; transcript downloaded from http://votesmart.org/speech_detail.php?sc_id=87377& keyword=&phrase=&contain=?q=print on October 30, 2009.

CHAPTER 4

1. I do not suggest that these are the only costs of secrecy. As noted in Chapter 2, secrecy can cause bureaucratic problems and the capacity itself must be invested in. However, I will emphasize the costs of the capacity for secrecy for public consent in democracies, as this is central to the secrecy dilemma.
2. Schuessler 2010.
3. Downes 2009, p. 12, emphasis added.
4. Desch 2002.
5. See also Rosato 2003.
6. See in particular pp. 19–22 from Desch 2002.
7. Waltz 1967, 1979.
8. See Desch 2002; Rosato 2003.
9. Waltz 1967.
10. Waltz 1979.
11. There is a disagreement within this literature about whether states seek security or must maximize their power because no amount of finite security is enough. At this point, the distinction is not crucial since both imply that all leaders are working uniformly toward the same solitary goal. I argue below that leaders may divert funds and priorities to selfish, nonsecurity ends, and thus take issue with theories that assume pure security-seeking behavior in all leaders. Colaresi (2004a, 2004b, 2005) includes arguments for why leaders and the opposition might inflate threats to enhance their own political ambitions within threatening situations.
12. Almond 1956, pp. 371–378, and de Tocqueville and trans., 2007, p. 122.
13. Lippmann 1922, 1927.
14. Morgenthau 1967.
15. Ripsman 2009.
16. Schweller 2009.
17. Ripsman 2009.
18. Others may disagree that this was indeed an imprudent decision; in fact, the reality of disagreements like this is one of the central points of this work (see below).
19. One might argue that this tension can be relieved by simply increasing an executive's power on national security issues, so that the public has no role, and taxes, drafts, spending, and terms of office could be unilaterally decided by an executive without elections or public accountability. However, this would simply turn the state into a non-democracy by my definition.
20. See Desch 2002, as well as de Tocqueville et al. 2007 (1835).
21. For example, Schweller 2009 suggests that Fascism is an optimal arrangement for effective foreign policy.

22. If the marketplace of ideas were fully functioning on foreign policy issues without transparency costs, and there were no active capacity for secrecy and the selective revelation of information, the public would not be as skeptical, because either (a) there would exist transparent exogenous proof of costs and benefits or (b) an executive's failing to reveal information would be a sign of incompetence or corruption. See the discussion of transparency costs in Chapters 3 and 4 as well as Colaresi 2005 and Colaresi 2012.
23. Analyzing whether changing a state's institutions from a democracy to an autocracy is beneficial is beyond the scope of this book. While repressing the opposition may work in non-democracies, it is not an available strategy in a democracy.
24. I use this phrase to delineate a secret whose classification is in the public interest. This is contrast to non-security-relevant secrets whose classification may bring a private benefit to a leader, but not a public security benefit.
25. Mearsheimer 2010, locations 226–228.
26. Downes 2009.
27. Knightley 2004, pp. 358–359.
28. Knightley 2004, pp. 358–359.
29. Knightley 2004, p. 360.
30. Quoted in Knightley 2004, p. 371.
31. Smith 1978, pp. 23–33.
32. Smith 1978; Dine 2006.
33. Knightley 2004, pp. 363–364.
34. Naylor 2000, p. 316. It eventually did become public.
35. Dine 2006.
36. Dine 2006, p. 178. Smith 1978 ultimately concludes that the conflict had large net public costs and that independence for Algeria was necessary a decade earlier.
37. Smith 1978; Naylor 2000; Knightley 2004.
38. Morgan 2002 and Knightley 2004, pp. 72–74.
39. Belfield 1975, p. 22.
40. Lowry 2000, p. 30.
41. Knightley 2004, p. 75.
42. Morgan 2002.
43. Knightley 2004, p. 77.
44. This was first designated MO7, then changed to MI7; the "b" represented the subsection on domestic and foreign propaganda.
45. Arter 2013.
46. See "Agony of AA Milne, the Reluctant Wartime Propagandist, and the 'Lies' About German Atrocities," available at http://www.telegraph.co.uk/history/britain-at-war/10015206/Agony-of-AA-Milne-the-reluctant-wartime-propagandist-and-the-lies-about-German-atrocities.html.
47. Arter 2013, location 1853/1855.
48. Arter 2013.
49. Original documents are now archived at http://cymruww1.llgc.org.uk/2013/04/15/mi-7b-the-discovery-of-a-lost-propaganda-archive-of-the-great-war.
50. Arter 2013, location 152/1855.

51. Arter 2013, location 1534/1855.
52. See the discussion of this point in Chapter 3.
53. Mayadas 1999.
54. See Brauer and Dunne 2004, p. 214.
55. Brauer and Dunne 2004, p. 214; "India Sells Back Helicopter Fleet to Britain," *The Guardian*, October 17, 2000, by Luke Harding, available at http://www.guardian.co.uk/uk/2000/oct/18/lukeharding.
56. See Smith 1994, p. 127; "Hermes for Scrap If India Says No," *Jane's Defense Weekly*, Vol. 3, No. 25, June 22, 1985, p. 1197; and "India Sells Back Helicopter Fleet to Britain," *The Guardian*, October 17, 2000, by Luke Harding, available at http://www.guardian.co.uk/uk/2000/oct/18/lukeharding.
57. A summary of the allegations can be found in "BAE Accused of Arms Deal Slush Fund" by David Leigh and Rob Evans, *The Guardian*, September 11, 2003, available at http://www.guardian.co.uk/world/2003/sep/11/bae.freedomofinformation; and "The Web Widens" by David Leigh and Rob Evans, *The Guardian*, June 7, 2007, available at http://www.guardian.co.uk/baefiles/page/0, ,2095864,00.html.
58. See Lord Goldsmith (December 15, 2006). "BAE Systems: Al Yamamah Contract." Hansard, December 14, 2006.
59. Johnson 1997 and Born and Leigh 2008.
60. Because the suppression of domestic opposition often involves infiltrating these groups and anticipating their arguments and political strategies, I treat these topics together in this section.
61. Gant 2004, p. 7.
62. The commission was officially titled the Royal Commission of Inquiry into Certain Activities of the Royal Canadian Mounted Police.
63. Lund Commission Staff 1996; Weller 2000.
64. Which was formally known as the United States Senate Select Committee to Study Government Operations with Respect to Intelligence Activities and was chaired by Frank Church, in the 1970s.
65. See Snider 1999/2000 and "Supplementary Detailed Staff Reports on Intelligence Activities and the Rights of Americans," Select Committee to Study Governmental Operations, Book III, Section IV B1a, April 23, 1976. Operation Shamrock predated the National Security Agency (NSA) and began in 1945 and was continued under Truman in 1952.
66. Snider 1999/2000, footnote 9.
67. See "Supplementary Detailed Staff Reports on Intelligence Activities and the Rights of Americans," Select Committee to Study Governmental Operations, Book III, Section IV B1a, April 23, 1976.
68. The latter of these was formally known as the Select Committee on Intelligence and was chaired by Otis G. Pike after Lucien Nedzi resigned in June 1975. These were the US Senate and House bodies tasked with investigating news stories about domestic spying and the misuse of intelligence and counterintelligence resources.
69. See Church 1976.

70. See, for example, Mayadas 1999; Knightley 2004, p. 77; Lord Goldsmith statement to House of Lords, "BAE Systems: Al Yamamah Contract," December 14, 2006, available at http://www.publications.porliament.UK/pa/id200607/idhansrd/text/61214-0014.htm; Church 1976; Snider 1999/2000; Lund Commission Staff 1996; and Gant 2004.

71. Read 2012. The gun did have limitations that were also revealed during World War I, and these are discussed in Chapter 5.

72. Read 2012.

73. See Doise 1994.

74. Read 2012, location 1285/9837.

75. Read 2012, location 2298/9837.

76. Read 2012, location 1280/9837.

77. Compare Hoffman 1980, p. 4, Doise 1994, and Read 2012, Chapter 5.

78. Read 2012, location 2296/9837.

79. Read 2012, location 2084/9837.

80. Read 2012, location 2088/9837.

81. Read 2012, location 2092/9837.

82. Read 2012, location 2153/9837.

83. Read 2012, location 2110/9837.

84. Read 2012, location 2115/9837.

85. Read 2012, location 2064/9837.

86. The change in the law was passed on February 12, 1895, without debate (Read 2012, location 2499/9837).

87. Read 2012, location 3465/9837.

88. Read 2012, locations 3479 and 3497/9837.

89. Read 2012, location 3506/9837.

90. Read 2012, location 3479/9837.

91. Read 2012, location 3530/9837.

92. Read 2012, location 3574/9837.

93. Read 2012, location 3596/9837.

94. Doise 1994.

95. Read 2012, location 3619/9837.

96. Read 2012, location 3628/9837.

97. Read 2012, location 3636/9837.

98. Picquart, seeing that he was being outmaneuvered, added to his will a note that a specific sealed envelope contained evidence that he had discovered of Esterhazy's spying and Dreyfus's innocence. It was to be delivered to the president of the Republic if he died (Read 2012, location 3719/9837).

99. Read 2012, location 3824/9837.

100. Read 2012, locations 3790 and 3816/9837.

101. Read 2012, location 4352–4357/9837.

102. Read 2012, location 4420–4421/9837.

103. Quoted in Read 2012, locations 4451 and 4430/9837.

104. This was the Italian Embassy document that had its content forged to implicate Dreyfus.

105. Read 2012.

106. He went on to rejoin the French army and fight in World War II.

107. In fact, there has been some speculation that the entanglement of the secret 75-mm gun and the Dreyfus Affair might be tighter still. Esterhazy claimed that he was a double-agent working for the Secret Section and that the orginal bordereau's mention of the short 120 gun was sent to deceive the Germans about the 75-mm triumph. French historian Doise, while noting ambiguities in the evidence, supports this story (see Doise 1994).

108. Read 2012.

109. The CIA was an evolution of the Office of Strategic Services, originally organized in 1942 to focus on foreign operation. For a history of the CIA and the many bureaucratic changes between 1942 and 1947, see Johnson 1997.

110. Johnson 1997.

111. Which produced the series of "Key Hole" Satellites that were used to view Soviet deployments (see Lewis 2002).

112. Polyakov has been described as "the jewel in the crown" or the intelligence agencies spies. He supplied evidence, for example, of the growing split between the USSR and China that helped persuade Nixon to communicate with Bejing and led to the opening in 1972. See "Death of the Perfect Spy," *Time Magazine*, June 24, 2001, by Elaine Shannon, available at http://www.time.com/time/magazine/printout/0,8816,164863,00.html.

113. Sharp 2012.

114. The full details of just how the CIA learned this information have not been publicly released at the time of this writing. The latest release of information on Project Azorian can be found in Sharp 2012, along with the documentary evidence available at the National Security Archive, http://www.gwu.edu/~nsarchiv/nukevault/ebb305.

115. Even if the USSR knew the location, they believed that it was irretrievable, as later events would make clear (see Sharp 2012, p. 257).

116. For years after the project became publicly known, people referred to it as Project Jennifer. However, we now know that Jennifer was the codename for the information compartmentalizaion for the project, which included very few people (see Sharp 2012, p. 43).

117. In his memoirs, Soviet Ambassador Dobrynin suggests that news of the salvage operation reached the Soviet Union after it was over (see discussion in Sharp 2012, p. 257).

118. See Sharp 2012, Epilogue.

119. White House Memorandum of Conversation, March 19, 1975, 11:20 a.m., available at http://www.gwu.edu/~nsarchiv/nukevault/ebb305/doc03.pdf.

120. Sharp 2012, pp. 257–260.

121. Freedom of information claims were met with what came to be known as the Glomar response, involving the CIA neither confirming nor denying the existence of the requested documents.

122. I do not take a position here about whether Project Azorian was good foreign policy or not, in the sense that the expected benefits would need to be greater than the costs. Instead, I am making the point that the secrecy surrounding Project Azorian was justified based on securing public benefits and intelligence and not

attempting to hide incompetence or promote narrow private interests, in contrast to the abuses surounding Watergate.

123. Komine 2008, p. 6.

124. Quoted in "The First Domino: Nixon and the Pentagon Papers," by Jordan Moran, Presidential Recordings Program, Miller Center, University of Virginia, available at http://whitehousetapes.net/exhibit/first-domino-nixon-and-pentagon-papers.

125. For example, he was given access to CIA camera equipment during this time. This fact led to some embarrassment in the White House when it was revealed that Hunt had returned the CIA camera they had brought to the burglary at Ellsberg's doctor's office, but left the film inside. See transcript of a recording of a meeting between the President and H. R. Haldeman in the Oval Office on June 23, 1972, from 10:04 a.m, to 11:39 a.m., available at http://www.nixonlibrary.gov/forresearchers/find/tapes/watergate/trial/exhibit_01.pdf.

126. See the letter "The Break-In That History Forgot," New York Times, June 30, 2007, by Egil Krogh.

127. See, for example, "FBI Finds Nixon Aides Sabotaged Democrats," Washington Post, A1, October 10, 1972.

128. Johnson 1997.

129. Quoted in Klein 2008, p. 121.

130. Klein 2008, p. 121.

131. See transcript of a recording of a meeting between the President and H. R. Haldeman in the Oval Office on June 23, 1972, from 10:04 a.m, to 11:39 a.m., available at http://www.nixonlibrary.gov/forresearchers/find/tapes/watergate/trial/exhibit_01.pdf.

132. Haldeman stated, "Ah, he'll call him in and say, 'We've got the signal from across the river to, to put the hold on this.' And that will fit rather well because the FBI agents who are working the case, at this point, feel that's what it is. This is CIA." See transcript of a recording of a meeting between the President and H. R. Haldeman in the Oval Office on June 23, 1972, from 10:04 a.m. to 11:39 a.m., available at http://www.nixonlibrary.gov/forresearchers/find/tapes/watergate/trial/exhibit_01.pdf. Perhaps surprisingly, the FBI operative they were going to use to plant the CIA story within the FBI was Mark Felt, who was later unveiled as "Deep Throat," the main source for press leaks on Watergate through the Washington Post.

133. Transcript of recording of a meeting among the President, John Dean, and H. R. Haldeman in the Oval Office on March 17, 1973, from 1:25 p.m. to 2:20 p.m., available at http://www.nixonlibrary.gov/forresearchers/find/tapes/watergate/trial/exhibit_10.pdf.

134. See, for example, "Nixon 'Smoking Gun' Tape Released," by Mike M. Ahlers, CNN, February 28, 2002. Available at http://archives.cnn.com/2002/ALLPOLITICS/02/28/nixon.tapes/.

135. See "The Watergate Report: Final Report of the Senate Select Committee on Presidential Campaign Activities," 1974, pp. 125–126.

136. The information kept secret included the fact that Hunt had directly asked the CIA a few months before the Watergate break-in whether it could supply

someone "who was accomplished at picking locks." See "The Keeper of Secrets Earned His Reputation," *The Washington Post,* June 27, 2007, by Bob Woodward, available at http://www.washingtonpost.com/wp-dyn/content/article/2007/06/26/AR2007062601965.html.

137. Page 4, Nixon's Web.

138. Schulman 2001, p. 121.

139. Schulman 2001, pp. 139–142.

140. Ronald Reagan, "Peace: Restoring the Margin of Safety," speech at Veterans of Foreign Wars Convention, Chicago, IL, August 18, 1980, available at http://www.reagan.utexas.edu/archives/reference/8.18.80.html.

141. However, while France was to continue its polarization and discontent for decades after the Dreyfus Affair, the United States suffered less due to active institutional steps to combat public distrust that we outline in the next chapter.

CHAPTER 5

1. Phythian 2007.

2. Fordham 1998.

3. Gaubatz 1999.

4. Reiter and Stam 2002.

5. As a case in point, if a sufficient majority felt aggreived, they could simply vote the repressive leader out.

6. This is similar to problems of adverse selection discussed by Akerlof (1970), where information asymmetries between an executive (seller) and the public (buyer) over the quality of a policy (product) can lead to market collapse. See Colaresi 2011 for a further description.

7. Moynihan and Combest 1997, Overview, p. 8.

8. See, for example, "Energy Bill a Special-interests Triumph," by Susan Milligan, *Boston Globe,* October 4, 2004, available at http://www.boston.com/news/nation/articles/2004/10/04/energy_bill_a_special_interests/.

9. Fordham 1998.

10. Belfield 1975; Smith 1978. On the difference between the endogenous and exogenous signaling of threats, see Colaresi 2007.

11. See Colaresi 2004b for a study of the risks of offering unreciprocated cooperation to a potentially threatening state.

12. See "Top Bush Officials Push Case Against Saddam," September 8, 2002, CNN, available at http://articles.cnn.com/2002-09-08/politics/iraq.debate_1_nuclear-weapons-top-nuclear-scientists-aluminum-tubes?_s=PM:ALLPOLITICS, as well as "Cheney Says Peril of a Nuclear Iraq Justifies Attack" by Elizabeth Bumiller and James Dao, *New York Times,* August 27, 2002. This is an example of one way that leaders attempt to mobilize additional public consent for a foreign policy, by releasing previously secret national security information. In fact, the selective release of information from the executive is a time-honored tradition in democracies. As *New York Times* reporter James Reston wrote in 1946 when discussing news coverage of peace negotiations, "governments are the only vessels that leak from the top"; see "Big 4's Press System Seen as Approved by Reporters" by James Reston, *New York Times,*

November 9, 1946, p. 4. It is not difficult to find quotes, on background, of unnamed government officials confirming an international threat or external troop strength numbers; see, for example, Simpson 2010 on the UK press and anonymous sourcing from within government, as well as "The 'Anonymous' Virus" by John McLaughlin, *The American Interest*, December 19, 2011, for a view into the leaking from within the executive classification system to the press. Many major foreign policy announcements are actually presentation of previously secret government information. Both Colin Powell's and Adlai Stevenson's presentation to the UN during the 2002/3 Iraq debate and the Cuban Missile Crisis, respectively, presented previously classified information. Similarly, sensitive information about the Boer War, Suez Crisis, and Iraq War was presented by the UK government to the public over the years in the hopes of buoying public opinion (see Simpson 2010). However, not only does this release of information have associated transparency costs, but any information provided by the executive to secure consent for policies will necessarily be partial. The remaining secrets may contradict or dilute the leaked information. This dilution of the apparent message could be due to actual secrecy concerns or pure political maneuvering. In either case, the public has a reason to doubt the credibility of the information they are receiving.

13. See "Senators Wary About Action Against Iraq" by Helen Dewar and Mike Allen, *Washington Post*, September 4, 2002.

14. See "Talk of War," PBS News Hour, October 7, 2002, http://www.pbs.org/newshour/bb/middle_east/july-dec02/iraqpolls_10-07-02.html and "Public Says Bush Needs to Pay to Weak Economy" by Adam Nagourney and Janet Elder, *New York Times*, October 7, 2002. The latter article included polls that showed that over 60% of the public preferred to wait, rather than authorize war now, and a majority of the public doubted the de-armament motive for the Iraq War.

15. Quoted in "Rumsfeld Says U.S. Has 'Bulletproof' Evidence of Iraq's Links to Al Qaeda" by Eric Schmitt, *New York Times*, September 28, 2002.

16. "Skepticism and Support Swirl Around Clinton," December 17, 1998, BBC News Report, http://news.bbc.co.uk/2/hi/events/crisis_in_the_gulf/latest_news/236582.stm.

17. Gustafson 1988, p. 149.

18. See Knightley 2004.

19. Waller 2006, pp. 111–113.

20. Quoted in Waller 2006, p. 112.

21. Ciment and Russell 2006, p. 989.

22. It is also possible that, at times, this trimming down of investments and support leads to better policy. For example, one might argue that public opposition helped to keep the United States out of a costly war with Iran late in George W. Bush's presidency. However, unconditional constraints can make significant errors of omission, as the cases of the United States, the United Kingdom, and France in the inter-war years, the French preparations for World War I, and the US reaction to the 1974 Cyprus conflict make clear below. This threat is explored further in Chapter 5.

23. See, for example, Ricks 2006, pp. 101, 108–110, 118, 144, 407.
24. Fisher 2004. See below for a discussion of post-Watergate executive credibility in the United States.
25. See "Security and Marketshare: Bridging the Transatlantic Divide in the Defense Industry," *European Security*, Vol. 10, Issue 1, 2001, Thomas Lansford, pp. 1–21.
26. Fordham 2002, 1998.
27. Fordham 1998.
28. This time period supplies a corollary to the exceptions mentioned above, where external threats can trigger domestic publics to support larger investments in defense. A skeptical public can remain skeptical if a revisionist power does not signal its bellicosity, as Kaiser Wilhelm did in the Agadir crisis; see below.
29. Jackson 2000.
30. Stavisky was a grifter who had significant connections among the political and military classes in France. His accusal and eventual death brought theories of a cover-up and significant scandal (see Large 1990).
31. The spiral could continue for democracies on national security, as it does with used cars. If unchecked, it might be the case that leaders fail to put forward costly but highly beneficial foreign policy plans—like the Marshall Plan—if they know that the public would not support them. As a result, the public becomes even more skeptical of expensive foreign policy price tags.
32. Maney 1998, p. 128.
33. Reynolds 2000. In fact, we have a name, sometimes used in a colloquial way, for public skepticism of national security mobilization: isolationism. Braumoeller (2010) makes a convincing case that is relevant to this discussion. He argues that isolationism is often a myth. For example, in the inter-war years the United States did not have a significant proportion of isolationists; instead, a large proportion of the public did not view Nazi Germany as a threat and thus only supported very modest spending. It was the inability of elites that perceived a higher threat level emanating from Berlin to convince others that caused the underspending, as opposed to a preexisting and unchanging value judgment to stay out of international affairs.
34. While public and congressional reaction to the Cyprus Crisis resembled post-Dreyfus distrust in France, the foreign policy paths of these countries soon diverged. After Cyprus, instead of decades of continuing and worsening polarization as in France, the United States undertook specific and important changes to increase public confidence that the capacity for secrecy was being used for public security, rather than abused. However, we must first understand the disease of withheld public consent before we can analyze a cure.
35. Stevenson 2004, p. 40.
36. See Porch 2003b, p. 43, and Chapter 1 for a discussion of the depth of distrust as well as the reorganization.
37. Krumeich 1987, pp. 14–15.
38. Krumeich 1987, p. 34.
39. Krumeich 1987, p. 37.
40. Krumeich 1987, pp. 14–15, 34–37.
41. Krumeich 1987, p. 21.

42. Castillo et al. 2001, p. 22.
43. Castillo et al. 2001, p. 26.
44. Krumeich 1987, p. 46.
45. Krumeich 1987, pp. 46–48.
46. Stevenson 2004, pp. 35–47; see also Audoin-Rouzeau et al. 2003, p. 22.
47. Porch 2003a, p. 245.
48. Porch 2003a, p. 212 and Audoin-Rouzeau et al. 2003.
49. Audoin-Rouzeau et al. 2003, p. 22.
50. Porch 2003a, p. 242.
51. That is, artillery that is hidden behind hills or in entrenched position.
52. Stevenson 2004, p. 42.
53. Audoin-Rouzeau et al. 2003, pp. 23–30. However, France did luck into an above
     average early air force due not to government policy but to idiosyncratic private
     air clubs (Porch 2003b).
54. Specifically, France would try to pierce the heavily fortified Metz-Strasbourg line
     as well as either initiate their own or repel a German thrust through Belgium. The
     French army could not do both of these things at the same time with their limited
     resources. By 1912, the plans called for British Expeditionary Forces, but London
     set specific and strict constraints on French policy vis-à-vis Belgium (Krumeich
     1987, pp. 24–25).
55. Krumeich 1987, p. 21.
56. Krumeich 1987, p. 31, Porch 2003a, Stevenson 2004, pp. 40–46.
57. Krumeich 1987, p. 16.
58. Krumeich 1987, p. 16.
59. Krumeich 1987, p. 19.
60. Krumeich 1987, p. 55.
61. Audoin-Rouzeau et al. 2003, p. 19.
62. Krumeich 1987.
63. Krumeich 1987, p. 17.
64. Details of the well-documented switch from a defensive to an offensive military
     strategy in France under General Joffre can be found in Krumeich 1987, Audoin-
     Rouzeau et al. 2003, and Porch 2003a.
65. Krumeich 1987, p. 17. The author goes even further and suggests that the French
     decision to risk war in 1914 was part of a domestic calculation whereby the gov-
     ernment forecast that the public was becoming increasingly distrustful of the
     military and that the mobilization would soon be reversed.
66. Doughty 2005, p. 14.
67. Krumeich 1987, pp. 50–54.
68. Audoin-Rouzeau et al. 2003, p. 20.
69. Audoin-Rouzeau et al. 2003, p. 20.
70. Krumeich 1987, pp. 10–11.
71. Audoin-Rouzeau et al. 2003, p. 19.
72. Porch 2003a, p. 249.
73. Porch 2003a, p. 243.
74. Porch 2003a, p. 243.
75. Porch 2003a, p. 243.

76.   Porch 2003a, p. 245.
77.   Porch 2003a, p. 244.
78.   Doughty 2005, pp. 29–30.
79.   Audoin-Rouzeau et al. 2003, pp. 29–30.
80.   Audoin-Rouzeau et al. 2003, p. 23. Even outside of heavy artillery, polarization in France doused rational calculation to the extent that Parliament blocked the use of camouflage due to bickering over patterns and colors, despite the fact that all other major power armies had switched to uniforms less conspicuous than the French red and blues (Stevenson 2004, p. 42).
81.   Porch 2003a, p. 254.
82.   Krumeich 1987, p. 11.
83.   Krumeich 1987, pp. 21–22. Further, there is some evidence that the divisions riven by the Dreyfus Affair continued even to the post–Cold War period: "In 1994, the Director of the Historical Section of the French Army stated that Dreyfuss innocence was merely 'a thesis generally admitted by historians.' He was sacked, and Dreyfuss' innocence was declared indisputable by his successor. It illustrated, once again, the difficulty of approaching with even-handed detachment this critical event in the history of France." See "France Is Still Fractured by the Dreyfus Affair" by Piers Paul Read, 2012, *The Telegraph*, available at http://www.telegraph.co.uk/news/worldnews/europe/france/9045659/France-is-still-fractured-by-the-Dreyfus-Affair.html.
84.   Krumeich 1987, p. 12.
85.   Porch 2003a, p. 250.
86.   Krumeich 1987, p. 52.
87.   Doughty 2005, p. 509.
88.   Krumeich 1987, p. 215.
89.   Enosis means fusion in Greek.
90.   The 1964 talks led to UN peacekeepers being stationed on the island, and the tensions in 1967 led to a stern warning from the United States to Turkey to avoid invasion of the island after a military coup in Greece (see Miller 2009).
91.   Warner 2009, p. 136; Miller 2009.
92.   Warner 2009, p. 136.
93.   Warner 2009, p. 136.
94.   Miller 2009, location 2650–2667.
95.   Warner 2009, p. 137.
96.   Warner 2009, p. 138.
97.   See *Foreign Relations of the United States*, Vol. XXX, Document No. 105.
98.   Warner 2009.
99.   Miller 2009.
100.   *Foreign Relations of the United States*, Vol. XXX, Document No. 128.
101.   *Foreign Relations of the United States*, Vol. XXX, Document No. 129.
102.   *Foreign Relations of the United States*, Vol. XXX, Document No. 128.
103.   Miller 2009, location 2748–2750.
104.   Kissinger 2000, location 11020/2336.
105.   See Mieczkowsk 2000, p. 276.
106.   Warner 2009, p. 141.
107.   Kissinger 2000, location 11020/2336; Bell 1977, p. 153.

108. Miller 2009, location 2774/4268.
109. Kissinger 2000, locations 3854–3862/23367; Miller 2009, location 2762/4268.
110. "Remarks of Congressman John Brademas (D-Ind.), 52nd Convention, Order of Ahepa, Boston, Mass," August 18, 1974, available at http://www.nyu.edu/library/bobst/research/arch/brademas/cyprus-740818f.htm.
111. Kissinger 2000, pp. 4004–4006.
112. "Washington Merry-Go-Round" by Jack Anderson, *The Ohio County Times*, Hartford, Kentucky, August 14, 1975.
113. Miller 2009, locations 2910–2911.
114. "Washington Merry-Go-Round" by Jack Anderson, *The Ohio County Times*, Hartford, Kentucky, August 14, 1975.
115. Foreign Relations of the United States, Volume XXX, Document 210, available at http://history.state.gov/historicaldocuments/frus1969-76v30/d210. Further discusion of the administration response and lobbying can be found in Document 230 in the same source, available at http://history.state.gov/historicaldocuments/frus1969-76v30/d230.
116. Further, the ambiguities and potential for abuse in the events leading up to the Cyprus crisis have led some to suggest that the United States helped to plan the regime change. See Miller 2009 for a summary.
117. "Remarks of Congressman John Brademas (D-Ind.), 52nd Convention, Order of Ahepa, Boston, Mass," August 18, 1974, available at http://www.nyu.edu/library/bobst/research/arch/brademas/cyprus-740818f.htm. Brademas made similar comments in a speech on the House floor, stating that Watergate happened "because of the defiance of the rule of law. Are we now to say that the Department of State is above the law?" Statement by Congressman Brademas on House Floor, as written, September 24, 1974, available at http://www.nyu.edu/library/bobst/research/arch/brademas/cyprus-740924c.htm.
118. See the discussion in Miller 2009, locations 2903–2904/4268.
119. Miller 2009, location 2884/4268.
120. "Whose Crisis" by William Shannon, *New York Times*, August 20, 1974. See also Mieczkowsk 2000, p. 276.
121. Miller 2009, location 2908; Mieczkowsk 2000, p. 277.
122. Kissinger 2000, location 4060/23367; Warner 2009.
123. Mieczkowsk 2000, pp. 276–277.
124. See Section 20(C) of the act. The relative importance of Greece and Turkey as alliance partners, even without the intelligence bases, favored Ankara. Congress set a 10:7 rule, whereby for every $7 of Greek military aid, Turkey receives $10. See Congressional Research Service Brief 86065, "Greece and Turkey: Current Foreign Aid Issues," December 3, 1996.
125. Doughty (2005), pp. 14.
126. Doughty (2005), pp. 42.
127. Doughty (2005), pp. 42–3.
128. For example, CIA Director Colby wrote in a follow-up report that "intelligence provide[d] explicit warning of growing confrontation." See FRUS, Vol. XXX, No. 171, as well as Vol XXX, No. 98. There is more ambiguous evidence about the accuracy in predicting the coup in Cyprus; see Vol. XXX, No. 148.

129.   William Hyland, Speech at Washington University Commencement, May 16, 1987.

130.   One counterargument to the possibility of nonsecurity motives for abuse is to suggest that leaders are inherently public serving and that even if they are abusing secrecy privileges at net public costs, this is simply a mistake rather than knowing corruption for private gain. Yet, from the public's point of view, it is immaterial whether a leader is pursuing deception due to the mistaken perception that the "honor of the army" can be protected by framing a Jewish officer or because he is afraid to lose his job. What matters are the net costs and benefits of policies to the public. Outright corruption leads to net public costs, but so does incompetence. Sandherr and Henry might have truly believed that they were protecting the French nation as they forged evidence, but the public did not benefit. In memoirs, Hunt and Gray both explicitly state that they were acting to protect the national interest. The truthfulness of these protestations does not change the secrecy dilemma for the public. The potential for abuse of information asymmetries means that the public has reason to be skeptical when told to support specific foreign policy initiatives or invest in military preparations.

CHAPTER 6

1.   Read 2012, location 2092/9837.

2.   Johnson 1997.

3.   As I will detail, retrospective oversight entails digging for information on national security that is classified and potentially costly to publicize. On most domestic issues which do not have obvious transparency costs, the public or legislators can demand information and approximate the real-time marketplace of ideas. Therefore the retrospective oversight tools I discuss have to be calibrated to reach into the capacity for secrecy and make information public. This is most easily seen with freedom of information laws. As Chapter 3 noted, every democracy analyzed had a capacity for secrecy. This capacity extends even to countries that have freedom of information laws. Every freedom of information law includes exemptions for national security secrets. Thus, the capacity for secrecy bulges into, and partially obscures, the transparency goals of freedom of information laws. However, not every exemption is the same. Some laws include the means by which a member of the public can access even exempted information—for example, if the request is in the public interest. This is discussed further in the next three chapters.

4.   The different relevant forms of costs that can be imposed on executives are discussed below.

5.   Which Disraeli was forced to take out a loan to invest in because his plans were blocked in parliament.

6.   Aldous 2007.

7.   Ames 1992.

8.   Manninen 2006, p. 33.

9.   Manninen 2006, p. 43.

10.   Manninen 2006, pp. 40–44.

11.   Manninen 2006, p. 45.

12. Manninen 2006, p. 34.
13. For a discussion of the law in its current formulation, see Banisar 2004.
14. See Chapter 6.
15. The infamous Star Chamber was in charge of delimitating and punishing this type of criticism until 1641 in England; however, even after the chamber's dissolution, political criticism was banned. While parliamentary privilege allowed members to criticize policies and not be arrested at Parliament, they did fear being harassed significantly once they left the House of Commons (see Hume 1983). Additionally, anyone not in Parliament had no such privilege.
16. Williams 1909, Vol. 16, pp. 415–416.
17. See Powers n.d., p. 13.
18. Laursen 1998.
19. Laursen 1998.
20. Powers n.d.
21. He also praised the King, since he did not know that the Struensse was in charge at the time.
22. In fact, in 2011, both Norway and Denmark were ranked by Freedom House as being among the top five countries with the freest presses in the world. See http://www.freedomhouse.org/report-types/freedom-press.
23. Barton 1986, p. 132.
24. Powers makes the case that news traveled swiftly to the new world in English-language newspapers, specifically in the Virgin Islands, where Alexander Hamilton was living at the time (Powers n.d., p. 55).
25. Cushman 1956, p. 2.
26. See Article 29 at http://www.un.org/en/documents/udhr/ and Powers n.d.
27. This specific language was used by a Tennessee delegation to complain about the tacit approval Lincoln had given to Andrew Johnson's oath that voters would take in the vote during the war in 1964. See Graf and Haskins 1983, pp. 203–204.
28. Tap 1998.
29. Burlingame 2013, Vol. II, p. 179.
30. Foote 1986, Vol. III, p. 559.
31. Trefousse 1997, p. 231.
32. James L. Morrison, quoted in Tap 1998, p. 21.
33. Tap 1998, p. 21.
34. Tap 1998, pp. 23–24.
35. Tap 1998, p. 34.
36. Tap 1998, p. 232.
37. The committee also played a role in publicizing battlefield events. In 1864 and 1865, the CCW's reports on the indiscriminate killing of Union soldiers that had surrendered at Fort Pillow, the treatment of Union prisoners of war, and the Sand Creek masacre of Native Americans in Colorado supplied credible information to the public on wartime events (see McKitrick 1967 and Tap 1998).
38. McKitrick 1967.
39. McKitrick 1967.
40. Tap 1998, pp. 230–245; see also the discussion in McKitrick 1967.
41. Tap 1998, pp. 230–245.

42. Bruce Tap's book takes a balanced view on the committee's effects, arguing that its immediate interference in war policy was negative, but its investigations of previous battles and of corruption and waste were positive. One problem with Tap's conclusions, however, is that he fails to separate the attitudes of the members of the committee from the work of the committee itself. For example, Tap is vigorous in his denunciation of the lack of military knowledge of Committee Chairman Wade and the other Republicans on the panel. He concludes that this lack of knowledge combined with meddling constituted the major cost the committee charged to the war effort. What Tap neglects, in my view, is that this lack of knowledge and meddling would have occurred, and did go on, even without the committee. For example, before the committee even existed, Benjamin Wade and Michigan Senator Zachariah Chandler and a group of other Republicans met with General McClellan and attempted to press him on strategy. The next day several of the group met with members of Lincoln's White House to have General-in-Chief Scott removed. This meddling occurred without the committee and would likely have continued if the committee had never existed. While investigations and testimony enhanced the power of some members of the committee, including Wade, some of the damage Tap worried about would have been done anyway. On the other hand, the thorough investigation of heavy artillery and procurement could only be accomplished by a vigorous committee empowered with the ability to compel evidence, meet in both secret and in public, conduct sight visits, and present public reports. See Tap 1998, pp. 17–19.

43. By 1864, most Radical Republicans, while still doubtful of Lincoln, supported his re-election. See Burlingame 2013.

44. Truman 1956, p. 168.

45. See Johnson 1997 and "Special Committee to Investigate the National Defense Program, Notable Senate Investigations, U.S. Senate Historical Office, Washington, D.C.," available at http://www.senate.gov/artandhistory/history/common/investigations/pdf/TrumanCommittee_fullcitations.pdf.

46. I believe the original quote is from Orwell and Angus 1968, p. 125.

47. Truman 1956, p. 168.

48. The strongest case that has been made for the transparency costs that accrued based on Yardley's publication of this fact is that it might have aroused greater distrust of the United States (see Schoenfeld 2010, pp. 88–91, 110–120). This is still a much lower price to pay for publicity than what would have occurred earlier.

49. Yet, even here the overall plan and deception proved valuable for months (see Chapter 2).

50. This is of course a spartan view of the secrecy involved in this crisis. There were many more secrets the United States held—for example, involving U-2 overflights and the rule of engagement for the blockage.

51. Which is "Castro" spelled backward.

52. Kennedy 1969.

53. Included in that book were details about the value the administration ascribed to the Jupiter missiles and the implicit deal that was struck (see Kennedy 1969).

54. This is just an example. The value of each of these secrets over time is open for debate. In fact, General LeMay is quoted as saying that he believed the Jupiter missiles continued to have significant value (see Mann 2011, p. 8). His position appears to be an outlier in the historical record.

55. Therefore, any secret is no more than twice the value of any other secret. This is assumed for simplicity.

56. In this example, p is .5. It is plausible that p increases over time. If p indeed increases over time, this would exaggerate transparency cost deflation further.

57. Using the average rather than the sum of all information is a trivial assumption since the relative pattern of transparency cost deflation is consistent across aggregation rules. However, using the average transparency costs is arguably more realistic (see below).

58. See Snider 1999/2000.

59. That information might reveal more obvious secrets.

60. See the report "Parliamentary Oversight of the Security Sector: Principals, Mechanisms and Practices" created by the International Parliamentary Union and the Geneva Center for the Democratic Control of the Armed Forces, as well as Willis 2011, "Understanding Intelligence Oversight: Guidebook" and "Compilation of Good Practices for Intelligence Agencies and Their Oversight: A Report to the UN Human Rights Council by the Special Rapporteur on the Promotion and Protection of Human Right and Fundamental Freedoms While Countering Terrorism."

61. See "Parliamentary Oversight of the Security Sector," p. 72, and "Understanding Intelligence Oversight," p. 34.

62. Kurian 1998; Fish and Kroenig 2009.

63. See, for example, Intelligence and Security Services Review Committee (2010), "Review Report on the Performance of the GISS on the Obligation to Notify, Kamerstukken II 2009/10, 29, 924, No. 49.

64. See Directorate General for Internal Policies 2011, pp. 127–128.

65. Banisar 2004.

66. See http://www.gwu.edu/~nsarchiv/nukevault/ebb367/index.htm.

67. See http://www.gwu.edu/\%7Ensarchiv/NSAEBB/NSAEBB365/index.htm.

68. More generally, see http://www.gwu.edu/\%7Ensarchiv/index.html.

69. See http://www.nationalarchives.gov.uk/information-management/legislation/section-46.htm.

70. However, a 2007 lustration law in Poland has significantly increased political pressure on journalists, as has the "El Pais" case (see Karlekar and Cook 2008). Costa Rica's press freedom improved with the repeal of a political libel law that made it a crime to insult public officials. Background on these changes can be found in Karlekar and Cook 2008 and http://www.rsf.org/Reporters-Without-Borders,4116.html, accessed November 10, 2009.

71. Karlekar and Cook 2008; Freedom House 2008. See also the various country–year reports from Reporters Sans Frontieres, www.rsf.org.

72. Prados and Portier 2004.

73. Shetreet 1991; Thompson 1999; Johnson 1997.

74. See, for example, the National Security Archive annual report for 2008, available at http://www.gwu.edu/~nsarchiv/nsa/2008 Annual Report.pdf.
75. Bueno de Mesquita et al. 2003; Bueno de Mesquita and Smith 2011.
76. Mayadas 1999.
77. Two earlier reports on Iraq, the Iraq Study Group report in 2006 and the Robb–Silvermann commission report in 2005, were focused on narrower questions of operation decisions in the future in the case of the former and the process of intelligence gathering in the latter. Each of these reports also was reported publicly only after the 2004 elections.
78. See Goulden 1969. I thank an anonymous reviewer for pointing out this citation.
79. See the discussion in Fisher 2003, 2004.
80. Laver and Shepsle 1990, 1996.
81. Goemans 2000; Choizza and Goemans 2011.
82. Laver and Shepsle 1996, p. 20.
83. See "Blair Narrowly Prevails in a Vote to Raise Tuition Fees" by Patrick Tyler, *New York Times*, January 28, 2004, available at http://www.nytimes.com/2004/01/28/world/blair-narrowly-prevails-in-a-vote-to-raise-tuition-fees.html.
84. See the discussion of the US and French cases in Chapters 5 and 6.
85. Ross Douthat, "The Iraq War and the GOP's Fortunes," October 28, 2008, Atlantic.com, available at http://www.theatlantic.com/personal/archive/2008/10/the-iraq-war-and-the-gops-fortunes/55729/.
86. "10 Years Later, Iraq's Impact Still Pervades Republican Party" by Tom Curry, NBC News, available at http://nbcpolitics.nbcnews.com/_news/2013/03/19/17360851-10-years-later-iraqs-impact-still-pervades-republican-party?lite.
87. Goemans 2000.
88. See "Bush's Legacy vs. the 2008 Election" by Kate Zernike, *New York Times*, January 14, 2007, available at http://www.nytimes.com/2007/01/14/weekinreview/14zernike.html. While Downes 2009 used this as an example of deception, it highlights that leaders can care about, and thus be vulnerable to, threats to their legacies.
89. Quoted in "George Bush's Legacy," January 15, 2009, the *Economist*, available at http://www.economist.com/node/12931660.
90. As we move forward with our investigation of oversight institutions, one reasonable objection is that leaders merely care about their political position. If that is the case, dynamic transparency costs and oversight may at times deliver information that is too little or too late to deter abuses.

CHAPTER 7
1. Thus, the existence of the capacity for secrecy.
2. Oversight must also have a benefit to the potential overseer. The public must reward those that discover and reveal genuine abuses, while providing disincentives for those that reveal information that would be useful to a competitor. I discuss the ramifications of this below and in Chapter 10.
3. Desch 2002 and Rosato 2003.
4. Ames 1992.
5. Banisar 2004. It should be noted that Costa Rica continued to maintain an intelligence service during this time.

6. For information on Costa Rica in 2006, see "Freedom House Narrative," available at http://www.freedomhouse.org/modules/mod_call_dsp_country-fiw.cfm?year=2006&country=6944.

7. Ravenal 1982.

8. Thus the executive can generate private benefits from the spending.

9. This can be seen formally in the Appendix.

10. This overspending might not be as bad as it sounds. Repressive autocracies usually have an even more expensive military apparatus, since this spending may be targeted at internal and external security as well as additional corruption. In Chapter 9 we will compare the overspending in democracies to that in non-democracies.

11. Due to the paradox of national security oversight discussed above.

12. Of course, neither researchers nor the public observe ability directly. Yet, if we assume that success in a crisis is a function of the relative latent abilities of the crisis actors, we can use information on the history of crisis outcomes to calculate whether, on average, democracies with retrospective oversight have higher latent foreign policy abilities. This is discussed in Chapter 9.

13. Reiter and Stam 2002; Schultz and Weingast 2003.

14. Act No. 78–753, passed July 17, 1978.

15. Porch 2003b.

16. Title 5 USC 552.

17. There were two subcommittees tasked with oversight of the CIA, but subcommittee oversight powers are weaker and include smaller staffs, by definition, than a full standing committee. See Johnson 1997 and Barrett 2005.

18. In the SPII index that is presented in Chapter 8 and runs from 0 to 1, the United States during this time scored 0.7. This reflects the improvement in the institutions as well as the lack of a balance test, along with select legislative investigative powers. While the data do not extend back to the 1940s, France would be scored around their value of .2 that they held until 1978. In categorical terms, the United States had moderate oversight, while France's oversight was low.

19. Hughes 2006, pp. 9, 108; Bloch 1999, p. 135.

20. Bloch 1999, p. 112.

21. Bloch 1999, p. 135.

22. Bloch 1999, p. 144. Even for the revisionist history of the period, May 2000 admits that one key contributing factor to the lack of organization and defeat for France was the political dysfunction and distrust of alarms of German threats from 1933 to 1937. See, specifically, May 2000, pp. 6–7.

23. Hughes 2006, p. 113; Bloch 1999, p. 141; see also Jackson 2003, p. 113.

24. Bloch 1999, p. 145; Hughes 2006, p. 108.

25. Martin 1999, p. 100.

26. Martin 1999, p. 100.

27. Martin 1999, p. 101; see also Hughes 2006, pp. 96–97.

28. Hughes 2006, p. 117–119.

29. Porch 2003b, p. 143.

30. Porch 2003b, p. 136.

31. The quote is from French General Henri Navarre and can be found in Porch 2003b, p. 143.

32. Porch 2003b, p. 137. See Porch 2003b, Chapters 4 and 5 for a description of the convoluted organization of the intelligence services and their management during the inter-war years.

33. Andrew, Aldrich, and Wark 2009, p. 22.

34. Porch 2003b, pp. 155–158.

35. The French intelligence services did play a role in helping the Polish intelligence services break the Enigma code. Hans-Thilo Schmidt had been working in the German Chiffrierstelle (Cipher Bureau) and contacted the French to sell them secrets when he was in need of money. These secrets turned out to be the instructions to the now famous Enigma machine, the first of which was turned over in November 1931. However, neither the French nor the British understood what they had, since they did not have a German Enigma machine. The French, luckily, did show the documents to the Poles, who had been working since 1929 on the Enigma and had built a replica. These instructions and several other similar deliveries of new details as the Germans changed the Enigma designs periodically from Schmidt aided the Polish efforts and then were passed to the British and French. Porch 2003b, pp. 156–158.

36. Porch 2003b, p. 150.

37. Porch 2003b.

38. Hughes 2006, pp. 111, 160.

39. Hughes 2006, p. 28.

40. Hughes 2006, pp. 36, 123.

41. Hughes 2006, p. 110.

42. Hughes 2006, p. 169.

43. Hughes 2006, pp. 109–111.

44. Jackson 2003, p. 113.

45. Jackson 2003, p. 115.

46. Jackson 2003, p. 119.

47. Jackson 2003, pp. 119–126.

48. This is usefully summarized in Jackson 2003.

49. Jackson 2003, p. 225.

50. Jackson 2003, p. 225; Porch 2003b, pp. 144–148, 163–167.

51. Porch 2003b, p. 148.

52. Porch 2003b, p. 145.

53. Porch 2003b, p. 145.

54. Porch 2003b, p. 163.

55. Porch 2003b, p. 166.

56. Porch 2003b, pp. 171–172. This is not to argue that any one weakness led to the defeat, but the late start to French armament and training increased the probability of defeat. For a historical account that suggests that France was prepared for war but was unlucky and failed to use sufficient imagination in planning, see May 2000. Convincing counterarguments can be found in Jackson 2003, pp. 187–196, as well as in Porch 2003b, pp. 140–168. As Jackson notes, "Although it might be true that the situation in 1939 was healthier than it had been a few years earlier, one is of course starting from a low base" (see Jackson 2003, p. 197).

57. Hughes 2006, p. 139; see also Bloch 1999, p. xi, and Porch 2003b, p. 148.
58. Alexander 1998, p. 179.
59. Alexander 1998, p. 179.
60. Jackson 2003, p. 24.
61. Alexander 1998, p. 179.
62. Maginot happened to be Minister of War during the debate in 1920 for a large tranche of funds for the fortifications. He was a proponent, but not a designer of the system.
63. Alexander 1998, p. 186.
64. Hughes 2006, p. 216.
65. Alexander 1998, p. 183.
66. Alexander 1998, p. 188. See also Hughes 2006, p. 211; Porch 2003b, p. 148.
67. Porch 2003b, Chapter 5.
68. Porch 2003b, pp. 166–168.
69. Hughes 2006, pp. 226–227; Bloch 1999, p. 51.
70. Bloch 1999, pp. 143–144.
71. Fitzgerald 2001, p. 88.
72. However, the treaties terms were observed, despite a lack of ratification.
73. Reed 2007, Chapter 16; Fitzgerald 2001, pp. 148–149.
74. Fitzgerald 2001, p. 149. In the first set of proposals, Reagan argued for a series of military budget increases from 1981 to 1984. The original 1983 presidential budget suggested a 10% increase in defense spending from a baseline of $214 billion, adjusting for inflation (Sweet 1982).
75. Reed 2007, Chapter 16.
76. Fitzgerald 2001, p. 149.
77. Hedrick Smith, "How Many Billions for Defense?" *New York Times Magazine*, November 1, 1981, p. 90.
78. Reed 2007, location 4678/6462.
79. He chose France reportedly because he had worked in that country. In addition, he spied through the French domestic law enforcement agency, the DST. While unorthodox, this had the practical benefit that it reduced the chances of him being discovered by the KGB; see Kostin and Raynaud 2011, Chapter 28.
80. Reed 2007, location 4699–4701.
81. Kostin and Raynaud 2011, Chapter 28.
82. Fitzgerald 2001, p. 156.
83. Hogan 1994, p. 31.
84. A summary of these early debates can be found in Posen and van Evra 1983.
85. Reed 2007, locations 4423–4428.
86. Fitzgerald 2001, p. 189.
87. Reed 2007, locations 4459–4461.
88. Quoted in "They Called it Star Wars," *Air Force Magazine*, June 2012, Vol. 95, p. 6.
89. Fitzgerald 2001, p. 130.
90. Quoted in Fitzgerald 2001, p. 211. See also Reed 2007, location 4480.
91. Circular error probability (CEP) reflected the accuracy of a missille, providing a radius for where 50% of missiles aimed at a point would land around that point.

92. See, for example, the discussion in "MX Missile Basing," September 1981, Institute of Advanced Study, NTIS order #PB82-108077, available at http://www.princeton.edu/~ota/disk3/1981/8116/8116.PDF.
93. See, for example, "Directed Energy Missile Defense in Space," April 1984, Institute of Advanced Study, NTIS order #PB84-210111, pp. 16, 25–26, available at http://www.princeton.edu/~ota/disk3/1984/8410/8410.PDF.
94. The public also had access to a stronger freedom of information law, as discussed above.
95. See, for example, "Soviet Strategic Force Developments," Senate Hearings, 99–335, and "The MX Missile and Associated Basing Decision: Hearing Before the Committee on Armed Services," United States Senate, Ninety-seventh Congress, second session, December 8, 1982.
96. "Special Panel on the Strategic Defense Initiative": Hearings Before the Strategic Defense Initiative Panel of the Committee on Armed Services, House of Representatives, One Hundredth Congress, Second Session, Hearings Held April 20, July 14, September 29, and October 4, 1988, Vol. 5.
97. "Soviet Strategic Force Developments," Senate Hearings, 99–335, p. 4.
98. In this case, two former CIA operatives were accused of working with Libyan intelligence. Libya at the time was considered a significant threat to US interests; see "CIA Denies Link to Former Agents," New York Times, February 2, 1982, available at http://www.nytimes.com/1982/02/03/us/cia-denies-link-to-former-agents.html.
99. See, for example, "The Qaddafi Connection: CIA Link to Terrorists" by Seymour M. Hersh, New York Times, June 15, 1982.
100. See Report on Iran-Contra Affair, 1987.
101. Saltoun-Ebin 2010, location 187.
102. See "Iran Contra Report," Part V.
103. "Iran-Contra Hearings: Poindexter Says He Withheld Iran-Contra Link from Reagan," New York Times, July 16, 1987.
104. See Report of the Congressional Committees Investigating the Iran-Contra Affair, House Report Number 100-433, Senate Report Number 100–216, published November 17, 1987.
105. "Iran-Contra Report," p. 13.
106. See "Supplemental Views of Senator James. A. McClure," in "Iran-Contra Report." One important point is missed by some of the dissents from the report. Senator McClure makes the point that a great part of the investigation merely confirmed what the executive revealed shortly before the investigation, and he suggests then that the investigation was unnecessary. This misses the key point that the Reagan administration decided to release details of what they knew because they expected significant investigations. If investigations were not credible, this information would have been less likely to be revealed.
107. "Iran-Contra Report," "Additonal View of Senator William S. Cohen," p. 673.
108. "Iran-Contra Report," "Supplemental Views of the Honorable Bill McCollum," p. 676.
109. The question of how to reassure the public while withholding information is not discussed in the memo; for quote and discussion, see "Iran-Contra Report," p. 619.

110. See "The Iran-Contra Report; The Countries Have Numbers," November 19, 1987, available at http://www.nytimes.com/1987/11/19/world/the-iran-contra-report-the-countries-have-numbers.html.
111. Fitzgerald 2001, Chapter 9; Anderson and Anderson 2009, location 5024.
112. The death of CIA Director Casey made uncovering evidence more diffcult; see the mentions of this event in the "Iran-Contra Report."
113. See "Iran-Contra Report," Part II and Part V.
114. Saltoun-Ebin 2010, pp. 151, 300, 312, 323–327, 359–363, 371, 430, 432.
115. Saltoun-Ebin 2010, p. 300.
116. Saltoun-Ebin 2010, p. 312; see also Fitzgerald 2001, p. 184.
117. Fitzgerald 2001, p. 129.
118. "Report to the Chairman Subcommittee on Federal Services, Post Office, and Civil Service, Committee on Governmental Affairs, US Senate," Government Accounting Office, GAO/NSIAD 94-219.
119. "Report to the Chairman, Subcommittee on Federal Services, Post Office, and Civil Service, Committee on Governmental Affairs, US Senate," Government Accounting Office, GAO/NSIAD 94-219, p. 32.
120. See the description in "General Details Altered 'Star Wars' Test" by Tim Weiner, New York Times, August 27, 1993.
121. "Report to the Chairman, Subcommittee on Federal Services, Post Office, and Civil Service, Committee on Governmental Affairs, US Senate," Government Accounting Office, GAO/NSIAD 94-219. In another twist, the same report publicizes the fact, unknown at the time, that the warhead was heated before being launched to increase its visibility. While the 1994 report suggests that this temperature still realistically simulated a Soviet ICBM, it provides another example of potential deception and the ambiguity it creates.
122. Bartels 1991.
123. Reed 2007, locations 4388–4396.
124. Reed 2007, pp. 4474–4478.
125. Fitzgerald 2001, p. 372.
126. Over 6000 Bradleys would eventually be moved to the Gulf War theater in 1991 and prove their worth. The research and program that led to the Bradley was almost killed off in the mid-1970s but was revived in 1978 and increased in the 1980s. See Haworth 1999.
127. Bartels 1991.
128. The Senate supported the program by a vote of 59 to 39 the next day. See Reed 2007, locations 4474–4478.
129. Reed 2007, locations 4523–4527; Fitzgerald 2001, p. 438.
130. Fitzgerald 2001, pp. 438–442.
131. See Blechman and Fried 1976.
132. Kinnard 1980, pp. 185–186.
133. Quoted in "Defense Budget Too Small Fired Schlesinger Claims" November 23, 1975, Associated Press, Daytona Beach Sunday News, p. 5A.
134. Hanhimaki 2004, p. 366.
135. McDonough, Rudman, and Rundlet 2006, p. 13.
136. Johnson 1997, p. 208.
137. See discussion in Fitzgerald 2001, Chapter 8.

138. Reed 2007, locations 3562–3565.
139. See "USS Theodore Roosevelt: History," US Navy Report, available at http://www.public.navy.mil/airfor/cvn71/Pages/Ship'sHistory.aspx.
140. Fitzgerald 2001, p. 410.
141. Kaufmann and Kaufmann 1997.
142. Reed 2007, location 4518.
143. Contrast Reed 2007 with Evangelista 2002.
144. See the discussion by Evangelista (2002, p. 335), who, while a critic of the role of Star Wars in the end of the Cold War generally, acknowledges that the Soviet leadership had increased incentives to avoid a world where the United States deployed weapons in space and continued their arms build-up.
145. Cannon (2000, p. 689) notes that the progress made in various weapons programs was discussed at crucial moments in the disarmament process and assured Reagan and others that a compromise would not sacrifice US security. While critics are correct to point out that these weapons programs themselves could not have been sufficient to bring Soviet cooperation—as a hardliner in Moscow could have used them to garner support for a reciprocal build-up—they appear to have been important on the US side. Further evidence of this can be found in Fitzgerald 2001, Reed 2007, and Gaddis 1997.
146. Gaddis 1997.
147. Nationalism plays a basic role in this formulation (see Desch 2002). In the next chapter we return to the role that nationalism might play in public opinion.
148. Schweller 2009; Ripsman 2009.
149. Downes 2009.
150. Schweller 2009; see also Ripsman 2009.
151. Reiter and Stam 2002, Reiter 2012.
152. Schultz 2001.
153. Bueno de Mesquita et al. 2003.
154. See Lake 1992 and Russett 1990.
155. To continue the analogy from a secrecy dilemma perspective, the classification procedure must hide some valuable information for solving the puzzles because if the public could solve for all the unknowns, so could potential competitors.
156. A fourth alternative that is also possible and sometimes espoused in the policy community is that retrospective oversight may be hurtful as opposed to helpful. If mistakes were made and ill motives colored policy, this perspective argues, it is best to move on and not dwell on the past. In direct contradiction to the idea of retrospective oversight, this idea pushes political debate forward rather than backward in time. Just as it is difficult to drive using only the rearview mirror, so democracies that rely too heavily on retrospective oversight are likely to be at a disadvantage. The Obama administration utilized some of this logic to deflect atttention from retrospective oversight on the causes of the Iraq War and onto the future instead. President Obama stated, "I don't believe that anybody is above the law. On the other hand, I also have a belief that we need to look forward as opposed to looking backwards ... My orientation is going to be to move forward." See "Obama: Time to Look Forward, but Bush Aides Aren't Above the Law," *USA Today*, January 11, 2001, available at

http://content.usatoday.com/communities/theoval/post/2009/01/61177294/
1#.Uqy-zRaARMl. In this perspective, oversight institutions such as strong legislative committee powers might be armed and ready, but their use is more
likely to backfire than propel accountability and public mobilization. In the
same interview, President Obama noted that his job entailed "[making] sure for
example at the CIA, [where] you've got extraordinarily talented people who are
working very hard to keep Americans safe ... I don't want them to suddenly
feel like they've got to spend all their time looking over their shoulders and law-
yering [up]." The quote was a response to an online question and is available at
http://change.gov/newsroom/entry/open_for_questions_round_2_response/.
Thus retrospective oversight not only is unwanted, but it could be dangerous,
causing intelligence officials to become distracted from their jobs of protecting
the country. This perspective is thus the liberal analog to the democracy
doubters' perspective. I will discuss this perspective in Chapter 10, in light of the
evidence.

CHAPTER 8

1. For example, by the Polity scale and Freedom House measures.
2. See Jaggers and Gurr 1995.
3. See, for example, Freedom House 2008.
4. Some specific components of these aggregated measures are sensitive to changes in
    national security information revelation patterns. For example, this is the case with
    the Freedom House civil liberties index, which includes an analysis of national se-
    curity tools and their uses in repressing dissent. See Freedom House 2008 country
    descriptions.
5. Interviews at Dáil conducted by the author.
6. See Schenker 1998.
7. Specifically, the measure is coded for all states, where information was available,
    that were coded above a 5 on the Polity democracy scale.
8. For example, some countries limit the revelation of information to those that can
    prove that they are "interested" parties. See Banisar 2004.
9. Banisar 2004.
10. We were able to verify the dates given successfully in all cases.
11. Herman and Mendel 1976; Union 1986.
12. Available at http://ipu.org/parline/parlinesearch.asp.
13. Kurian 1998.
14. Doring 1995.
15. These are listed at http://www.ipu.org/english/parlweb.htm, last accessed on
    January 30, 2010.
16. See description on http://www.freedomhouse.org/template.cfm?page=
    351&ana_page=363&year=2010, accessed June 10, 2010. While data on press
    freedom have been collected by Freedom House, it is limited in its coverage.
    Alternatively, the Freedom House political rights index includes a measure of
    freedom of information laws and thus would duplicate the indicator above.

Further, the component on freedom of information laws in the Freedom House political rights data is not publicly available and thus could not be purged.

17. At this point, the equal weighting is reasonable. In the future, alternative indices, weights, and measurement strategies could be applied.

18. Sources come from Norton 1990, Copeland and Patterson 1994, Doring 1995, Herman and Mendel 1976, Union 1986, Kurian 1998, and Fish and Kroenig 2009, as well as the PARLINE database at http://www.ipu.org/parline/parlinesearch.asp, last accessed on January 30, 2010, and country-specific parliamentary webpages.

19. Sometimes the language of the law used the language of a harm test but did not include any avenue for appeal; these were coded as .5 on the exemption indicator.

20. See Kurian 1998, pp. 112–128, as well as the House of Commons Guide to Committees, available at http://www.parl.gc.ca/information/about/process/house/CommitteesPracticalGuide/PDF/CmtesPG2008_all-e.pdf, accessed January 7, 2010.

21. Kurian 1998, p. 128.

22. Kurian 1998; on Parliamentary and Relations n.d., pp. 205–210. See also PARLINE entry on Denmark, available at http://www.ipu.org/parline/reports/CtrlParlementaire/2087_F.htm.

23. Union 1986; Kurian 1998; Fish and Kroenig 2009.

24. Union 1986, pp. 1210–1211.

25. Franks 1987, pp. 161–165, 169–170.

26. Oversight was strengthened in 1991 when a permanent subcommittee on intelligence oversight was set up and the principal of organizations such as the Canadian Security Intelligence Service (CSIS) reporting to Parliament at regular intervals was established (Rosen n.d., *Farson 1996*).

27. Banisar 2004.

28. Kurian 1998; Rubinoff 1996.

29. See the discussion in Chapter 6.

30. I use the Polity dataset to define democracies here as those states that score either as a 9 or a 10 on their democracy scale. This means that we are including strong democracies like the United States and Japan today, but omitting weaker democracies such as Argentina in the 1980s. We relax this rule later, but the current high threshold helps us use the average of oversight over time, instead of allowing weak democracies that emerge over or below a lower threshold to affect the ability to compare across time.

31. As explained in the previous section.

32. See Banisar 2004 and Born and Leigh 2008.

33. While it may be a technical detail, I have scaled these variables so changes from 0 to 1 are comparable, if the institutions themselves are equally important for oversight. For example, I have assumed that passing a new freedom of information law that is fully implemented and includes a balance test with no other restrictions (a change from 0 to 1) improves oversight at the same rate as instituting a new national-security-specific committee with full investigatory powers that presents minority reports and is fully staffed (a change from 0 to 1). In the later sections, I relax this assumption at various times by separating out the indices and weighing

and comparing their relative oversight power. In most cases, this assumption holds up remarkably well. Where it does not, I discuss it in the text.

34. "Parliamentary Oversight of Security and Intelligence Agencies in the European Union" by Aidan Wills and earlier in the report "On the Parliamentary Oversight of the Intelligence Services in the WEU Countries—Current Situation and Prospects for Reform" from the now-defunct Assembly of the Western European Union.

35. Greater than .6 on the overall security policy information institutions scale. I am using "stronger" here in the relative sense. A score of .6 or even .7 still denotes that significant oversight tools are missing. For example, the United States during the Reagan years had moderate but significant oversight, despite having a higher SPII score than many other democracies at the time. Stronger relative institutions can still lead to only moderate oversight in an absolute sense.

36. As well as non-democracies.

37. Spain was not a functional democracy at the time.

38. I use four regions that allow a relatively equal distribution of state-years, and particularly years of democracy, to facilitate comparison. I used the Correlates of War project region definitions.

39. The SPII index is categorized into seven ranges for illustration of the underlying patterns.

40. As defined in the previous section as over .6 on the security policy information institution scale.

41. Separating Africa from the Middle East does not change the trends that are apparent here.

42. At first glance, one might want to explain Australia's oversight by reference to her relationship with the United Kingdom. However, Australia has consistently had stronger oversight over national security than did the United Kingdom during this entire period.

43. Tobler 1970.

44. The slope graph, as concocted by Edward Tufte, includes all states that scored six or above on the Polity scale in 1975 and 2005.

45. South Africa would also be in this group, but it did not have a Polity score of at least 6 in 1975. However, in 2005 it has a SPII index of .57, up from .17 in 1992.

46. With a Polity score above or equal to 6 in both periods.

47. The 2002 Intelligence Authorization Act amended the Freedom of Information Act in the United States by allowing intelligence agencies to question whether a requester was acting as a "representative" of another country or intergovernmental organization such as the World Bank or the United Nations. This allows these agencies to limit the release of information to some persons on the grounds that they may be acting for non-US governmental groups, which is a weakened form of interest restriction that is used in other countries.

48. And in fact Costa Rica had a slip in civil liberties between 1993 and 2003, and Colombia between 1989 and 2003, that lowered the SPII index to .41 in Costa Rica and .23 in Colombia for that time.

49. Although as we will see in the concluding chapter, this has begun to change, both with the implementation of the freedom of information act there and with

proposed changes in the way select committees operate, particularly regarding the intelligence and national security services.

50.   Greece, Turkey, and Ireland, as of this date, have large disparities between oversight over domestic matters and national security issues. This can be seen in Greece's standing orders of Parliament as well as in the fact that parliaments in Greece and Ireland have no committee or subcommittees tasked with oversight and review of intelligence and executive national security information that was previously classified.

51.   The Polity 2 measure varies from –10 to 10. See Jaggers and Gurr 1995 for greater detail on the coding of the democracy measure.

Chapter 9

1.   See Bueno de Mesquita et al. 2003, Russett 1993, Martin 2000, and Schultz 2001 for a summary of arguments and evidence.

2.   See Martin 2000 and Fearon 1994, 1998.

3.   See Kennedy 1969 and Schlesinger 1978.

4.   The literature on the rally-'round-the-flag effect is too voluminous to cite comprehensively. Hetherington and Nelson 2003 includes a succinct summary of the patriotism arguments, while Brody 1991 explores the logic of the opposition criticism perspective.

5.   See Mueller 1970. Even the opposition criticism model (Brody 1991) assumes that the public follows elite cues rather than constraining policy from the bottom up; see below.

6.   Waltz 1967, p. 272; Morgenthau 1967; and Rosato 2003, p. 599.

7.   See Lippmann 1922, 1927.

8.   Morgenthau 1967, p. 558.

9.   It is possible that the public may rally and then recoil after a crisis. However, if publics rally everywhere equally, and not based on varying institutional incentives, then oversight institutions would not be correlated with immediate support.

10.   Gibbs 1995 and Stiglitz 1999.

11.   " 'Wag the Dog' Has Tongues Wagging," *New York Times*, by Frank Bruni, August 21, 1998.

12.   Although even in this case the details may be ambiguous. For example, the public might still wonder about provocations as in the Cenepa War between Ecuador and Peru, where both countries claimed that the other entered their territory first, or even more blatantly the Gleiwitz incident in 1939 where the Nazi forces posed as Polish forces and attacked a German radio station in Germany so as to provoke war.

13.   This was specifically complained about recently in debates to change the committee into a parliamentary committee; see Hansard, Nov. 21, 2011, HC Deb.

14.   The data are taken from Lai and Reiter 2005 for the United Kingdom, Chapman and Reiter 2004 for the United States, and Conley 2006 for France. Each of these papers tended to use a slightly different version of what a foreign policy crisis/potential rally event might be. I ensured that crises from the International Crisis Behavior Project were included in each definition and added the crises that were

identified by each other. In a few places where coding did not seem to fit or when the pre and post polls did not align with the crisis coding, I fixed these problems to ensure maximal comparability across time and context. In addition, I follow Lai and Reiter in using the UK vote intention series to measure the rally. It is also possible to use a similar question about whether respondents are satisfied with the prime minister. These results are substantively identical and presented in the Appendix.

15. Both in a simple difference in means test and in a multivariate regression controlling for prior approval, election timing, and annual trend, the differences were significant at the .05 level.

16. The difference between the means is not statistically significant at the .05 level or the .10 level. The difference between periods is also not significant in a multivariate regression context where prior approval, election timing, and an annual trend are controlled for.

17. Specifically, these are Loess smooth plots that estimated the expected value at a given value of x, here a crisis, by weighting the points to the left and the right of that observation and conducting a local linear regression.

18. Two points are not shown for the United States to keep the scales consistent across plots. These were rallies above 15, namely, the Persian Gulf War rally event (18) and the Afghanistan rally event (33). Note that even when we exclude the Afghanistan rally from the estimation, the United States still has a significantly larger rally post-1974 as compared to pre-1974.

19. The difference between the United States and France and between France and the United Kingdom is statistically significant at the .10 and .05 level, respectively.

20. Chapman and Reiter 2004.

21. Colaresi 2007 provides further evidence in the US context, using a slightly different list of rally events and more detailed information on crisis-specific variation in post hoc verification.

22. Fordham and Walker 2005.

23. The data come from Fordham and Walker 2005, and I define autocracies as states that score a −10 on the Polity scale and define democracies as those states that score above 7. Changing these numbers does not alter this picture, as Fordham and Walker explicate. I use the Fordham and Walker data because I want to zoom in on their finding that while democracies spend less than autocracies, there are explicable and differential spending patterns in democracies. Future work can extend this analysis to other data sources.

24. The executive does not want to offer a high military budget that will be rejected for certain, so a low budget is offered and accepted under these circumstances. See Appendix for formal details of this equilibrium. When the public believes with sufficient clarity that there is a crisis, they will support high military spending that is offered. However, they will also support low spending because a leader would only offer low spending if there was actually no crisis.

25. By Bayes' rule; see Appendix.

26. In this mixed strategy; see Appendix.

27. Specifically, the executive's strategy set in this mixed strategy equilibrium is to offer the high spending budget whenever a signal of an imminent crisis is received. However, if the signal for a more pacific time is received clandestinely by the leader,

he or she will randomize between offering the high budget and at other times the appropriate lower figure.

28. This proportion is then multiplied by 100 for interpretability and logged. The log is taken, as in other studies, for two reasons. First, there are extreme outliers in the data, with some states spending 100 times more than other states, leading to a large deviation from the assumption that spending is normally distributed. Second, several useful economic specifications suggest that errors enter military spending in a multiplicative fashion; taking logs makes these multiplicative errors additive. See Knight et al. 1996.

29. Although we would still await the final section on foreign policy success to ensure that this spending was indeed inadequate and states were not just being extremely efficient.

30. I do not include the United States or the USSR during the Cold War in these calculations because their spending levels, as part of their superpower competition, were much greater than others'.

31. Here I define repressive autocracies as those countries that score −10 on the Polity scale.

32. This is the subset of democracies that score greater than 6 on the Polity scale.

33. This is multiplied by 100 for comparability to subsequent analyses.

34. This is calculated by exponentiating the median logged spending value and subtracting the small start-up value.

35. The SPII scale is split into 9 equal-length groupings, and the points included in each interval are used to create the boxplot. Outliers are not shown.

36. Specifically, the lines are drawn from the 25th (75th) percentile (one end of the box) to the last data point that is more (less) than 1.5 times the inter-quartile range.

37. Where the Polity score is equal to 10.

38. This sample includes all states with Polity scores above 7 to increase the variance across the SPII index in each case.

39. The assumption is that if x_i is the SPII score for country i, then military spending is a function of x_i and x_i^2.

40. Wood 2006 provides details of the estimation.

41. According to both AIC.

42. This is described further in the Appendix.

43. Waltz 1979, p. 152.

44. As measured again by the Correlates of War material capabilities data.

45. Shlaim 2001, pp. 241–242.

46. These models are similar to logit or probit models of success, but allow for more flexibility. First, they allow me to add additional uncertainty about the underlying ability of states. As is shown in the Appendix, this increases the uncertainty around the estimates. Analogous results from a non-Bayesian perspective can be found in the Appendix.

47. See Maoz 2005.

48. Success is coded when one side either is victorious or forces the other side to yield. We cannot use the smaller subset of all-out wars because there are so few of them during the study period. Specifically, there are only eight cases of democratic wars since 1970.

49. I utilize battle deaths for this coding (see Ghosn, Palmer, and Bremer 2004).
50. The boundaries of the interval categories are −749, −225, −75, −24, 0, 24, 75, 225, 749. These become the observed cut-points of the interval-level Bradley–Terry model described in the Appendix.
51. Specifically, I set the capability advantage to 2 and the national security oversight index to .8 and 0, respectively. The posterior estimates are taken from the model 2 specification.
52. Here the 90% highest posterior interval is (0.03, 0.07).
53. A full mediation analysis is beyond the scope of this work.
54. Interestingly, the outlier on the bottom right of the graph fits the explanation quite well. This point was the Whiskey on the Rocks crisis between Sweden and the Soviet Union in October 1981. A Soviet submarine hit rocks near the Swedish coast and also in close proximity to military exercises. Despite the large capability gap between Sweden and the USSR, Sweden was able to manage a draw in the situation quite well. In fact, some commentators suggest that the incident should instead be seen as a "brilliant success." See the discussion in Bynander 1998, p. 374.
55. Replacing wins, draws, or losses with an interval that matched the scale of net own versus enemy fatalities as discussed above.
56. The mean of the posterior distribution for the national security oversight coefficient was 293.5 with a standard error of 136.2 and a 90% HPD of (119.8, 468.2).
57. An analysis of the posterior predicted probabilities from this model, which is not dependent on assuming equal variances across models, is similar but slightly more dramatic than those shown in Figure 9.14.
58. A discussion of the random effects can be found in the supporting materials. I ran similar BOB-T models with and without the random effect terms and found that the uncertainty estimates around the coefficients shrank by approximately 23% if the random effects were omitted from the specification. Less dramatically, the mean value for the posterior distribution for national security oversight institutions was 1.96 with the random effect terms and 2.36 without them.
59. Colaresi 2006.
60. Colaresi 2011.
61. Bueno de Mesquita et al. 2003.
62. Guisinger and Smith 2002.
63. Fordham and Walker.
64. Reiter and Stam 2002.

Chapter 10
1. As a movement toward one side necessarily means being farther from the other side.
2. I discuss this point below further.
3. See "Journalism That Knows No Shame" by Max Boot, November 28, 2010, *Commentary Magazine*, available at http://www.commentarymagazine.com/blogs/index.php/boot/382682.
4. "Why Do Editors Committed to Press Freedom Attack Wikileaks?" by Roy Greenslade, *The Guardian*, November 28, 2010, available at guardiannews.com/media/greenslade/2010/nov/28/wikileaks-national-newspapers.

5. "Edward Snowden Hailed as Hero, Accused of Treason—As It Happened" by Paul Owen and Tom McCarthy, *The Guardian*, June 10, 2013, available at http://www.guardian.co.uk/world/blog/2013/jun/10/edward-snowden-revealed-as-nsa-whistleblower-reaction-live.

6. "Edward Snowden: 'Hero or Traitor'" by Geoffrey Stone, *Huffington Post*, available at http://www.huffingtonpost.com/geoffrey-r-stone/edward-snowden-hero-or-tr_b_3418939.html.

7. "Edward Snowden Hailed as Hero, Accused of Treason—As It Happened" by Paul Owen and Tom McCarthy, *The Guardian*, June 10, 2013, available at http://www.guardian.co.uk/world/blog/2013/jun/10/edward-snowden-revealed-as-nsa-whistleblower-reaction-live.

8. Moynihan 1999, p. 227. For the commission report, see Moynihan and Combest 1997.

9. "Pelosi Gets Poor Marks for Handling Interrogation Matter" by Jeffrey Jones, *Gallup*, May 21, 2009. Among all respondents, only President Obama had approval numbers above the CIA on the issue.

10. "On WikiLeaks and Government Secrecy" by Jordan Stancil, *The Nation*, December 3, 2010, available at http://www.thenation.com/article/156835/wikileaks-and-government-secrecy#axzz2WgDlQC00.

11. Interview with Charlie Rose, *Charlie Rose Show*, June 17, 2013.

12. "Edward Snowden: 'Hero or Traitor'" by Geoffrey Stone, *Huffington Post*, available at http://www.huffingtonpost.com/geoffrey-r-stone/edward-snowden-hero-or-tr_b_3418939.html.

13. "CNN/ORC Poll," conducted June 11–13, 2013, released June 17, 2013, p. 20, available at http://i2.cdn.turner.com/cnn/2013/images/06/17/rel7a.pdf.

14. Quoted in "On WikiLeaks and Government Secrecy" by Jordan Stancil, *The Nation*, December 3, 2010, available at http://www.thenation.com/article/156835/wikileaks-and-government-secrecy#axzz2WgDlQC00.

15. Winston Churchill, speech broadcast on October 1, 1939.

16. See Chapter 4. Additionally, the Maher Arar case involved Canada working with the United States to detain a Canadian citizen for two weeks in the United States and one year in Syria where he was tortured according to the SIRC report. The Treholt case involved Arne Treholt, who had been convicted of spying for the Soviet Union in Norway. He was also a Labour politician. In 2012, doubts surfaced as to the authenticity of the evidence brought at trial, particularly by the intelligence services. The EOS committee undertook a significant investigation that uniquely publicized the fact that the security services had used illegal means to attain information and had attempted to avoid the disclosure of that information. See Treholt Investigation, available at http://www.eos-utvalget.no/filestore/TreholtENG.pdf.

17. "Judge Alito's View of the Presidency: Expansive Powers" by Jess Bravin, *The Wall Street Journal*, January 5, 2006, p. A1.

18. The Blair government had tried to increase this to 90 days. "Blair Defeated on Terror Bill," *The Guardian*, November 9, 2005, available at http://www.guardian.co.uk/politics/2005/nov/09/uksecurity.terrorism.

19. See, for example, the articles by Henry Porter at the *Observer*, as well as Tony Blair's responses, "Britain's Liberties: The Great Debate," available at http://www.guardian.co.uk/commentisfree/2006/apr/23/humanrights.constitution.

20. See Discussion in Chapter 4.
21. Named after the parliament in Poland that typified this arrangement at the time.
22. Pew Research for the People and the Press.
23. See "Partisan Divide on Iraq Exceeds Split on Vietnam" by Robin Toner and Jim Rutenberg, *New York Times*, July 30, 2006, available at http://www.nytimes.com/2006/07/30/washington/30war.html. When the partisan gap began to recede it was only because Republicans also increased their opposition to the conflict (see Jacobson 2007).
24. See Jacobson 2007.
25. The figure for conservatives was 30% and for liberal Democrats 16%. This was in the case where no UN approval was given. See "Iraq: The Last Pre-War Polls" by Roger Mortimore, IPSOS-MORI, March 21, 2003, available at http://www.ipsos-mori.com/newsevents/ca/287/Iraq-The-Last-PreWar-Polls.aspx.
26. See Geoff Hoon and Michael Boyce testimony at Chilcot Inquiry, available at http://www.iraqinquiry.org.uk/media/45042/20100119-hoon-final.pdf and http://www.iraqinquiry.org.uk/media/51818/20110127-Boyce.pdf, as well as Prados and Portier 2004, p. 144.
27. See Chapter 4.
28. See Church Committee Report, November 20, 1975, Section B Covert Action as a Vehicle for Foreign Policy Implementation, p. 11.
29. The Intelligence Oversight Act of 1980 made the notification of select members of Congress mandatory. From the perspective of retrospective oversight, this type of notification is problematic. First, the members of the legislature cannot share this information with their colleagues by law in the United States. Second, if the legislatures do not leak the details and the operation fails to provide security benefits or, worse, has larger costs, these politicians may be seen as complicit in the planning. A problem of this sort has arisen in the NSA wiretapping scandal.
30. P.L 98-473 Stat. 1935–1937.
31. Contemporaneous reports include "Iran-Contra Investigation: Joint Hearings Before the Senate Select Committee on Secret Military Assistance to Iran and the Nicaraguan Opposition and the House Select Committee to Investigate Covert Arms Transactions with Iran" in 1987/1988; "Report of the Congressional Committees Investigating the Iran-Contra Affair with Supplemental, Minority and Additional Views," also in 1987/1988; "Preliminary Inquiry into the Sale of Arms to Iran and Possible Diversion of Funds to the Nicaraguan Resistance" in 1987; and "Were Relevant Documents Withheld from the Congressional Committees Investigating the Iran-Contra Affair" in 1989. Additionally, the Reagan administration appointed the Tower Commission, which issued a report in 1987.
32. Quoted in Jamieson 1993, p. 86.
33. In 2005 the head of the DGSE, Pierre Lacoste, claimed that President Mitterrand authorized the action. The DSGE might have gotten away with the sinking except there was a casualty as a cameraman reentered the boat after the first bomb exploded but before the second and was drowned. See Born and Caparini 2007, p. 138.
34. GCHQ is the Government Communications Headquarters and is the evolution of the Bletchley Park codebreaking operation.

35. See "Politicians Demand More Power Over Intelligence Agencies" by Richard Norton-Taylor, *The Guardian*, July 13, 2011.

36. Canadian oversight here should be credited with creating SIRC very early. However, even here there is room for improvement, as the linkages between national security committees and SIRC could be strengthened. See SIRC Report 2005.

37. Another potential drawback of legislative oversight conducted purely by elected politicians is that the oversight functions can be used for partisan gains. This is much less of a problem if more than one party is included on the committee in a meaningful role and if minority reports are possible, as measured in the security policy information institution index discussed in the previous two chapters.

38. Portugal also has the Council for the Oversight of the Intelligence System of the Portugese Republic, but this committee only has one staff member to date. One recent EU study concluded that "[s]pecialized non-parliamentary bodies have a number of advantages in comparison to parliamentary oversight committees, which are the inverse of the drawbacks associated with parliamentary oversight . . . . First, they are normally professional bodies whose members do not have other occupations. This means that they have more time to dedicate to oversight. Second, members of non-parliamentary oversight bodies usually have a much longer tenure of membership, which gives them the opportunity to develop expertise over time. Third, in many cases, members are selected on the basis of their qualifications rather than their positions within a political party or parliamentary caucus. Fourth, members of specialized non-parliamentary oversight bodies are generally regarded as being more independent than members of parliamentary bodies because they do not hold political office and/or operate in an environment where oversight can be used for political gain." The report goes on to note that these bodies do suffer from a lack of accountability themselves. See "Parliamentary Oversight of Security and Intelligence Agencies in the European Union" by Aidan Wills and Mathias Vermeulen, *Report for the European Parliament*, 2011, pp. 32–33.

39. The logic was that rendition was a transnational problem that needed a transnational oversight net. See Activity Report, Belgian Standing Intelligence Agencies Review Committee, 2006/7, available at http://www.ennir.be/sites/default/files/pictures/pdf_9.pdf.

40. Leigh and Harding 2011, p. 183.

41. See "Blueprints of NSA's Ridiculously Expensive Data Center in Utah Suggest It Holds Less Info Than Thought" by Kashmir Hill, *Forbes*, July 24, 2013, available at http://www.forbes.com/sites/kashmirhill/2013/07/24/blueprints-of-nsa-data-center-in-utah-suggest-its-storage-capacity-is-less-impressive-than-thought/.

42. For quote and figures see "The WikiLeaks Illusion" by Alasdair Roberts, *Wilson Quarterly*, summer 2011.

43. "Americans Want More Information on NSA Surveillance—Could They Get It?" by Phil Bump, *The Atlantic*, June 19, 2013, available at http://www.theatlanticwire.com/politics/2013/06/americans-want-more-information-nsa-surveillance-could-they-get-it/66389/.

44. Danielle Cailloux, *EuroIntel Proceedings*, 1998.

45. Hansard, November 21, 2011, p. 73. "Belgian Observations on Intelligence Oversight and Strategic Opportunities for Change," presented at EuroIntel

Conference, 1998, by Danielle Caillioux. Available at http://www.oss.net/
dynamaster/file_archive/040319/7b5d1c82c2b955ddb845a1837ed05f0/
OSS1998-E1-10.pdf.
46. See Pew Research Center Poll, September 1–4, 2011.
47. Pew Research Center, March 30–April 3, 2011.
48. See the online Polity data for Hungary at http://www.systemicpeace.org/polity/
hun2.htm. It also scored very high on the Freedom House "Freedom in the World"
values.
49. Other changes include mandatory retirement of judges so they can be replaced and
changes to the independence of the central bank.
50. See "Civil Liberties Committee Coverage," *BBC*, February 9, 2012, available
online at http://news.bbc.co.uk/democracylive/hi/europe/newsid_9693000/
9693944.stm.
51. As discussed in Chapter 2.
52. A particularly interesting extension would be to analyze post-conflict settings.
Oversight theory would suggest that the previous focus on the time of elections
and power-sharing is incomplete. Instead, the question of whether an executive
can be trusted with effective national security tools is highly salient. Retrospective oversight would be one useful mechanism for an executive to be able to
credibly commit to utilizing the military and intelligence services toward producing a greater proportion of public rather than private goods. On accountability
avoidance and the organization of repression, see Carey, Colaresi, and Mitchell
2014.
53. Carey, Colaresi, and Mitchell 2014.
54. Gaubatz 1999.
55. "Counter-Terrorism Powers: Reconciling Security and Liberty in an Open Society," Home Department, UK, pp. 1 and 16.
56. This is discussion paper number 6147.
57. June 26, 2006, Speech to the Centre for Policy Studies.
58. See Stone 2007, p. xiii. See also the unabridged information in Stone 2004.
59. See Bueno de Mesquita et al. 2003, as well as Chapter 3 herein.

APPENDIX
1. See Colaresi 2007.
2. Some may object to a model of the rally that treats the public as responding to a
leader's action. However, both the opposition and foreign policy restraint (defensive) goals hypotheses rely on a similar, though unstated, assumption. For example,
in the opposition criticism argument, a crisis arrives, then the leadership and opposition act and comment, and the public rallies or not conditional on this dynamic.
Similarly, in the foreign policy restraint/defensive goals hypothesis, the rally depends on the previous government explanation of its goals and the press coverage
of that explanation.
3. If this inequality is reversed, the distinction between the β and θ worlds breaks
down, as does the uncertainty. Regardless of the state of the world, the public
would like to avoid α if possible.

4. There are a multitude of simplifications within this model and theory. I follow other work in suggesting that the worth of a model should be measured by the usefulness of its empirical predictions rather than the truthfulness of its assumptions. As noted by Morton (1999), all models, by design, include false assumptions.

5. One slight difference is that I interpret the uncertainty in the model as reflecting private information about the crisis situation rather than private information about the "type of player." This is similar to the Lupia and McCubbins 1998 model that separates uncertainty about the situation and the player.

6. This game includes a continuum of mixed strategy equilibria when

$$p = \frac{-\tau_p + (\theta - \gamma)}{\theta}$$

These are described by $(\alpha, \alpha, \sigma_p(S) > \bar{m})$, where

$$\bar{m} = \frac{-\tau_a}{((\frac{-\tau_p+(\theta-\gamma)}{-\theta})(\beta - \epsilon - \theta)) + \theta + \tau_a}$$

and $\sigma_p(S)$ is the probability with which the principal plays support.

7. More details about the game and proofs are contained below. Note that the notation changes as compared to the first game.

8. Formally, the optimum spending level can be seen as the vertex of a quadratic function of the form $y = a(\hat{\gamma} - \dot{P})^2 + c$, where $a < 0$. Therefore, $\dot{P}$ is the value of actual spending $(\hat{\gamma})$ that maximizes public benefits, y. Public benefits at that optimum are equal to c and are defined below conditional on the state of the world. The shape of the quadratic function represents the trade-off of spending relative to the optimal security level. Spending that is insufficient to secure the national interest could be increased and lead to a greater economic return to the public if offered and accepted. Spending that is over and above securing the national interest is inefficient and could be better allocated to domestic programs. In this way the curvilinear relationship represents the domestic consequences of the guns-versus-better trade-off (Duval 1993, Powell 1999).

9. The order of the items in the payoff vector is executive, public, and then legislature.

10. Importantly, this mirrors the political process being modeled. The executive has classified information about the security threats facing a country that the public does not have, but the public and legislature both observe the total suggested price of security as suggested by the executive, which may or may not reflect the underlying security situation.

11. Rational beliefs are defined as following Bayes' rule for updating beliefs conditional on previous choices in the game.

12. Akerlof 1970.

13. This set of equilibria vary only in the choice of the executive, since the executive is indifferent between proposing $\hat{\gamma} = \gamma$ or $\hat{\gamma} = \alpha$ when opposition is played by the public with certainty.

14. This would only fail to occur when security is sufficiently inexpensive even when $\overset{.}{P} = \gamma$, which obviates the difference between the states of the world in the model, or when the public is already sufficiently convinced that security was expensive, which is untrue by definition for new and emerging threats. Partisan differences within an electorate also raise p.

15. Morgenthau 1948, p. 60.

16. Herring 1941.

17. Kennan 1951.

18. See Millett 1996, pp. 324–325.

19. Berend 1998.

20. "The Report on the Covert Activities of the Central Intelligence Agency, September 30, 1954," pp. 6 and 7, declassified in 1976, available at http://www.foia.cia.gov/helms/pdf/doolittle_report.pdf, accessed October 20, 2010.

21. Johnson 2006, pp. 5–15.

22. See also Johnson 1997, pp. 207–209.

23. See Reiter and Chapman 2004, Lai and Reiter 2005, and Conley 2006. The rally events were coded by looking at the updated International Crisis Behavior dataset (Brecher and Wilkenfeld 2000) as well as the original data for each country. Where there was a conflict, I utilized the International Crisis Behavior dataset to improve the comparability of the definition of an event across cases.

24. Bayesian estimates using conjugate priors provide nearly identical results.

25. I use superscripts D and W to represent whether the indicator is referring to democracies or all states in the world.

26. Jervis 1976; Diehl 1983; Walt 1987; Gross-Stein 1991; Brzoska and Pearce 1994.

27. Goldsmith 2007.

28. Moran's I calculations with the military expenditure data and the weights matrix defined below provided further evidence of this spatial dependence.

29. The number of states includes both democracies and non-democracies.

30. I use i and j here to represent the number of democratic states and all states, respectively.

31. This setup merely subsets the analysis to measure neighborhood spending for each democracy while taking all neighbors' military spending into account. The spatially weighted average is lagged one year because budget cycles generally follow a fiscal year and a reaction time of one year is reasonable, and this specification fit the militarized expenditure data better than the analogous model estimated by IV with the simultaneous spatial lag and evaluated through cross-validation.

32. Rivals are coded using Thompson's definition and the list and dates contained in Colaresi, Rasler, and Thompson 2007, pp. 37–51. Allies are coded from the Alliance Treaty Obligations and Provisions Project (ATOP) data (see Leeds et al. 2002), for any pairs of states that have offensive or defensive commitments. Using the average of rival and ally spending, instead of the sum, for each state does not change the inferences presented below. Just as with neighbors, rivals and allies come from the superset of all states, not just democracies.

33. Fordham and Walker 2005.

34. Number of borders is coded using the Correlates of War contiguity data (see Stinnett et al. 2002).

35. Correlates of War Project n.d.
36. Brecher and Wilkenfeld 2000.
37. Olson and Zeckhauser 1966; Sandler and Hartley 1999.
38. The data come from the Correlates of War capabilities dataset (Singer 1987).
39. Jo and Gartzke 2006; see their Table 1.
40. Correlates of War Project n.d.
41. Simultaneity is less of a problem in this analysis because changing the institutional structure of national security oversight takes a significant period of time (see above). Therefore it is unlikely that increases in military spending in a given year lead to institutional changes that same year. To further probe the possibility of simultaneity bias, I ran several two-stage least squares models that used the 1975 value for oversight in a given country as an instrument for oversight. The results were substantively identical to those reported here. Another salient concern is that a potential confounder such as international threat could lead to both large military spending and increased oversight over time. This is one of the strong motivations for including rivalry, alliance ties, major power status, and international conflicts as control variables. As is shown below, the inclusion of these variables does not reduce the substantive impact of oversight institutions on military spending in democracies.
42. See the discussion in Goemans 2008 for the potential domestic relevance of these variables.
43. Here we are assuming that the greater the difference in the latent foreign policy ability of two states, the greater the probability that the stronger state gains a positive outcome of the dispute, subject to ceiling and floor effects.
44. For example, in one analysis below there are 6 control variables and thus C_i would be a $6 \times N$ matrix (N being the number of observations) and β_C would be a 1×6 matrix of weights. Each element of β_C is a coefficient in a generalized linear mixed model framework.
45. Agresti 2002.
46. Stigler 1994.
47. Stuart-Fox et al. 2005.
48. See Agresti 2002 and Turner and Firth 2010 for additional details.
49. Turner and Firth 2010 includes a useful discussion of Springall 1973, where the random effects are assumed to be zero.
50. Tutz 1986.
51. More thresholds can be added if additional categories are relevant. This point is returned to in the discussion of net fatalities.
52. Other binomial-family link functions such as the probit or Cauchy are also possible. A probit specification leads to an ordered version of the Thurstone–Mosteller model.
53. The priors for the normal distribution are given with precisions, rather than variances.
54. The setup of this model can be compared to a Bayesian ordered logit model as explicated in Jackman 2010.
55. Another way of handling ties is to either drop these observations, as in Reiter and Stam 2002, or include these as losses and model an order effect measuring

the difficulty of winning, versus losing or drawing. In each case there would be a substantial loss of information. Regardless, if we carry through with these approaches, our inferences remain either substantively identical or more dramatic.

56. This is discussed in the next section in more detail.

57. Note that point differentials are not count data because they include positive and negative integers. In the future, an application of Skellam regresson might be useful, but this falls beyond the scope of the current work.

58. This quantity was assumed to be one in the BOB-T model, as in conventional ordered logit models, for identification. Similar priors are used with the addition of $\sigma \sim \mathcal{U}(0, 10{,}000)$.

59. Note that these variables enter the ability equations for a dispute participant, i or j, measuring λ_i or λ_j, respectively.

60. It is important to note that several of these variables including material capabilities may be post-treatment, in the sense that oversight institutions aid in mobilizing foreign policy resources. If, as expected, higher values of the r-SPII index lead to greater mobilization and material capabilities and both then lead to higher foreign policy ability, the partial effect of the oversight institutions index when controlling for material capabilities will be attenuated. We should be able to see this when comparing the substantive size of the r-SPII coefficients across specifications. I include these variables in select specifications because they may give a conservative picture of the empirical benefits of oversight institutions.

61. Major power is coded dichotomously. The information comes from the COW project (Correlates of War Project n.d.).

62. Power capabilities come from the well-known COW capabilities index, version 3.02 (Singer, Stuart, and Stuckey 1972; Singer 1987). See also Desch (2002).

63. Coded from Thompson's list of strategic rivalries (Thompson 2001). Specifically, external threat/rival strength is measured by taking the natural log of the sum of all rival capabilities. A small start-up value is added to all threat observations (.01). This represents the theoretical expectation that all states feel some small quantity of external pressure, even if they are not involved in a rivalry.

64. This implies that the state is on "side a" in the MID data.

65. This was coded as a three or above on the hostility level variable in the DYADMIDs data (Maoz 2005).

66. This point is further explored in a robustness test where all cases of US involvement are dropped from the analysis.

67. Plummer n.d.

68. Heidelberger and Welch 1983.

69. Raftery and Lewis 1992.

70. These are taken from model 2.

71. The results here were produced with the polr function in R. This output is then presented in an analogous way to the BOB-T models, with the identifying constraint switching from the intercept in each model being equal to zero, the default in R, to the thresholds for winning and losing being equal in absolute value. This does not change any of the estimated coefficients, only the estimates of the intercept ($\mu_1 - \mu_2$) and the threshold (τ). This is merely a reorganization of the

information in the data given a theoretically informed, rather than atheoretical, identifying constraint (see Jackman 2010).

72. The association p-values for each Brant test were .57 for model 1, .25 for model 2, .31 for model 3, and .26 for the final model. Score tests for each specification lead to substantively identical inferences.

73. This quantity was assumed to be one in the BOB-T model, as in conventional ordered logit models, for identification. Similar priors are used with the addition of $\sigma \sim \mathcal{U}(0, 10{,}000)$. Additionally, the range of the uniform prior on the random effect variances was increased to $(0, 10{,}000)$.

74. This was done by running ordered logit models for each specification and testing the equality of the coefficients across the models. The χ^2 value was 5.3, with a p value of .45.

75. These results use the specification in model 4 above.

BIBLIOGRAPHY

Agresti, A. 2002. *Categorical Data Analysis*, 2nd ed. New York: Wiley.

Akerlof, George. 1970. The Market for "Lemons": Quality Uncertainty and the Market Mechanism. *The Quarterly Journal of Economics* **84**(3):488–500.

Aldous, Richard. 2007. *The Lion and the Unicorn: Gladstone vs. Disraeli*. New York: WW Norton and Company.

Alexander, Martin. 1998. In Defense of the Maginot Line. In *French Foreign and Defence Policy, 1918–1940: The Decline and Fall of a Great Power*, ed. Robert W. D. Boyce. New York: Routledge.

Almond, Gabriel. 1956. Public Opinion and National Security Policy. *Public Opinion Quarterly* **20**(2):371–378

Ames, Barry. 1992. *Political Survival: Politicians and Public Policy in Latin America*. Berkeley, CA: University of California Press.

Anderson, Martin and Annelise Anderson. 2009. *Reagan's Secret War: The Untold Story of His Fight to Save the World from Nuclear Disaster*, Kindle edition. New York: Crown Publishing Group.

Andrew, Christopher and Oleg Gordiesky. 1990. *KGB: The Inside Story of Its Foreign Operations from Lenin to Gorbachev*. London: Hodder and Stoughton.

Andrew, Christopher, Richard Aldrich, and Wesley K. Wark. 2009. *Secret Intelligence: A Reader*. Abingdon, UK: Routledge.

Andrew, Christopher and Vasili Mitrokhin. 1999. *The Sword and the Shield: The Mitrokhin Archive and the Secret History of the KGB*. New York: Basic Books.

Arter, Jeremy. 2013. *MI7b: The Discovery of a Lost Propoganda Archive from the Great War*. Amazon Digital Services, INC.

Audoin-Rouzeau, Stéphane, Annette Becker, Leonard V. Smith, and William Beik. 2003. *France and the Great War*. London: Cambridge University Press.

Bamford, James. 1983. *The Puzzle Palace: Inside the National Security Agency, America's Most Secret Intelligence Organization*. New York: Penguin.

Banisar, David. 2004. "Global Survey: Freedom of Information and Access to Government Record Laws Around the World." Available at www.freedominfo.org.

Barrett, David M. 2005. *The CIA and Congress: The Untold Story*. Lawrence, KS: University Press of Kansas.

Bartels, Larry. 1991. Constituency Opinion and Congressional Policy Making: The Reagan Defense Buildup. *American Political Science Review*, pp. 457–474.

Barton, Hildor Arnold. 1986. *Scandinavia in the Revolutionary Era, 1760–1815*. Minneapolis, MN: University of Minnesota Press.

Belfield, Eversley. 1975. *The Boer War*. Hamden, CT: Archon Books.

Bell, Coral. 1977. *Diplomacy of Detente: The Kissinger Era*. London: Martin Robertson.

Bennington, Geoffrey. 2011. Kant's Open Secret. *Theory, Culture and Society* **28**(7):26–40.

Bennis, Warren and Patricia Ward Biederman. 1998. *Organizing Genius: The Secrets of Creative Collaboration*. New York: Basic Books.

Bentham, Jeremy, John Bowring (ed). 1843. *The Works of Jeremy Bentham*. Edinburgh: William Tait.

Berend, Ivan T. 1998. *Decades of Crisis: Central and Eastern Europe Before World War II*. Berkeley: University of California Press.

Bernstein, Jeremy. 2010. John von Neumann and Klaus Fuchs: An Unlikely Collaboration. *Physics in Perspective* **12**(1):36–50.

Biddle, Stephen. 2004. *Military Power: Explaining Victory and Defeat in Modern Battle*. Princeton, NJ: Princeton University Press.

Blechman, Barry M. and Edward R. Fried. 1976. Controlling the Defense Budget. *Foreign Affairs* **10**(1):1–24.

Bloch, Marc. 1999. *Strange Defeat: A Statement of Evidence Written in 1940*. New York: WW Norton.

Bok, Sissela. 1989. *Secrets: On the Ethics of Concealment and Revelation*. New York: Vintage.

Born, Hans and Marina Caparini. 2007. *Democratic Control of Intelligence Services Containing Rogue Elephants*. England: Ashgate Publishing Limited.

Born, Hans and Ian Leigh. 2008. *Intelligence Accountability: A Comparative Perspective*. Burlingame: Born and Leigh Intelligence Accountabiity, Vol. 5 in Strategic Intelligence (Westport, CT: Praeger), pp. 141–164.

Brauer, Jurgen and Paul Dunne. 2004. *Arms Trade and Economic Development: Theory, Policy and Cases in Arms Trade Offsets*. New York: Routledge.

Braumoeller, Bear F. 2010. The Myth of American Isolationism. *Foreign Policy Analysis* **6**(2):349–371.

Brecher, Michael and Jonathan Wilkenfeld. 2000. *A Study in Crisis*. Ann Arbor: University of Michigan.

Brody, Richard A. 1991. *Assessing the President: The Media, Elite Opinion, and Public Support*. Palo Alto, CA: Stanford University Press.

Brooke, Heather and Ian Hislop. 2006. *Your Right to Know: A Citizen's Guide to the Freedom of Information Act*. London: Pluto Press.

Brown, Kevin W. 2004. *Penicillin Man: Alexander Fleming and the Antibiotic Revolution*. Scarborough, Canada: Sutton Publishers.

Brzoska, Michael and Frederic S. Pearce. 1994. *Arms and Warfare: Escalation, De-escalation, Negotiation*. Columbia: University of South Carolina Press.

Bueno de Mesquita, Bruce and Alastair Smith. 2011. *The Dictator's Handbook: Why Bad Behavior Is Almost Always Good Politics*. New York: Public Affairs.

Bueno de Mesquita, Bruce, Alastair Smith, Randolph Siverson, and James Morrow. 2003. *The Logic of Political Survival*. Cambridge, MA: MIT Press.

Bueno de Mesquita, Bruce and David Lalman. 1992. *War and Reason: Domestic and International Imperatives.* New Haven, CT: Yale University Press.

Burlingame, Michael. 2013. *Abraham Lincoln: A Life,* Vol. 2. Baltimore, MD: Johns Hopkins University Press.

Bynander, Fredrik. 1998. The 1982 Swedish Harsfjarden Submarine Incident: A Decision-Making Analysis. *Cooperation and Conflict* 33(4):367–407.

Campbell, Craig and S. S. Radchenko. 2008. *The Atomic Bomb and the Origins of the Cold War.* New Haven, CT: Yale University Press.

Cannon, Lou. 2000. *President Reagan: The Role of a Lifetime.* New York: Public Affairs.

Carey, Sabine, Michael Colaresi, and Neil Mitchell. 2014. "The Organization of Repression: Pro-Government Militias and Accountability Avoidance." Working Paper.

Castillo, Jasen, Jullia Lowell, Ashley J. Tellis, and Jorge Munoz. 2001. *Military Expenditures and Economic Growth.* Washginton, DC: Rand.

Chapman, Terrence L. and Dan Reiter. 2004. The United Nations Security Council and the Rally-Round the Flag Effect. *Journal of Conflict Resolution* 48(6):886–909.

Chen, Jian. 2001. *Mao's China and the Cold War.* Chapel Hill: North Carolina University Press.

Choizza, Giacomo and H. E. Goemans. 2011. *Leaders and International Conflict.* Cambridge, UK: Cambridge University Press.

Chowdhury, Shyamal K. 2004. Do Democracy and Press Freedom Reduce Corruption? Evidence from a Cross-Country Study. University of Bonn, Center for Development Research (ZEF), number 18769.

Church, Frank. 1976. *Church Committee Report: Supplementary Detailed Staff Reports on Intelligence Activities and the Rights of Americans, Book III.* Washington, DC: United States Senate.

Ciment, James and Thaddeus Russell. 2006. *The Home Front Encyclopedia.* New York: ABC-CLIO.

Colaresi, Michael. 2004a. When Doves Cry: International Rivalry, Unreciprocated Cooperation, and Leadership Turnover. *American Journal of Political Science* 48(3): 555–570.

Colaresi, Michael. 2004b. Aftershocks: Postwar Leadership Survival, Rivalry and Regime Dynamics. *International Studies Quarterly* 48(4): 713–728.

Colaresi, Michael. 2005. *Scare Tactics: The Politics of International Rivalry.* Syracuse, NY: Syracuse University Press.

Colaresi, Michael. 2007. The Benefit of the Doubt: Testing an Informational Theory of the Rally. *International Organization* 61(1):99–144.

Colaresi, Michael. 2011. Adverse Classification. Paper presented at the American Political Science Meeting.

Colaresi, Michael. 2012. A Boom with Review: How Retrospective Oversight Increases the Foreign Policy Ability of Democracies. *American Journal of Political Science* 56(3): 671–689.

Colaresi, Michael P., Karen Rasler, and William R. Thompson. 2007. *Strategic Rivalries in World Politics: Position, Space and Escalation.* Cambridge, UK: Cambridge University Press.

Conley, Richard. 2006. From the Elysian Fields to the Guilliotine?: Presidential and Prime Ministerial Approval in Fifth Republic France. *Comparative Political Studies* 39(5):570–598.

Copeland, Gary and Samuel C. Patterson, eds. 1994. *Parliaments in the Modern World*. Ann Arbor, MI: University of Michigan Press.

Correlates of War Project. 2011 State System Membership List, v2004.1. http://correlatesofwar.org.

Correll, John T. 2005. Airpower and the Cuban Missile Crisis. *Airforce Magazine* **88**(8):78–83.

Crickmore, Paul. 2004. *Lockheed Blackbird: Beyond the Secret Missions*. London: Osprey Publishers.

Crisis in Parliament in Flux: Politics and Canada's Intelligence. 1996. "Committees in Congress." *Journal of Conflict Studies* **16**(1).

Cushman, Robert E. 1956. *Civil Liberties in the United States: A Guide to Curent Problems and Experience*. Ithaca, NY: Cornell University Press.

Debs, Alexandre and H. E. Goemans. 2010. Regime Type, the Fate of Leaders and War. *American Political Science Review* **104**(3):430–445.

Desch, Michael. 2002. Democracy and Victory: Why Regime Type Hardly Matters. *International Security* **27**(2):5–47.

de Tocqueville, Alexis, J. P. Mayer (ed.), and George Lawrence (trans.). 2007 (1835). *Democracy in America*, abridged edition.

Diehl, Paul F. 1983. Arms Race and Escalation: A Closer Look. *Journal of Peace Research* **22**(3):205–212.

Dine, Phillip. 2006. *Artful Deceptions: Verbal and Visual Trickery in French Culture*. Bern, Switzerland: International Academic Publishers. Chapter: "Deception as Demystification in the French Literature of the Algerian War."

Directorate General for Internal Policies. 2011. *Parliamentary Oversight of Security and Intelligence Agencies in the European Union*. Brussels, Belgium: European Parliament.

Doise, Jean. 1994. *Une Secret Bien Garde: L'Histoire Militaire de L'affaire Dreyfus*. Paris, France: Seuil.

Doring, Herbert, ed. 1995. *Parliaments and Majority Rule in Western Europe*. New York: Campus Verlag/St. Martin's Press.

Doughty, Robert A. 2005. *Pyrrhic Victory: French Strategy and Operations in the Great War*. Cambridge, MA: Harvard University Press.

Downes, Alexander B. 2009. How Smart and Tough are Democracies? Reassessing Theories of Democratic Victory in War. *International Security* **33**(4):9–51

Doyle, Michael W. 1997. *Ways of War and Peace*. New York: WW Norton and Company.

Duval, R. and J. Mok. 1992. Trading Deficits for Defense and Domestic Programs: The Guns and Butter Hypothesis Revisited. In *The Political Economy of Military Spending in the United States*, ed. Alex Mintz. London: Routledge.

Edgar, Harold and Benno C. Schmidt. 1973. The Espionage Statutes and Publication of Defense Information. *Columbia Law Review* **73**(5):930–1020.

Ellis, Elisabeth. 2005. *Kant's Politics: Provisional Theory for an Uncertain World*. New Haven, CT: Yale University Press.

Elsea, Jennifer. 2011. "Criminal Prohibitions on the Publication of Classified Defense Information." *Congressional Research Service* (7-5700).

Evangelista, Matthew. 2002. *Unarmed Forces: The Transnational Movement to End the Cold War*. Ithaca, NY: Cornell University Press.

Farson, Stuart A. 1996. In Crisis in Flux?: Politics, Parliament and Canada's Intelligence Policy. *Journal of Conflict Studies* **16**(1):1–21.

Fearon, James D. 1994. Domestic Political Audiences and the Escalation of International Disputes. *American Political Science Review* **88**(3):577–593.

Fearon, James D. 1995. Rationalist Explanations for War. *International Organization* **49**(3):379–414.

Fearon, James D. 1998. Bargaining, Enforcement, and International Cooperation. *International Organization* **52**(2):269–306.

Fish, M. and M. Kroenig. 2009. *The Handbook of National Legislatures*. New York: Cambridge University Press.

Fisher, Louis. 2003. Deciding on War Against Iraq: Institutional Failures. *Political Science Quarterly* **118**(3):389–410.

Fisher, Louis. 2004. *Presidential War Powers*. Lawrence, KS: University of Kansas Press.

Fitzgerald, Frances. 2001. *Way Out There in the Blue: Reagan, Star Wars and the End of the Cold War*, Kindle edition. New York: Simon and Schuster.

Fledman, Shai. 1997. *Nuclear Weapons and Arms Control in the Middle East*. Boston: MIT Press.

Foote, Shelby. 1986. *The Civil War*, Vol. III. New York: Vintage.

Fordham, Benjamin. 1998. *Building the Cold War Consensus: The Political Economy of US National Security Policy, 1949–51*. Ann Arbor, MI: University of Michigan Press.

Fordham, Benjamin. 2002. Domestic Politics, International Pressure and the Allocation of American Cold War Military Spending. *Journal of Politics* **64**(1):63–88.

Fordham, Benjamin and Thomas Walker. 2005. Kantian Liberalism, Regime Type and Military Resource Allocation: Do Democracies Spend Less? *International Studies Quarterly* **49**(1):141–157.

Forsythe, David P. 1992. Democracy, War and Covert Action. *Journal of Peace Research* **29**(4):385–395.

Franks, C. E. S. 1987. *The Parliament of Canada*. Toronto: University of Toronto Press.

Freedom House. 2008. *Freedom in the World: Country Reports*.

Freille, Sebastian, M. Emranul Haque, and Richard Kneller. 2005. "A Contribution to the Empirics on Press Freedom and Corruption." Globalization and Economic Working Policy Working Paper.

Frontius, Sextus Julius, and Bennett Charles. 1925. *Stratagemata*. New York: Loeb.

Gaddis, John Lewis. 1997. *We Now Know: Rethinking Cold War History*. Oxford, UK: Oxford University Press.

Gannon, James. 2001. *Stealing Secrets, Telling Lies: How Spies and Codebreakers Helped Shape the Twentieth Century*. Washington, DC: Potomac Books.

Gannon, Robert. 2006. *Hellions of the Deep: The Development of American Torpedoes in World War II*. State College, PA: Penn State University Press.

Gant, Patrick. 2004. *Reflections*. Security Intelligence Review Committee.

Garfield, Brian. 2007. *The Meinertzhagen Mystery*. Washington, DC: Potomac Books.

Gaubatz, Kurt. 1999. *Elections and War: The Electoral Incentive in the Democratic Politics of War and Peace*. Palo Alto, CA: Stanford University Press.

Ghosn, Faten, Glenn Palmer, and Stuart Bremer. 2004. The MID3 Data Set, 1993–2001: Procedures, Coding Rules, and Description. *Conflict Management and Peace Science* **21**(1):133–154.

Gibbs, David N. 1995. Secrecy and International Relations. *Journal of Peace Research* **32**(2):213–226.

Goemans, H. E. 2000. *War and Punishment: The Causes of War Termination and the First World War*. Princeton, NJ: Princeton University Press.

Goemans, H. E. 2008. Which Way Out: The Manner and Consequences of Losing Office. *Journal of Conflict Resolution* 52(6):771–794.

Goldsmith, B. E. 2007. Arms Racing in "Space": Spatial Modeling of Military Spending Around the World. *Australian Journal of Political Science* 42(3):419–440.

Gorelik, Gennady. 2011. The Riddle of the Third Idea: How Did the Soviets Build a Thermonuclear Bomb So Suspiciously Fast? *Scientific American* **August 21**. Online: available at http://blogs.scientificamerican.com/guest-blog/2011/08/21/the-riddle-of-the-third-idea-how-did-the-soviets-build-a-thermonuclear-bomb-so-suspiciously-fast/

Goulden, Joseph C. 1969. *Truth Is the First Casualty: The Gulf of Tonkin Affair, Illusion and Reality*. New York: Rand McNally.

Graf, Leroy P. and Ralph W. Haskins. 1983. *The Papers of Andrew Johnson, Volume 6, 1862–1864*. Knoxville, TN: University of Tennessee Press.

Gross-Stein, Janice. 1991. Calculation, Miscalculation and Conventional Deterrence: The View from Cairo. In *Psychology and Deterrence*, eds. Richard Ned Lebow, Robert Jervis and Janice Gross-Stein. Baltimore: The Johns Hopkins University Press.

Guisinger, Alexandra and Alastair Smith. 2002. Honest Threats: The Interaction of Reputation and Political Institutions in International Crises. *Journal of Conflict Resolution* 46(2):175–200.

Gustafson, Lowell S. 1988. *The Sovereignty Dispute Over the Falkland (Malvinas) Islands*. Oxford, UK: Oxford University Press.

Hanhimaki, Jussi. 2004. *The Flawed Architect: Henry Kissinger and American Foreign Policy*. New York: Oxford University Press.

Haworth, W. Blair. 1999. *The Bradley and How It Got That Way: Technology, Institutions, and the Problem of Mechanized Infantry in the United States Army*. New York: Praeger.

Haynes, John Earl and Harvey Klehr. 1999. *Venona: Decoding Soviet Espionage in America*. New Haven, CT: Yale University Press.

Haynes, John Earl, Harvey Klehr, and Martin Alexander. 2009. *Spies: The Rise and Fall of the KGB in America*. New Haven, CT: Yale University Press.

Heidelberger, P. and P. D. Welch. 1983. Simulation Run Length Control in the Presence of an Initial Transient. *Operations Research* 31(3):1109–1144.

Heikal, Mohamed H. 1973. *The Cairo Documents: The Inside Story of Nasser and His Relationship with World Leaders, Rebels, and Statesmen*. New York: Doubleday and Company.

Herman, Valentine and Francoise Mendel, eds. 1976. *Parliaments of the World: A Reference Compendium*. New York: Walter de Gruyter.

Herring, Pendleton. 1941. *The Impact of War: Our American Democracy Under Arms*. New York: Farrar and Rinehart.

Hetherington, Marc and Michael Nelson. 2003. Anatomy of a Rally Effect: George W. Bush and the War on Terrorism. *PS: Political Science and Politics* 36(1):37–42.

Hoffman, Robert L. 1980. *More than a Trial: The Struggle over Captain Dreyfus*. New York: Free Press.

Hogan, J. Michael. 1994. *Nuclear Freeze Campaign: Rhetoric and Foreign Policy in the Telepolitical Age.* East Lansing, MI: Michigan State University Press.

Holloway, David. 1996. *Stalin and the Bomb.* New Haven, CT: Yale University Press.

Holt, Thadeus. 2004. *The Deceivers: Allied Military Deception in the Second World War.* New York: Scribner.

Howard, Michael, and F. H. Hinsley. 1990. *British Intelligence in the Second World War,* Vol. 5. New York: Cambridge University Press.

Hughes, Judith. 2006. *To the Maginot Line,* 2nd ed. Cambridge, MA: Harvard University Press.

Hume, David. 1983. *The History of England,* Vol. 5. Indianapolis, IN: Liberty Fund.

Huntington, Samuel. 1993. *The Third Wave: Democratization in the Late Twentieth Century.* Norman, OK: University of Oklahoma Press.

Huth, Paul and Todd Allee. 2003. *The Democratic Peace and Territorial Conflict in the Twentieth Century.* Cambridge, UK: University of Cambridge Press.

Ikenberry, G. John. 2000. *After Victory: Institutons, Strategic Restraint and the Rebuilding of Order after Major Wars.* Princeton, NJ: Princeton University Press.

Jackman, Simon. 2010. *Bayesian Analysis for the Social Sciences.* New York: Wiley.

Jackson, Julian. 2003. *The Fall of France: The Nazi Invasion of 1940.* Oxford, UK: Oxford University Press.

Jackson, Peter. 2000. *France and the Nazi Menace: Intelligence and Policy Making, 1933–1939.* Oxford, UK: Oxford University Press.

Jacobson, Gary C. 2007. *A Divider, Not a Uniter: George W. Bush and the American People.* New York: Pearson/Longman.

Jaggers, Keith and Tedd Robert Gurr. 1995. Transitions to Democracy: Tracking Democracy's Third Wave with the POLITY III Data. *Journal of Peace Research* 32(6):469–482.

Jamieson, Kathleen Hall. 1993. *Dirty Politics: Deception, Distraction, and Democracy.* Oxford, UK: Oxford University Press.

Jervis, Robert. 1976. *Perception and Misperception in International Politics.* Princeton, NJ: Princeton University Press.

Jo, Dong-Joon and Erik Gartzke. 2006. *Codebook and Data Notes for "Determinants of Nuclear Weapons Proliferation: A Quantitative Model.* Online: available at http://pages.ucsd.edu/~egartzke/data/jo_gartzke_0207_codebk_0906.pdf

Johnson, Loch K. 1997. *America's Secret Power.* Cambridge, UK: Cambridge University Press.

Johnson, Loch K. 2007. *Strategic Intelligence,* Vol. 4. Westport, CT: Praeger.

Johnson, Robert David. 2006. *Congress and the Cold War.* Cambridge, UK: Cambridge University Press.

Kahn, David. 2004. *The Reader of Gentlemen's Mail: Herbert O. Yardley and the Birth of American Codebreaking.* New Haven, CT: Yale University Press.

Kant, Immanuel. 1957. *Perpetual Peace.* New York: Bobbs-Merrill.

Kant, Immanuel. 1979. *The Conflict of the Faculties, translation by Mary J. Gregor.* New York: Abaris Books.

Kant, Immanuel. 1983. *Perpetual Peace and Other Essays, translated by Ted Humphrey.* New York: Hackett.

Karlekar, Karin D. and Sarah G. Cook. 2008. *Freedom of the Press 2008: A Global Survey of Media Independence*. New York: Freedom House.

Kaufmann, Chaim. 2004. Threat Inflation and the Failure of the Marketplace of Ideas: The Selling of the Iraq War. *International Security* 29(1):5–48.

Kaufmann, J. E. and H. W. Kaufmann. 1997. *The Maginot Line: None Shall Pass*. New York: Praeger.

Kennan, George. 1951. *American Diplomacy, 1900–1950*. New York: Penguin.

Kennedy, Robert. 1969. *Thirteen Days: A Memoir of the Cuban Missile Crisis*. New York: WW Norton.

Khrushchev, N. 1970. *Khrushchev Remembers*. Boston: Little, Brown Publishers.

Kinnard, Douglas. 1980. *The Secretary of Defense*. Lexington, KY: University of Kentucky Press.

Kissinger, Henry. 2000. *Years of Renewal*, Kindle edition. New York: Simon and Schuster.

Klein, Woody. 2008. *All the Presidents' Spokesmen: Spinning the News—White House Press Secretaries from Franklin D. Roosevelt to George W. Bush*. New York: Praeger.

Knight, Malcolm, Norman Loayza, and Delano Villanueva. 1996. *The Peace Dividend: Military Spending Cuts and Economic Growth*. New York: World Bank Policy Research.

Knightley, P. 2004. *The First Casualty*, 3rd ed. Baltimore: Johns Hopkins University Press.

Komine, Yukinori. 2008. *Secrecy in US Foreign Policy: Nixon, Kissinger and the Rapprochement with China*. Aldershot, UK: Ashgate.

Kostin, Sergei and Eric Raynaud. 2011. *Farewell: The Greatest Spy Story of the Twentieth Century*, Kindle edition. AmazonEncore.

Krumeich, Gerd. 1987. *Armaments and Politics in France on the Eve of the First World War: The Introduction of Three-Year Conscription, 1913–1914*, translated by Stephen Conn. Berlin, Germany: Berg Press.

Kuhn, Thomas. 1970. *The Structure of Scientific Revolutions*. Chicago: University of Chicago Press.

Kurian, George Thomas. 1998. *World Encyclopedia of Parliaments and Legislatures*, Vol. 2. London: Inter-Parliamentary Union.

Lai, Brian and Dan Reiter. 2005. 'Rally' Round the Union Jack? Public Opinion and the Use of Force in the United Kingdom, 1948–2001. *International Studies Quarterly* 49(2):255–272.

Lake, David. 1992. Powerful Pacifists: Democratic States and War. *American Political Science Review* 86(1):24–37.

Large, David Clay. 1990. *Between Two Fires: Europe's Path in the 1930s*. New York: W. W. Norton and Company.

Laursen, John Christian. 1998. David Hume and the Danish Debate about Freedom of the Press in the 1770s. *Journal of the History of Ideas* 59(1):167–172.

Laver, Michael and Kenneth A. Shepsle. 1990. Coalitions and Cabinet Governments. *American Political Science Review* 84:874–890.

Laver, Michael and Kenneth A. Shepsle. 1996. *Making and Breaking Governments. Cabinet and Legislature in Parliamentary Democracies*. Cambridge, UK: Cambridge University Press.

Leeds, Brett Ashley. 1999. Domestic Political Institutions, Credible Commitments, and International Cooperation. *American Journal of Political Science* 43(4):979–1002.

Leeds, Brett Ashley, Jeffrey M. Ritter, Sara McLaughlin Mitchell, and Andrew G. Long. 2002. Alliance Treaty Obligations and Provisions, 1815–1944. *International Interactions* **28**(1):237–260.

Leigh, David and Luke Haring. 2011. *Wikileaks: Inside Julian Assange's War on Secrecy.* New York: Public Affairs.

Lewis, Jonathan E. 2002. *Spy Capitalism: Itek and the CIA.* New Haven, CT: Yale University Press.

Lippmann, Walter. 1922. *Public Opinion.* New York: Free Press.

Lippmann, Walter. 1927. *The Phantom Public: A Sequel to Public Opinion.* New York: Macmillan.

Lowry, Donald. 2000. *The South African War Reappraised.* Manchester, UK: Manchester University Press.

Lund Commission Staff. 1996. *Rapport til Stortinget fra kommisjonen som ble nedsatt av Stortinget for å granske påstander om ulovlig overvåking av norske borgere (Lund rapporten). Dok. Nr. 15.* Oslo, Norway: Stortinget.

Lundstrom, John B. 2006. *Black Shoe Carrier Admiral: Frank Jack Fletcher at Coral Sea, Midway and Guadalcanal.* Annapolis, MD: Naval Institute Press.

Lupfer, Timothy T. 1981. *The Dynamics of Doctrine: The Changes in German Tactical Doctrine During the First World War.* Fort Leavonsworth, KS: Leavonsworth Papers.

Lupia, Arthur and Mathew D. McCubbins. 1998. *The Democratic Dilemma: Can Citizens Learn What They Need to Know?* Cambridge, UK: Cambridge University Press.

Macintyre, Ben. 2011. *Operation Mincemeat: How a Dead Man and a Bizarre Plan Fooled the Nazis and Assured an Allied Victory.* New York: Broadway.

Mahon, James Edwin. 2003. Kant on Lies, Candour and Reticence. *Kantian Review* 7(1):102–133.

Mahon, James Edwin. 2009. Kant on Keeping a Secret. *Listening: Journal of Religion and Culture* **44**(1):21–36.

Maney, Patrick J. 1998. *The Roosevelt Presence: The Life and Legacy of FDR.* Los Angeles: University of California Press.

Mann, Robert. 2011. *Daisy Petals and Mushroom Clouds: LBJ, Barry Goldwater and the Ad That Changed American Politics.* Baton Rouge, LA: LSU Press.

Manninen, Juha. 2006. Anders Chydenius and the Origins of the World's First Freedom of Information Act. In *The World's First Freedom of Information Law,* ed. Juha Mustonen. Kokkola, Finland: Anders Chydenius Foundation, pp. 18–50.

Maoz, Zeev. 2000. The Street Gangs of World Politics: Their Origins, Management and Consequences, 1816–1986. In *What Do We Know About War?,* ed. John Vasquez. Lanham, MD: Rowman and Littlefield.

Maoz, Zeev. 2005. Dyadic Militarized Interestate Disputes (version 2.0). Online: available at http://psfaculty.ucdavis.edu/zmaoz/dyadmid.html

Martin, Benjamin F. 1999. *France and the Après Guerre, 1918–1924: Illusions and Disillusionment.* Baton Rouge, LA: Louisiana State University Press.

Martin, Lisa. 2000. *Democratic Commitments.* Princeton, NJ: Princeton University Press.

May, Ernest R. 2000. *Strange Victory.* New York: Hill and Wang.

Mayadas, M. (Lt Gen). 1999. *How the Bofors Affair Transformed India 1989–1999.* New Delhi: South Asia Press.

McDonough, Denis, Mara Rudman, and Peter Rundlet. 2006. *No Mere Oversight: Congressional Oversight of Intelligence Is Broken*. Washington, DC: Center for American Progress.

McKitrick, Eric L. 1967. Party Politics and the Union and Confederate War Efforts. In *The American Party System*, eds. William Nisbet Chambers and Walter Dean Burnham. New York: Oxford University Press, pp. 117–151.

Mearsheimer, John J. 2010. *Why Leaders Lie: The Truth About Lying in International Politics*. New York: Oxford University Press.

Mieczkowsk, Yanek. 2000. *Gerald Ford and the Challenges of the 1970s*. Lexington, KY: University of Kentucky Press.

Mill, John Stuart. 2013. *The Works of John Stuart Mill: On Liberty, Representative Government, Utilitarianism*, Kindle edition. Amazon.

Miller, James Edward. 2009. *The United States and the Making of Modern Greece: History and Power, 1950–1974*, Kindle edition. Chapel Hill: University of North Carolina Press.

Millett, Allan R. 1996. Patterns of Military Innovation in the Interwar Period. In *Military Innovation in the Interwar Period*, eds. Williamson Murray and Allan R Millett. Cambridge, UK: Cambridge University Press, pp. 329–340.

Milner, Helen V. 1997. *Interests, Institutions and Information: Domestic Politics and International Relations*. Princeton, NJ: Princeton University Press.

Mitchell, Sara McLaughlin, Scott Gates, and Havard Hegre. 1999. Evolution in Democracy-War Dynamics. *Journal of Conflict Resolution* 43(6):771–792.

Montinola, Gabriella R. and Robert W. Jackman. 2002. Sources of Corruption: A Cross-Country Study. *British Journal of Political Science* 32(1):147–170.

Morgan, Kenneth. 2002. The Boer War and the Media. *Twentieth Century British History* 13(1):1–16.

Morgenthau, Hans. 1948. *Politics Among Nations*. New York: Knopf.

Morgenthau, Hans. 1967. *Politics Among Nations*, 4th ed. New York: Knopf.

Morton, Rebecca. 1999. *Methods and Models*. Cambridge, UK: University of Cambridge Press.

Moynihan, Daniel Patrick. 1999. *Secrecy: The American Experience*. New Haven, CT: Yale University Press.

Moynihan, Daniel Patrick and Larry Combest. 1997. *Secrecy: Report of the Commission on Protecting and Reducing Government Secrecy*. Washington, DC: United States Printing Office.

Mueller, John E. 1970. Presidential Popularity from Truman to Johnson. *The American Political Science Review* 64(1):18–34.

Naylor, Phillip Chiviges. 2000. *France and Algeria: A History of Decolonization and Transformation*. Gainesville, FL: University of Florida Press.

Norris, Robert S. 2009. George Koval, Manhattan Project Spy. *Journal of Cold War Studies*. Paper Presented at Woodrow Wilson Center Conference, Cold War International History Project.

Norton, Philip, ed. 1990. *Legislatures*. Oxford, UK: Oxford University Press.

Olson, Mancur and Richard Zeckhauser. 1966. An Economic Theory of Alliances. *Review of Economics and Statistics* 48(3): 266–279.

On Parliamentary, Committee and Public Relations. n.d. Parliamentary Oversight of the Intelligence Services in the WEU Countries—Current Situation and Prospects for

Reform Parliamentary Oversight of the Intelligence Services in the WEU Countries—Current Situation and Prospects for Reform. Technical report, European Security and Defense Assembly.

Orwell, Sonia and Ian Angus. 1968. *The Collected Essays, Journalism and Letters of George Orwell: In Front of Your Nose, 1945–1950*. London: Harcourt Brace Jovanovich.

Parker, Frederick D. 1993. *A Priceless Advantage: US Navy Communications Intelligence and the Battles of Coral Sea, Midway and the Aleutians*. Center for Cryptolotical History, National Security Agency.

Phythian, Mark. 2007. The British Experience with Intelligence Accountability. *Intelligence and National Security* **22**(1):75–99.

Plummer, Martyn. n.d. *Just Another Gibbs Sampler.*

Porch, Douglas. 2003a. *The March to the Marne:The French Army, 1871–1914*. Cambridge, UK: Cambridge University Press.

Porch, Douglas. 2003b. *The French Secret Services: A History of French Intelligence from the Dreyfus Affair to the Gulf War*. New York: Farrar, Straus and Giroux.

Posen, Barry and Stephen van Evra. 1983. Defense Policy and the Reagan Administration. *International Security* **8**(1):3–45.

Powell, Robert. 1999. *In the Shadow of Power: States and Strategies in International Politics*. Princeton, NJ: Princeton University Press.

Powers, Elizabeth. n.d. *Freedom of Speech: The History of an Idea.*

Prados, John. 1995. *Combined Fleet Decoded: The Secret History of American Intelligence and the Japanese Navy in World War II*. New York: Random House.

Prados, John and Margaret Pratt Portier. 2004. *Inside the Pentagon Papers*. Lawrence, KS: University of Kansas Press.

Prich, Anthony. 2000. *The Burning of Washington: The British Invasion of 1814*. Annapolis, MD: Naval Institute Press.

Raftery, A. E. and S. M. Lewis. 1992. One Long Run with Diagnostics: Implementation Strategies for Markov Chain Monte Carlo. *Statistical Science* **7**(1):493–497.

Rasmusen, Eric and J. Mark Ramseyer. 1994. Cheap Bribes and the Corruption Ban: A Coordination Game Among Rational Legislators. *Public Choice* **78**(1):305–327.

Ravenal, Earl C. 1982. *Reagan's 1983 Defense Budget: An Analysis and an Alternative*. Washington, DC: CATO Institute Paper, No. 10.

Read, Piers Paul. 2012. *The Dreyfus Affair: The Story of the Most Infamous Miscarriage of Justice in French History*. London: Bloomsbury.

Reed, Thomas. 2007. *At the Abyss: An Insider's History of the Cold War*, Kindle edition. New York: Random House.

Reed, Thomas and Danny B. Stillman. 2010. *The Nuclear Express: A Political History of the Bomb and Its Proliferation*. New York: Zenith Press.

Reiter, Dan. 2003. Exploring the Bargaining Model of War. *Perspectives on Politics* **1**(1):27–43.

Reiter, Dan. 2011. A Closer Look at Case Studies on Democracy, Selection Effects, and Victory. *H-Diplo Roundtable* **11**(12):4–34.

Reiter, Dan. 2012. Democracy, Deception, and Entry Into War. *Security Studies* **21**(4):594–623.

Reiter, Dan and Allan C. Stam. 2002. *Democracies at War*. Princeton, NJ: Princeton University Press.

Reynolds, David. 2000. *Britannia Overruled: British Policy and World Power in the 20th Century*. London: Pearson.

Rhodes, Richard. 1995. *Dark Sun: The Making of the Hydrogen Bomb*. New York: Simon and Schuster.

Rich, Ben R. and Leo Janos. 1996. *Skunk Works: A Personal Memoir of My Years at Lockheed*. Boston: Back Bay Books.

Richardson, Douglas. 1991. *Northrop B-2 Spirit*. New York: Smithmark Publishers.

Ricks, Thomas E. 2006. *Fiasco: The American Military Adventure in Iraq*. New York: Penguin Press.

Ripsman, Norrin. 2009. Neoclassical Realism and Domestic Interest Groups. In *Neoclassical Realism, the State, and Foreign Policy*, eds. Steven Lobell, Norrin M. Ripsman, and Jeffrey Taliaferrro. Cambridge, UK: Cambridge University Press.

Rosato, Sebastian. 2003. The Flawed Logic of the Democratic Peace. *American Political Science Review* 97(4):585–602.

Rose-Ackerman, Susan. 1978. *Corruption: A Study in Political Economy*. New York: Academic Press.

Rosen, Philip. 2000. *The Canadian Security Intelligence Service*. Ottawa: Library of Parliament.

Rozell, Mark. 2002. *Executive Privilege: Presidential Power, Secrecy, and Accountability*, 2nd ed. Lawrence, KS: University of Kansas Press.

Rubinoff, Arthur G. 1996. India's New Subject-based Parliamentary Standing Committees. *Asian Survey* 36(7):723–738.

Russett, Bruce. 1990. *Controlling the Sword*. Cambridge, MA: Harvard University Press.

Russett, Bruce and John Oneal. 2000. *Triangulating Peace*. New York: WW Norton and Company.

Russett, Bruce M. 1993. *Grasping the Democratic Peace*. Princeton, NJ: Princeton University Press.

Russett, Bruce M. and John R. Oneal. 2001. *Triangulating Peace: Democracy, Interdependence, and International Organizations*. New York: Norton.

Saltoun-Ebin, Jason. 2010. *The Reagan Files*. Washington, DC: CreateSpace.

Sandler, Todd and Keith Hartley. 1999. *The Political Economy of NATO: Past, Present and into the 21st Century*. Cambridge, UK: Cambridge University Press.

Schecter, Jerrold L. and Peter S. Deriabin. 1995. *The Spy Who Saved the World*. New York: Brassey's Inc.

Schenker, Hillel. 1998. The Rocky Road from Big Brother's Helper to Government Watchdog. *Palestine-Israel Journal* 5(3):2–11.

Schlesinger, Arthur Jr. 1978. *Robert Kennedy and His Times*. New York: Houghton Mifflin.

Schoenfeld, Gabriel. 2010. *Necessary Secrets: National Security, the Media and the Rule of Law*. New York: WW Norton and Company.

Schuessler, John M. 2010. The Deception Dividend: FDR's Undeclared War. *International Security* 34(4):133–165.

Schulman, Bruce J. 2001. *The Seventies: The Great Shift in American Culture, Society, and Politics*. New York: The Free Press.

Schultz, Kenneth. 2001. *Democracy and Coercive Diplomacy*. Cambridge, UK: Cambridge University Press.

Schultz, Kenneth A. and Barry R. Weingast. 1998. Limited Governments, Powerful States. In *Strategic Politicians, Institutions, and Foreign Policy*, ed. Randolph M. Siverson. Ann Arbor, MI: University of Michigan Press, pp. 15–49.

Schultz, Kenneth and Barry Weingast. 2003. The Democratic Advantage. *International Organization* **Winter**(1):3–42.

Schumpeter, Joseph A. 1947. *Capitalism, Socialism and Democracy*, 2nd ed. New York: Harper.

Schweller, Randall L. 2009. Neoclassical Realism and State Mobilization: Expansionist Ideology in the Age of Mass Politics. In *Neoclassical Realism, the State, and Foreign Policy*, eds. Steven Lobell, Norrin M. Ripsman, and Jeffrey Taliaferro. Cambridge, UK: Cambridge University Press.

Scott, Len. 1999. Espionage and the Cold War. *Intelligence and National Security* **14**(1):23–47.

Sharp, David H. 2012. *The CIA's Greatest Covert Operation: Inside the Daring Mission to Recover a Nuclear-Armed Soviet Sub*. Lawrence, KS: University of Kansas Press.

Shetreet, Shimon. 1991. *Free Speech and National Security*. Boston: Nijhoff.

Shlaim, Avi. 2001. *The Iron Wall: Israel and the Arab World*. New York: Norton and Company.

Shleifer, Andrei and Robert W. Vishny. 1993. Corruption. *Quarterly Journal of Economics* **108**(2):599–617.

Silverstein, Ken and Jeff Moag. 2000. The Pentagon's 300-Billion-Dollar Bomb. *Mother Jones* **January/February**. Online: available at http://www.motherjones.com/politics/2000/01/pentagons-300-billion-dollar-bomb

Simpson, John. 2010. *Unreliable Sources: How the 20th Century Was Reported*. London: Macmillan.

Singer, J. David. 1987. Reconstructing the Correlates of War Dataset on Material Capabilities of States, 1816–1985. *International Interactions* **14**:115–132.

Singer, J. David, Bremer Stuart, and John Stuckey. 1972. Capability Distribution, Uncertainty, and Major Power War, 1820–1965. In *Peace, War, and Numbers*, ed. Bruce M. Russett. Beverly Hills, CA: Sage.

Smith, Chris. 1994. *India's Ad Hoc Arsenal: Direction or Drift in Defence Policy?* Oxford, UK: Oxford University Press.

Smith, Tony. 1978. *The French Stake in Algeria: 1945–1962*. London: Cornell University Press.

Smyth, Denis. 2010. *Deathly Deception: The Real Story of Operation Mincemeat*. Oxford, UK: Oxford University Press.

Snider, L. Britt. 1999/2000. Unlucky Shamrock: Recollections from the Church Committee Investigation of NSA. *Central Intelligence Agency Studies in Intelligence*, winter.

Snyder, Jack and Erica D. Borghard. 2011. The Cost of Empty Threats: A Penny, Not a Pound. *American Political Science Review* **105**(3):437–456.

Springall, A. 1973. Response Surface Fitting Using a Generalization of the Bradley–Terry Paired Comparison Model. *Applied Statistics* **22**(1):59–68.

Stam, Allan. 1996. *Win, Lose or Draw: Domestic Politics and the Crucible of War*. Ann Arbor, MI: Michigan University Press.

Stevenson, David. 2004. *Cataclysm: The First World War as Political Tragedy*. Cambridge, MA: Basic Books.

Stigler, Stephen. 1994. Citation Patterns in the Journals of Statistics and Probability. *Statistical Science* **9**(1):94–108.

Stiglitz, Joseph. 1999. On Liberty, the Right to Know, and Public Discourse: The Role of Transparency in Public Life. Oxford Amnesty Lecture, Oxford, UK.

Stinnett, Douglass M., Jaroslav Tir, Philip Schafer, Paul F. Diehl, and Charles Gochman. 2002. The Correlates of War Project Direct Contiguity Data, Version 3. *Conflict Management and Peace Science* **19**(2):58–66.

Stone, Geoffrey. 2007. *War and Liberty: An American Dilemma, 1790 to the Present.* New York: W. W. Norton.

Stone, Geoffrey. 2004. *Perilous Times: free Speech in Wartime, from the Sedition Act of 1798 to the War on Terrorism.* New York: W. W. Norton.

Stuart-Fox, D. M., D. Firth, A. Moussalli, and M. J. Whiting. 2005. Multiple Signals in Chameleon Contests: Designing and Analysing Animal Contests as a Tournament. *Animal Behavior* **71**(4):1263–1271.

Suvorov, V. 1984. *Inside Soviet Military Intelligence.* London: Macmillan.

Sweet, W. 1982. Defense Spending Debate. *Editorial Research Report* 1.

Szasz, Ferenc Morton. 1992. *British Scientists and the Manhattan Project: The Los Alamos Years.* London: Palgrave.

Tap, Bruce. 1998. *Over Lincoln's Shoulder.* Lawrence, KS: University of Kansas Press.

Thompson, Dennis. 1999. Democratic Secrecy. *Political Science Quarterly* **114**(2): 185–200.

Thompson, William R. 2001. Identifying Rivalries in World Politics. *International Studies Quarterly* **45**(2):557–586.

Thorp, D. J. 2011. *The Silent Listener—Falklands 1982: The Inside Story of British Electronic Surveillance and Intel Controversies.* London: The History Press.

Trachtenberg, Marc. 2010. Review of "The Deception Dividend: FDR's Undeclared War." *H-Diplo* **10**(3):1–7.

Trefousse, Hans L. 1997. *Andrew Johnson: A Biography.* New York: W. W. Norton.

Truman, Harry. 1956. *Memoirs.* Garden City, NJ: Doubleday and Company.

Turner, Heather and David Firth. 2010. *Bradley–Terry Models in R: The BradleyTerry2 Package.* Unpublished manuscript.

Tutz, Gerhard. 1986. Bradley–Terry–Luce Models with an Ordered Response. *Journal of Mathematical Psychology* **30**(3):306–316.

Tzu, Sun. 2005. *The Art of War.* New York: Shambhala Publications.

Union, Inter-Parliamentary, ed. 1986. *Parliaments of the World: A Comparative Reference Compendium,* Vol. 1 and 2, 2nd ed. New York: Facts on File.

Vincent, John. 1998. *Secrecy in Great Britain.* Cambridge, UK: Cambridge University Press.

Waller, Maureen. 2006. *London 1945: Life in the Debris of War.* New York: St. Martin's.

Walsh, Michael. 2009. George Koval: Atomic Spy Unmasked. *Smithsonian Magazine* **May**. Online: http://www.smithsonianmag.com/ist/?next=/history/george-koval-atomic-spy-unmasked-125046223/

Walt, Stephen. 1987. *The Origins of Alliances.* Ithaca, NY: Cornell University Press.

Waltz, Kenneth. 1967. *Foreign Policy and Democratic Politics.* Boston: Little, Brown.

Waltz, Kenneth. 1979. *The Theory of International Politics.* Reading, MA: Addison Wesley.

Warner, Geoffrey. 2009. The United States and the Cyprus Crisis of 1974. *International Affairs* **85**(1):129–143.

Weller, Geoffrey R. 2000. Political Scrutiny and Control of Scandinavia's Security and Intelligence Services. *International Journal of Intelligence and Counterintelligence* **13**(2):171–192.

Williams, Henry Smith. 1909. *A Historians' History of the World: A Comprehensive Narrative of the Rise and Development of Nations as Recorded by the Great Writers of All Ages*, Volume 16. London: Hooper and Jackson.

Wood, Simon N. 2006. *Generalized Additive Models: An Introduction with R*. Boca Raton, FL: Chapman and Hall/CRC Group.

Wright, Peter. 1987. *Spy Catcher*. Sydney, Australia: William Heinemann.

Yardley, Jonathan. 2004 (1931). *The American Black Chamber*. Annapolis, MD: US Naval Institute Press.

Zubok, Vladislav and Constantine Pleshakov. 1996. *Inside the Kremlin's Cold War: From Stalin to Khrushchev*. Cambridge, MA: Harvard University Press.

"A Secret Article for Securing Perpetual Peace" (Kant), 289n6

security. *see* national security issues

Security Intelligence Review Committee (Canada), 20, 84–85, 238, 244t, 246, 300n60–62

Security Policy Information Institutions, 180–190 *passim,* 185f, 189f, 192t, 200, 200f, 202, 209, 211, 212–219f, 321n1–324n51 *passim,* 323n39, 326n35

Security Policy Information Institutions index, 315n18

Sejm–ocracy, 241, 329n21

Senate Select Committee on Intelligence, 142, 314n77

Serbia, secrecy laws in, 68t

75–mm artillery gun, 86–94 *passim,* 108, 301n71–302n107 *passim,* 307n51, 307n53

Shamrock, Operation, 85–86, 300n64

Shane, Scott, 282n24

Shanker, Thom, 284n57

Shannon, Elaine, 302n112

Shannon, William, 116, 309n120

Sharp, David H., 96, 302n113–120 *passim*

Shepsle, Kenneth A., 142, 314n80

Shetreet, Shimon, 313n73

Shlaim, Avi, 217, 288n97, 288n100

Shleifer, Andrei, 285n17

Sicily, Operation Mincemeat and, 54–55, 56f, 292n57–293n61 *passim*

Silverstein, Ken, 296n104, 296n113

Simpson, John, 305n12

Sinai conflict of 1956, 38

Singer, J. David, 334n38, 335n58

SIRC. *See* Security Intelligence Review Committee

Six Day War, 5, 283n29

skepticism. *see also* credibility; opposition parties

Cyprus crisis and, 105–106, 112–116, 306n34, 308n89–309n124

Dreyfus Affair and, 105–112, 306n30, 306n34–308n83

Ford administration and, 170

freedom of information laws and, 19

institutional oversight and, 146–147

investment and, 104–105, 305n22–306n33

Iraq War (2003) and, 102–104, 304n12–305n14

isolationism and, 306n33

Maginot line and, 161

marketplace of ideas and, 299n22

Nixon administration and, 170

surveillance programs and, 8–9, 283n43

Watergate and, 105–106, 112–116, 306n34, 308n89–309n124

skepticism of government, 7–9

Skunk (Skonk) Works, 52, 63, 65, 95, 296n105

Slovakia, secrecy laws in, 68t

Slovenia, secrecy laws in, 68t

Smith, Alastair, 229, 313n75, 327n58

Smith, Chris, 300n56

Smith, Hendrick, 317n77

Smith, Tony, 81, 299n31–37 *passim,* 304n10

Smyth, Denis, 293n59–65 *passim*

Snider, L. Britt, 85, 300n65–66, 301n70, 313n58

Snowden, Edward, 2, 4, 237, 246, 281n7–8, 282n24, 327n5–328n12 *passim*

Snyder, Jack, 292n57

Sobell, Morton, 60

Solomon, Gerald, 104

South Africa

arms industry scandals and, 83

Boer War and, 82

institutional oversight in, 186f, 187

secrecy laws in, 68t

Southern Christian Leadership Conference, 85

South Korea

national security oversight index and, 183

secrecy laws in, 67t

Spain

Dreyfus Affair and, 92